REFLECTIONS
ON THE LIFE AND DREAMS OF C.G. JUNG

BY ANIELA JAFFÉ
FROM CONVERSATIONS WITH JUNG

HISTORICAL COMMENTARY
BY ELENA FISCHLI

Reflections
on the Life and Dreams of C.G. Jung

by Aniela Jaffé
from conversations with Jung

Historical Commentary
by Elena Fischli

English translation by Caitlin Stephens

DAIMON
VERLAG

Reflections
on the Life and Dreams of C.G. Jung

by Aniela Jaffé
from conversations with Jung

Historical Commentary
Elena Fischli

English translation
Caitlin Stephens

ISBN 978-3-85630-792-9

First edition 2023

Cover Design: English edition adaptation by Robert Imhoff from the original German edition design by Peter Volkart of Zürich, using a photograph made at Eranos by Margarethe Fellerer

List of Illustrations and copyrights on page 374

Contents

On Psychiatric and Analytical Practice

On the Here and the Beyond

Human Image, God Image, Worldview

Historical Commentary by Elena Fischli

Preface

"Have I led a meaningful life? What have I learned? What part of my work is significant and might endure? And what interests me now, at the end?"

These and other questions were reflected upon by C.G. Jung in wide-ranging conversations with Aniela Jaffé over the final five years of his life. Many of his insights can be found in *Memories, Dreams, Reflections by C.G. Jung* (hereafter *MDR*)[1].

He had considerably more to say, however: *Reflections* is actually a continuation, comprising a sizeable and never-before-published selection of Jung's ruminations on his life's work, his late thoughts and his self-awareness as they percolated during these conversations. Jaffé considered this additional material too essential to be neglected and she assiduously endeavored to prepare it for future readers.

The collection of Jung's memories and stories here presented has experienced a long and labyrinthian evolution. Ultimately, thanks to the acuity and tenacity of Aniela Jaffé, these precious pages are at last seeing the light of day. I would like to briefly explain how this posthumous publication of *Reflections* ultimately came to be.

Though familiar with some of her writings, I did not meet Aniela Jaffé personally until late 1975 during my student years at the Zürich C.G. Jung Institute. Assigned by the editor of *Spring,* James Hillman, to translate her recent Eranos lecture, "C.G. Jung und die Eranos-Tagungen"[2], into English for publication in the journal, I soon

1 Jaffé, Aniela, Ed., *Memories, Dreams, Reflections by C.G. Jung*, 1962, Pantheon, New York.

2 Jaffé, Aniela, "C.G. Jung und die Eranos Tagungen", in Portmann, Adolf and Ritsema, Rudolf, Eds., *Eranos Jahrbuch*, 1975, Vol. 44, E.J. Brill, Leiden, pp. 1ff; "C.G. Jung and the Eranos Conferences" in *Spring, An Annual of Archetypal Psychology and Jungian Thought*, 1977, Zürich, pp. 201ff.

found myself at Frau Jaffé's Hochstrasse doorstep in Zürich Fluntern, seeking consultation regarding various details of her essay. This first encounter marked the beginning of an ever deepening friendship that continued until her death at age 88 in October, 1991. I came to know a lively and cultured spirit, ripened with hard-won life experience and generous in the sharing of it.

During those late years of her life, while continuing with her Jungian analytic practice, teaching at the Jung Institute and participating in activities of the Psychology Club, Aniela Jaffé was also in the process of carefully arranging her papers and archival documents, writing or reworking numerous essays and carrying on a prodigious and often profound international correspondence, some of which is chronicled in the accompanying commentary.

Her greatest regret and concern during these final years was that significant portions of what C.G. Jung had shared with her in conversation, as recorded in her notes made while preparing her biography of Jung in the late fifties, had been lying dormant ever since, unpublished and practically inaccessible. A substantial portion of her compilations from these intense sessions had not found place in *MDR*, with its page-count limited by the publishers, among other reasons (see Introduction, pp. 6ff). How could the remaining material simply be left languishing in an archive? She worked through this unique collection of late thoughts and dreams again and again, chapter by chapter weaving a unique new volume of biography.

The result was a manuscript that she believed not only should be, but *must* be published – she owed it to Jung to carry out his wishes in this way. After all, he had shared his recollections, dreams and anecdotes in an often deeply reflective process with the understanding that she would then carry on to form and shepherd the fruits of this labor into print. For more than a decade, Jaffé periodically returned to work on the manuscript. However, not everyone shared her conviction and in the face of unresolved copyright challenges, she refrained from proceeding with its publication.

Growing older and seeing no imminent possibility for publication on the horizon, she ultimately made a decision in 1986 to place the manuscript in younger hands, naming me her literary executor and requesting that I persevere in the quest to publish it.

Many years later (2013) an agreement was reached with representatives of the Jung family (Foundation for the Works of C.G. Jung) for the editing and publication of her original 'protocol' notes, as they came to be called, a development that had long been desired by Jungian scholars and others who were aware of their existence. These 'protocols' – Jaffé's raw notes which served as her basis for the writing of both of the biographical volumes – are actually copies that Jaffé made and sent to publisher Kurt Wolff in the late 1950's; despite explicit requests, they were never returned to the author. Not anticipating today's great interest in the history of this process, Aniela Jaffé destroyed her original shorthand notes. In the late 1970's, the copies of Jaffé's notes were given by Wolff's widow, Helene Wolff, to the former director of the Bollingen Series, John Barrett, who subsequently turned them over to Princeton University Press (in the meantime, publisher of Jung's *Collected Works*). In 1983, they were deposited in the Library of Congress with restricted access. It is highly doubtful whether Jaffé herself would ever have published this raw material, but after decades of curiosity and interest by Jungian historians and others, arrangements have now been made for them to be edited by Sonu Shamdasani of the Philemon Foundation and published by Princeton University Press.

It was also agreed that Jaffé's carefully edited manuscript, based on previously unpublished sections of material from the 'protocols', would appear independently with Daimon Verlag – the result, *Reflections*, is now before you. Just as *MDR* had gone through a long and arduous process extending over many years, so, too, did this second volume of Aniela Jaffé's edited notes from her conversations with Jung have a highly challenging path to master.

Over the course of Aniela Jaffé's final years, reticent though she was to divulge her personal story, we had a number of conversations about her life and work. In the beginning, this was primarily in relation to the editing and preparation of revised editions of her writings. As time went on, we also began to speak of more personal matters, including some aspects of her own biography. She introduced me to what remained of her family and some of her closest friends. I was invited to occasional simple lunches or tea at her apartment, for example when Julie Neumann, Violet de Laszlo, Laurens van der Post or other international friends passed through town or when her nephews Frank and Luke Herrmann from England, the sons of her sister Gabriele, were visiting. The latter would later prove to be most helpful in providing family history, factual context and further contacts that were crucial for the biographical aspects of this book. While her personal history continued to be a reluctant topic, Aniela Jaffé was always ready to discuss questions concerning the unpublished manuscript and to provide invaluable background information for the footnotes and explanations.

When it came time to prepare the manuscript for publication (originally in German), I was fortunately able to entrust this task to Elena Fischli, co-founder and editor of Daimon Verlag, whose myriad talents, expertise and tenacity were well-suited not only for finalizing the text and copious footnotes, but also for the necessary wide-ranging research and ordering of the considerable archival material gathered. In the process, this corpus of information organically evolved to become the "Historical Commentary" comprising the second part of this book and very relevant to the genesis of the biographical material. The behind-the-scenes story of how *MDR* and *Reflections* came to be, along with in-depth commentary illustrating the complexities involved in their publication and a detailed biography of Aniela Jaffé, can thus finally be presented.

For me personally, Aniela Jaffé was a mentor and friend of the finest sort: calm, deep and compassionate. Her wise and modest presence elicited the trust of her analysands and students throughout the decades of her analytic work. An apt listener of the highest order, she could bring forth an observation or reflection with just the right timing and tone so that it could be accepted and acknowledged, even in the presence of an activated complex.

She would spend as much of her own time reflecting on cases as during the actual sessions. Arriving at her apartment, I would often find her pondering over dreams of her clients, noting points for attention in sessions to come. Analysands could be certain there would be insightful questions and observations awaiting them every week. She brought this same degree of care and sensitive intensity to her work with Jung and on his memoir, both during and after his lifetime.

On her long and eventful path, Aniela Jaffé was repeatedly challenged by incredible adversity, particularly during the period of Nazi domination and persecution in Europe. Even while later living in Zürich, she had faced near-poverty and also prejudice from critics and occasionally some of her analyst colleagues, not to mention the intrigues that played out during the time of her collaboration with Jung and preparation of *MDR*. *"Let the dogs bark – it is a sign that we are moving!"*[3], as Jung consoled her more than once when the tribulations were all too painfully present.

Steadfastly she continued, guided by her inner compass, an innate wisdom and patience, and her compassion for others. She leaves us with an inspiring legacy, some of which is to be found within the pages of this volume, but also in *MDR, The Myth of Meaning, Death Dreams and Ghosts* and numerous other publications, and not least in the fruits of her decades of dedication to accompanying analysands and students on their individual journeys.

May the fulfillment of her final wish attest to the remarkable spirit and life of C.G. Jung and his biographer and friend, Aniela Jaffé.

Robert Hinshaw, Publisher

3 Attributed to Johann Wolfgang von Goethe, among others.

Introduction

C.G. Jung was 81 years old in 1956 when we began the series of conversations during which I made notes that would after much work become the book, *Memories, Dreams, Reflections by C.G. Jung.*[1] Our conversations took place at varying intervals over the course of more than four years. By writing some valuable contributions of his own, Jung also added to the project that had been allocated to me. In addition, he entrusted me to complement certain aspects based on other documents and letters that he made available. For various reasons, some of the notes I recorded during our talks and used as starting material for writing the book were not included in the published work.

In the meantime, more than three decades have passed. Looking today at the unpublished notes with a renewed perspective, one views them as precious fragments. Many of these spontaneous remarks and comments reveal so much about the personality, development and thought-world of Jung that I concluded it would be worthwhile to make them available to interested readers. The present book, *Reflections on the Life and Dreams of C.G. Jung*, has been collated from edited extracts of the notes I made at the time of our conversations. Despite their fragmented nature, they provide valuable insights into the world of C.G. Jung's thoughts and experiences. Prior knowledge of *Memories, Dreams, Reflections by C.G. Jung* is not necessary, but would be helpful in terms of understanding the overall context.[2] Memories recounted more as anecdotal asides or in a chain of associations, and

1 Jaffé, A., (Ed.), *Memories, Dreams, Reflections by C.G. Jung*, 1963.

2 See also Jaffé, A., "From Jung's Last Years", in *From the Life and Work of C.G. Jung*, 1971 (3. Aufl. unter dem Titel *Aus C.G. Jungs letzten Jahren und andere Aufsätze*, 1987).

observations on specific topics, at times did not fit in with the flow of the previous book. Some other reflections were deemed too intuitive, perhaps even audacious or hypothetical – for example, Jung's reflections on life after death, reincarnation, karma, etc., as well as certain religious questions. Their 'unscientific' character needs to be seen in relation to the situation in which these observations were made: they were spontaneous spoken thoughts that arose within an explicit context – sometimes related to writing and scientific papers that Jung was working on or reading at the time, or to personal encounters, letters or book publications or new editions. In most cases, the remarks related to inner images and current preoccupations. It should be remembered that these conversations took place during the last years of Jung's life; his wife Emma Jung and his companion of many years Toni Wolff had died not long before, and he himself was at the threshold of death.

Jung allowed his thoughts to flow freely during our conversations, according to the situation and his interests of the moment. When speaking with me he was not hindered by intellectual considerations of possible criticism from his contemporaries. It didn't concern him that his words and insights might require further thoughtful reflection before they could be deemed coherent or valid. Perhaps he could speak so freely because he trusted my knowledge of his scientific work and my style of editing and writing. Sometimes it seemed as if he were facing in my direction and talking to himself.[3]

In the time since our conversations took place, attitudes toward spontaneous thoughts like these have changed. There is now growing interest and understanding of the embryonic and emergent stages, of associations and processes leading to a later coherent result. Thus, certain notes have been included which are valuable for a broader understanding of Jung's scientific works: they are thoughts *in statu nascendi* – attempts to get closer to the meaning of challenging problems by circling around them.

Much of it is of a personal subjective nature. In our conversations, Jung almost always used the word 'God' in accordance with

3 Jung was a great storyteller. When I managed – which wasn't always the case – to interest him with my observations or questions, he responded with a flood of memories and thoughts.

the common parlance of the time, whereas in his letters and essays he emphasized that human words or ideas referring to God always express an image of God in the human soul. However, even in his academic writing, Jung did not completely rule out the objective validity of certain religious assertions – he thought it was not possible to say whether such religious expressions, by referring to something inherently unknowable and mysterious, related to an actual God or exclusively to human ideas of God.[4]

A final – at the time, decisive – reason for holding back a portion of these notes was their personal nature. It seemed too early for publication of some of our conversations, in particular those relating to Jung's colleague and companion Toni Wolff (1889-1953), with whom he was very close for many years. Since the publication of *Memories, Dreams, Reflections by C.G. Jung,* much has been reported, true and false, about this relationship in books, films and the press. Now would perhaps be the time to report what Jung himself said about their relationship in our conversations. As was his wont, he did not refer to external events, but rather the psychological background. He told of dreams that persuaded him to initiate the relationship, and of others after Toni Wolff's death which seemed to indicate a postmortem development.

With regard to our conversations and work on the memories book, this was never, as has sometimes been falsely assumed, a "dictation of autobiographical material". Jung did not dictate a single line of *Memories* to me; rather, he spoke freely and left it up to me to record what I chose. I sometimes asked questions or made remarks, and on rare occasions there were others present who did the same. If I managed to touch upon a point of interest, Jung did not just answer my question, but followed his train of thought further. One conversation often involved a variety of topics. There were some themes to which he returned again and again over the months and years of our work together, and thus many different thoughts could circle around a particular question. Jung also frequently added further ideas later, when we again found ourselves discussing the same or a related topic. Jung's

4 See also C.G. Jung, Collected Works (CW) vol. 11, *Psychology and Religion: West and East*, 1958, p. 661ff. On the God image see also: Adler G./Jaffé A. (Ed.), *C. G. Jung – Letters*, Vol. I, 1953, Vol. II, 1953. And Jaffé, A. (Ed.), *C.G. Jung: Word and Image,* 1979, p. 207ff.

pattern of talking in our conversations was largely associative, and I did my best to keep this flow of associations moving with my questions and comments, otherwise it would run dry.

After working together for many years, Jung knew that I was familiar with most of his writing and with his thought processes and points of reference. He thus took it for granted that I would understand his reflections and allusions during our conversations without explanation. Where necessary, I have therefore sparingly added some explanatory information when writing up my notes.

With a self-devised method of note-taking, I was able to record what I felt was important. To transcribe and type up free-flowing speech word for word, it would have been necessary to use professional shorthand, which I unfortunately had not mastered. Whenever possible, however, I did write up and edit my notes later the same day, adding any additional recollections of what Jung had said, and rendered everything into a readable state while endeavoring to maintain Jung's direct and free style of expression. It was a priority for me to retain the character of spontaneously formulated remarks, but I was keenly aware that the spoken and the written word differ considerably. When transferring the spoken into writing, modifying and rearranging the words to create a readable text was inevitable. In addition, it has to be said that every session and every situation played out differently, and it would not be accurate to claim that Jung had a single consistent manner of speaking.

At the request of the publisher, a major part of my task was to extract from my notes of various dates the themes that belonged together, group them by content and assemble them in such a way that they formed a coherent text. The publisher had insisted from the beginning that as much of the text as possible should sound like direct statements by Jung, similar to an autobiographical report.[5] Jung himself consid-

5 From the start Kurt Wolff, editor at Pantheon Books, wanted a book that would be as close as possible to a work by C.G. Jung and would give the impression of an autobiography, for which reason he wanted me to use direct speech in the first person. While Jung had at that time agreed to work on a biographical project and even wrote some texts himself for the book, he always remained ambivalent about the idea of an autobiography, mainly for psychological and philosophical reasons. In the fall of 1958, after reading drafts of some chapters from *Memories, Dreams, Reflections by C.G. Jung*, Jung expressly asked me to integrate my questions, comments and reactions into the manuscript so that it would reflect the form of a conversation. I therefore revised the text to that

ered me at one point the 'co-author' and editor responsible for the project, and even suggested that the book should appear solely under my name because, despite our collaborative work, we did not consider it to be an autobiography.

In preparing these additional notes for publication, I was not restricted by the need for thematic coherence, as I had been for *Memories*. I have therefore been able to make the fragmentary character of the statements much more clearly evident. The notes are dated and the book thus has the more suitable feel of a diary. In certain cases, a short introductory comment or note explains the relevant context of the situation in which the remarks were made. The sections are not in chronological order, but have been arranged according to four general topics.

Not much time remains for me at my present age. I wish to thank all those who have encouraged and supported me in producing this book and share my belief in the value of publishing these notes, in particular Sir Laurens van der Post of London, as well as Robert Hinshaw and Elena Fischli, publishers at Daimon Verlag, Einsiedeln, who are editing the text according to my instructions in preparation for a future publication.

Aniela Jaffé
Summer 1991

effect, but unfortunately the publisher did not agree to the changes. I then again revised the entire manuscript, with Jung's agreement, to make it solely his side of the conversations. That structure is possibly what often led to the false assumption that Jung had dictated the text to me word for word. [Ed.: see the "Historical Commentary" of this publication for a full editorial epilogue, pp. 197 ff.]

On Personality and Life Experience

Accepting What Life Presents Me With

October 20, 1959

People do not realize just how much they are putting at risk when they don't accept what life presents them with, the questions and tasks that life sets them. When they resolve to spare themselves the pain and suffering they owe to their nature. In so doing, they refuse to pay life's dues and for this very reason, life then often leads them astray.

If we don't accept our own destiny, a different kind of suffering takes its place: a neurosis develops, and I believe that *that* life which we have to live is not as bad as a neurosis. If I have to suffer, then let it be from *my* reality. A neurosis is a much greater curse! In general, a neurosis is a replacement for an evasion, an unconscious desire to cheat life, to avoid something.

One cannot do *more* than live what one really is. And we are all made up of opposites and conflicting tendencies. After much reflection, I have come to the conclusion that it is better to live what one really is and accept the difficulties that arise as a result – because avoidance is much worse.

Today I can say: I have been true to myself, I have done what I could to the best of my knowledge and conscience. Whether it was right or not, I cannot say.

Suffering was inevitable in any case. But I want to suffer for *those* things which really belong to me. A decisive factor for me in choosing this path was the knowledge that if I did not respond fully to my life's purpose and challenges, then they would be inherited by my children,

Islands of calm in the flow of time were her afternoons with the biographical conversations: C.G. Jung in the summer of 1959; photo © Aniela Jaffé.

who would have to bear the burden of my unlived life in addition to their own difficulties.

I am aware of what a heavy burden was passed on to me by my parents. Such a burden cannot simply be shaken off. You find yourself weighed down with an inheritance that you have to accept and carry around like a snail carrying its house on its back. Being "smart" and behaving reasonably are not enough to get you through life. You may well spare yourself some trouble, but you cut yourself off from your own life in the process.

I have seen the fate of those who have not lived their own lives, and it is simply horrible. People who live out their destiny and fulfill it to the best of their knowledge and abilities have no reason for regret. In a way, Voltaire was right when he said one only has to regret "*surtout ce que l'on n'a pas fait.*"[1] It is of immense importance that we as humans accept the debts incumbent on us. In old age it is not the wonderful things that we perhaps missed out on seeing or experiencing that we will regret, but rather the moments when we let life pass us by.

1 C.G. Jung liked to sprinkle his speech with expressions and phrases in English and French, especially when speaking High German – as he usually did with me – and not the Basel dialect. The aphorism "one regrets not what one has done, but what one has not done" is attributed to the Roman emperor and philosopher Marcus Aurelius (121–180). Here Jung emphasizes the *regret* for matters left undone. [Ed.: Jung often quoted freely in conversation, sometimes simply drawing casually on his broad knowledge as a well-educated intellectual. As it is not always possible to find out which editions he used as sources, exact bibliographical references cannot be given apart from for Jung's own works. For a more precise study of the sources in C.G. Jung's library see Shamdasani, S., *C.G. Jung – A Biography in Books*, 2012].

Insight, Secrecy and Community

December 6, 1957

True connection with other people, with the world, with the cosmos, is impossible unless we know what is going on inside ourselves. It was only my understanding of what is common to all people, the unconscious with its collective contents, the archetypal, that enabled me to relate to others. As a young man, of course I thought I understood people and had relationships. But other people basically meant nothing to me!

However, the urge to understand the mysteries of the soul would not let me go; I felt compelled to reflect on these things. It did not simply come down to a compulsion, but to my own will, my temperament. It was actually what I always wanted. Because of this intense desire to understand the soul, as a young doctor I even wished that I could experience schizophrenia myself, or at least have a love affair with a schizophrenic woman, so that I could find out what went on in these people.

I became lonely, not on account of my desire for insight, but because of what this led me to – the acquisition of insight. At first there was no one around me who could understand. And, strictly speaking, even now I am talking to you about matters I was never able to explain before – to anyone. If you gain something from it, you too will be set apart from others. Knowledge can make you feel alone, cause a loneliness.

The opposite is also true, however: knowledge of the archetypal forces is necessary to understand the deeper meaning of community and companionship. True community comes through shared knowledge and insight.[1] There is little point in finding community through shared banalities. Some special exclusive insight that can be shared with a few others is what binds people together. For primitive people,[2] therefore, community is always linked with secrecy. Community is a kind of mystery cult.

1 See also C.G. Jung's comments on secrets and societies bound together by archetypal experiences in Jaffé, A. (ed.), 1962, p. 342ff. and p. 355f. The above remarks were made in the context of Jung's recollection of dreams and reflections after his illness of 1944, ibid. p. 289ff.

2 For Jung the terms "primitive" and "Negro" – which from the 18th century onward were broadly used in everyday speech as well as literary and academic language – did not have the negative connotations they have today. From the 1970s the discriminatory connotations of these terms, closely connected with colonialism, began to be discussed. They are now considered ethnocentric, racist descriptors. Jung's use of these words here and in later chapters about his experiences in Africa has been kept by Aniela Jaffé, just as they were kept in the original in Jung's *Collected Works*. [Ed. note]

True Encounters

The publisher Kurt Wolff, in his initial letters to me about the biography project, said he would like Jung to talk about his relationships and contact with other well-known contemporaries. Although I immediately responded that Jung clearly preferred to speak about inner experiences and not outer ones, Kurt Wolff repeatedly returned to the matter and even wanted an entire chapter dedicated to the subject. When I mentioned it occasionally in our conversations, Jung's reactions ranged from wearily unenthusiastic to downright irritated. In response to my last two attempts to bring up the matter, he explained in no uncertain terms the kind of encounters that were meaningful for him.

May 23, 1958

I enjoy meeting people. Many come to me with concerns that I cannot or may not discuss with others. But if subsequently people are seized by an idea that they cannot drop or that leads to failure, it has nothing to do with me.

Encounters with famous contemporaries? I met with Toynbee[1] twice and told him something about my ideas. But he gave away nothing about himself. And I never heard whether the conversation had any effect on him... I got to know Lowell, the famous astronomer, in my younger years – he was my sponsor when I received the doctorate

1 Arnold J. Toynbee (1889–1975), British historian, cultural theorist and philosopher of history.

at Clark University[2]... My relationship with Pauli?[3] Would I be able to talk about that...?

(After a long period of silent reflection)

You'd think I had no friends and no relationships. Not true! I have very individual relationships with each of my children, children-in-law and grandchildren. But the decisive encounters in my life were those with quite ordinary people – or people we do the disservice of calling "patients." They were the encounters from which I learned something. The same is true of my meetings with Mountain Lake[4] and with a simple pandit in India.[5]

The significance of these "insignificant people" is that they are human beings who gave of their essence in the encounter. It was revealed or became obvious without them wanting it to; I encountered their true selves. You only find this when people fully experience their life and events. It has nothing to do with particular achievements in the outer world. That is only the foreground.

I always wanted the *background*. That was decisive, what I looked for. And I found people with whom I could have such a relationship. I have numerous relationships, many with people I count as friends.

February 6, 1959

My true encounters are so profound that it is hardly possible to speak of them. Others would not be able to understand why certain people were important to me, what they meant to me and why they

2 Percival Lowell (1855–1916), American astronomer. C.G. Jung was awarded an honorary doctorate from Clark University, Worcester, Massachusetts, on September 13, 1909 together with William Stern (1871–1938) and Sigmund Freud (1856–1939).

3 Physicist Wolfgang E. Pauli (1900–1958) received the Nobel Prize for Physics in 1945 in recognition of his Exclusion Principle. He and C.G. Jung had a longstanding relationship. See Jung, C.G./ Pauli, W., *The Interpretation of Nature and the Psyche*, 1955; Meier, C.A. (Ed.), *Atom and Archetype: The Pauli/Jung Letters 1932–1958*, 1992.

4 A chief of the Taos Pueblo, in the indigenous language Ochwiä Biano, otherwise known as Antonio Mirabal. In 1925 Jung visited a group of Native Americans in New Mexico and talked with Mountain Lake. He vividly described this encounter to me in mid-May 1958. Cf. also Jaffé, A. (ed.), 1962, p. 246ff., and Jaffé, A. 1979, p. 155, illus. 147.

5 Cf. Jaffé, A. (ed.), 1962, p. 277ff.

were so significant. There are stones with gold hidden inside – nobody knows about it because they look like quite ordinary stones, apparently of no use to anyone. But with the right methods it is possible to extract the gold.

Encounters were most important to me when they illuminated the hidden depths of the soul. I could also put it like this: when I can access what is in the background, I can relate to others – if not, they do not really interest me. I was and am able to find access to people where one would least expect it, to unusual and wondrous people. That was the case with Babette for example.[6]

I can be in an intense relationship with the most unlikely people, an inner relationship. I know people who interest me greatly because they are seized by these background processes or because these dynamics and influences shine through them. This enables me to relate to them. Then nothing about a person can be trivial or ugly or repulsive enough to frighten me off.[7] I can develop the patience of a saint because I am able to sense the background. You cannot explain it if you have not experienced it yourself.

I appreciate positive human qualities very much, but decisive for me is always whether I sense this otherness – the background – or its absence. If that is missing, I will not even look twice at someone. Of course, there are great human qualities which I value highly, but it is only when someone is connected to the background forces that I find them fascinating. Everything else pales in comparison. Living with some of these people, however, would be another matter...

---

6 A schizophrenic patient whom Jung treated at the University Hospital of Psychiatry Zürich (Burghölzli). Cf. C.G. Jung "On the Psychology of Dementia Praecox" and "The Content of the Psychoses" both in CW 3, *The Psychogenesis of Mental Disease*, trans. R.F.C. Hull, 1960. Cf. also Jaffé, A. (ed.), 1962, p. 125ff.

7 C.G. Jung alludes here to Sigmund Freud's question when visiting Burghölzli in 1908 as to how Jung could bear "spending hours and days with this phenomenally ugly female" (referring to Babette). See ibid., p. 128.

On My Mother's Second Voice

June 7, 1957

On this day, C.G. Jung talked about his mother. Since early childhood, and again during significant phases of his adulthood, he had been aware of two personalities in her. The usually visible one was a warm-hearted, conventional and affable woman, but at decisive moments a second voice with powerful, unassailable authority could emerge, stirring simmering, deep-seated contents in Jung, e.g., the issue of the anima or his research ambitions.[1] *In January 1958, a few months after this description of his mother's twofold personality, C.G. Jung wrote, in "From the Earliest Experiences of My Life,"*[2] *about his own twofold personality, calling the two aspects number 1 and number 2.*

As a young assistant physician at Burghölzli[3] in Zürich, I lived on Zollikerstrasse. I was working on the association experiments[4] at the time, and my whole room was plastered with graphs. One day my mother visited me, with no idea of what I was doing. She looked

1 Cf. Jaffé, A. (ed.), 1962, p. 48ff.
Anima: Personification of a feminine nature in the unconscious of a man, often projected onto a woman. This dual sexuality of the psyche postulated by Jung corresponds to the biological fact that a person's sex is determined by having a greater number of male or female genes. The smaller number of genes of the opposite sex seem to form an opposite-sex personality, but one which often remains undeveloped and therefore unconscious.

2 Cf. Jaffé, A. (ed.), 1962, p. vi.

3 University Hospital of Psychiatry Zürich (also called the Forel Clinic by Jung), at that time under the directorship of Eugen Bleuler. See also fn. p. 44.

4 Cf. C.G. Jung, CW 2, *Experimental Researches*, trans. R.F.C. Hull, 1973, para. 1350ff.

around the room and then asked: "What's all this then?" – "These are the graphs from the experiments I'm working on at the moment." I was feeling rather proud of my efforts. But at that point I had no idea yet whether my results would come to anything. I was just at the point of discovering what the disturbances in the experiments might mean, and assumed they were connected with feeling-toned, autonomously acting complexes.[5] My mother looked at all the drawings again and suddenly stood up – like a judge – and with her "second" voice asked me: "Well, do you think it could be something?"

My mother rarely spoke in this tone – but when she did, she would intuitively and unexpectedly say something of great significance. At those times she often hit exactly on an unacknowledged or unconscious feeling of mine. And sometimes what she said sounded something like an ambiguous oracle. In this case, I could have taken her question to mean either that I was not valuing my work highly enough, or that I was overestimating its worth. But in any case, she gave voice to an unrecognized doubt within me.

Her question affected me so much that I could not lift a pen for the next three weeks. Her words had unflinchingly exposed my own doubts about the importance of my undertaking, and now I asked myself in all seriousness whether what I was doing really made sense. I always find it hard to accept that my own judgment can deceive me. My mother, in that very moment, had expressed my own unacknowledged apprehension. And she did so in that grave serious voice, so different from her usual way of speaking – as if she wanted to make me realize that my work really did have something worthwhile, but at the same time raise the doubt about whether it amounted to anything. Almost in the same breath, she added: "I don't understand any of it!"

---

5 In the work of C.G. Jung, complexes do not have the same meaning as in everyday language. He describes them as "(...) psychic fragments which have split off owing to traumatic influences or certain incompatible tendencies. As the association experiments prove, complexes interfere with the intentions of the will and disturb the conscious performance; they produce disturbances of memory and blockages in the flow of associations; they appear and disappear according to their own laws; they can temporarily obsess consciousness, or influence speech and action in an unconscious way. In a word, complexes behave like independent beings, a fact especially evident in abnormal states of mind. In the voices heard by the insane they even take on a personal ego-character like that of the spirits who manifest themselves through automatic writing and similar techniques." See C.G. Jung, CW, Vol. 8, *The Structure and Dynamics of the Psyche*, trans. R.F.C. Hull, 1969, para. 253.

It was like a Delphic oracle: "Thus, or just not thus." Ambiguous and pregnant with meaning like the prophecy: "If you cross the Halys you will destroy an empire!"[6] Actually, my mother emphasized the great significance of what was present.

6 C.G. Jung quotes the ambiguous prophecy of Pythia (the Oracle of Delphi) to Croesus, King of the Lydians, who failed to consider that his attack on Persia might lead to his own empire being defeated (546 BC); Jung mixes up the Halys river with the Rubicon river, which Caesar crossed before taking over Rome. For an earlier, divergent, description of this event, see also McGuire W. (ed.), *Dream Analysis, Notes of the Seminar given in 1928–30 by C.G. Jung*, 1984, p. 97.

Time Out Before Marriage: Paris and Oxford

October 4, 1957

At the end of September 1957, Kurt Wolff visited Zürich and read some of my notes for the first time. He requested that Jung add more about the role of art, music and literature in his life. He was also interested in hearing Jung describe his relationship to some of the paintings hanging in his house in Küsnacht. A few days later, Jung was ready to talk to me about these subjects.

When I was in high school, I often visited the Basel art collection.[1] I already admired Holbein and Böcklin, even then, and I loved the old Dutch masters. People in Basel at that time were very interested in art, thanks to the influence of Jakob Burckhardt.[2] Later I started my own collection of old etchings, including some pieces by Boucher and some early German color woodcuts. An etching and a woodcut by Dürer are among them.[3] When I was in Paris in 1902, I spent hours ambling around the *bouquinistes'* stalls and bought a few things.[4] That is where I stumbled across the Dürer engraving. For a whole year I ded-

1 The collection has been in the Kunstmuseum Basel since 1936; in Jung's youth it was housed in the museum on Augustinergasse which is now the Natural History Museum.
2 The cultural and art historian Jakob Burckhardt (1818-1897) held the professorial chair for history and art history at the University of Basel from 1858 to 1893.
3 François Boucher (1703–1770); Albrecht Dürer (1471–1528).
4 *Bouquinistes*: Booksellers of antiquarian books, in particular at the street stalls along the banks of the Seine in Paris.

icated myself almost exclusively to art. That was before I returned to Burghölzli after my "sabbatical" – later on I no longer had enough free time. I had taken up my duties at Burghölzli at the age of twenty-five, straight after passing the state examination for medicine in 1900. In fall 1902, I took a break from my post and went first to Paris for six months and then to England for two months.[5] In Paris I attended lectures by Janet at the *École des Hautes Études*[6], but I did not know him personally. Charcot was already dead by then. I did meet Binet in person, but nobody else apart from him.[7] I also visited the asylums and a few hospitals. At that time the French were at the forefront of psychiatry and I was well-versed in the French literature on the subject.

But as far as possible, I put medicine to the side. Instead I immersed myself in the museums and soaked up the art. I went to the Louvre almost every day and gazed innumerable times at *La Gioconda*[8] and paintings by the Italian renaissance artists. I enjoyed chatting to the copyists there and had a copy of a Frans Hals done.[9] I also commis-

5 In a later conversation on 11 April 1958 Jung said that in 1902 he had "been in Paris for about four months – from September to December." We know from his correspondence with his cousin Hélène Preiswerk that he was still in Paris at the beginning of January 1903, traveling from there to London on January 19. A few weeks later he returned to Switzerland via Ostend; he and Emma Rauschenbach were married in Schaffhausen on February 14, 1903.

6 In 1902 Pierre Janet (1859-1947) held a professorial chair for psychology at the *Collège de France*, but was also head of the *Laboratoire de psychologie expérimentale et comparée* at the *Salpêtrière*. When Jung mentioned attending Janet's lectures, he twice said that they had been at the École des Hautes Études. The *Hôpital de la Salpêtrière* is affiliated with the École Pratique des Hautes Études. It is possible that Jung also attended lectures by Alfred Binet at his *Laboratoire de la psychologie physiologique* at the Sorbonne. (See next footnote on Jung's contact with Binet.) On another occasion he distanced himself from Janet, saying that his lectures had been "terribly boring" and that as a young psychiatrist he had not been able to learn much from him. In a letter to Freud on September 11, 1907 Jung wrote: "Janet is a vain old buffer, though a good observer. But everything he says and does now is sterile." (McGuire, W. (ed.) *The Freud/Jung Letters*, trans. Ralph Mannheim and R.F.C. Hull, 1979, p. 85). However, elsewhere Jung said that Janet's publications had been important for him, and during his time as attending physician at Burghölzli he gave lectures on Janet at the University of Zürich.

7 Jean-Martin Charcot (1825-1893) was a neurologist and anatomical pathologist who ran the research laboratory at the *Hôpital de la Salpêtrière*, Paris; psychologist Alfred Binet (1857–1911) was one of the main founders of psychometrics. After several years under Charcot at the *Salpêtrière* he switched to the *Laboratoire de psychologie physiologique* at the Sorbonne, which he directed from 1894 until his death. In 1902 C.G. Jung had talked with him about the association experiments and a possible collaboration, but it never came to pass.

8 Leonardo da Vinci's Mona Lisa – said to be a portrait of the Florentine merchant's wife Lisa del Giocondo.

9 The family portrait *Van Beresteyn-van der Eem* was sold to the Louvre in 1885 as a Frans Hals (1581/1585–1666) painting. According to art history analyses, it is now thought to have been painted by Pieter Claesz Soutman (1593/1601–1657), a contemporary of Frans Hals. In 1902 C.G.

sioned a copy of Ghirlandaio's painting *Vieillesse et Jeunesse*[10] as a birthday gift for my fiancée. It is the portrait of an old man looking at a child of around four years old. The expression on both of their faces is wonderful. They are reading themselves in each other's eyes. The old man embodying the past, the boy embodying the future. The quizzical look on the child's face is unbelievably tender. I had the copy of Fra Filippo Lippi's *The Adoration in the Forest* done later, in Florence.[11] The Egyptian art that I saw in the Louvre also left an indelible impression on me.

In Paris, two phenomena touched me deeply: one was the beautiful art and the other was *la misère qui a froid, la misère noire.*[12] I read various statistical works in an attempt to get a better picture of the social conditions. Paris made an enormous impression on me. On the one hand such beauty and on the other such terrible squalor.

Actually, I found myself in a terrible state, I'd never seen anything like it before. The whole of human misery...[13] I was completely occupied with dark thoughts about the suffering of humankind, about the gaping black abyss. Feelings of a *grande compassion* surged in me. I often thought of the Buddha, about whom I had read in Schopenhauer. That people could find Paris *amusant* baffled me. I was far too affected by the social tragedy. I visited the Paris Morgue, went to *Les Halles*, spent time in the poor parts of the city.[14] Paris was either wonderfully beautiful, tasteful and elegant – or it was a pit of squalor. I found it very difficult to bear. I lived on one franc a day, even though I was already a doctor. I stayed in a student hotel, *Hôtel des Balcons*, in Rue Casimir

---

Jung commissioned a copy by Léontine Lemée of a detail from the right-hand side of the painting showing the family's nanny with the four small children. The copy hung above the marble fireplace in the dining room of the Jung family home at Seestrasse 228 in Küsnacht. Cf. Foundation C.G. Jung Küsnacht (ed.), *The House of C.G. Jung*, 2009, pp. 70, 74, 75 (there listed erroneously as a copy of a Frans Hals painting).

10 Domenico Ghirlandaio (1449–1494), *Ritratto di vecchio con nipote*, ca. 1490, Louvre, Paris.

11 Fra Filippo Lippi (1404–1469), *Adorazione del Bambino di Annalena*, completed between 1453 and 1455, Uffizi Gallery, Florence, Italy. Copy by Giulia Cheli Capella. This and the Ghirlandaio copy also hung in the Jung family's dining room.

12 "The misery that is cold, the black misery."

13 Picasso at the same time was experiencing and exploring his "Blue Period," with paintings depicting the loneliness and poverty he encountered in Paris.

14 *La Morgue* was a public attraction in Paris until it closed in 1907. Bodies found on the street or pulled out of the Seine were publicly displayed so that visitors could help with their identification. *Les Halles* was the central fresh food market in Paris.

Delavigne. I would not wish to have missed this time of poverty.[15] It taught me to appreciate the simple things.

I also painted my own pictures at that time. Landscapes of northern France, small watercolors. And once a large picture of clouds.[16] Also a few smaller sketches, not that many. One night I stayed up until four in the morning painting – a landscape painted from memory. This foreign landscape had made a powerful impression on me – the colors, the atmosphere.

Often I wandered alone around Paris and the surrounding area – Fontainebleau, Versailles, Trianon, and so on. I had to think of Napoleon. I was totally *imbued by French*,[17] and also read a lot of French novels. Later I subscribed to the French newspaper *Le Matin* for a long time, and acquired a wide vocabulary. In Paris I spoke like a Frenchman. I always ate in small, relatively simple bistros and talked with ordinary people – in the street, in shops, or wherever the opportunity presented itself. In that way I even more or less mastered the *argot*.[18]

From Paris I went to England, where I found it difficult to adjust. At that time my English was still very limited. I did not attend any lectures there, just visited some hospitals, and spent most of my time in museums and galleries again. Oxford was the high point of my stay in England. It was a city that suited me very well. The thrill I felt upon seeing the colleges for the first time is unforgettable. And the conversations that went on there! After dinner a silver snuff mull was passed around. Then came black coffee with cigars and liqueurs, followed by intellectual discussions in the style of the 18th century. Only men were present, because the discourse was supposed to be exclusively intellectual.

15 After finishing university Jung had to repay a considerable debt to his uncle (3,000 francs – equivalent to about 30,000 dollars today) as well as support his mother and sister.

16 Cf. Jaffé, A., 1977, Illus. 35-36. [Ed.: see also *C.G. Jung. The Red Book*, Museum Rietberg exhibition catalog, 2010, pp. 4, 5, and Hoerni, U., Fischer, Th., Kaufmann B./Foundation of the Works of C.G. Jung (ed.), *The Art of C.G. Jung*, 2019, p. 85]

17 Trans. note: Jung said the phrase "imbued by French" in English. Hereafter, where Jung used English words in his speech, this has been indicated by italics in the text.

18 *Argot* originally referred to a historical sociolect spoken by French thieves and beggars in the Middle Ages, a kind of secret language. Later the term came to mean simple or bawdy slang. Victor Hugo used *argot* for many passages in his novel *Les Misérables*.

Early Reading Experiences

October 4, 1957

When asked which works of literature most influenced his development, C.G. Jung had the following recollections:

Two books are among my earliest memories. The first story to leave a deep and lasting impression on me was the Grail legend. It was my favorite book as a child, I thought it was really wonderful. I read it twice in a row. The Grail figures have accompanied me ever since, I found them mysteriously fascinating. However, I seldom mentioned them in my writings, as my wife had begun quite early on to write about the Grail legend.[1]

The second work of literature to affect me deeply was Goethe's *Faust*. But I was fifteen or sixteen by then. It was my mother who told me: "Now you really must read *Faust*." This book then made the greatest impression on me. Yes, it was *the* book, everything else paled in comparison. There were also a few poems by Goethe that stood out, but in my opinion nothing reached the heights of *Faust*. *Faust* always felt like a personal bequest to me. Goethe did not really complete the story. Some issues remain unanswered.[2] His other plays and his style, however, this "distinguished style" of his, I found too *ponderous*, too overdone. True, *Wilhelm Meister* is a really good book, but it did not

1 Jung, Emma/von Franz, Marie-Louise, *The Grail Legend*, Princeton University Press, Princeton, 1970.

2 Jung refers above all to the unatoned murders of Philemon and Baucis. Cf. Jaffé, A. (ed.), 1962, p. 235ff.

really impress me that much.[3] Later I read his *Conversations with Eckermann* with interest, but I always found them rather awkward, too.[4]

When I was a student, I discovered Hölderlin and got to know his poem "Patmos." At the time I held it to be a high point of German lyric poetry.

"...But high in the light
Blossoms the silver snow,
And, witness to life everlasting
On attainless walls
The immemorial ivy grows..."[5]

A lot of Hölderlin's other work is stylized or has a somewhat exaggerated emotionality, but for me "Patmos" is unsurpassable.

And then I came across Mörike's "Orplid"[6] – an exquisite poem! It stood out way above all his other poems, which seemed surprisingly average to me. Hugo Wolf turned "Orplid" into a wonderful song.[7] "Patmos" and "Orplid" – both of those poems are indelibly etched in my memory.

Curiously, Vischer's *Auch Einer* also inspired me then.[8] I came across this novel at the same time as I began reading Schopenhauer.

3 *Wilhelm Meister's Journeyman Years, or the Renunciants*, first German edition 1821, complete edition 1829, Stuttgart, Cotta; English edition 1989, New York, Suhrkamp (in Goethe's collected works; v. 10).

4 Johann Peter Eckermann (1792–1854), German writer, *Conversations with Goethe in the Last Years of His Life*, Boston and Cambridge, 1852. See also p. 80.

5 Friedrich Hölderlin (1770-1843), German poet. "Patmos" is the title of a hymn completed in 1803. Translation here by Michael Hamburger, 1952. C.G. Jung writes comprehensively about the poem in CW 5, *Symbols of Transformation*, 1967, para. 630–642; see also CW 6, 1971, para. 446 and Jung's note in CW 13, *Alchemical Studies*, 1967, para. 300.

6 Eduard Mörike (1804–1875), German poet and theologian; his poem *Gesang Weylas* about the fantasy island of Orplid was written in 1831: "You are Orplid, my land! / That shines afar; / Your sunlit shore sends up sea – / Mists, that moisten the cheeks of the gods. / Ancient waters climb, / Rejuvenated, child, about your waist! / Kings, who attend you, / Bow down before your divinity." (Eduard Mörike, *Gedichte*, Stuttgart, 1867; trans. Richard Stokes, *The Book of Lieder*, Faber, 2005).

7 Hugo Wolf (1860–1903), Austrian composer of Slovenian heritage, set *Weylas Gesang* to music in 1888 as part of his series of compositions of Mörike's poems (no. 46, D-flat major).

8 Friedrich Theodor Vischer (1807–1887), German writer and philosopher. *Auch Einer* [Also One] was the title of his very successful novel published in 1879 about a fictional eccentric Swiss protagonist. In his essay on the trickster figure, Jung writes that Vischer's novel was previously considered part of German general education (GW 9/I, *Die Archetypen und das kollektive Unbewusste*, 1985, p. 271ff. – no reference to Vischer could be found in the English edition).

He was the first of the modern philosophers that I read.[9] Schopenhauer's vision of the world, his pessimistic world view, was something I sometimes shared and other times rejected.

Schopenhauer was followed by Kant.[10] I studied Kant very seriously. With him it was about this careful detail work and accuracy in distinguishing what belongs to me or is within my sphere of influence, and what goes beyond it, to whence we cannot reach without causing damage.

After that I became interested in Nietzsche.[11] Above all *Zarathustra* – that moved me deeply.[12] This book brought a troubling problem for me: what happened to Nietzsche with *Zarathustra*? It is about Nietzsche's encounter with the archetypal figure of the wise old man, but an encounter that remained hanging in the air, in an unreal netherworld. Other works by Nietzsche moved me intellectually, but *Zarathustra* touched me personally. *Faust* and *Zarathustra*, in a way both are on the same level – both provided a connection to something within me.

I could not really connect to more contemporary German literature. I found it somehow too psychological, and although there were some interesting things, they did not move me deeply. Of course I read Shakespeare's plays and sonnets, but I always found them to be typical "literary" creations. The poetry is very good, but it did not really touch me. I had more of a connection to Schiller with his ethical pathos. I felt a particularly genuine and positive connection with his prose writing.[13] Of course I also recognized the beauty of individual poems,

9 On the significance of Schopenhauer (1788–1860) for the young C.G. Jung see also Jaffé, A. (ed.), 1962, pp. 69, 74f., 80. See also p. 75 in this book.

10 Immanuel Kant (1724–1804), German philosopher of the enlightenment. C.G. Jung refers mainly to *Critique of Pure Reason*; as a young man however, he was also impressed by *Dreams of a Spirit-Seer*. See also Jaffé, A. (ed.), 1962, pp. 70, 71f., 74, 99, 101.

11 Friedrich Wilhelm Nietzsche (1844–1900), philosopher, poet, writer. See also Fn. 6, p. 22. Four months after this conversation, C.G. Jung wrote about his own youth and the books that had influenced him and referred in more detail to the influence of Schopenhauer, Kant and Nietzsche. Cf. also Jaffé, A. (ed.), 1962, p. 69ff.

12 *Thus Spoke Zarathustra. A Book for All and None.* Parts 1 and 2 1883, Part 3 1884, Part 4 1891. C.G. Jung studied this book intensively: from spring 1934 until the end of 1939 he gave seminars in English on *Nietzsche's Zarathustra*. The notes of the seminars were first published in book form in 1988 by Princeton University Press, ed. James L. Jarrett, and in 1989 by Routledge, London. See also in CW 6, 1971, "The Apollonian and the Dionysian," para. 223–240.

13 See ibid., "Schiller's Ideas upon the Type Problem," para. 101–222.

but they were like flowers that one chances upon. I could not say that one or another left a special impression on me.

When I asked about his impressions of classical Greek and Roman literature, Jung answered:

I loved the world of the Odyssey.[14] Also parts of Virgil's *Aeneid* and his *Eclogues*, especially the fourth,[15] and some poems of Horace.[16] Later on, Apuleius was very significant for me. In his writing I always sensed the problem of the transformation of the soul as it presented itself in ancient times. It therefore had a strong impact on me, but I came to it quite late, when I had already started researching the psychology of the unconscious.[17] The Greek dramas, meanwhile, held little attraction; even Plato did not really interest me, did not really speak to me.[18] Of the Greek philosophers Heraclitus was my favorite.[19] He had amazing intuition and insight.

14 The epic poem ascribed to the Greek poet Homer tells of the adventures of Odysseus and his companions on their return journey to Ithaca from the Trojan war.

15 Virgil's *Eclogues*, part of the *Bucolics*, were written in around 40 BC. The fourth eclogue describes a new era ushered in by the birth of a boy, for which reason it was later often seen as a Messianic prophecy. Cf. C.G. Jung's words in CW 10, 1970, para. 250: "A direct result of slave influence was the strange melancholy and longing for deliverance that pervaded imperial Rome and found striking impression in Virgil's Fourth Eclogue." Cf. also CW 5, 1967, para. 119.

16 Horace (65 BC–8 BC), one of the most important Roman poets alongside Virgil and Ovid. His philosophical standpoint was well received in Renaissance humanism and neoclassicism.

17 Lucius Apuleius Madaurensis, born in the second century. Roman writer, known mainly for *Metamorphoses*. C.G. Jung refers here to *Liber XI* of *Metamorphoses* and the story "The Golden Ass." See CW 5, 1967, para. 56–175 ("The Hymn of Creation," "The Song of the Moth"). A few years before this conversation, Jung had also read Erich Neumann's work on Apuleius, *Amor and Psyche: The Psychic Development of the Feminine*, with great interest; cf. Neumann, E., 1956.

18 Jung's distancing of himself from Plato here would appear to be a circumstantial reaction. In the chapter "The Problem of Types in the History of Classical and Medieval Thought," CW 6, 1971, para. 8ff., he discusses Plato's work at length. Cf. also CW 9/I, 1968, para. 149: "'Archetype', far from being a modern term, was already in use before the time of St. Augustine, and was synonymous with the 'Idea' in the Platonic usage."

19 Heraclitus of Ephesus, pre-Socratic philosopher, 535–475 BC. Jung repeatedly referred to Heraclitus in connection with the dynamic polarity of the soul, in particular to Heraclitus' idea of the *enantiodromia* as the constant opposing forces contained within all living things as a basic principle of existence and of the cosmic rhythm. Jung's library contained a copy of Diels, Hermann, *Die Fragmente der Vorsokratiker*, 1903.

Reminiscences of Bachofen, Burckhardt and the City of Basel

October 1, 1957

The following was C.G. Jung's response to a question of Kurt Wolff about Bachofen and Burckhardt during a visit to Bollingen.

My grandfather was from the same generation and era as Jakob Burckhardt[1] and Bachofen.[2] When attending the *Gymnasium* [high school] in Basel I often came across both men, Burckhardt on a daily basis in fact, as he taught at the school. He shuffled around absent-mindedly, always sunk deep in his own thoughts. His style of dress was not particularly elegant, with his large neckties and *Vatermörder* collars.[3] Bachofen, in contrast, drove around the city in a wonderfully fine carriage. He was very rich, a multi-millionaire, which really meant something in those days, and owned the famous "White House." I often saw him there, it was next to the "Blue House."[4] He always wore trousers that were too tight – those thin trousers with stripes – and a kind of *redingote*, a fitted frock coat. He was very elegant and had a

1 Cf. on Burckhardt also Jaffé, A. (ed.), 1962, p. 101, p. 111.
2 Johann Jakob Bachofen (1815–1887), historian of law, classicist and anthropologist, professorial chair at the University of Basel. His most important work *Das Mutterrecht* (Mother Right) was published in 1861.
3 *Vatermörder* was the name for stiff high collars worn in the 19th century.
4 The "White House" and the "Blue House" are two neighboring mansions built by architect Samuel Werenfels for the patricians Lucas and Jakob Sarasin on the street Rheinsprung in Basel, and are considered to be the most significant baroque buildings in the city.

potbelly, but his round face made him look like a little boy – he really had the face of a child. He had a great sense of humor.

Basel was rife with stories and rumors about the two of them, such as this one: Burckhardt once had to move apartments. As he entered the house, he came across one of the movers, a huge man who had simply hoisted Burckhardt's baby grand piano onto his back. Burckhardt cried out in great astonishment: "Criminy, the Atlas!"[5] Burckhardt's sister was the grandmother of a friend of mine – Albert Oeri.[6] It was he who told me all these stories and *bonmots* about Burckhardt – some were serious, but others were just childish nonsense. My friend had the same round face as his great uncle, and also lisped like him.

Burckhardt did not appear to have close relations with women. He was a very sensitive introvert and never married. His sensitivity kept him at a distance, he was far too shy to initiate and develop a relationship with a woman. Because of this, he remained childlike, infantile.

Burckhardt always made sneering comments about Bachofen, which enticed me to become very interested in the latter.[7] All the derogatory remarks that Burckhardt let slip about Bachofen and Nietzsche piqued my interest in them. I never saw Nietzsche. He had already stepped down before my family came to Basel.[8] But I did take an interest in him and his work before turning to psychiatry. The parents of another friend of mine – Andreas Vischer – had realized that Nietzsche was anything but well-off and supported him financially.[9]

5 In Greek mythology, Atlas was a Titan who was condemned to hold up the heavens for all eternity.

6 Albert Oeri (1875–1950), historian, publicist and politician and long-time friend of C.G. Jung.

7 In his writings and letters, Jung alluded only rarely to Bachofen and Burckhardt, the latter mainly in connection with the term "primordial images." Jung: "[Archetype] embraces the same idea as is contained in 'primordial image' (an expression borrowed from Jakob Burckhardt)." (CW 6, *Psychological Types*, 1971, para. 624). On August 15, 1952 Jung wrote to Hans Schär in response to his review of *Answer to Job*, in which Schär noted Jung's spiritual affinity to Burckhardt (Schär, H., "C.G. Jung und die Deutung der Geschichte," 1952): "Your idea of my spiritual affinity or at least sympathy to Burckhardt is amazingly true. Burckhardt's pessimistic forebodings were undoubtedly right." (*Letters II*, 1971, p. 80). Jung refers here to their shared skepticism about human capacity for culture. Bachofen is mentioned even less often in Jung's work. In a letter to Professor Eugen Böhler of May 16, 1956 (*Letters II*, 1971, p. 299), Jung compares himself with Bachofen, as he "... took infinite pains to be persuasive. All in vain. His time had not yet come." On his inner relationship to the two characters, only implied by Jung, cf. also the contribution by Wolff-Windegg, P., "C.G. Jung – Bachofen, Burckhardt, and Basel," in Spring, *An Annual of Archetypal Psychology and Jungian Thought*, Zürich, 1976, pp. 137–147.

8 From 1869 to 1879 Nietzsche held a professorship in classical philology at the University of Basel.

9 Jung refers to the parents of the friend from his youth Andreas Vischer (1877–1930), a surgeon who from 1905 worked in Turkey. Vischer was socially and politically active his whole life.

Wolff had recently published a book about Jakob Burckhardt in the USA[10] *and remarked that Burckhardt's measure of aesthetic value differed greatly from modern assessments. Jung said the following in response:*

What Burckhardt overlooked in Italy and how he perceived the country is astonishing. He was not even able to appreciate Ravenna![11] It shows how aesthetic values are conditioned by a particular time. Just as Goethe did not 'see' Giotto.[12] It is a psychological prejudice pertinent to a time period. Even the genius succumbs to what is in vogue, as a mouthpiece of the times. But it is astonishing how limited Burckhardt was in his judgment: this inability to grasp Ravenna!

All in all, the Basel of my childhood, youth and student years had a cosmopolitan and sophisticated atmosphere. When I moved to Zürich, I could feel the difference: I felt like I had landed in a provincial village. Zürich's relationship to the world is not intellectual, but commercial.

Of course there were also businessmen in Basel, the "Bändeliherren."[13] They made the necessary money for the others, who had an intellectual connection with the world. The wealth of the Basel industrialists and money-makers was used to fund the university. And Basel is a border town, don't forget, which led to this curious syncretistic hybrid spirit between France, Germany and Switzerland. The language spoken, however, even in the upper echelons, was strictly Basel German dialect and not French as in Bern, for example. As Basel was not only geographically but also culturally somewhat isolated, its

10 In 1955 *Letters of Jakob Burckhardt*, ed. Alexander Dru, was published by Pantheon. Wolff was also planning an American edition of Johann Jakob Bachofen's *Mutterrecht und Urreligion* [published in English as *Myth, Religion and Mother Right* by the Bollingen Foundation, New York, 1967, with a foreword by Joseph Campbell], and in February 1954 had asked C.G. Jung to recommend further essays by Bachofen. Jung did not want to be involved in the project and suggested that Karl Kerényi write a new foreword for the book.

11 C.G. Jung refers here to the early Christian churches, baptisteries and mausoleums of Ravenna – in particular the mausoleum of the Empress Galla Placidia with its late-antique Byzantine mosaics. Cf. Jaffé, A., (ed.), p. 284ff. The main focus of Burckhardt's attention was the Italian renaissance.

12 Giotto di Bondone (1266/67–1337), Florentine painter, pioneer of the Renaissance and founder of the Tuscan fresco painters; his most significant work can be found in Rome, Florence and Padua.

13 Entrepreneurs and factory owners in the silk ribbon business, the major industry in Basel in the 19th century. The development of silk-dyeing techniques led to the start of the chemical industry in Basel.

local flavor was used as a protective shield. This phenomenon is very characteristic of the whole of Switzerland by the way. It's an expression of the mistrust that characterizes Swiss people.

In Basel those who live on the outskirts of the city toward the countryside are said to be from "across the Birs."[14] Those who do not live in Basel must therefore be miserable. When I went to Zürich people always asked me: "So, when are you coming back? Can you really live in Zürich?" That is Basel! I still have a soft spot for the city, but it's no longer like it was before. I still belong to that time when Bachofen was part of the town, and Jakob Burckhardt.

May 4, 1957

C.G. Jung also mentioned the difference between the intellectual atmosphere of Basel and Zürich on another occasion when he was recounting some memories of his early days at Burghölzli.

I was terribly spoiled from living in Basel – there was a very cultivated tradition there which was evident in conversation. You could tell people were well educated. There I belonged to the "intellectual aristocracy," so to speak. With Bleuler – who was a cross between a farmer and a schoolteacher – there was none of that.[15] What I appreciated about Zürich was that the air was free. There was no centuries-old stuffiness – but the people in Zürich often seemed to me like a conglomerate of peasants. In my early days in Zürich I mostly came across as very unlikeable to my colleagues. A few admired me, but others hated me. I was a *Basler*, I had the Basel *médisance* – the sharp tongue – and I liked to make off-color jokes. But they did not understand my critique and my ideas. They had never heard of theological discussions – in Basel I was used to having ideological debates. There, you could count on the other having had a classical education. For example, even we medical students could debate among ourselves about the different

14 The Birs is the river that forms the border between the cantons of Basel-Stadt [Basel city] and Basel-Landschaft [Basel countryside].

15 Eugen Bleuler (1857–1939), from 1898 to 1927 director of the University Hospital of Psychiatry, Burghölzli, in Zürich and professor of psychiatry at the University of Zürich. C.G. Jung worked under his directorship from 1900 to 1909.

styles of Ciceronian rhetoric. It was taken for granted. As medical students we argued about Schopenhauer, about Kant, about various theological approaches. It was a cultured and intellectually stimulating environment. That did not exist in Zürich.

Transference, Willingness to Follow and Responsibility

March 19, 1958

The following comments came a short time after Jung had told me how Freud had exhorted him – like father to son – to uphold the latter's theory of sexuality; Jung, however, had very early on fostered his own ideas which deviated from Freud's. Just before this conversation, Jung had looked through a collection of essays written by Toni Wolff and sent them to the publisher Daniel Brody, including the two articles "The Individuation Process in Women" and "Structural Forms of the Feminine Psyche." He had also recently received some letters and publications dealing with the topic of nationality.[1]

The attitude of men and women in the case of transference onto a man is very different. I have often experienced that a man with a positive transference toward me wants to act like me, or rather wants to adopt my psychology, while a woman wants to live out the feelings. The man may then display a boundless, crazy enthusiasm. In cases of idealistic transference of a man toward me, there was the danger that he would try to extend himself beyond the limits of his own being. He would lose all sense of proportion and follow his projection enthusiastically and often blindly, functioning from then on as a kind

1 Cf. Jaffé, A., (ed.), 1962, "Sigmund Freud" on the relationship between Freud and Jung, p. 146ff.; the essays by Toni Wolff first appeared in 1959 with Rhein Verlag in *Studien zu C.G. Jungs Psychologie,* 3rd ed., Einsiedeln, 2003; see also C.G. Jung *Letters II,* Jung to Daniel Brody, 18.3.1958, a letter of recommendation in which the year of Jung's split from Freud and the beginning of analytical psychology is described as "the fateful year."

of follower or "henchman," with me as the "general." Such a man has to learn that this "general" is basically a part of himself. I have often perceived this follower phenomenon in the souls of the Germans, in whom it plays a major role. It has something to do with their dangerous tendency to absolutism.

I once had an experience which was very telling, indeed downright comical, in this regard. When I was still working at Burghölzli, a young doctor joined our ranks, a psychiatrist from Stuttgart. He had come to Burghölzli to find out about new psychological and psychiatric viewpoints. He soon realized that I had something to say.[2] He immediately assumed the role of an acolyte. What I said was gospel! He was a nice fellow by the way, a real Swabian from a very good family.

At the time at Burghölzli, we had our own clinical jargon, a witty medics' slang, in which we used all the unlikely and funny phrases that schizophrenic patients came out with. For example, if we had to be particularly friendly to an older woman patient, we would say "Today I oiled my aunt!"[3] or "Today I made a nerve attachment with her." That was supposed to mean: I made an emotional connection with her. If you managed to convince the boss to grant you leave, you would say: "I oiled the boss so that he would give me a vacation." Normally you might say you buttered him up or soft-soaped him, i.e., got him in the right mood. If we wanted to particularly ingratiate ourselves with someone, we would say: "I'll make a nerve attachment with him."

We used these expressions and turns of phrase in casual conversation and of course always in jest. We would exclaim, for example: "My God, now I've had a thought withdrawal!" Or say, playing on Schreber's expression: "Damn it, *scilicet* again!" and other such inanities.[4] If an idea suddenly occurred to us, we might say: "One of them

2 C.G. Jung was assistant medical director at the University Hospital of Psychiatry Zürich from 1905 to 1909.

3 When a machine is oiled it runs better, so "greasing" and "oiling" here refers to dealings that are designed to curry the favor of the other person through flattery, money, etc. [Trans. note: *Tante* (aunt) is a colloquial German expression for a woman].

4 Daniel Paul Schreber (1842–1911) was a German judge and writer best known for his book *Memoirs of My Nervous Illness*, Leipzig, 1903, in which he describes his own psychosis in precise detail. In 1911 Sigmund Freud published an essay about the book, "Psycho-Analytic Notes on an Autobiographical Account of a Case of Paranoia (Dementia Paranoides)," in Freud, S., *Zwang, Paranoia und Perversion*, 1911. The mentally ill Schreber used to see little men walking on his skin. From time to time, one of these little men would invade his body and disappear with the cry

has invaded me," referring to the little men that according to Schreber crawled around on the skin.

Some time later I saw the young Swabian doctor again, and we chatted in our medics' jargon like in old times. It was *good fun*. A while after that, he died.[5] A few years after his death, a young doctor, also a psychiatrist, visited me. He said that he had learned a lot about psychology from said German physician and was very interested in the subject. In all seriousness, he then claimed that one could see how important psychology was when, for example, one "made a nerve attachment" with schizophrenics. My ears pricked up! And then he started talking about "thought withdrawal"! "My God, what expressions are you using? That was just our medics' jargon!" "Dr. X taught me these expressions!" he answered. My erstwhile colleague had actually believed they were technical terms!

There you see what effect an unconscious transference can have when it takes the form of this desire to follow. "Watching him spit and watching him cough..."[6] The worrying thing, though, is not so much the ludicrous mimicry, but the fact that the follower ventures too far beyond his own limits. He is no longer himself – and therein lies the danger.

I experienced another case like that, with a certain Mr. von X. He was homosexual. I hardly knew him personally; I was only introduced to him once. But apparently an immediate transference onto me had taken place. Incidentally, he was also a psychiatrist. I had no idea about his transference. He was in analysis with someone else, I don't know who. The analyst had apparently gone to great lengths to talk him out of his homosexuality! In his transference onto me, Mr. von X always thought that would particularly please me. So he suppressed his ho-

---

"Ei verflucht...!" ["Damn it...!]. At first, these little men had called out *"Ei verflucht noch einmal!"* ["Damn it, again!"]. Schreber was annoyed by the last words being left out and added: *"scilicet, noch einmal!"* (*scilicet*: specifically, namely).

5 Jung is probably referring to the psychiatrist Wolfgang Stockmayer (1881–1933), who was resident physician at Burghölzli in 1907 under Jung as assistant director. From 1913 Stockmayer practiced in Berlin before leading his own renowned clinic in Tübingen. Jung remained friendly with Stockmayer after his return to Germany and also gave him copies of parts of *The Red Book*. Stockmayer died at the age of 52.

6 Quote from Friedrich Schiller's *Wallenstein*. A rifleman mocks a cavalry sergeant who in eager servitude tries to imitate his commander's bearing and expressions: "Watching him spit and watching him cough, you've learned to mimic him well enough..."

mosexuality and even got married to a woman. Of course the marriage went wrong and he had to get divorced.

One day he came to me and threw the whole mess at my feet, so to speak, claiming it was all my fault. "But I don't even know you," I said to him. No, no, it was my fault that everything had gone so badly, that he had married and was now divorced. Since then he had been a nervous wreck. But I had never even worked with him, I had had nothing to do with any of it!

Here too, the man had this particular kind of transference: "He knows. He is right, so I will blindly follow him – and absolve myself of all responsibility." In doing that, he lost himself.

That, by the way, is exactly what happened in Germany. How "glorious" it was when Hitler came! Until then one always had to take care of oneself and take personal responsibility. But then along comes a man who says to everybody: "I will bear the responsibility!" And they followed the devil as far as Moscow! Are we now "the land of poets and thinkers"[7]?

It can happen to individuals that they venture too far, live in an illusion and lose themselves in the process. And then the resistances manifest themselves. In the case of Mr. von X, that happened right off the bat. The other examples show the danger of transferring responsibility onto another person, of seeing the responsibility as someone else's. Just think about what the Germans said after the Second World War: "The British should have invaded!" Yet another attempt to evade responsibility! But what would have happened if the British had actually done that? How would the Germans have reacted then? All of their hate would have come down on the British.

Someone with a transference of this type onto another person needs to recognize the danger involved and to acknowledge their own reality and responsibility – to enable them to really represent themselves and not someone else.

7 The phrase referring to Germany's self-image of cultural and intellectual greatness, often used with sardonic irony in the 20th century to evoke the intellectual values and ideals of German classicism and romanticism which had been lost. On the inflationary aspect of this German self-image and its dissociative character cf. also C.G. Jung, "After the Catastrophe," CW 10, 1970, para. 400ff.

At one time I jumped into the fray and flew the banner for Freud, but only up to the point where I could still accept responsibility for it. I had always, from the very beginning, had a *reservatio mentalis*[8] in relation to his concept of sexuality.

In transference situations, a man must know where he himself stands. And know that only he is responsible for himself. That is hard for German people. They easily fall into the intoxication of following and stumble into a kind of drunken consciousness. Then an ambivalent barbarism emerges which as a result of the lack of freedom and independence can have a very negative effect. One does not just endanger others, but also oneself. People with this desire to follow are just waiting for someone to obey and run after. They wait, like the Germans, for their monarch or supreme commander, to be wonderfully freed from their own task, from the need to think independently and bear responsibility for themselves. It was diabolical when Hitler said: *I* will bear the responsibility! That is exactly what a follower is waiting for. But it does not work – no one can take on another person's responsibility. People who want to be or become wholly themselves must bear their own responsibility and be accountable for their own lives and actions.

8 Mental reservation

Memories of the Young Einstein

March 21, 1958

> *From early January 1958, C.G. Jung dedicated himself intensively to recording the memories of his childhood, adolescence and student years. Much of the text was written at Bollingen. I was allowed to read the manuscript as it developed. At that time Jung and I often spoke about the dual nature of his personality number 1 and number 2 – he described the latter as being deeply connected with the unconscious and the archetypal. In his recollections of the young Einstein, Jung now emphasized the scientist's dual nature.*

Have I ever told you about meeting Einstein?[1] He was a guest at my house a few times during the period when he was working on his general theory of relativity, and he talked about his theory and explained its basic concepts to me. That must have been in about 1910.[2] As a person he did not leave much of an impression on me at the time. He had a soft, feeling-toned character, incredibly naive, endearingly so. But next to this, he possessed an extraordinarily autonomous mathematical understanding. This plunged him into a world of ideas, and as a person

---

1 Albert Einstein (1879–1955), theoretical physicist, Nobel Prize for Physics 1921.

2 In 1909 Albert Einstein was appointed lecturer in theoretical physics at the University of Zürich, and from October 1912 to spring 1914 held a professorship at ETH Zürich. The visits presumably took place during this period. The physicist Ludwig Hopf, also on several occasions Eugen Bleuler and once the theologian Adolf Keller were present at the dinners at the Jungs' house. See C.G. Jung, *Letters II*, 1971, pp. 108-109 (25.2.1953 to Carl Seelig). In 1905, at the age of 26, Einstein had already published the research work that was later named the *special* theory of relativity. After being invited to work with Max Planck in Berlin, he published his general theory of relativity in 1916.

he was just kind of hitched on behind. When encountering him in a personal context, it was impossible to get a grasp of his personality, and he seemed terribly soft. I experienced him as a person who consisted only of his theory: the rest was sentiment – a kind of sentimental idealism with shallow intelligence. He was probably a feeling type. His thinking was in the unconscious and functioned autonomously.

Einstein was not somebody whose ideas shone out through his personality – at least not at that time. He had something of a gentle youth about him and fostered socialist ideas;[3] one could well imagine him doing his children's mathematics homework for them as a tremendously loving, kind and indulgent but weak father. His marriage was no different from that of any average Joe. That's the conclusion I came to from my little psychological "test" anyhow.

The theory, however, made a very strong impression on me.[4] I had the feeling it was something highly significant. The *extent of it*, of its reach, however, I could not grasp; my understanding of mathematics was far too limited. As soon as Einstein began to talk about it, he was

3 Einstein, who was already an anti-militarist in his youth, was politically active from the outbreak of the First World War. He joined the German human rights league and in 1918 was one of the first signatories of the left-liberal *Deutsche Demokratische Partei*. From 1922 he was a member of the committee on intellectual cooperation at the League of Nations. At the league's request, in September 1932 he exchanged letters with Sigmund Freud on the question *Why War?*, a correspondence that has been widely read right up to this day (Einstein A./Freud S., *Warum Krieg? – Ein Briefwechsel,* 1933). Together with Heinrich Mann, Käthe Kollwitz, Ernst Toller and others, he was signatory in 1932 to the *Dringende Appell für ein antifaschistisches Bündnis* [urgent appeal for an anti-fascist alliance] to try to prevent the rising threat of National Socialism. After Hitler came to power, Einstein amended his anti-militarist stance. From 1945 he was committed to international armaments control and cooperation, and established the Emergency Committee of Atomic Scientists. In 1949 he published an essay entitled *Why Socialism*, in which he predicted the danger of an all-powerful and giant bureaucracy in a far-reaching centralization of political and economic powers, and vehemently argued for the protection of the rights of the individual and of democracy. See also: Einstein, A., Nathan, O., Norden, H., *Einstein on Peace,* Random House, New York, 1988.

4 In a letter of February 25, 1953 to Carl Seelig, patron of Robert Walser and biographer of Albert Einstein, Jung wrote of his meeting with Einstein that it was "the simplicity and directness of his genius as a thinker that impressed me mightily" and that this "exerted a lasting influence on my own intellectual work. It was Einstein who first started me off thinking about a possible relativity of time as well as space, and their psychic conditionality. More than thirty years later this stimulus led to my relation with the physicist Professor W. Pauli and to my thesis of psychic synchronicity." (*Letters II*, 1971, p. 109). In 1954, Carl Seelig's *Albert Einstein. A Documentary Biography*, based on the symposium in Bern in 1955 *50 Years of the Theory of Relativity* led by Wolfgang Pauli, was published; in 1956 Carl Seelig also published *Helle Zeit – Dunkle Zeit. In memoriam Albert Einstein*. Jung knew these publications and remarked in October 1957 that Einstein in his old age had not been able to understand the ideas of younger physicists, but had been able to accept them as a further development of the theory.

another person; he was the process itself, the equation itself. It was like with a musician who in private may be a feeble fellow but as soon as he plays, you realize: he *is* the music, his greatness is in the music. That is how it was with Einstein – he *was* the equations, he *was* mathematics. Then you got the feeling of something inexorable, something inevitable driving him, of a greatness to which there can essentially be no emotional connection. Einstein was his ideas, or his ideas were him.

With me, it is similar. I have had much trouble asserting myself alongside my ideas.[5] I was forced to follow the inner law that was imposed upon me. It left me no freedom. It was clearly the same with Einstein. He drifted off in his mathematical calculations like in a Noah's ark.

Freud was quite different in this respect. He was probably also a feeling type. But he was tougher, despite having that typical Viennese courtesy. Whereas Einstein displayed a somewhat shallow optimism and was a good-hearted philanthropist, Freud was rancorous and resentful, hard, cynical.[6] But Freud's personality was much stronger than Einstein's. Freud definitely had a striking personality.

5 See Jaffé, A. (ed.), 1962, p. 356ff. for further thoughts in this regard.

6 We had already talked about Freud at the beginning of this conversation. It is conceivable that Jung mentioned Freud again here because of his awareness of the exchange of letters between Einstein and Freud on the question *Why War?* See fn. 3, p. 42.

On the Importance of Space in a Marriage

June 27, 1958

For a creative person, marriage is a terrible risk. I had the indescribably good fortune to find a wife who gave me ample space to breathe.[1] Without that I would not have been able to do my work at all. I need to be able to think thoughts that transcend all limits, and for another person this could be devastating. Someone imprisoned in standard ways of thinking, in a relationship with a person like that, might simply lurch from one crisis to the next.

The essential question in any marriage is whether each of the partners is able to be their true selves, to self-actualize, and also allow the other partner – the husband or the wife – the freedom to follow his or her own path of individuation. A woman who is further ahead and more mature than her husband calls the tune without him knowing it, because she gives him so much space that he never even notices.

1 Emma Jung-Rauschenbach (1882–1955) was married to C.G. Jung from 1903 until her death.

Languages

September 19, 1958

The last time Kurt Wolff and I visited Bollingen together, C.G. Jung defended his use of Latin and Greek expressions, which the publisher was reluctant to include in view of the North American readership.

You can only understand the Middle Ages if you understand Latin. I would not have understood anything about psychology if I had not been able to read the old Latin texts in the original. It is incredibly important to feel part of that, to know about this period of European history and to be connected with this part of our past. One can see from American history how rootless the Americans are, how unconnected to something historical. If awareness of history is lacking, then an overemphasis on science and technology all too easily arises, which in some respects can be fatal. As professor of internal medicine, my scientifically educated grandfather published the announcements for his students in Latin, it was without question.[1] Knowledge of both Latin *and* Greek is a prerequisite for understanding alchemy. I read hundreds of manuscripts that had not been translated and that are still

1 Carl Gustav Jung (1794–1864) studied natural sciences and medicine in Heidelberg, was an assistant surgeon at the Charité hospital in Berlin and lecturer at the *Königlich-Preussische Kriegsschule* (Prussian War Academy). For political reasons, he was forced to leave Prussia in 1818 (cf. also footnote 13 on p. 57 in this regard). After a stay in Paris, in 1822 he was appointed to a professorship at the University of Basel, where he engaged in a wide variety of activities. See also Jaffé, A. (ed.), *Erinnerungen, Träume, Gedanken von C.G. Jung*, 1962, p. 400ff. The Jung family history, compiled by Aniela Jaffé, was not included in *Memories, Dreams, Reflections by C.G. Jung*. It was later translated by R.G.S. Weber and published separately in Spring Journal, Dallas, 1984, p. 35ff.

not translated today. I also preferred to read the original Latin when those texts had been translated; I found them easier to understand.[2]

Original German texts or original editions of documents from the Middle Ages are on the whole much more confusing than the Latin manuscripts because the German language of the baroque period was not so suited to crystallizing and clearly expressing thoughts as the pure structure of Latin. Whereas Latin has a rigid syntax, German is more random and freer in its structure.

I also read Greek alchemical manuscripts in the original, of course. Many of them had been translated into French by Marcellin Berthelot.[3] But the translations are not reliable, the translator did not understand the meaning of alchemy.

The last language I learned was Swahili.[4] I first learned it from a grammar book. But when I arrived in East Africa I had to relearn much of it because they speak a Swahili pidgin[5] there. Classic Swahili is no longer understood. My *headman* had been an *officer de liaison* in Tanganyika in the First World War, but his English was totally incomprehensible.[6] My *palavers*[7] with the local people were all held in this pidgin Swahili.[8] I want to give you an example of the imagistic quality

2 In one of our first conversations for the biography project, C.G. Jung told me that his father had taught him Latin from the age of five; when he went to high school his Latin teacher often asked him to fetch Latin texts and books from the university library, which the young student would "snoop into" with delight as he made his way slowly back to school while his classmates were struggling with their exercises in the classroom.

3 Marcellin (also Marcelin) Berthelot (1827–1907), French science historian, chemist and politician. C.G. Jung refers to Berthelot's translations (*Collection des anciens alchimistes grecs*, 3 vols., Paris 1887/88, *La Chimie au moyen âge*, 3 vols., Paris, 1893, and *Les Origines de l'alchimie*, Paris, 1885) in CW 5, *Symbols of Transformation*, 1967, and CW 12, *Psychology and Alchemy*, 1968.

4 Swahili is a Bantu language spoken in many parts of East Africa with many loanwords from Arabic and other languages.

5 Swahili pidgin is Swahili mixed with a variety of borrowed words from Arabic, Indian languages, Portuguese and English.

6 *Headman* = guide; *officer de liaison* = liaison officer or official. Tanganyika was a previous name for the mainland part of present-day Tanzania without Zanzibar and Pemba, or for a large part of the former German East Africa. It was introduced as a country name when the larger part of the German colonial territory was transferred by mandate to Great Britain. Since April 1964, the territory together with Zanzibar has formed the United Republic of Tanzania.

7 The word *palaver* (originally from the Greek *paraboli*) came from Portuguese usage as an expression for dealings with African business partners, and in local African usage ultimately came to mean a parley or improvised conference on a specific topic, or talks to exchange important thoughts. This is in contrast to the pejorative meaning in everyday British or American English of "idle never-ending talk or fuss."

8 See the chapter on "Spirits in Kenya" in the present volume, p. 101.

of the language: once I was getting changed for dinner and I could not find my tie. I asked my *boy*, a native of Mozambique: "Wapi necktie?" – "Where is the tie?" He answered: "Ndanya mtoto." I stopped short, as the literal translation is: "Inside the child." With a questioning tone I replied: "Mtoto?" – "Child?" to which he answered: "Ndio. Ndanya mtoto ya mesa" – "Yes, in the child of the table." This image referred to the drawer in the table.

On Wholeness and the Limits of Language

March 13, 1958

Language forms a continual hindrance and limitation to our ability to express thoughts, feelings or experiences. On the one hand, language equals idea; it is a method of passing on knowledge. On the other, it is merely made up of words and a particular syntax and grammar, and is therefore limited by its forms.[1] Thus the alchemists, for example, said of the stone they sought, the *lapis philosophorum*, that it had a thousand names – "*habet mille nomina*." And even a thousand names were not enough to express its mystery: it is the mystery of wholeness. But nevertheless, the alchemists tried to define this wholeness and named the stone *Mercurius*, or diamond, or carbuncle, and invented countless other images. One can produce a thousand words, a thousand descriptions, and yet the essential is still not expressed, the entirety is not portrayed. It transcends knowledge and language, and remains a mystery.

All instincts and drives, not only sexuality but also aggression or will to power, are expressions of a striving toward wholeness and contain an enigma. Like the psyche as a whole, every natural drive is a mystery. We do not know how these drives are constructed, just as we do not know how the psyche is constructed. The psyche always also includes the whole; the same is true of matter, and it cannot be expressed

1 Later Jung wrote in a letter that both our powers of conception and our language were lacking in the necessary "simplicity" to combine the many individual aspects of conscious cognition. Only "numinous experiences retain their original simplicity or oneness which still gives us intimations of the Unus Mundus." *Letters II*, 1971, p. 509 (to Traugott Egloff, 8.6.1959).

with words. Take power, for example: it is also a very subtle affair. One licks the other's boots and uses such behavior to gain power – it is true when one says that behind every tyrant stands an all-powerful valet. Sexuality is also an expression of a striving for wholeness, or can be. Many people do not understand that I can fully accept sexuality as an essential expression of wholeness, but not as the exclusive explanation. It is nature, it is primitive, that is its essence. At the same time, it is also a spiritual mystery, in which all that is individual is extinguished in favor of an overarching wholeness. But the essence of this wholeness remains hidden. That is the *mysterium coniunctionis.*

One must never overlook the fact that wholeness appears in many forms, but it remains a *numen*. If one does not acknowledge the truth that sexuality is numinous – it is a god and a demon – one remains stuck in the narrow, exclusively biological understanding of it. However, the *numen* cannot be described or grasped with words.

Matter is only *one* aspect of reality, as is the psyche. But the whole is present in both of them. We just cannot express it. Both are aspects of the One, of the inexpressible.

On Toni Wolff

June 14, 1957/August 1958

In connection with a recollection of his final visit with Richard Wilhelm,[1] *Jung came to speak about transgressions and sins, which were necessary and for which a debt had to be paid. He said that some transgressions were ordained by fate. Only by humbly acknowledging the transgression could redemption become possible.*

There are things in life which herald a stroke of fate. I knew this the moment I was confronted with the problem of Toni Wolff.[2] After our analytic work came to an end, I discharged her appropriately, even though I felt a very strong connection with her. Then a year later I had a dream: we were together in the Alps, and we found ourselves in a val-

1 Richard Wilhelm (1873–1930), theologian and Sinologist, lived in China for many years with his wife, a daughter of evangelical theologian Christoph Blumhardt of Bad Boll. Wilhelm, in collaboration with C.G. Jung, published the Chinese text *The Secret of the Golden Flower* in 1929. Cf. CW 13, 1967. In late fall 1929, prior to Wilhelm's death on March 2, 1930, Jung had paid him a final visit after experiencing a vivid vision; see Jaffé, A. (ed.), 1962, p. 377. According to Jung, their last conversation had revolved around Wilhelm's position between East and West, and the two men had discussed whether Wilhelm's ascetic renunciation of a love affair with a Chinese woman had been in contravention of fate.

2 Toni Wolff (1888–1953), analytical psychologist, co-founder of the Psychology Club Zürich in 1916 and club president for many years, lecturer at the C.G. Jung Institute Zürich. For forty years, until her death, Toni Wolff was personally and professionally very close to C.G. Jung. Jung said that the narrower tower at Bollingen built in the thirties represented Toni Wolff, while the earlier tower characterized his wife Emma. For a collection of Toni Wolff's essays on analytical psychology, see Wolff, T., 1959. Jung wrote an introduction for this book which was published posthumously in August 1958; see CW 10, 1970, para. 887–902. Cf. also "On the Idea of Rebirth as a Mythical Concept" and "On Dreams of Toni Wolff and Emma Jung after their Deaths" in the present work, p. 161ff.

ley surrounded by cliffs. Suddenly from inside the mountain, I heard elves singing and Toni was about to disappear into the mountain. I was deeply shocked and thought: no, it cannot be! That is when I wrote to her again.

Around that time, I had a series of dreams that preoccupied me greatly. One terrible dream was the following: I saw a woman whose body from the middle down was stone, while her top half was still alive. I knew I had given this woman an injection into her spine that had paralyzed her. I was appalled I had done such a thing, and felt racked with guilt.

And then I had a real-life experience one day when I swam out in the lake and got a cramp in my leg. I made a vow: if the cramp went away and I was able to swim back, I would give in.

The dream about the mountain cliffs reminded me of the Elf King.[3] I heard the quiet calling of the elves and saw how Toni was disappearing into the mountain – and I pulled her back. Then I knew: now it is inevitable. The anima demands her victim, I cannot avoid it any longer. It was a decision of life or death, also for me.

Of course, by taking up the relationship with her, I was thrown into such chaos that I no longer knew which way was up and which was down. But what a power drive might have been unleashed if I had evaded the anima! I would never have been able to get beyond it. Instead, it led to a relationship of great significance. During my difficult time of inner seeking[4] she accompanied me with profound psychological and human understanding, considerable natural intel-

3 The *Erlkönig* or Elf King is a legendary figure which inspired J.W. Goethe's ballad of the same name. The poem tells of a child caught between two male figures, one of whom is depicted as the savior-father, the second as a seductive nature spirit who tries to entice the child away from the father. The ballad ends in the death of the youngster. [Ed. note: As a student, Toni Wolff was close friends with fellow student William Wolfensberger; the pair exchanged poems they had written and had intimate discussions on philosophical and theological questions. To what extent Jung's dream could be taken to relate to this friendship must remain open here. On Wolfensberger's literary work and his love for Toni Wolff in the years 1910 to 1913, see Lejeune, Robert, Ed., *William Wolfensberger – Ausgewählte Werke*, 1964. Cf. also Linsmayer, Charles, Probst, Rudolf, Ed., *Eingeklemmt zwischen Unmöglichkeit und Sehnsucht*, 2007.]

4 Here Jung is referring to the years following his separation from Freud (1912 to 1919) when he was dealing with the stream of images from his unconscious. Cf. in this regard *The Red Book* and the chapter "Confrontation with the Unconscious," Jaffé, A. (ed.), 1962, pp. 170–199. Toni Wolff was Jung's patient for a few months from September 1910; he resumed contact with her in August 1911 whereupon she increasingly became part of his close circle and assisted him in his work.

ligence and great sensitivity. In giving me a firm hold, she fulfilled the role of anima in a most beautiful sense.[5] She was fertile ground for me.

5 Shortly before her death in 1955, Emma Jung referred to this support, saying: "I will always be grateful to Toni for doing for my husband what neither I nor anyone else could have done for him at a most critical time." From: Van der Post, L., 1976, p. 178. Dieter Baumann, a grandson of C.G. Jung, recalled how his grandfather had once told him at a family gathering in 1945 how important Toni Wolff's help had been to him for his discovery of the anima. Cf. BBC Broadcast, Carl Gustav Jung: 1875–1961, recording 14 July 1975, editor: Ean Begg.

The Last Desperate Attempts of Aristocracy to Be Heard: Count Keyserling

June 28, 1957

Kurt Wolff asked C.G. Jung several times to describe his encounters with Count Keyserling, probably because they had first met at gatherings hosted by Keyserling in Munich in the twenties. Jung did not display any spontaneous interest in the subject. However, when he did finally choose to talk about the count, Jung's reflections provided an example of his interest in how background influences were expressed in a person.

I became acquainted with Count Keyserling[1] in the twenties at a conference at his "School of Wisdom" in Darmstadt.[2] I already knew

1 Hermann Keyserling (1880–1946), philosopher and writer. C.G. Jung wrote reviews of three of Keyserling's books between 1928 and 1934 (see CW 10, Civilization in Transition, 1964, p. 479ff. "The Swiss Line in the European Spectrum"; ibid., p. 489ff., "The Rise of a New World"; ibid., p. 496ff., "La Révolution Mondiale"). See also C.G. Jung, *Letters I*, 1971, for various letters from C.G. Jung to Keyserling between 1927 and 1932. In Jung's "Religion and Psychology: A Reply to Martin Buber" (CW 18, 1958, para. 1499ff.), first published in *Merkur, VI*, 1952, he briefly responds to Keyserling's charge that he was "unspiritual."

2 The "School of Wisdom" was founded in Darmstadt in 1920 as a private academy of philosophy. Alongside initiator Hermann Keyserling, the publisher Otto Reichl, who was also Jung's publisher at that time, and Grand Duke of Hesse Ernest Louis were heavily involved in the founding of the school, the latter as one of the principal financial sponsors. From 1920 to 1927, the "Gesellschaft für Freie Philosophie" [Society for Free Philosophy], which was founded primarily in order to promote the School of Wisdom, hosted annual conferences that were the subject of considerable public attention. The lectures from the conferences were subsequently published by Otto Reichl Verlag in volumes entitled *Der Leuchter. Weltanschauung und Lebensgestaltung.* Thomas Mann was a prominent supporter, and notable speakers were Richard Wilhelm, Leo Frobenius, Paul Dahlke, Rabindranath Tagore, Max Scheler and C.G. Jung. Jung here refers to the lecture that he gave there

him as an author from his *Travel Diary of a Philosopher.*[3] I had also heard about him from Oscar Schmitz before I met him in person.[4] Schmitz told me a humorous story about how Keyserling had once almost challenged him to a duel because Schmitz called him an extravert based on my theory of psychological types. Keyserling had angrily insisted that he was an introvert.

No one could be less of an introvert than Keyserling! Every time I met him, I was completely swamped. He talked at me like a raging torrent. Completely without interruption, every time we met. I could not get a word in edgewise, so to speak. I could not help but think of the famous meeting between Professor Windelband and Thomas Carlyle in Heidelberg. When Windelband was asked after the meeting "So professor, how was the visit?" he answered "Well now, Carlyle talked for two hours straight about the holy virtue of silence."[5] Keyserling was exactly like that! Some things he said were very amusing and witty, but everything was presented as the incontrovertible truth. It was futile to try to have a real conversation with him, one was simply *snowed under.* This continuous onslaught so exhausted me that I could no longer concentrate on what he was saying. I used to ask myself why he had such a compulsion to talk. Was he trying to prove something? Why this urgent need to so impress upon others that he was present and had something important to say? I could never find any coherent thread running through his utterances. It was impossible to remember

in 1927 with the title "Die Erdbedingtheit der Psyche" (first published in *Mensch und Erde*, vol. 8 of *Der Leuchter. Weltanschauung und Lebensgestaltung*, 1927). The first section of the lecture appeared in 1928 under the title "Die Struktur der Seele" in *Europäische Revue IV.* A revised and extended edition of this was published in 1931 in C.G. Jung, *Seelenprobleme der Gegenwart*; the other part became the essay "Mind and Earth." See CW 8, "The Structure of the Psyche," 1960, para. 283ff. And CW 10, "Mind and Earth," 1964, para. 49ff.

3 New York, 1925.

4 Oscar A.H. Schmitz (1873–1931), German writer, in contact with C.G. Jung from the early 1920s. Schmitz gave Jung his book *Fairy Tales from the Unconscious.* See in this regard C.G. Jung, *Letters* I, 1971, p. 39ff. (letter of 26.5.1923). In 1932, Jung wrote a foreword to "The Tale of the Otter," see CW 18, *The Symbolic Life*, 1950, para. 1716ff.

5 Wilhelm Windelband (1848–1915), German philosopher and historian, professorial chair at the University of Heidelberg from 1903. Thomas Carlyle (1795–1881), Scottish philosopher and historian; in his novel *Sartor Resartus* he postulated that "speech is of time, silence is of eternity" and in his publication *Past and Present* he wrote that "'the talent of silence' is our fundamental one."

what he had talked about and I would not have been able to repeat a single one of our conversations. It was just too much.

Now and again, quite unexpectedly, Keyserling could display great humility. These were rare moments, revealing that he also had a surprisingly humble side. Unfortunately, this aspect was almost always drowned out by the great torrent of words. However, I never had the impression it was tasteless vanity. It was more like a genuine, involuntary demand for respect coming from someone who could not help but assert himself against the tribulations of the time he was living in. He was an aristocrat, and it was this background that wanted to assert itself, that had to assert itself *à tout prix*. It was his nature and he was driven by it. For this reason, I once wrote that he was not a person but a phenomenon.[6] That pleased him enormously.

He was less pleased, however, with my comment on his idea of founding a cultural monastery for intellectuals. I wrote that I found it hard to imagine Count Keyserling as a lay brother "charged with working in the kitchens."[7] Life in a monastery requires submission and humility... But he did not like hearing these words.

He was a significant and impressive phenomenon who simply could not help but try to assert himself. Aristocracy was embedded within him, and fate dictated that he *must* express it. But it was not really clear to what end. It seemed to me like the last gasp of an aristocratic claim for recognition being asserted by a nobleman *at the tail end of aristocracy*. His speeches and writings had little in the way of content, he had no message that needed to be heard. It was the reaction of an aristocrat *at the end of his rope*. You could sense in him the all-powerful

6 See C.G. Jung, CW 10, 1964, para. 903ff.

7 Inspired by the *Entretiens sur l'avenir de l'esprit européen* chaired by Paul Valéry in Paris in 1933, Keyserling had proposed as a future solution Nietzsche's idea of a cultural monastery whose members would live on a higher plane, free of earthly considerations, "ascetics forming a nobility of a kind hitherto unknown." Jung criticized this idea in his review of *La Révolution mondiale*: "Those noble souls [...] will constitute an order, or will be fit to be received into such, when [...] they are conscious of their lack of freedom, humbly recognize their dependence, have forgotten their so-called uniqueness; [...] have their natural centre of consciousness in their earth, in their race, and in social and political necessities, and (lastly) when [...] there has grown up in them a need for true human fellowship from a profound experience of the nullity of human existence. If our esteemed author, Count Keyserling, were to become a lay brother charged with working in the kitchens of the cultural monastery, then I would believe in the feasibility of this idea, but not before." See C.G. Jung, CW 10, para. 935ff.

Baltic baron, a *grand seigneur* who was now a *roi sans royaume*. He had originally been a shy person, or so he claimed. But the needs of the times had forced him to become a very loud man with a booming voice, as if he wanted to knock a wall down. It flowed out of him as the reaction of a feudal personage relinquishing power. This is what he represented, with all the advantages and disadvantages of nobility.

His wife was a granddaughter of Bismarck.[8] So in Darmstadt I got some insight into German nobility, in particular of north Germany. There were interesting people around, such as the older sister of Countess Keyserling, who lived in Potsdam.[9] She was a real character, a true lady of aristocratic bearing, very commanding; she reminded me of the English aristocracy, they had the same expansive gestures. When the Russians came, she wrapped them effortlessly round her little finger, knowing exactly how to deal with scoundrels. Those Bismarcks had quite some caliber. With Keyserling on the other hand, you could sense a clear undercurrent of brutality. You could feel the whip; sense the violent nature.

Through Keyserling, my wife and I were once invited by the Grand Duke of Hesse to stay at the ducal palace.[10] The Grand Duke was a very friendly gentleman. In his free time he liked to sit sewing at his embroidery frame.

On one occasion a brother of the Kaiser was among the dinner guests, his name was Heinrich.[11] He told the story of how he had fled from Berlin during the Spartacist uprising of 1919. Outside the city one of the revolutionaries had suddenly jumped onto the running board of his car. Heinrich had single-handedly shot him down.[12] I was greatly struck by the barbaric background that was clearly in evidence.

8 Countess Maria Goedela von Bismarck-Schönhausen (1896–1981).

9 Hannah Leopoldine Alice von Bismarck-Schönhausen, married to von Bredow (1896–1971).

10 Ernest Louis, Grand Duke of Hesse and by Rhine (1868–1937). In November 1937, following the Grand Duke's death on October 9 of the same year, C.G. Jung wrote an obituary for the memorial book dedicated to the Duke (Jung Archive, ETH Zürich).

11 Albert Wilhelm Heinrich von Preussen (1862–1929), younger brother of Emperor Wilhelm II.

12 The Spartacist uprising refers to the general strike and armed battles in Berlin from 5 to 12 January 1919 (also called the January uprising): the left wing of the independent Social Democratic Party and the communists wanted to topple the government of Ebert and Scheidemann and take power following the November Revolution of 1918 which had forced Emperor Wilhelm II to take exile in the Netherlands. On the government's orders, the uprising was violently crushed by the Freikorps soldiers, in the course of which Rosa Luxemburg and Kurt Liebknecht were executed.

There was another character in Darmstadt who also interested me: an occultist! He was like an 18th-century character at a royal court. He was an educated aristocrat, Count Hardenberg,[13] and wore a wide-brimmed black hat; he reminded me of Count Cagliostro or the mysterious Comte de Saint Germain.[14] I noticed this man in particular because his style was so fitting. As a dark figure, a *tenebrio* – rather than an *éminence grise* – he complemented the innocuousness of the Duke's court. He had something of a Rosicrucian or an alchemist about him.

I got along well with these people – as long as the brashness they all shared, that particular cynicism that in many cases was actually a front for their over-sensitivity, did not take over the proceedings.

13 Cuno Ferdinand von Hardenberg (1871–1938), Major-Domo of Grand Duke Ernest Louis, art historian, painter; together with Hermann Keyserling published *Das Okkulte*, Darmstadt, 1923. In a later conversation with Kurt Wolff at the beginning of October 1957, C.G. Jung mentioned a forefather of Cuno von Hardenberg. In 1820, this relative had apparently accused C.G. Jung's liberal-minded grandfather Carl Gustav Jung (1794–1864) of being a "demagogue" and incarcerated him for 13 months in the Berlin *Stadtvogtei* prison due to his friendship with Karl Ludwig Sand – murderer of the conservative-reactionary German poet and councilor August Kotzebue – and then banished him from Prussia (see also Jaffé, A. (Ed.), *Erinnerungen, Träume, Gedanken von C.G. Jung*, 1962, p. 402, German edition only; English see Spring Journal, 1984, p. 37ff.). Hardenberg had therefore been the *bête noire* of Jung's grandfather for the rest of his life.

14 Both aristocratic adventurers with connections to the Rosicrucians operating in many European royal courts. They make appearances in many literary works (Goethe, Schiller, Tolstoy, Dumas, etc.). Saint Germain (dec. 1784) claimed to be three thousand years old. His pupil Alessandro di Cagliostro (1743–1795) claimed to be able to produce gold. *Tenebrio* signifies a mysterious sinister figure.

Experiences at Yale and Harvard

Hoping for a successful reception of C.G. Jung's memoirs in the USA, Kurt Wolff repeatedly asked us to write more about Jung's experiences in North America. The events of those times, however, no longer held much interest for Jung and he responded to my inquiry with anecdotes about the response he had received when invited to lecture in the USA in the thirties.

April 11, 1958

In 1937, I was invited to speak at the Terry Lectures at Yale University in America.[1] My lectures were a huge success. The event was open to the public, and at first I was worried about the size of the enormous auditorium where the lectures were to be held – it is very unpleasant to speak in a room that is barely a quarter full. Moreover, I had been warned that the audience numbers were likely to decrease after the first lecture. So I was very annoyed.

1 C.G. Jung was invited by the Dwight Harrington Terry Foundation to Yale University, New Haven, Connecticut, in October 1937 to give the fifteenth annual lecture series on the subject *"On Religion in the Light of Science and Philosophy."* He spoke on October 20 on *"The Autonomy of the Unconscious,"* on October 21 on *"Dogma and Natural Symbols,"* and on October 22 on *"The History and Psychology of a Natural Symbol."* In 1938 Yale University Press published, simultaneously with Oxford University Press, London, all three lectures which had originally been written by Jung in English. A German translation by Felicia Froboese was revised by Toni Wolff and C.G. Jung. In the foreword written in October 1939, C.G. Jung stressed that the printed versions in both English and German contained "considerably more" than the lectures he had delivered, as substantial additions had been made in particular to the second and third lectures. See also CW 11, "Psychology and Religion," para. 1–168. Subsequent well-known speakers at the Terry Lectures included Erich Fromm, Paul J. Tillich, Margaret Mead and James Hillman.

For the first lecture the auditorium was maybe a tenth full, with around three hundred people. The next evening six hundred were there, and on the third occasion it was so full that the police had to close the hall. I was really amazed. That auditorium could hold around three thousand people.[2]

At the time I put it down to the Americans having a sort of subterranean connection with me. They have a faculty for intuition that is not to be underestimated. It means they can follow my thoughts without understanding the individual components on an intellectual level. The American academics, however, rarely comprehend me because most of them only understand things in terms of statistics. But I have always been enormously popular among the general public in the USA. The other professors could not explain my success, precisely because they were not able to grasp what I was actually talking about.

While there, the following amusing incident occurred: after the third lecture, I returned to our guest accommodation on the university campus. It was still quite early, so we were invited to tea with one of the deans, Professor Dudley French. Our hostess was his wife, an elderly, very formal lady. For example, she put on a hat to serve the tea – so absurd!

When I entered the sitting room, I found her crying behind her mountain of silverware and teacups. Of course I tried to leave discreetly, but she said: "No, no, stay, come on in. I'm just crying, don't worry about it." I asked her what had moved her so. She answered: "I was at your lecture. It was so beautiful! I hardly understood any of it, but it was so wonderful!" She could not express it, but something had struck her deeply which I had also sensed in other audience members. I did feel that I had reached people. But many had a reaction like hers: they could not really get to grips with it. I did not meet anyone with whom I

2 In contrast to C.G. Jung's recollection, an article that appeared in the *New York Times* on October 21, 1937, "Jung views Dreams as Key to 'Isms'," reported that the opening lecture on October 20 in Woolsey Hall at Yale University was attended by more than two thousand people. Even though Kurt Wolff had pushed Jung to comment on the Terry Lectures, he decided to omit the whole of the section reproduced here because Cary Baynes – a student of C.G. Jung for many years and close friend of Kurt Wolff – who had attended the lectures, remembered the audience numbers decreasing rather than increasing.

could have a halfway intelligent conversation about it. But the listeners were moved. Something in my words had affected them.

That was something extraordinary about my visit to Yale. The success really surprised me. I had the feeling of making contact there – this did not happen to me often in life. In fact most of the time I felt like my words were going straight out the window.

Something similar to what happened at Yale had also occurred during a previous lecture at Harvard University.[3] There the lecture was only for selected guests; the audience was made up of specialists, around two hundred and fifty people. My subject was: "*Factors Determining Human Behavior.*" It was primarily about the unconscious. When my lecture was over, I made my way out of the building. Two young audience members were so close in front of me going down the stairs that I was able to overhear their conversation. One asked the other: "Did you understand that lecture?" The answer has stayed with me: "Well, I couldn't follow it, but that fellow knows what he is talking about!"

3 C.G. Jung's lectures there in September 1936, part of the Harvard Tercentenary Conference of Arts and Sciences, were entitled "Psychological Factors Determining Human Behavior." They were first published in English in 1937 in the conference publication, *Factors Determining Human Behavior,* Harvard University Press, Cambridge, Massachusetts. See C.G. Jung, CW 8, 1960, para. 232ff.

Archaic and Uncouth Aspects of Antiquity

June 7, 1957

In connection with his observations about the personality of his mother, who sometimes seemed like an "archaic priestess in a bear's cave," and his own difficulties with the anima, Jung mentioned an episode that took place in Naples when he was thirty-seven.

To visit Rome and come face to face with the spirit of antiquity that is still so alive there, and the equally vital spirit of early and late Christianity, would have caused in me such excitement and agitation that I was never able to bring myself to go, even though I so wanted to.[1] What does Rome mean to me? An anima to be avoided, which I am not developed enough to face. Like the seat of the fire. But I was able to visit Pompei. After I had managed to visit northern Italy without trouble, in 1912 I took the ship from Genoa to Naples, from where I was to sail for New York.[2] During my stay in Naples I visited Pompei. That was when I had just finished writing "*Wandlungen und Symbole der Libido.*"[3] I was deeply impressed by Pompei's ancient culture and

1 Cf. Jaffé, A. (ed.), 1962, p. 287ff.

2 At the invitation of Dr. Smith Ely Jelliffe, at the end of September 1912 Jung gave a series of nine lectures at Fordham University, New York, on the subject *The Theory of Psychoanalysis* (see CW 4, "The Theory of Psychoanalysis," para. 203–522). He also received an honorary doctorate in law for his association experiment studies and his work on *Dementia praecox*.
According to his correspondence, it is also possible that Jung's visit to Naples and Pompei took place in the spring of 1913.

3 "Wandlungen und Symbole der Libido" first appeared in German in the *Jahrbuch für psychoanalytische und psychopathologische Forschungen*, vol. III and IV, in 1911/1912. In 1912, Franz Deuticke Verlag, Vienna/Leipzig, published it in a special edition book. The English translation appeared in

art, by the frescoes and paintings in the *Villa dei Misteri*.[4] They unleashed a state of internal excitation in me, and moved me in an erotic way. In Naples I experienced a particular aspect of the ancient world – a sense of its uncouthness. When I looked at people and studied their physiognomy, I kept getting an impression of a base nature which reminded me of the mysteries of Persephone on Samothrace – a sort of Samothracian Kali.[5] I saw faces that were purely animalistic, unnaturally demonic shapes, grotesque ugliness. At every turn I sensed the strange and dangerous ancient spirit. I was constantly afraid of becoming contaminated with it.

I had dinner with the Neapolitan guide who had shown me around the city, and had a couple of hours to spare before I had to board the ship again. He said to me quietly, in a polite tone, that he could show me something very interesting: a brothel. "No thank you!" He took a sidelong glance at me and after a short pause said, again very politely: "There are also very attractive boys!" "No, certainly not!" Then he sank into deep reflection. He looked at me again, this time rather unsure and doubtful, and then once more with that quiet polite tone said he knew of a place with especially beautiful goats!

There in Naples I could sense the spirit of antiquity, the frightening aspects of the coarse and ruthless, and the concealed animal spirit – it had not remained in the past. I also felt it in Pompei, which did not surprise me. Just think of Rome: the blood sports and the gladiators of

1916 under the full title *Psychology of the Unconscious: a study of the transformations and symbolisms of the libido, a contribution to the history of the evolution of thought* (Kegan Paul Trench Trubner, London; trans. Beatrice M. Hinkle). In 1952 a revised version of the work with the new title *Symbole der Wandlung* (*Symbols of Transformation*, CW 5, 1956) was published.

4 The *Villa dei Misteri* is an ancient Roman villa near Pompei and with its famous frescoes depicting Dionysian mysteries, one of the most significant sites of classical archeology. It is thought that the frescoes show a ritual of initiation into the Dionysus mystery cult. At C.G. Jung's request, Linda Fierz-David wrote a comprehensive interpretative study of the frescoes, which was issued by the Psychology Club as a mimeograph manuscript: Fierz-David, L., *Psychologische Betrachtungen zu der Freskenfolge der Villa dei Misteri*, 1957, Zürich. [English translation published 1988, Spring Publications, Dallas, trans. Gladys Phelan, as *Women's Dionysian Initiation: the Villa of Mysteries in Pompei*].

5 Samothrace, an island in the northern Aegean, was the location of the sanctuary of the Cabeiri or *Kaberoi*, the chthonic deities which were later worshipped as Persephone, Demeter, Hades and Hermes. Kali, in Sanskrit literally "the black one," is a Hindu goddess of death, destruction and renewal.

the ancient cults. The cruelty is unimaginable. And its spirit can still be felt today.

A Darkness Revealed

October 12, 1957/January 14, 1959

The dark has played a significant role in my life ever since childhood. Just think of my experience with God and the Basel Münster.[1]

Once when I was still a young student and very unsure of myself, something happened that unsettled me greatly. Back then I harbored this desire to experience the eternal spirit directly, to see God! Then I had a dream in which I felt, or rather I *knew*: now it is coming, now I will finally experience it!

There was a door. And I knew that when I opened this door, I would have the experience, then I would see. So I opened the door, and what did I see? A pile of manure, and a great mother sow lying on top of it!

Can you imagine what a tremendous shock it was? Not quite as bad as the Basel Münster experience, but nearly.

The sow is a widespread symbol of Demeter, of the Earth Mother and her fertility. She is also an aspect of Isis, but of course I did not know any of this at the time. The primordial mother appears in a shocking form as long as consciousness, under the influence of patriarchal thinking, has not yet recognized and accepted the value of the feminine principle. The feminine numen is a compensation for

1 Cf. Jaffé, A. (ed.), 1962, p. 36ff. Here Jung describes his long-resisted vision of God sitting high above on a throne and letting an enormous turd fall on the sparkling roof of the cathedral. As a child he had found it extremely difficult to allow himself to think something that contradicted religious convention and tradition. At that point, he had begun to realize "that God could be something terrible"; ibid. p. 40.

our masculine God-image. A God-Mother complements a God-Father. The animal form is simply an early stage. With the expansion and differentiation of consciousness, the image of a divine mother is transformed into its highest sublime form.

In a way, the dream image also corresponded to the symbolism of the alchemists, who believed that the treasure they sought was to be found in the basest of materials, indeed in sewage and feces: "*In stercore invenitur.*"[2]

Back then, as a young student, I had no inkling of these meanings. It was a frightful experience and I was quite shaken up.

2 In filth it shall be found. Cf. CW 13, para. 182, fn. 61 [there "*in stercore eiectus*"].

Seclusion, Solitude and Eternity

End of April 1958

As I was preparing the draft of my chapter about Bollingen, I asked Jung whether the separate room in the second tower, which was added in 1931, was intended as a kind of chapel. He then told me about his longing for a place of seclusion and timelessness, a longing which had been with him since his student days.

I never intended to build a chapel, rather I wanted to create a place I could withdraw to, and where I could be completely alone, by myself. A place of retreat, like a kind of meditation room. In India, having this kind of space for withdrawal is an absolute necessity because people live crowded so closely together. For us Europeans, this place of retreat is perhaps the *locus*[1] or privy. Who knows how many good ideas have occurred in the privy! We tend to be disparaging of this *retirade*, however, and it sounds disrespectful when I say it is nevertheless a place of being without any other, an *adytum*.[2] No one else is allowed to enter.

In the separate tower room I can be totally alone, only very few people are given access. The paintings in there are not for display. I always have the key to this room on my person, no one else is allowed to enter. On the walls I have painted what leads me into a state of solitude. It is a den for meditation, sometimes a very unpleasant meditation. It

1 Old expression in German for toilet, from the Latin for place.

2 The *adytum* (Latin, from the Greek *adyton*, "the place not to be entered"), was the innermost sanctuary in Greek and Roman temples. *Retirade*, from the French *retirer*, literally retreat, is also an old-fashioned euphemism in German for toilet.

contains all of what enables me to be transported out of time, to leave the present behind...[3]

The first time I experienced this particular kind of withdrawal and deep contemplation was in the crypt at Oberzell, amid the vineyards on Insel Reichenau.[4] As a young man I made a regular pilgrimage to this small crypt during my vacations. It was my place. As a student, I went on this pilgrimage every year, always in spring or summer. There I felt removed from the world and transported beyond into a place of timelessness, into eternity – you could also call the place a tomb.

That is what I had in mind when I designed the tower room. It was also supposed to be a kind of tomb. At the 18th-century hermitage in Arlesheim, there is a bench in a romantic spot with an inscription above it that has remained etched in my memory, as it expressed my feelings so precisely: "*o beata solitudo, o sola beatitudo.*"[5] At first I thought about inscribing these words onto the outer wall of the room, but in the end I decided in favor of the dictum of Saint Ambrose: "*In patientia vestra habetis animam vestram.*"[6]

3 See Jaffé, A. (ed.), 1962, p. 224

4 The crypt of the early medieval church of St. George on the island of Reichenau in Lake Constance, the walls of which are adorned with 10th century murals. Certain figures from these murals may have served as inspiration for C.G. Jung's later depictions of Philemon in *The Red Book*.

5 Oh blissful solitude, oh solitary bliss.

6 In your patience you have your soul.

Thoughts on the Memoir Project

On Number 1 and Number 2

From November 1957 onward, C.G. Jung often mentioned how the conversations for the biography were stirring up further thoughts and memories. Much had become clearer to him as a result of these talks, but he was not yet able to put it into words. When he spoke to me about his past, the memory was always combined with a reflection from his current standpoint. Toward the end of 1957, he expressed, explicitly now, how hard he was trying to find an "objective view" of his childhood and youth. I had the impression he was wrestling not just with the analysis of a deep-seated structure, but equally with the problem of how to express it in words. This would soon be confirmed in a very personal piece of writing. The following extracts from correspondence throw some light onto the beginnings of this process. On December 30, Jung wrote to his old Basel schoolfriend Gustav Steiner:

"When we are old, we are drawn back, both from within and without, to memories of youth. Once before, some thirty years ago, my pupils asked me for an account of how I arrived at my conception of the unconscious. I fulfilled this request by giving a seminar.[1] During the last years the suggestion has come to me from various quarters that

1 English seminar, 23 March to 6 July 1925. McGuire, W. (ed.), *C.G. Jung, The Seminars. Vol. III, Analytical Psychology. Notes of the Seminar given in 1925*, 1989. [Ed. note: Revised edition by Shamdasani, S. (ed.), *Introduction to Jungian Psychology; Notes of the Seminar on Analytical Psychology given in 1925 by C.G. Jung*, 2012.]

I should do something akin to an autobiography. I have been unable to conceive of my doing anything of the sort. I know too many autobiographies, with their self-deceptions and downright lies, and I know too much about the impossibility of self-portrayal, to want to venture on any such attempt. Recently I was asked for autobiographical information, and in the course of answering some questions I discovered hidden in my memories certain objective problems which seem to call for closer examination. I have therefore weighed the matter and come to the conclusion that I shall fend off my other obligations long enough to take up at least the very first beginnings of my life and consider them in an objective fashion. This task has proven so difficult and singular that in order to go ahead with it, I have had to promise myself that the results would not be published in my lifetime. Such a promise seemed to me essential in order to assure for myself the necessary detachment and calm. It became clear that all the memories which have remained vivid to me had to do with emotional experiences that stir up turmoil and passion in the mind – scarcely the best condition for an objective account!"[2]

Jung went on to emphasize how vividly his early "inner experiences" were coming back to him – they were the "essential" part of his life, in contrast to outer events which were only significant when they coincided with his inner experiences and phases of development. However, he did not yet know how these could be described in words:

"Fate will have it – and this has always been the case with me – that all the 'outer' aspects of my life should be accidental. Only what is interior has proved to have substance and determining value. As a result, all memory of outer events has faded, and perhaps these 'outer' experiences were never so very essential anyhow, or were so only in that they coincided with phases of my inner development. An enormous part of these 'outer' manifestations of my life has vanished from my memory – for the very reason, I now realize, that I was never really

2 C.G. Jung, *Letters II*, 1971, p. 406. Gustav Steiner, who together with C.G. Jung had been a member of the Zofingia student fraternity, had recently asked Jung to write a description of his student days.

'in' them, although it seemed to me then that I was participating with all my powers. Yet these are the very things that make up a sensible biography: persons one has met, travels, adventures, entanglements, blows of destiny, and so on. But with few exceptions they have become phantasms which I barely recollect, for they no longer lend wings to my imagination. On the other hand, my memories of the 'inner' experiences have grown all the more vivid and colourful. This poses a problem of description which I scarcely feel able to cope with, at least for the present. (...)"[3]

I had long realized from our conversations that a chronologically coherent biography in the usual sense was not to be expected, but that readers would instead be richly rewarded by insights into the inner world afforded by the reflections of an elderly C.G. Jung. In order to indicate even in the title that this was no conventional biography, and to give us more freedom in shaping the book, in December 1957 I suggested calling it "Erinnerungen, Träume, Gedanken" [Memories, Dreams, Reflections], which Jung liked very much. On December 31, C.G. Jung ensconced himself in the tower at Bollingen and began writing his text "From the Earliest Experiences of My Life."
When I visited him there on January 10, 1958, he gave me the burgeoning handwritten text to read, which went as far as his ninth year of life. I offered to give him my notes from our conversations of the previous year about his early life, but he declined, saying he wanted to write the text completely afresh. He still had no idea where it was all going to lead, however.
I urged him to write as much and for as long as possible. But despite the writing he was doing himself, he still wanted to continue the biographical conversations with me. During a subsequent visit on January 21, he again said how engrossed he was with his work on the text. When he returned to Küsnacht from Bollingen at the end of January, he continued writing. His intensive daily concentration on the past had unleashed streams of memories, for which he had now also found the appropriate structure: he was writing about an "inner

3 Ibid., p. 407.

personality" which belonged to a "spirit of the depths" and did not merely complement his "outer personality" but took precedence over it. With the narrative of a dual perspective embodied by "personality number 1" and "personality number 2", he was now able to get the "objective viewpoint" he had been trying so hard to find. Now he could describe things from two perspectives – one personal and subjective and the other in terms of fate and the archetypal background.

Initially, however, he still had many doubts about this narrative form. In response to an approving letter from Cary Baynes regarding my conversation notes, Jung expressed his misgivings, writing to her:

"It consists in the most peculiar and to me unexpected fact that I try to work out the history of my early days, seen as I have seen it in my youth without knowing what it meant and unable then to express it in words. Now I have the memories and the words but I am continuously disturbed by my own subjectivity. It is curious how one has an absolutely certain feeling of value on the one side and on the other an equally certain doubt about its value..."[4]

January 31, 1958

Prior to the conversation on the above date, C.G. Jung allowed me to read his text which had in the meantime progressed as far as his fifteenth year of life. I was very impressed with the narrative form he had found for a two-fold personality, number 1 and number 2, and the way in which he described the early and significant effect of personality number 2. Jung's text seemed to me like the impressive avowal of a person who had been spiritually moved even as a child. He made a connection between his personality number 2 and the representation in alchemy of the "old man" as the "age-old son of the mother." This "age-old son" he had later personified with the figure called Philemon. Looking back at his time of confrontation with those powerful inner images and their consequences, Jung now said:

4 Ibid., p. 411, C.G. Jung to Cary Baynes, 24.1.1958.

In my life I *always* had to follow my inner personality, the number 2. Thus, I also had to give up my academic career. I had two alternatives: either I forge a career as an academic – a path which lay smooth before me – or I follow my higher calling.[5] The higher calling told me to follow those strange fantasies which had begun to emerge, but which I could not make public.[6] So, I either forge a career ... or I focus on what seems to me more important, *sub specie aeternitatis*. To have been a professor or not – what does that really matter? It is just as insignificant as whether I have a doctorate or not. Of course it was frustrating to have to renounce a career – I raged against the decision, and it was painful in many respects. But those are all transitory emotions, fundamentally they are meaningless. Remaining in touch with the unconscious, that is what is important. And if one concentrates on what number 2 wants and says, then all the pain fades away. I have had this kind of experience many times, not just in those younger years when I turned away from an academic career, but throughout my whole life. For example, I was very hot-tempered; but whenever matters came to a head, something flipped and I entered a place of total stillness. I was far removed from everything, as if the annoyance was long past and as such I could regard it only as something of utter insignificance.

Personality number 2 increased in importance over the course of the years. At all decisive moments of my life there was this reaction – the voice of my second personality. I came to the conclusion that it must be connected with a very powerful archetype which I then identified as the "wise old man" – a character who is able to consider everything *sub specie aeternitatis*, as if it had occurred long ago and already disappeared. The things that mattered to him, the essential aspects, were dreams, and reflections on the totality of all things. From

5 From 1905 to 1913, C.G. Jung lectured in psychiatry at the University of Zürich. Following his marriage to Emma Jung however, the family's finances were secure and there was no pressing economic need for him to pursue permanent employment in academia.

6 C.G. Jung refers to the phase from 1913, see in this regard "Confrontation with the Unconscious," Jaffé, A. (ed.), 1962, p. 170ff. and p. 188: "I wrote these fantasies down first in the Black Book; later I transferred them to *The Red Book*, which I also embellished with drawings." The *Black Books* consist of several smallish black-bound leather notebooks; *The Red Book*, a red-leather folio volume, contains the same fantasies in elaborate form and language, written out in calligraphic Gothic script, in the style of medieval manuscripts. [See also C.G. Jung, *The Red Book*, 2009, ed. Sonu Shamdasani for Philemon Series/Foundation of the Works of C.G. Jung; C.G. Jung *The Black Books*, 2020, ed. Sonu Shamdasani.]

that perspective, the question of whether or not to pursue an academic career was totally irrelevant!

When I aligned myself with Freud, I also knew that I was risking my career.[7] But even then, number 2 said: To pretend you do not know Freud is an act of deceit. You cannot base your life on a lie. And that settled the matter. Later, when I had successfully established myself in a teaching position at the university, the question raised itself again – this time, the inner figures called to me: "You, teach us the deep things!"[8] Then I had to make a decision, and I had to risk throwing away my academic career. It was as if from one moment to the next I had been dragged out of the outer world by the "Old One." "You know well that all this means nothing. It is all just pompous showmanship. What you are doing in that intellectual establishment has no value. The sole thing of value is your access to the depths." And with that, I had to say: goodbye, academic career!

I have often surprised myself: number 1 wanted something, and number 2 voiced something quite different but true. With number 1, I always had the feeling of uncertainty – something could always happen that one had not foreseen. After all, its world is only relative. The truth, what counts, lies in the world of number 2. That was also the case with my writing – what I wrote was always an order, so to speak, from number 2. It was always about issues that didn't tolerate adaptation or consideration of worldly public opinion. It started with my work on alchemy[9] – and then just think of my book on Job![10] It

7 In 1903 Jung had read Freud's *The Interpretation of Dreams* for the second time and been deeply impressed by it, and in 1906 he sent Freud his association studies. This marked the beginning of an intensive correspondence and a personal relationship between the pair. Cf. various essays by C.G. Jung on Freud in CW 4 and CW 15; see also Jaffé, A. (ed.), 1962, chapter "Sigmund Freud," p. 146ff., and McGuire, W. (ed.), *The Freud/Jung Letters. The Correspondence between Sigmund Freud and C.G. Jung*, 1974, trans. Ralph Manheim and R.F.C. Hull.

8 Jung refers here to the call of the dead in his essay "*Septem Sermones ad Mortuos,*" which appeared in a private printing in 1916; see also Jaffé, A. (ed.), 1962, p. 378ff.; cf. also fn. 6, p. 91.

9 From 1928, Jung studied alchemy intensively and acquired a comprehensive library of alchemical texts. His publications in this regard can be found in CW 12, 13, 14.

10 "Answer to Job", Rascher, 1952, in CW 11, 1969, para. 561ff. C.G. Jung wrote the text following an illness in spring 1951; in the introduction he explains that the passionate tone of the language reflects "the shattering emotion which the unvarnished spectacle of divine savagery and ruthlessness produces in us" through the God-image portrayed in the Book of Job. Jung was heavily criticized (not only in theological circles) for writing of the antinomy of the light and dark aspects of the numinosum and for exposing the complementary existence of a dark spirit alongside the light. The historical period in which the text was written is also significant – in chapter XVII Jung discusses

is still just the same today: when I write about flying saucers, I risk putting myself in an impossible position with every intellectual;[11] and ultimately the same applies now with the autobiographical text and what I am trying to relate there as honestly as possible.

At the moment I am writing primarily about my inner experiences. They eclipse the more insignificant memories, which have too little to say. Right now, I am describing how I moved from theology, which so fundamentally disgusted me, to philosophy. *That* is where my life and my passion is to be found. Presenting this in words, however, is proving to be extremely difficult, as it relates only to the inner personality, the one I have called number 2, who at that time led a totally isolated life inside of number 1 because he was completely unable to talk to anyone. It was a secret and strange life, and caused me to experience episodes of considerable depression.

It has become vitally necessary for me to write down my memories now. If I miss just one day of working on them, I immediately experience highly unpleasant physical symptoms – nausea, loss of appetite and so on. As soon as I start writing, these symptoms disappear and my head becomes clear.

There is something unpredictable about what I am writing. Each of my books has somehow had a stroke of fate about it – it is impossible for me to write to order or plan. This book has already taken a different direction from the one I imagined at the beginning – it is on a very different path!

Now I have arrived at the point where I discovered Schopenhauer and I do not quite know how it happened. It occurred to me that I

the paradoxical idea of God in the context of having lived through two World Wars: "We have experienced things so unheard of and so staggering that the question of whether such things are in any way reconcilable with the idea of a good God has become burningly topical. It is no longer a problem for experts in theological seminaries, but a universal religious nightmare..." ibid., para. 736.

11 "Flying Saucers. A Modern Myth of Things Seen in the Skies," in CW 10, 1970, para. 589ff. In this essay C.G. Jung conducts a psychological analysis of the phenomenon of UFOs and flying saucers and elaborates their meaning as a modern myth. In the introduction he admits that "such reflections are not only exceedingly unpopular but even come perilously close to those turbid fantasies which becloud the minds of world-reformers and other interpreters of 'signs and portents.' But I must take this risk, even if it means putting my hard-won reputation for truthfulness, reliability, and capacity for scientific judgment in jeopardy." CW 10, 1970, para. 590.

began by reading about the history of philosophy, and Schopenhauer was the first of the modern philosophers with whose work I became familiar. Schopenhauer's pessimism struck a strong chord with me – this was certainly linked to the depression I suffered at the time. Schopenhauer was the first person I came across, so to say, who spoke *my* language.[12]

Even though I told Jung I would be delighted if he were to write about the whole of his life, he insisted on continuing our conversations about his life and work. On February 1, 1958, he wrote to the publisher and informed him that our talks had awakened in him the wish to occupy himself with his early years on his own. But as long as it remained a work in progress, he refused to say anything about the developing text and its possible scope. He also refused to speculate about the future use of what he was writing:

"(...) I myself don't know how far my preoccupation with my early memories will lead me. At the moment I feel I would like to carry my account of them only up to the point where they join up with my scientific work. For me every book is a kind of fate, and for this reason I cannot say with any certainty where the boundary line will set itself. [...] I realize that in a certain sense I am coming into collision with Frau Jaffé's work, but I think this difficulty can be obviated by our entering into a collaborative relationship. I would contribute my bit, so to speak."[13]

It later emerged that the publisher saw this not only as a positive development, but also as a potential "catastrophe" – he was concerned about an autobiography written personally by C.G. Jung being published by a competitor such as Rascher Verlag at the same time as the publication of Pantheon's "so-called autobiography" under my editorship.[14] *To avert such a turn of events, Wolff flew to Zürich in*

12 See also fn. 9, p. 29.
13 C.G. Jung, *Letters II*, 1971, p. 414.
14 Kurt Wolff to Aniela Jaffé, letter of 9.11.1958, Aniela Jaffé Archive, Daimon Verlag; hereinafter AAJD.

mid-February 1958 and convinced Jung to combine his and my notes, calling it a "conjunctio of the written and spoken word."[15]
After reading Jung's text, Wolff said he found the narrative form of a number 1 and number 2 somewhat alienating and also felt number 2 was disproportionately represented in our conversation notes. He asked Jung to talk and write more about number 1. To me, Wolff expressed concern that readers might perceive Jung as having a split personality with schizophrenic traits. Below was Jung's response when I told him of Wolff's reaction.

May 20, 1958

The question is not whether such a diagnosis could be made, but what is being expressed through such an assumption. Should we then say, for example, that religions, which have always spoken to people's inner beings as opposed to their outer shells, were all talking nonsense? On the contrary, religions regard the inner being as a normal figure residing in everyone. This does not prove that every individual with an inner and outer personality is schizophrenic! If all of us have the same "illness," then it is a natural human characteristic and not a disorder. All religions presume the existence of such a structure. Otherwise there never would have been a phenomenon as widespread as religion.[16]

I do not fit into a conventional pattern. What I told you and have now written down is the meaning of my life, and if the story is dominated by the inner world, it is because this is what has shaped my life. For many, this is hardly comprehensible.

But if I were not to portray that inner life, my biography would be a mere apologia. What I am recounting about my childhood, youth and early adulthood are facts – this is who I am. The meaning and essence of such a biography would be completely lost if I had to force it into a

15 Kurt Wolff to C.G. Jung, 26.1.1958, Beinecke Library Yale, hereinafter BLY.
16 See also Jaffé, A. (ed.), 1962, p. 45.

conventional structure. My biography is what it is. The most one could say is that I am a "freak of nature."

May 23, 1958

Opposing the idea of a "split personality," Jung added regarding number 1 and number 2:

It only looks like two from the outside. When one looks at oneself from outside, one sees two. But it is actually merely the perception: "you are also that." If we see it as a duality it is simply that *our conscious understanding is not capable* of seeing that we are also that inner part. One might think: "Either it is the ego or it is the Self." But it is actually both. The conception of a split only comes from the inability of our consciousness to see both in one. Remember how the "Cherubinic Wanderer" asks: "How can it be that both are both?"[17]

March 21, 1958

When some of those closest to Jung expressed misgivings or resistance to the publication of this unusual life story, Jung insisted, despite his understanding for their reluctance, that with this project as well, he had to "tread his own path".

If my children say the biography belongs in the family, not in public, I simply have to look beyond it. Their attitude is completely normal, I know that. The daemon in me, the creative urge, expressed itself absolutely and ruthlessly. If people around me do not understand the daemon and its effect in me and cannot bear the fact that it leads me to disconnect from them at times, I have to carry on regardless. Only when the daemon leaves me in peace can I live as the average person does. Then I can relate to others and have what people call

17 C.G. Jung quotes from *The Cherubinic Wanderer* by Angelus Silesius: "*Die widergiltliche Kind- und Vatterschaft: Ich bin Gotts Kind und Sohn/Er wider ist mein Kind: Wie gehet es doch zu/dass beide beides sind?*" ["The reciprocal father-son bond: I am God's child and son/He in turn is my child: How can it be that both are both?", trans. CS] (Chapter VI, Verse 256).

my warmth of feeling. The ordinary had no place in me. But when a person expresses the extraordinary, it makes others anxious – it is uncomfortable, uncanny. People always want everything to be understandable even for the smallest of minds. What I have is *amor fati* – a feeling for fate, a love of fate.[18]

A few weeks earlier, Jung had used the metaphor of a "raging torrent" to describe a life shaped by the daemon:

That is how I experience life – as an immense torrent. Being outside the torrent is agony, being in it is agonizing rapture. But being outside of it brings no joy, no true relief. Of course one breathes a sigh of relief, so to speak, at being out of it – but this is merely a reward for one's own cowardice. The price is spiritual constipation. How anyone can live so half-heartedly is a complete mystery to me.[19]

On the Publisher's Requests

After Kurt Wolff had read a long article about C.G. Jung in the Saturday Evening Post at the end of May 1958 revering Jung as a therapist,[20] he wrote asking Jung to say more about William James "in a simple and colloquial way," since for the English readership, James was the best-known figure after Freud.[21] In a letter of June 17, 1958, Jung set out his position and again expressed his critical attitude toward conventional biographies and personal memoirs:

"As for my meeting with William James, you must take into account that I saw him only twice and talked with him for a little over an hour, but there was no correspondence between us.[22] Apart

18 *Amor fati,* literally love of fate, is a term used by Friedrich Nietzsche to refer to an unconditional acceptance of life and one's own fate.

19 Cf. A. Jaffé to Kurt and Helene Wolff, 18.3.1958, AAJD, BLY.

20 *Saturday Evening Post*, 24.5.1958, "He probes the Human Soul," by Ernest O. Hauser.

21 William James (1842–1910), American philosopher and psychologist, professor at Harvard University. [Ed. note: cf. Kurt Wolff to Aniela Jaffé, 28.5.1958, Kurt Wolff to C.G. Jung, 3.6.1958, BLY]. See the following three footnotes.

22 C.G. Jung had met William James on September 10, 1909, one year before the latter's death, at

from the personal impression he made upon me, I am indebted to him primarily for his books. We talked mostly about his experiments with Mrs. Piper, which are well enough known,[23] and did not discuss his philosophy at all. I was particularly interested to see what his attitude was to so-called 'occult phenomena'. I admired his European culture and the openness of his nature. He was a distinguished personality and conversation with him was extremely pleasant. He was quite naturally without affectation and *pomposity* and answered my questions and interjections as to an equal. Unfortunately he was already ailing at the time, so I could not press him too hard. Aside from Théodore Flournoy, he was the only outstanding mind with whom I could conduct an uncomplicated conversation.[24] I therefore honor his memory and have always remembered the example he set me.

Incidentally, I have discussed James at some length in my book on types.[25] If I were to write an appreciation of James from my present standpoint it would require an essay in itself, since it is impossible to sketch a figure of such stature in a few words. It would be an unpardonable exercise in superficiality if I presumed to do so.

I regret that my biography, as I envisage it, is in many respects unlike other biographies. It is utterly impossible for me, without expressing value judgments, to remember the millions of personal details and then have such a conceit of them in retrospect as to tell them again in all seriousness. I know there are people who live in their own

Clark University, Worcester, Massachusetts, and again on September 12, 1909 at Lake Placid, NY, during Jung's trip to the USA with Freud. A walk during which William James had spoken to Jung about his heart problems probably took place at Lake Placid; Jung had incorrectly dated this meeting as taking place in 1912 when he mentioned it a few months earlier. On that occasion Jung had described William James as a "contemplative person" with whom he had had an "excellent understanding with regard to his estimation of the religious factor in the psyche" (Jaffé's conversation notes of June 14, 1957, Library of Congress, Washington, LoC).

23 William James, president of the Society for Psychical Research from 1894 to 1895 and a member of the Theosophical Society Adyar, also conducted research into parapsychological phenomena and worked for several years with the medium Leonora Piper (1857–1950). C.G. Jung briefly mentions Mrs. Piper in his "Commentary to the 'Secret of the Golden Flower,'" see CW 13, 1967, para. 60. He devoted an entire chapter to William James' theory of typology in CW 6, 1971, para. 505-541.

24 Théodore Flournoy (1854–1920), Swiss psychologist, professor at the University of Geneva, was, alongside Freud, a positive formative figure for C.G. Jung. I wanted to integrate a section about Jung's meetings with William James and Théodore Flournoy into the chapter about Freud, but the publisher found this inclusion to be "disturbing and unfitting" and removed it. For this reason, Jung's inspirational mentor and father-like friend Flournoy is only mentioned in the appendix of the German edition, Jaffé, A. (ed.), 1962, p. 378f.

25 Jung devoted an entire chapter to William James' theory on types in CW 6, 1971, para. 506-533.

biography during their lifetime and act as though they were already in a book. For me, life was something that had to be lived and not talked about. Also, my interest was always gripped by a few but very important things, of which I anyway couldn't talk, or had to carry around with me for a long time until they were ripe for putting into words. In addition, I have been so consistently misunderstood that I have lost all desire to recall 'significant conversations.' God help me, when I read Eckermann's *Conversations* even Goethe seemed to me like a puffed-up turkey.[26] I am what I am – a most unsatisfactory autobiographer."[27]

When, in August and September 1958, the publisher wanted to expunge the formulation of personality number 1 and number 2 from Jung's text, a good deal of tension arose. I fought against this editorial intrusion, while Wolff justified it by saying the book had to be made more understandable for the average American reader. I pointed out to him that every change would have to be authorized by Jung and reminded him that Jung had shown rare and great trust in me by providing the manuscript for "From the Earliest Experiences of My Life." Unfortunately, the publisher regarded my insistence on the unique nature of Jung's text as a power struggle and said that I was overlooking the weaknesses in Jung's writing: Wolff claimed that I considered Jung to be a "great thinker and great writer," idealized him and thus defended his every word, in contrast to Wolff, who believed Jung was indeed an outstanding thinker and visionary, "but no writer. Il n'est pas du métier.*" For Wolff, Jung was so assailed by thoughts and images that "his pen can hardly follow," resulting in sentences that needed to be "brought to order, explained." As a publisher, he wanted "to take on, as the most modest of servants, the delicate task of editing" to "smooth out jumbled formulations, ambiguities and unclear sentence constructions, and balance the unbalanced."*[28] *Neither Jung nor I agreed.*

26 See also footnote p. 28.

27 C.G. Jung to Kurt Wolff, 17.6.1958, *Letters II*, 1971, pp. 451–453; translation modified.

28 Kurt Wolff to Aniela Jaffé, 18.10.1958, AAJD [copy of letter also in BLY, cf. Historical Commentary, fn. 79, p. 288]

In mid-October 1958, after he had read the drafts of my chapters "Confrontation with the Unconscious" and "The Work," a lengthy conversation about the form of the memoir project took place between Jung and me. Jung was disturbed by the way I had thematically bundled together fragments of conversations from different dates and written connecting sentences in the first person, supposedly in his style. He could not really find himself in the text, thought the tone was often too feminine, and wished to be heard more "purely" – this was more important to him than completeness and flow. During this discussion he also said he would rather not have the material divided into chapters. Doing without chapters had in fact been an early suggestion of mine, but this had been rejected by the publisher. Jung now wished for me to make myself more present in the text – with questions and reactions to his statements, even in the form of my dreams. I understood his reaction to the language and the form, but found it hard to imagine bringing in more of myself.

Shortly after this conversation, I presented Jung with a draft of the Freud chapter written according to his instructions, and he was pleased with the result. We then agreed not to have a question-and-answer structure, but rather to include brief comments from me regarding the content and style, or introductory notes for certain topics. Jung attached great importance to having the origin and formation of the book's content explained transparently in the foreword, so that readers would clearly understand our collaboration and how the book had taken shape.

Erich Neumann was in Europe for a few months in October of 1958 and he read my draft chapters.[29] *On the twenty-sixth of that month, he visited Jung at Bollingen, and discussed the manuscript, including the draft chapters with him in detail. His positive assessment, coming from a man Jung esteemed greatly and who had not previously been involved in the process, led Jung to feel more confident about both the content and form of the book. He subsequently asked Neumann to*

29 Erich Neumann (1905-1960) spent several months in Europe in the summer of 1958, during which time he was invited to speak at the International Congress for Jungian Psychology in Zurich, at the Eranos Conference and at a congress in Barcelona. He and C.G. Jung had a longstanding friendship of many years, and Neumann and I had also long been close.

write an addition to the Freud chapter together with me – which in fact we did, but this draft was later rejected by the publisher as being too defensive and out-of-place.[30]

On the Imagined Reception of the Book

In early 1959, C.G. Jung corrected and expanded several of my draft chapters, and read a few more for the first time. We had recently discovered that the publisher had sent parts of the manuscript to an English translator, even though we were still in the midst of producing the text. Jung made it clear that he – and I – did not want to work under time pressure and emphasized how important it was to him to be able to check and approve the content.[31] *The ongoing approval process of my chapter drafts had stirred something in him. It was "working in him," he told me, and he wanted to add something again but was unable to really get hold of it yet. After he subsequently read the chapter "On Life after Death" (the German title of which was at that point "Jenseitskapitel" [Afterlife Chapter]), he began to write a further text while at Bollingen. This evolved into part of the chapter "Late Thoughts." The extent to which his engagement with the biography project had evolved into an intensive process of self-reflection was now becoming clear. At this point, he also realized just how much of himself he was divulging with such a publication. He now expressed his uncertainty – which he had already voiced previously on occasion – and exhibited a certain shyness about the endeavor:*

30 Ed. note: no copy of this text could be found in the papers of Aniela Jaffé. On this development see also the Historical Commentary p. 197ff.

31 In a letter of November 11, 1958, C.G. Jung wrote in unmistakable terms to Kurt Wolff's wife Helene Wolff that he "as the main person involved in this undertaking" had "the right to check what has been recorded and produced." He wrote that he had found several parts to be "still shaky" and that correcting them could only be beneficial. "My current activity is essentially restricted to correcting the existing chapters in which I am clearing up all positive errors and also adding new sections [...] I have complete trust in the work of Frau Jaffé, not just in her ability to do a good job, but also in her understanding of the material which is not the simplest of propositions." But he said he felt responsible for the material that had come from him and therefore would "make sure that nothing goes out that I do not feel to be authentic." AAJD. [Cf. Historical Commentary, p. 291f.]

In our conversations about my memories and when looking through these chapters, I have learned a lot, because I was forced to reflect upon myself. It has been like purgatory for me! Now I can only hope that I will be spared this later on. The endeavor was and is so complicated because it exceeds my powers of judgment.

I expect absolutely no success at all with this book. On the contrary: I expect a chain of misunderstandings, similar to those after the book on Job. But *Answer to Job* simply had to be written, for God's sake! The biography didn't have to be. Yet, when the suggestion comes to one from outside: why not a biography? It is a reasonable question. Something should be done in this regard. And then it turned out that I began to get interested in it myself, in how everything happened the way it did in my life and how I got to where I am now; and then I wrote about the first twenty-five years of my life myself.

I never would have done this if you had not been here. That is, I cannot say it came from an inner need. It was only because you wrote about me, and then I thought I could contribute something myself that I started with the writing.[32] It interested me as a "posthumous" matter, so to speak.

Now I find myself in a situation like none I have known before. I have never experienced anything similar to this in my life. That is why I thought: well then! But when I was at Bollingen and read the latest pages you wrote,[33] I was strongly affected, it gave me a jolt. It had a shock effect: what, that is in there too?! I encountered my inner situation in black and white. And what will happen after it is printed? But here it is, as if it were written not with printers' ink but with my blood. Actually, it was the same with *Job*, but that was not a book about my personal situation.

32 C.G. Jung refers to his text "From the Earliest Experiences of My Life," about his childhood, schooldays and student life, which he wrote between January and April 1958. He began the chapter with a dedication to his children. Kurt Wolff deleted this, despite my opposition, at the recommendation of Cary Baynes. I used Jung's text in *Memories* with as few changes as possible and expanded it with a few extracts from my conversation notes about his childhood, youth and student years. See also Jaffé, A. (ed.), 1962, p. vi. [Cf. Historical Commentary, p. 285f.]

33 Jung refers to the chapter "On Life after Death," in which he talks about "scientifically unprovable thoughts" regarding the "interplay between the 'here' and the 'hereafter'" and describes his attempt to document his thoughts as telling stories, mythologizing. In addition to myths about the hereafter, his own experiences and dreams are also described and reflected on, cf. ibid., p. 299ff.

My uncertainty stems from a prophecy that my anima gave me once in a dream: that I would be cut up into bits and sold piecemeal. That would top it all!

My "negative" attitude to the autobiography[34] is of course a defense, or a kind of self-preservation. I dare not think positively about it. If I did, I would be unprepared in my naivety for the reception that it will meet out there. It would probably hurt me so much that I *have* to tell myself right from the start: to the world you have fallen from the Devil's cart. With your thoughts you look like a mere fool speculating about causing uproar. But there is another part of me that believes in this endeavor. I have to believe in my own significance, otherwise my life would be a complete waste, and I cannot see it like this, I cannot comprehend it in this way. I find it very difficult to be critical in this regard; I have to stick to my path come hell or high water, irrespective of criticism or praise.

But all my life I have basically gone my own way, as well as I could anyhow, with an inner consequence, not thinking of any childish advantage or recognition I might gain. Of course one does occasionally think of such things, it is only human, but they were not my main motivation. That caused me no suffering. I know about the positive, but because I know it – and no-one else really does – I will always be at fault in the view of others. Because I do not say what pleases the many, but what displeases them. I am at cross-purposes with the world, like Jacob Böhme.[35] As a result I am unpopular.

34 C.G. Jung referred to the project in a variety of different ways – sometimes he called it a "biography," seldom it was a "so-called autobiography," the latter probably because Kurt Wolff from the very start had been so insistent that it be written in the first person and as far as possible in the style of an autobiography. However, Jung welcomed the fact that the book's title would reflect its fragmentary, memoir-like character. In the final years of the project, Jung made it more and more clear that he saw me, as editor, as being responsible for the book for which he had merely provided some contributions and assistance. He closely accompanied the development of the text in many phases. [See the Historical Commentary, p. xxx ff. and the correspondence between Aniela Jaffé, C.G. Jung and Kurt Wolff, 1957-1961, BLY, AAJD.]

35 Jacob Böhme (1575–1624), German mystic and philosopher; Jung made repeated references to Böhme in his work. He felt connected with the ideas of Böhme for whom "God's love" and "God's wrath" belonged together in incomprehensible, divine antithesis. In the language of the psychology of the unconscious, Jung referred to this antithesis with his concept that the consciousness-transcending Self encompasses good and bad aspects.

Some three months previously, on October 18, 1958, C.G. Jung had spoken with me briefly about the exposure to which he would be subjected with the publication of the planned book. On that occasion, he had also anticipated that reactions may be critical, but did not seem so concerned about them:

I have been thinking again about the possible publication of what I have been telling you about my life. One cannot write a biography without telling the truth. There are already untold numbers of false biographies. Of course one can also say: *mysteria revelata vilescunt* – revealed mysteries lose their value. What I have experienced is indeed very unusual.

But actually, I do not lose anything by describing it. I belong to the world, not to myself. One is somewhat exposed by a biography with this level of truthfulness. And naturally one has to ask oneself if one might not feel somehow wounded by the reactions to it...

But so much rubbish has already been said about me! So a little bit more or less won't bother me.

The Dream of the Abandoned House

October 12, 1957

This chapter shows strikingly how Jung never ceased to reflect on his dreams.

Yesterday I dreamed of something I have often dreamed about before. I keep having this same dream. There is a long story where I am doubtful about something or something remains undecided. Now I remember that it had to do with cooking.

The dream is about a house. I would like to call this house "Bollingen number 2." I have long had this idea that I had two Bollingens.[1] The other one is not by a lake, but on a plateau, in a relatively flat landscape. Maybe there is a river nearby, but the house is not next to water. Often I see it surrounded by meadows. In the recurring dreams I am never quite satisfied with the house. It was not built by me, and that is why I abandoned it. But there is also some doubt about it, and some unanswered questions. The only thing I know for sure is that I keep forgetting its existence and therefore I have a kind of bad conscience about it. You can also have a bad conscience toward objects. For example, I think mournfully of my sailing boat which I no longer use and sometimes even forget about. You know about the importance of the objects at Bollingen for me. I relate to them as to living creatures.

1 "Bollingen" is the name of a tower-shaped stone building built by Jung himself near the village of Bollingen on the Upper Lake Zürich. It was Jung's place of retreat and many of his books were written there. Cf. Jaffé, A. (ed.), 1962, p. 223ff.

The 83-year-old wood-chopper; photo © Aniela Jaffé.

That contributes greatly to my feelings of well-being and relaxation there. I have to ask the objects what they want – they tell me and I have to serve them. In this way, one experiences what it means to have a *participation mystique* with objects. They issue a *call* to me that I have to answer. If I see a pair of swans here in Küsnacht I do not feel I have to feed them, but at Bollingen, I do. When I am there, I live the way people lived thousands of years ago. In olden times, objects told people what they wanted and what they would give in return. That is how I live at Bollingen. For example, I see that the oil lamp is empty and wants to be filled. The wood wants to be chopped and stacked, the stone wants to be carved, a pipe is blocked and wants to be repaired, many such things. So passes the day, with the objects making *claims* on me. I am always waiting for a call – *what next*?[2] Writing is also like a kind of *claim* on me. The piece of paper says: "I want to be written on." Then, and only then, do I have the right attitude and am able to write.

It is the same with this house in the dream. How could I leave a house abandoned for so many years? The thought that immediately follows is: now I must finally take care of it again. But do I really own such a house? Of course it exists, but many years have passed since I last saw it. What state is it in? All these thoughts and questions continue to be repeated in this dream. However this time, one little detail was different: an old farmer's wife from the neighborhood had the keys. It is an old house, maybe it is near a village. It does not have its own garden, or any private land around it, it simply stands right in the middle of the pasture. It is also not clear whether there is a road nearby, or whether it is on a hill. It is rather lacking in character – it has four walls and an absolutely undistinguished door. Inside it is divided into simple rooms. Downstairs is a large room with a fireplace. In earlier dreams, there was also something particular in the house – something I had painted a long time ago and forgotten again, things like that. The house is always rather spartan, because I had cut corners or needed to save money. In yesterday's dream the house has two wings built at

2 C.G. Jung also tried to be, as he put it, "polite" to objects when he was in Küsnacht. See Jaffé, A., 1989, p.125ff. He set store by orderliness, which as an intuitive type did not always come easily to him. "Things take their revenge," he used to admonish himself and me, meaning that lack of order had consequences.

right angles to one another. The downstairs windows are small, those upstairs are somewhat larger. The shutters are closed. It is a bit like the abandoned farmhouses one sees in northern Italy or the South of France – they have farmhouses with smaller windows downstairs than upstairs.

There is one important detail in this recent dream: the keys are in the hands of an old woman, a farmer. Now, this is a place where not much happens, where an isolated abandoned house would barely be noticed. Only if it were near a town might someone think of using it.

I never know exactly what I have left behind in the house. How is it furnished? It has only the bare minimum of necessities. And everything is a bit drab and forlorn. It is not really to my taste, it has little originality: an ordinary, practical door, everything done on the cheap. It is as if I did not have enough money at the time I built it. It is a kind of first draft of something.

In earlier dreams I thought the kitchen was downstairs. Now the big room is on the upper floor. In the dream, I am now inside this house and want to look around. Because I thought: you cannot just leave something like that, just abandon it! It was as if I were to tell my children that there was some other part of me about which they knew nothing. Next I went upstairs, although I do not remember a staircase, and up there was a relatively large, but also cozy, room. Beautiful Persian carpets covered the floor. The room was arranged as a kind of living room with a certain degree of comfort. Actually, it looked surprisingly comfortable. But for what? It was a first attempt of mine to get back to the countryside, to where nothing could bother me, where I could be alone – I always suffer if I cannot be alone. In the dream it feels as if I have finally found the house again and regret that I do not go there more often, that it is always closed up. I feel sad that I forgot about it. But I simply cannot understand what this house could actually mean.

Being in a house is like being in a particular situation in life. It is somehow connected to Bollingen, it is like a shadow of it, maybe a counterpart or a preliminary stage. In contrast to Bollingen, this house is nothing special – it is rather conventional. I was thinking about the dream in the night. Although it nearly escaped me, there was one detail that helped me recall it. This dream is always mixed up with an active imagination that begins during the dream: how could I perhaps redesign the house? But in such a way that it would stay the same old house and keep its particular character and history? Strangely I cannot connect any experiences with this house, sometimes it seems like a fantasy. This time it was as if I now really wanted to solve the puzzle of what this house means, to do something about it. It was similar to the feeling I had in the past when I felt a pressing need to finally complete Bollingen. But if I only knew what it might be about!

(I then suggested as an interpretation that it could have something to do with the "Black Books" and the "Red Book," and with the fantasies and images contained in them.[3] *This topic had come up again in the course of our conversations for Memories.)*

Of course, that is it, *it clicks*! *The Red Book* was never finished, and it is unfinishable.[4] I saw immediately from the very beginning that what I say in that book would first need to be brought into a suitable form before it could be shown to the public. I knew from the beginning that the fantasies in their original form could never be presented to the world. They had a kind of prophetic nature, and I certainly did not want to be a prophet. They were raw materials that streamed out of the unconscious. But these things do not constitute the whole person. One should not overestimate the unconscious.

Nietzsche, for example, did not realize this. He identified entirely with his Zarathustra, the archetypal figure of the Wise Old Man,

3 Jung wrote and illustrated his fantasies in *The Red Book*, a red leather-bound folio manuscript created between 1914 and 1920. He had first noted them down in the "Black Books." See also p. 72, fn. 6 and Jaffé, A. (ed.), 1979, p. 65ff. Although the fantasies as such remained unfinished, they formed a significant foundation for much of Jung's later work. The tower in Bollingen was also the realization of a fantasy, "a piece of a realized dream." Jung painted some of the walls of the tower in the style of the illustrations in *The Red Book*. The book and the tower have an archetypal, historical character.

4 In 1959, Jung did actually attempt to complete a final painting associated with death, but also left this picture incomplete. Instead he wrote, after an interval of nearly three decades, a final fantasy conversation which linked back to one of the earliest ones with Elias/Philemon, Salome and the snake which later turned into a bird. See Jaffé, A. (ed.), 1962, p. 387 (only in the German edition).

and thought it was his whole being.[5] But I have always taken a critical stance toward my fantasies. I am no poet-philosopher like Nietzsche, who believed in his involuntary visionary creation. I always said: *it* said that, but not I. I just hear it and deplore its meagerness. Back then, I was simply pulled into this flood from the unconscious and felt as if I were inside it. But I always maintained my conscious critical voice. It was with gnashing teeth that I allowed the fantasies to come and wrote them down, because basically I did not agree with them. That is why, apart from *Septem Sermones ad Mortuos*, I did not let any of them out into the world.[6] They were finished, something complete in themselves.

And so the "house" remained unfinished – to this day!

5 See p.37

6 "Seven Sermons of the Dead" was written in 1916 and was circulated only to a small circle of friends in a private printing. It is a psychological fantasy about the creation of the world written in poetic language and in the style of gnostic creation myths, in which a new God-image combining light and dark is symbolically born. The text summarizes the main ideas from the imaginative fantasies that preceded it, and can be seen as a preview of Jung's subsequent work. Cf. Jaffé, A. (ed.), 1962, p. 378ff., and Jaffé, A., "The Creative Phases in Jung's Life," p. 154ff., in Jaffé, A., From the Life and Work of C.G. Jung, 1989, Daimon, Einsiedeln. [See also C.G. Jung, *The Red Book*, Shamdasani, S. (ed.), 2009, p. 333ff.].

Snake and Fish

April 30, 1958

In 1936, I spent the entire summer here at Bollingen writing my text about the Mass.[1] The topic gripped me tremendously. The main part had already been written, but I still found myself very emotionally involved. Around that time I was naturally often reflecting on the symbol of the fish, and *Aion* later emerged from these reflections.[2]

During that summer I found behind the wall here, at the back by the small water hole, a meter-long snake. It was draped motionless over a branch and had its head in the water. Then I noticed that it had a fish in its jaws and thought: "Good God, how can that be, there are no fish in this pool!" The fish was bigger than the snake's mouth – it was a young perch.[3] How on earth did the fish get there? I imagined something like this must have happened: the snake had probably slithered down to the lake to drink, and it had caught the fish. But perch have spikes on their fins! The fish must have stuck out its fins in the snake's mouth in self-defense, driving the spikes into its throat and thereby killing it. When I found them both, the perch had already started to rot, but the snake had not. The fish's fins were pushed deep into the

1 "Transformation Symbolism in the Mass," first published in *Eranos Jahrbuch 1940/41*. See CW 11, 1969, para. 296ff.

2 First publication in 1951 with Rascher, then in CW 9/II, 1968. *Aion* addresses the development of the two-thousand-year-old Christian aeon as concomitant with the astrological age of the fish (Pisces).

3 Perch, called *Egli* in Swiss German, can be found in most lakes in Switzerland. Grass snakes and dice snakes, which can be over a meter in length, are protected reptiles living in the vicinity of many Swiss lakes and are not uncommon; they eat primarily fish.

snake's throat so that the snake could not swallow it. It had probably struggled for hours in agony.

And now just think: the fish, the symbol of Christian love, perishes because it is eaten by the chthonic black snake. But the snake also perishes as a result of catching the fish. Both perish at the hands of the other, because one is the complete opposite of the other. There is no link between them. That is why they both have to die. They represent the unconscious early forms, on the animalistic level, of the great pair of opposites.

The black snake is a symbol of *Mercurius*, it is the philosophical animal in alchemy.[4] As a symbol, it is often seen as something adverse, something evil. It is a dark spirit. The fish as a symbol is something that is "only good." It is a symbol of Christ and connected to the love feast.[5] Both of them, snake and fish, perish, because each is the total opposite of the other. Together they form an unconscious opposition, in the same way as occurs when the theriomorphic background of Christianity is not recognized: its animalistic, libidinal nature. In other words, when it is not acknowledged that both belong together as two sides of the whole.

Because I was occupied with these ideas in connection with the Eucharist at the time, my discovery of the two creatures seemed like a synchronistic event.[6]

---

4 On Mercurius and snakes see C.G. Jung "The Spirit Mercurius," CW 13, 1967, and his studies on alchemy, CW 12, 1968 and CW 14, *Mysterium Coniunctionis*, 1970.

5 "Love feast" or Agape feast refers to the Last Supper that Jesus shared with his apostles the night before his crucifixion and which he instructed them to repeat in remembrance of him. For C.G. Jung on fish as a symbol of Christ and in alchemy, see especially CW 9/II, 1968.

6 In a letter to Wolfgang Pauli of January 13, 1951, C.G. Jung also mentions this discovery at Bollingen and writes: "Like the time when I was working on the psychology of "*Das Wandlungssymbol in der Messe*" [Transformation Symbolism in the Mass], approaching it from the angle of alchemy, it happened that a serpent tried to swallow a fish that was too large for it and consequently choked. Fish is the other eucharistic food, and in this case, it is seized not by a person but by the chthonic spirit, the mercurial serpent. (Fish = Christ. Serpent = Christ and the feminine darkness principle.) At the time, I was the observer on the outside who could only see the coincidence but not the common archetypal basis; i.e., I did not understand how the serpent corresponded to the Mass. But I did feel very strongly that the case was one of meaningful coincidence – i.e., not just an irrelevant 'so-it-is' situation." In Meier, C. A. (ed.), 1992, p. 68-69.

I gave the snake a proper burial and marked its grave. Here – next to the entrance gate to the tower – I carved it in stone, with the fish in its mouth, and wrote an inscription.[7]

7 Cf. Jaffé, A., 1979, Illus. 137, p. 142. The Latin inscription reads: "*Piscis devorati nimis magna causa anguis suffocatus est. Hoc modo ambo simul perierunt in testimonium missam operisque magisterium esse idem et non idem quia mors eorum erat cogitationis meae coincidentia ac correspondentia. In huius facti memoriam anno MCMXXXVI posui CGJ*" En.: "Because it devoured a fish too large the snake suffocated. In this way, both perished simultaneously, to testify that the Mass and the [alchemical] opus are the same and not the same, namely their death was an event coinciding and corresponding with my thoughts. In memory of this event, I, C.G.J., placed this stone in the year 1936."

The Call to Allah in Islam

May 16, 1958 / April 24, 1959

For a long time I had no real understanding of Islam. I could not really relate to it. But in Sudan I experienced a meaningful connection, and this was confirmed to me in India.

As we were traveling down the Nile on a paddle-wheel river steamer, two small boats were attached to its side. In one of the boats lay a sick man, a Muslim, and in the night I heard him from time to time calling out: "Allah!" It sounded like a pleading cry to the universe! Then I understood: this is it! This far-reaching voice, going out into endless space, that was living Islam for me. It contained the whole of the Arabic soul, a deeply moving expression of intense relationship to God, of the Islamic eros and the wonderful Arabic poems of love.[1] I heard this call again in the great mosque of Delhi.[2] The all-penetrating voice of the muezzin was singing the name of God: "Allah." It evoked the broad presence of the heavens, of the universe. I also experienced it in the Ibn Tulun Mosque in Cairo, when thousands of birds flew up into the air at the sound of the call. Ibn Tulun is one of the most

1 Evidence of C.G. Jung's awakened interest in the spiritual world of Islam can be found in his impromptu lecture in the summer of 1939 at the Eranos Conference, "*Die verschiedenen Aspekte der Wiedergeburt*," cf. "Concerning Rebirth," CW 9/I, 1968, para. 199ff. In it he discusses the Eighteenth Sura of the Quran, especially the figure of Khidr – the Green One – which he calls a "symbolization or incarnation of Allah." See also CW 12, 1968, para. 155.

2 Jama Masjid or Masjid-i Jahan Numa Mosque – the world-reflecting mosque – in the center of Shahjahanabad, the old town of Delhi, is one of the biggest mosques in the world. Jung visited it in 1938; see also Jaffé, A. (ed.), 1962, p. 274ff. [On Jung's trip to India, see also Sengupta, Sulagna, *Jung in India*, Spring Journal Books, 2013]

sublime buildings imaginable for a house of God.[3] I am convinced that the word "Allah" is a call in itself, like the Indian "Om." *Om* expresses a totality, while *Allah* expresses a deep longing. For me as a European, *Om* is easier to grasp. It is meditative, contemplative, while *Allah* expresses something much different. It is eros and feeling. *Om* is about being deeply moved – but not a cry of longing. It contains some sense of fulfillment. *Allah* does not express fulfillment. *Allah* is a cry in the desert, under an endless sky. It is a call to a Being which is omnipresent, like the wind that one senses everywhere. When the sun rises and the muezzin's song rings out from every tower, it is a call of nature coming from the bottom of the heart – like the birds taking flight and singing in the morning. It isn't a contemplative view, but rather a feeling experience of the deepest sort.

For Muslims, the religious commandments are not what is decisive. Rather, it is this yearning; a longing directed toward the great wide heavens and an unconditional and indeterminate fate.

3 Jung visited the largest mosque in Cairo at the end of his African expedition in the winter of 1926 and again in spring 1933 on a short trip to the Middle East. See also CW 12, 1968, para. 155.

On Experiencing Africa

May 16, 1958

I can hardly express what I experienced in Africa.[1] From the very beginning, I thought I would have to be quite an artist to convey it. This was my first encounter with an original, primitive, timeless world. It was like being bewitched. It is impossible to describe such emotions. It felt like being set back in time around a hundred thousand years – a feeling that accompanied me in many parts of Africa. I was grateful to heaven for this opportunity to see the living primeval world. This going-back-in-time generated curiously conflicting feelings in me: as a white man I always had to maintain self-awareness and on the other hand, I lived in an unconscious identity with everything around me, like in a *participation mystique*. I felt I had dropped into a world in which humans and animals and everything belong together – in an incredible unity. There was no dissonance, nothing out of place, no cultural awareness interrupted the scene. Every time I came across a trace of the white man, for example if the women were carrying old gasoline containers on their heads instead of earthenware pots, I felt a jolt. Curses, now we have stepped on a reminder of civilization and have a splinter of glass in our foot! It all sounds so exaggerated, but that primordial time was so present, so real, and like a beautiful dream

1 In December 1925 and January 1926, the then fifty-year-old Jung visited Kenya and Uganda. Cf. Jaffé, A. (ed.), 1962, p. 253ff. See also Jaffé, A. (ed.), 1979, *C.G. Jung: Word and Image*, p. 160ff.; Illus. 151 is a map showing the route of the expedition.

– only to be suddenly interrupted by the incongruous blaring of a gramophone or something of that sort.

This primordial atmosphere was in no way romantic, however: one sensed a tremendous barbarity and meaninglessness. Millions and millions of animals are born, lower their heads to graze, and then die – and this for countless millions of years. Clusters of tiny huts cling to hillsides like wasps' nests. It is a world that is imperturbable, complete, a world of immense, terrible futility and infinite beauty. I often felt an indescribable bliss.

It was as if I had fallen out of time altogether. But then naturally I had to come back to the here and now and think about what we would eat and where we would buy provisions, where we should go next and so on. And then I suddenly heard my two friends speaking English! This contrast was dreadfully irritating: these white pigs here in the middle of it all, people belonging in quite another time! And this was true for me as well. I myself was this insane disturbance. But if I had not been, then this overwhelming experience would not have been possible – that is incredibly emotional. There was something about the experience that led me to wish I could stay in it forever. I could not imagine that I would ever cease longing to go there again, where the world is as it always was. I always wanted to return, always, it is so wonderful! On Mount Elgon, for example, when I heard the *bellbird*[2] singing every morning at dawn, its bell-like song ringing out across the horizon, I believed that if I ever heard this sound again someday I would surely die of homesickness. The bird's song was like the chiming of a small bell – a lovely clear ring – and I sat there every morning and listened. It was most precious. You can live in Africa ten years and never experience something like this if you resist it in a European way. But something in me found an open door, enabling me to have these experiences. It was naturally the primitive consciousness in me. Then one experiences nothing only as it appears: everywhere there are countless unseen possibilities, and everywhere one encounters – poetically speaking –_a "scent of the wondrous." Of course one can also experience this in other places. I have also felt it in remote parts of

2 A tropical bird that also lives in South America and Australia.

the Alps where nature reigns. After some time in such places, nature also begins to reign in oneself, like in a kind of *abaissement du niveau mental.*[3] In civilized life here one is always expending energy – we use energy. As if you were constantly spending out of a full wallet. But there, in nature, you are not full but rather empty, and nature is abundantly full. You do not expend, you receive. The potential is reversed. It is not I who is dealing with nature, but rather nature is dealing with me. The African atmosphere, the loneliness of Africa – these were the unexpected, satisfying experiences which moved me deeply at the time, *the satisfactory answer.* And that was more valuable to me than a collection of ethnological trophies to be shown off later, weapons and cooking pots and heaven knows what else. None of that mattered to me. I wanted to know what effect Africa would have on me.

Experiencing the primitive consciousness is of course not without danger. My two friends and I were very careful in our relations with one another, and when we were walking, we always maintained a distance of some twenty meters between us.[4] Europeans, when alone among black Africans, tend to react much more sensitively to one another. I remembered a warning dream I had dreamed a long time before, at least seven years before my African journey: I was climbing a huge jungle tree like a monkey, pulling myself up with my arms. I had very short legs. And as I sat high up in the tree – it was a gigantic *cottonwood* tree, about a hundred meters tall – I suddenly became frightened, and I realized the forest ranger could see me and would shoot me down. Not because I was a monkey, but because I had falsely acted as a monkey. That felt like a great sin.

All of my dreams during the expedition were on the side of my conscious ego and not on the side of the *primeval darkness* – of the original darkness or the maternal mystery. The dreams always disappointed me at the time. I had expected that the unconscious would embrace this

3 A lowered state of consciousness; C.G. Jung adopted the term coined by Pierre Janet (on Pierre Janet see p. 24).

4 C.G. Jung was at first accompanied by Helton Godwin (Peter) Baynes (1882–1943) and George Beckwith (1896–1931). Ruth Bailey (1895–1980) later joined the expedition group when they reached their camp at Mount Elgon.

opportunity with pleasure. But no, not at all! With a single exception, no dream related to the dark continent.[5]

5 On this phenomenon and the interpretation of it see also Jaffé, A. (ed.), 1962, p. 272f.

Spirits in Kenya

September 19, 1958 / June 22, 1957

In my palavers with the natives in East Africa I had to tread very carefully.[1] As soon as they know what you want, they tell you exactly what they think a European would like to hear. If you're not careful, they'll make up stories out of thin air. It is better to feign boredom, then you have more of a chance. But it is enormously difficult to steer the conversation to the essential questions. There are certain matters they will not discuss under any circumstances. For example, I was never able to speak with them about ghosts or spirits – the *selelteni*. That would have been equivalent to making an inappropriate remark in an English *drawing room*. Once, before I was aware of it, I broke this rule. The people were so upset that I had to break off the palaver. Such things may not be invoked. The black man fears the technological power of the whites. But he also feels spiritually plundered. He is ashamed of his spiritual traditions, which seem just as pathetic to him as his weapons. What value does the African *dawa* [medicine] have compared to the magic methods of the white doctors? What value do his religious views have compared to the richly equipped missions? He dreams of guns, of shirts and shorts, and the women dream of colorful European clothes.

No one wants to admit ever having heard of gods, demons, spirits, or tribal lore. They even wanted me to believe they had never seen ghost houses! But that just went too far for me. We had, after all, already found numerous ghost houses, including a few very new ones.

1 Regarding the word "palavers" see fn. 7 on p. 46, as well as Jaffé, A. (ed.), 1962, p. 264.

One had just recently been built in the next *kraal* [village], a very nice one made of stones. It was built because our water-bearer was ill. Our people – the porters – asked us for help. I sent my friend, who had more practical experience than I. He diagnosed a septic miscarriage. We were in rather a quandary, as we were not equipped for such a case.

But as I later heard from one of my African friends, the people had also called a *mganga* [medicine man] from the western side of the mountain. He looked at the feverish patient, began circumambulating the house in larger and larger circles and finally declared the trail leading down from the mountain to be a ghost path. The sick girl's parents had evidently both died young and she was their only daughter. Up in the bamboo forest, which was apparently the forest of the dead, the parents felt very lonely and sad and wanted to fetch their daughter to them.

To defend against them, a ghost trap had to be built on the *trail.* A clay figure of the patient was placed in a little hut. Water and *posho* [food] were also provided in fragments of pots. As was customary, the little hut was placed at a sharp bend in the path, so that the ghosts would have to go directly into it. Meanwhile, the real patient was recovering, free of the damaging influence of the ghosts. She actually recovered within two days and appeared in the camp again on the third day with her water jug, free of fever. I was unable to learn if the *mganga* had also used other methods.[2] In this case, an African friend told me who had built the ghost house and what its purpose was. I tried to bring it up in various palavers, but no one dared to acknowledge it, so awestruck were they before the white man – or before the spirits?

I saw how deep-seated this fear of spirits was during an expedition to a bamboo forest which extended up to an altitude of 2,800 meters. As we arrived at the forest, the porters came and beseeched me to grant them leave: they were so tired they could not carry on. Didn't I want to turn around? There was nothing to be seen here, only trees. And if I did want to continue, would I not at least allow them to sleep here for a while and wait for me? I laughed at them, I even threatened them. All

2 Cf. also "The Psychological Foundations of Belief in Spirits," CW 8, para. 575, fn. 2; there the medicine man is called the *nganga*.

in vain, they were completely demoralized. I could do nothing but leave them lying there. Only one porter, a Masai called Sabié, a courageous and strong young man, agreed after some hesitation to accompany me and my friends.

The bamboo forest cast a murky green light and was traversed by game trails[3] of buffalo and rhinos. For a long time, we followed a rhino trail, hunched down because the thick canopy of branches began at one and a half meters – the height of a rhinoceros' back. As usual, I was unarmed, in order to demonstrate my harmlessness to humans and animals. I scrupulously avoided destroying any living creature. Apart from a tiny puff adder which I found on a path and associated with a child's foot, I never killed any animals. The Masai porter followed tight on my heels and the further we went, the closer he was behind me. He seemed agitated and was sweating heavily. His eyes were twitching. Finally I asked him: "What is wrong with you Sabié?" He whispered in my ear: "*Selelteni*, ten thousand." It was not the rhinoceroses or buffaloes that he feared, but the invisible dead. The spirits took him to the limits of his courage! I never missed an opportunity to go to those places described by the Africans as *mbaja*, or unfavorable. As well as meaning "bad," *mbaja* has a magical connotation, a kind of: "there is something uncanny here," "something odd is going on here." I went to all those places where *sheitani* – which in Arabic means something like "evil spirit" – allegedly dwelled.

In many cases, I was able to uncover a real circumstance which people had misinterpreted, making it feel uncanny to them. But once we came to a place where I myself discovered and sensed the numen. It was a purely subjective experience. On the side of Mount Elgon one can still see an old lava stream which previously flowed there. It ends abruptly above the valley, and there the jungle begins. Growing in the area of the lava mass, where nothing else grows far and wide, were a few tall trees towering over the jungle. They looked like bastions, like safe places providing a good overview of the area and enabling things like snakes to be seen. We wanted to set up our camp near one of these trees. Suddenly, however, I felt very uncomfortable. It was as

3 Game trails are routes regularly used by animals which over time form clearly visible paths.

if someone were staring directly at me from the jungle. It looked like a huge bird of perhaps two meters height was staring at me. I peered through the binoculars, but saw nothing. The figure of the bird turned out to be a play of light and shadow in the leaves. But the eerie feeling stayed with me and was so strong that I needed to get away from there. One becomes like this in Africa! To my *boys*, I said just one word – *mbaja* – and they understood immediately. No one contradicted me, and we quickly departed. I was extremely relieved to get away from that place, but to this day I do not know what it was that unsettled me. That was the only place in Africa to which I felt such an aversion. The unprejudiced way in which the Negroes accepted my intuition made a great impression on me.

Hauntings and Externalized Archetypal Energy

January 26, 1957

During a talk with a group of theologians at his house in Küsnacht, Jung was asked about the phenomenon of haunting phenomena and ghost sightings – this was the first time I heard him mention the experience in Kenya described above.

When nature appears in its genuine form and the usual veil of familiarity is torn away, ghostly phenomena can occur. For example, if you lose your way in the jungle. Or you are in distress at sea and the situation becomes critical. This is when such phenomena can occur.

There is a story about a man who wanted to sail alone to America. He injured himself, a sepsis developed and he was no longer able to steer the boat. Thanks to the trade winds, it was likely that the boat would keep its course. So he set the helm accordingly and tied it fast so that the boat, driven by the trade winds, could keep sailing without his participation. Then he lost consciousness. From time to time, he awoke and looked toward the helm. And he saw someone standing there. The figure holding the wheel appeared to be an old sailor wearing a strange medieval dress.

It was evidently the splitting off of an archetypal figure, a projection. It was a situation so critical that the veil of familiarity usually concealing nature was torn. In a moment like this, everything suddenly appears to be different, and such splits can occur; the archetypes become autonomous, as it were. There is no longer a relationship to nature. When, for example, a situation at sea becomes perilous, something like this can happen.

Or you go mountain-climbing and think nothing can go wrong. You take a rope, an icepick, you are an experienced climber, and so on. But something unforeseen happens and suddenly everything changes. You have lost the connection with nature – and then comes the splitting-off, then come the demons.

War also leads to situations where ghost sightings can be observed. Think of the Central Swiss Regiment during the Second World War, when a rumor arose that the hands of Saint Nicholas of Flüe[1] had been seen holding back the German armies at the border! Today we are again in a situation where nature, because of our loss of relationship with it, shows us how *inhuman* it can be and reveals its unforgiving, violent and immense power: our planetary existence is now threatened. Nature is showing its terrible face. If just one world leader goes crazy, the Earth will be drenched in radiation, and then it is all over. Wars today are global affairs with global consequences. It is extremely dangerous. If just one political leader or responsible party starts running around with a flaming torch, we are lost.[2] It is no longer of human proportions – and when such situations are constellated, phenomena like those just described can appear. We are currently experiencing the phenomenon of flying saucer sightings in many places around the world, although the question of whether they really exist is controversial and rather unlikely.[3] Seen mythically, they are *praesagia* – portents, in mythological language, the intervening gods.[4] The Semitic expression *El Gabiros* or *Akbar* indicates the meaning of these apparitions: "small in form but great in force." It is the great power appearing in an in-

1 Nicholas of Flüe, also Niklaus von Flüe or Brother Klaus (1417–1487), was a 15th-century Swiss hermit and mystic canonized by Pope Pius XII in 1947. He is the patron saint of Switzerland.

2 During 1956 and early 1957, C.G. Jung had been working on the essay "The Undiscovered Self (Present and Future)". In the introduction he writes: "What will become of our civilization, and of man himself, if the hydrogen bombs begin to go off, or if the spiritual and moral darkness of State absolutism should spread over Europe? [...] Everywhere in the West there are subversive minorities who [...] hold the incendiary torches ready..."; see CW 10, 1970, paras. 488-489.

3 On the phenomenon of unidentified flying objects (UFOs) cf. C.G. Jung: "Flying Saucers: A Modern Myth of Things Seen in the Skies." Jung was working on this essay at the time he met with the theologians. It first appeared as a pamphlet with Rascher, Zürich, in 1958. See CW 10, 1970, para. 589ff.

4 *Praesagium* = omen, presentiment, premonition, prophecy

conspicuous form when one is confronted with unforgiving, inhuman nature. When we become conscious of our true relationship to nature, of our inability to dominate or control it, such phenomena may occur. When I was in Africa, I too found myself in situations where nature showed its wild face. I found myself in a completely altered psychic state and am almost embarrassed to describe what I experienced there. My reactions, however, proved to be on the mark. Once we arrived at a place I inexplicably felt was "unfavorable," "bad," "dangerous for the soul." It took just a single word from me to one of the Negroes and he understood straight away, without question. It was a signal to get out of there as quickly as possible. From a European perspective, we would call it a crazy reaction. But under those circumstances, it was quite different. We were forced to take such irrational impressions seriously and to heed inner warnings. It might also have been an intuitive sense of latent danger. One could come across a large *mamba* snake, they can be found everywhere in Africa, or a herd of elephants might suddenly appear, or a huge *hippopotamus* with its enormous weight. Unlike here, where everything is so civilized, I can stroll through the garden without having to worry about a *hippopotamus* appearing and devouring my pants, there one is always exposed to danger. That is why you also have to reckon with irrational impressions, including ghosts and spirits and all sorts of uncanny tales. When I talk about it here, it sounds ridiculous; but when you are in such a situation, it is as serious as hell. It is absolute reality.

Of course you can say there is no such thing. They are simply hallucinations or sensory illusions or projections of the psyche. That is all well and good when you are ensconced in your study. But out there, in nature, they are undeniable facts, whether purely psychological or not. From a psychological point of view, these are realities of the soul. Illusion, too, is something real.

I am reminded of the case of a philosophy professor who had a huge fear of cancer. He knew he did *not* have a carcinoma, but the fear that he might have one remained. His malady was real – he just called it by the wrong name. Nowadays we call such phenomena pathologies – in earlier times, they were called gods. The names are not important, they are mere sound and smoke – the phenomenon is genuine and has a real effect. Think of the so-called *poltergeist,* for example.[5] Only when the attitude changes do the ghosts and hauntings suddenly disappear. And then we speak of illusions, of splitting-off, or of archetypal projections. The archetype is always present as energy, but not always perceived. What we understand by the term archetype is a transcendent reality that we cannot comprehend.

June 23, 1956

The following notes were made when I was engaged in writing the book Death Dreams and Ghosts, a project which Jung had asked me to undertake.[6] *I have always been interested in reports of spirits and ghost sightings in which strange things present themselves as psychological realities. Then the complexes really run wild and come pounding on the door, like ghosts! With my cousin, the medium, the enormously impressive thing was that her trance pronouncements about an important, prominent personality, whom she had also seen in spirit form, were not just empty random fantasies, but corresponded to an inner reality, to her psychological structure. It made a great impression on me.*[7] *Such realities can also be found in people who are mentally ill.*

5 A *poltergeist* is a kind of ghost or spirit considered responsible for physical disturbances, like loud noises or objects being moved. On the *poltergeist* phenomenon see also C.G. Jung, "On the Psychology of the Trickster-Figure," CW 9/I, 1968, para. 457, 469.

6 Jaffé, A., *Geisterscheinungen und Vorzeichen*, Rascher, 1958 (first published in English as *Apparitions and Precognition*, University Books, 1963; present English edition published with the title *Death Dreams and Ghosts*, Daimon Verlag, 1999); the book included a collection of over 1,200 letters about premonitory dreams, precognitions, apparently meaningful coincidences, etc., which had been collected as part of a survey by a Swiss magazine and then given to Jung for a psychological investigation. In 1955, he entrusted me with this task, which entailed categorizing the scientifically informative material and examining the various problems from a psychological perspective. He supported and was interested in my work, and we had many conversations about the difficult subject of extrasensory perception or "occult" experiences.

7 Jung wrote his dissertation about the experiences of his cousin Helene Preiswerk: "On the Psychology and Pathology of So-Called Occult Phenomena" in CW 1, 1970, para. 1-150 Cf. also his essay "The Psychological Foundations of Belief in Spirits" in CW 8, 1969, para. 570-600. While he had originally explained "spirits" – as in the above notes – as projected complexes of the collective unconscious, he later did not completely exclude the possibility that ghosts and spirits were aspects of a transpersonal reality. Cf. ibid., para. 600, fn. 15. In the summer of 1920, he had personally experienced ghostly phenomena in a haunted country house in England, which could not be explained as a projected complex. In: F. Moser, *Spuk, Irrglaube oder Wahrglaube?*, 1950. Also published in CW 18, 1976, para. 764-781

That is what makes the delusion so unshakable. One cannot counter it with reason. It is as hard as stone. Something is there, is really present, is not just an opinion. The psyche is an irrefutable reality, even if it cannot be weighed or measured.

I myself had experiences with dreams which left me with the feeling: now something has happened! The dream indicated that something important had happened or would happen. It was not always an outer event, but often related to an inner experience, a transformation, the emergence of a previously unacknowledged idea. It usually turned out that such dreams had a deep effect. They were often a precursor to difficult, creative work.

With my cousin, I realized early on that those things which are normally dismissed as opinions or empty fantasies must be understood as a living inner reality. They are complexes externalized as hauntings or ghosts, so appear to be outside. You can camouflage the fact of the matter with preconceived opinions, or you can also simply disregard it. But then you have not understood the reality of the soul.

Father Hubertus Heals the Little Elephant of Circus Knie

September 19, 1958

C.G. Jung told the following story during the final visit Kurt Wolff and I made together to Bollingen in 1958, after speaking of the great reticence he had encountered in Africa when he tried to ask people about spirits and ghosts. Swiss farmers behaved similarly and would vehemently deny such events if one addressed them directly, he said.

Supernatural manifestations and magic are familiar matters for Swiss farmers. But I lived here in Bollingen for ten years before I realized there is a haunted stable very close by. In almost every village around here live alleged sorcerers. That is true everywhere. Also in England, in Germany, in Italy, and so on, such incidents occur but are not talked about.

Near Bollingen is a Capuchin monastery which is home to two exorcists.[1] Father Hubertus, a Franciscan monk who once healed a little elephant from Circus Knie with Franciscan love, also lived there. The Knie family circus and all their animals spend their winters in Rapperswil, not far from here. The Rapperswil district veterinarian was called to treat the young elephant, but was unable to help. Then someone said: "Why don't you call Father Hubertus?" And the old Franciscan monk came. He went to the little elephant, scratched the animal's head, looked into his eyes, stroked his back and then said: "Why, he doesn't *want* to get well!" Then he scratched the elephant's

1 C.G. Jung is probably referring to the Capuchin monastery near Rapperswil.

head again, stroked his back, and looked into his eyes for a long time. And again he said: "Nothing can be done. He still doesn't want to." Father Hubertus simply stayed with the animal. After an hour and a half, he said: "Now he wants to!" And from then on, the little elephant was healthy. The diarrhea stopped. He had disliked living in a pigsty environment, and perhaps the trainer or the animal keeper was unkind, so he thought: "We're not going to go along with this!" The little elephant had let himself go, given up. The Franciscan then evidently convinced him that his keepers loved the little creature very much. And that restored his will to live. As a local farmer told me, this same Hubertus also once managed to resolve a strange situation on his farm. One day this farmer came to me and was in a very bad mood. "Is someone sick?" I asked. "No." "And how are the cattle?" "I know what is wrong." "What is it then? Is a cow sick?" "If you have gotten thirty liters of milk every day from a cow and today only ten, what do you say?! I know what I'm going to do: I'm going to Father Hubertus." The monk said to him: "Now then, Karli, what is the matter?" "Well, yesterday I had twenty-five to thirty liters from this cow, and today only ten." Then Hubertus said to him in the local dialect: "Take a piece of paper and write all her names on it." The best cow often has a lot of names, but one of them is always *Venes* – from Venus. So our farmer wrote these names on a piece of paper, which Father Hubertus then tucked into the sleeve of his habit. "There," he said, "you can go now, everything is alright." The farmer gave him a five-franc coin and went back to the barn. And it was true: everything was back to normal. The cow gave her usual thirty liters again.

Such treatments are one of the main sources of income for the Capuchins. They heal with Franciscan love. "Brother Wolf"![2] This Catholic influence lives on in the countryside in this area and creates a relationship between the Church and the farmers, even the Protestant ones. The land here belongs to the Catholic diocese of St. Gallen.

2 C.G. Jung refers here to the legend of Saint Francis of Assisi and the wolf of Gubbio. The wolf was terrorizing the town until Francis sought him out, talked to him and called him "Brother Wolf," and negotiated with him, promising him food in return for peace. The story comes from the collection of legends *I Fioretti di San Francesco*, an anonymous Italian manuscript from the late 14th century. In the 19th and early 20th century, the *Fioretti* was a popular devotional book and was significant in shaping the image of Saint Francis.

The Witch and the Goat

August 3, 1957

Once when I was feeling very melancholic, I decided to go on a long hike in the Lower Engadin, starting from Scuol. As I entered the Val Sinestra or Val di Stria – *stria* in Romansh[1] means witch – I sat down on a bench and lit a cigarette. Then I suddenly sensed something behind my head, and when I turned around I saw a goat sniffing at the cigarette smoke. So I stuck the cigarette in her mouth and – look at this – she held it between her lips! It looked very comical of course. Afterwards I gave her another one, but she ate it. I sat there a while longer and then I suddenly felt something on my cheek: the goat was nuzzling her head very gently against mine! Naturally, all of my melancholy vanished.

Of interest here is that in symbolic imagery and mythology, witches often appear as goats.

Many years later in the Grisons valley of Calanca near the Pizzo delle Streghe – the witch's summit – a man was pointed out to me. This man was said to have encountered a *strega,* a witch, many years before, and had not spoken a single word since.

If you get lost in the mountains and come across a goat, you might easily think of following it, believing it is heading to its barn and will lead you back to the village. Big mistake! Goats can lead one into total confusion. That is apparently what happened to this man. He had

1 Romansh is a Rhaeto-Romance language spoken in the Swiss canton of Graubünden/Grisons, and is an official language of Switzerland.

been out hunting and came home totally broken and bewildered after several days of wandering. He had even thrown away his gun. He had not uttered a single word since.

Dream Images in Sickness and Convalescence

February 6, 1959

In 1919 I had a very bad case of influenza with a forty-degree fever. It was the "Spanish flu." It felt like a matter of life or death.[1] I had a dream – though I couldn't say for sure if it was a dream or a vision. I was in a small sailing boat in a wild choppy sea. In the boat was a ball. It lay inside the boat and I knew I had to bring it to safety. Behind me a huge wave swelled and was going to engulf me and the boat.

Then I landed on an island. It was volcanic, barren like a lunar landscape or a land of the dead. Nothing was growing there. I no longer remember: was the ball now lying on the ground of the island or floating above it?

Later came a beautiful image. It must have been during my convalescence – or maybe the dream image marked the start of my recovery. A wonderful evening sky arched over the island. The ball was floating between two trees, or had landed there.

And a final dream image: it was in the harbor of Sousse, in Tunisia.[2] A luxurious tent had been erected and the ball lived inside the tent, or was lying in state there. The typical African sailing boats were moored in the harbor. My impression of this harbor was very distinct and clear.

---

1 The "Spanish flu" epidemic, which is thought to have originated in the US midwest, swept across Switzerland between July 1918 and June 1919 in three waves. It claimed 25,000 victims altogether in Switzerland, more men than women. Many men on military service duty died of the influenza. C.G. Jung fell ill during the third wave of flu in the summer of 1919.

2 Sousse is a harbor city approximately 140 km south of Tunis; Tunisia was a French colony until 1956.

When I really did visit Sousse sometime later, the harbor was exactly as I had seen it in the dream. However, at the time of the dream I did not yet know that I would go to Africa. This came about only two or three months later.[3] When I arrived in Sousse for real, I saw immediately: it is my dream! There are the boats like in the dream![4]

C.G. Jung later painted several of these dream images.

3 Cf. Jaffé, A. (ed.), 1962, p. 238ff. C.G. Jung was invited by his friend and neighbor Hermann Sigg at the beginning of 1920 to accompany him on a business trip to Tunis. The voyage took place in March 1920. See also C.G. Jung's letter from Sousse to his wife Emma from March 20, 1920, ibid., p. 371ff.

4 [Ed. note] Stiftung der Werke C.G. Jungs, ed. Hoerni, U., Fischer, T., Kaufmann, B., *The Art of C.G. Jung*, 2019, p. 131-137; cf. also Museum Rietberg Exhibition Guide (Ed.), 2010, illustrations p. 39-41.

A Vision of Colors as Inspiration to Paint

February 1960

One morning recently, after some stomach trouble, I was playing patience. The sun was shining and suddenly my cards were saturated in wonderful colors. The pictures seemed to have a three-dimensional quality which I have never experienced before. Wonderful – like a mescalin experiment! The objects in the room were also incredibly vivid and suffused with color. Like a fantastical painting!

I realized that the colors were forcing me to take notice of them, but I did not understand immediately what the vision could mean. So now I must think about it. [1]

---

1 A short time later Jung began to paint again. The motifs were fantasies from the unconscious. As he wrote in an extensive letter in 1955, Jung never took mescalin himself and had misgivings against its application as a means to get closer to psychic contents (*Letters* II p. 222f.). As a physician he was aware of the mescalin experiments by psychiatrist Hans Prinzhorn and by Kurt Beringer. The latter evaluated the experiences of medical colleagues and students recorded after self-experimentation with mescalin. In a letter of 1954 to Father Victor White, C.G. Jung emphasized how pointless it would be to try and find out more about the unconscious than was disclosed through dreams and intuitions: "I should hate the thought that I had touched on the sphere where the paint is made that colours the world, where the light is created that makes shine the splendour of the dawn, the lines and shapes of all form, the sound that fills the orbit, the thought that illuminates the darkness of the void. There are some poor impoverished creatures, perhaps, for whom mescalin would be a heavensent gift without a counterpoison, but I am profoundly mistrustful of the 'pure gifts of the Gods.' You pay very dearly for them"; *Letters* II, p. 172f. In his last work on schizophrenia, Jung writes that it is unlikely that mescalin causes identical symptoms to a psychosis. CW 3, para. 570.

Inner Music

January 31, 1958

When I was a student on clinical placement, I came home one day extremely tired. I sat on the sofa and almost fell asleep. Then I heard, very softly and as if from far away, a beautiful alto voice. She was singing an aria in the style of Handel. I sank gradually deeper toward sleep, without *really* sleeping, however. In this curious state, I heard the voice very close by, much closer than before. As if the singer had entered the room next door. A wonderful alto voice! I listened for a long time and then heard instruments too, like a distant musical accompaniment. "That's strange," I thought, "there is no one there. And anyway: no one can sing like that. Nobody has such an exquisite voice. This is the voice of a great artist."

Then I started to become more awake, and the voice immediately retreated further away. But the enchanting tones could still be heard. I could not comprehend what it was.

I remembered this voice when I was sitting that winter evening in Bollingen listening to the kettle of boiling water singing merrily.[1] I had a similar experience yesterday evening. With my inner ear I heard a song by Brahms. As if a great singer would have kindly taken care of me and said amiably: "I'll sing you this Brahms piece, then you will surely sleep." Just like that! It was wonderful, simply wonderful. And afterward, I slept like a baby.

1 Cf. Jaffé, A. (ed.), 1962, p. 229.

Am I the Reincarnation of a Buddhist?

February 15, 1958

I have sometimes asked myself if I am perhaps the reincarnation of someone from India. If that were so, I'm sure I would have been a Buddhist. That's certain. I recall my indescribable enthusiasm on reading Schopenhauer because I learned something about India and Buddhism from him; I felt similarly moved when I read the *Lalitavistara.*[1] When I then visited India myself, I became quite overwhelmed with emotion at the sight of the stupas of Sanchi. It went far beyond a natural reaction.[2] There is also the dream I had in which an Indian man is meditating me, and as long as he keeps meditating, I continue to live.[3] This man was also a Buddhist. The aspect of India that moved me the most was without doubt Buddhism. It aroused a terrible agitation in me. In Benares I visited the grove where Buddha held the Fire Sermon.[4] There had originally been a stupa there which was later

1 A legendary life of the Buddha in the Mahayana tradition from the 2nd or 3rd century. Jung mentions the *Lalitavistara* in "The Type Problem in Poetry," CW 6, 1971, para. 297.

2 Cf. Jaffé, A. (ed.), 1962, p. 278f. Jung was invited, along with some ninety European scholars, by the Indian Science Association to their Silver Jubilee Congress which took place at the University of Calcutta in early January, 1938. After arriving in Mumbai (then Bombay) in mid-December, the delegation traveled via Hyderabad and Ellora to the Buddhist site of Sanchi in the state of Bhopal. A stupa is a structure built to symbolize Buddha and his teachings (dharma). Circumambulation of the stupa is an important ritual for Buddhists. [For a detailed description of C.G. Jung's travels in India see also Sengupta, S., 2013.]

3 Cf. Jaffé, A. (ed.), 1962, p. 323.

4 The delegation arrived in Benares (Sanskrit: Varanasi) on December 27, 1937, and visited the grove in Sarnath where according to tradition Buddha had attained enlightenment and given the sermon *Saccavibhanga Sutta*. The Fire Sermon, the *Adittapariyaya Sutta*, is a famous later speech by the Buddha about generosity and renunciation.

rebuilt in Sanchi – in a wonderful place.[5] And I was so overcome there that I had to take my leave from the others. I was so emotional, I had to hide from them. It was a tremendous shock. Later it also became one of my life's tasks to bring together the spirit of East and West. Richard Wilhelm was astonished at my knowledge of the "Eastern soul." "How do you know about all of this?" I had not read much, all I knew came from inside myself, from my own inner experiences.

If I had lived in India, I would without a doubt have been a Buddhist, of that I am sure. Buddhism was really what moved me most of all in India.

That also explains the running theme in my relationship to Europe, to the West: my feeling of alienation or of being a stranger. I never understood how people here could find the inner world and what I said about it strange or alienating. But it was so, and still is.

And there's another curious thing: the multiplicity of the archetypes and their fantastical forms corresponds exactly to the Buddha's situation. He challenged it, that is he questioned the never-ending and unexamined flow of images from a matriarchal realm, exactly as I call for reflection on what is observed and experienced. For me, it is about *reflecting* on the infinite archetypal image forms. Both mean the process of making conscious and of individuation.

Naturally in Buddhism the same thing has happened as in Christianity: Buddha has become the imago of self-actualization, even though he said that by breaking the Nidana chain[6] a person can attain Bodhi[7] and can thereby also become a Buddha.[8] Through meditation

5 See CW 10, 1970, para. 991. "Not very far from Agra and Delhi is the hill of Sanchi with its famous stupa. [...] There, on the top of a rocky hill, with a distant view over the plains of India, you behold a huge globe of masonry, half-buried in the earth. According to the *Maha-Parinibbana-Sutta*, Buddha himself indicated the way in which his remains were to be buried. He took two rice bowls and covered the one with the other. The visible stupa is just the bowl on top. One has to imagine the lower one, buried in the earth. The roundness, a symbol of perfection since olden days, seems a suitable as well as an expressive monument for a Tathagata. It is of immense simplicity, austerity, and lucidity, perfectly in keeping with the simplicity, austerity, and lucidity of Buddha's teaching. There is something unspeakably solemn about this place in its exalted loneliness, as if it were still witnessing the moment in the history of India when the greatest genius of her race formulated her supreme truth." (Tathagata is one of the names for Buddha, see also p. 127.)

6 Nidana: in Sanskrit the twelve-link chain of dependent origination, or chain of causation.

7 Bodhi: awakening/enlightenment, or the conscious understanding of a Buddha about the true nature of all things.

8 In 1939, C.G. Jung wrote a foreword for the German edition of Daisetz Teitaro Suzuki's *Intro-*

anyone can become a Buddha. That is similar to Christianity, in which Christ is the image that lives in everyone. But in the West, it led to an *imitatio Christi*, just as in the East it led to an *imitatio* of the Buddha. Hence, the Buddha statues everywhere. Why? Because *he* is now a role model – and as soon as that happens, the possibility of degeneration is present. It just happens – *tout sort parfait des mains du créateur, tout dégénère entre les mains de l'homme.*[9] We should be honest with ourselves about that for once. These things are mysterious and difficult. "The world is deep, deeper than one had been aware."[10] I don't know why all these quotations are coming up in me today!?

duction to Zen Buddhism. A new edition was issued in 1958, the first of many reissues. For Jung's foreword see CW 11, 1969, *Psychology and Religion: West and East*, para. 877–907.

9 C.G. Jung here adapts the words of Jean-Jacques Rousseau: "*Tout est bien sortant des mains de l'Auteur des choses, tout dégénère entre les mains de l'homme*" – everything is good when it leaves the hands of the creator, everything degenerates in the hands of humans. (In *Émile ou De l'éducation*, 1762)

10 "*Die Welt ist tief und tiefer als der Tag gedacht*" ("The world is deep, deeper than day had been aware"; trans. Walter Kaufmann, 1954) is the actual quote from Nietzsche's *Thus Spoke Zarathustra*.

On Psychiatric and Analytical Practice

On Working with Patients Diagnosed with Schizophrenia

June 16, 1956

> *Following his dissertation and his clinical work as a doctor at Burghölzli, schizophrenia continued to be a topic of interest for C.G. Jung in later years. His last contribution on the subject was made at the 2nd International Congress for Psychiatry in September 1957.*[1] *As a matter of principle when treating patients, I make no distinction between on the one hand schizophrenics and neurotics, and on the other, the so-called "normal people" who might come to me to talk about a philosophical or religious question. In all cases, I proceed in the same way.*

A diagnosis – for example the diagnosis of "schizophrenia" – interests me at most in connection with the question of whether the patient is treatable or not. The diagnosis does not show me what is *really* going on with these people. It is a clinical classification tool, one which may sometimes serve to orient the doctor somewhat but which is often nothing more than a *flatus vocis*.[2] When doctors diagnose "schizophrenia" or "hysteria," they think it tells them something about the patient. But such classifications do not help the patient nor

1 At the 2nd International Congress for Psychiatry held in Zürich from September 1 to 7, 1957, C.G. Jung was honorary president of a symposium on "Chemical Concepts of Psychosis." His grandson Dieter Baumann presented Jung's contribution, "Schizophrenia." See CW 3, 1960, para. 553–584.

2 *flatus vocis*: literally "breath of the voice" – a metaphor for the pointlessness of trying to pin down living particularities with names and generalizations. *Flatus* in medical terms means intestinal gas or "wind."

do they show what form the treatment will take. I am more likely to find that out through the dreams. Maybe also through the patient's emotional or psychological difficulties, but these can also occur in other people. I therefore have no fixed general tenets and no theories regarding the treatment. Every patient presents me with a new task, and I have to approach each case individually. Of course you have to take an anamnesis, but the true case history always reveals itself only at the end. With neurotics, it is best to start exactly at the point where they are in the moment. With this, you save a lot of time. In fact, one really saves time when one does not proceed according to fixed rules, but waits until the life story and all its complications gradually unfold.

I never relate to the pathology but rather talk to these patients as I would talk to healthy people. My aim is to establish a relationship like between healthy people. You can only treat ill persons from the perspective of their health. They are not medical objects – we have to be aware that we are dealing with specific individuals.

Usually these patients extend a hand, so to say, and one has to grab it in order to hold on to them. You have to give them something to pull them out of their unreal state. You have to let them know again and again not only that you are there for them, but that you know how they feel and understand what is happening to them. In order to understand them, however, all theoretical assumptions have to be set aside. The only reliable guide to follow is nature, then one will not go astray. But theoretical preconceived notions are never correct.

The problem is always one of bringing the patients back to earth from their unreal world, from their fantasy realm. The doctor's most important task is to accompany the patients on their way back to earth.

It is said that modern psychotherapy consists of the doctor activating, as it were, the patient's projections. But we need to look at it in a more differentiated way. In principle, it is indeed true: one cannot prevent the doctor becoming a carrier of the patient's projections or representing a certain figure for the patient. One *is* this figure, whether one wants to be or not, and whether one consciously activates it or not. As I got older, I became a father figure, "*the wise old man*" or the like, sometimes even a mother. One has to accept these projections to give the patients a bridge to reality. They send out feelers in the form of these projections. The patients want to know if they will reach the doctor in this way. As a doctor, then, one should not discourage a patient's projections, should not dishearten the patient by rejecting or interpreting the projections. One is forced, as it were, to play a role. But only for *this* purpose: helping the patient to find a way back to reality. The patients later discover for themselves that their projections do not correspond to reality. At this point they also need help, otherwise they would remain stuck in their transference and possibly in their psychosis. But at first the patients are dependent on their projections. If the projections are accepted by the doctor, it gives the patient a certain security.

Once a twenty-four-year-old man came to Burghölzli from a German psychiatric clinic with a diagnosis of schizophrenia. He had been admitted because he had thrown a red and white bouquet into the carriage of the *Kaiserin* in Berlin and shouted: "*Les couleurs Suisses pour l'Impératrice!*" – Swiss colors for the Empress! He was arrested by the police. Because he was Swiss, he was sent back to Switzerland as quickly as possible. That is how he arrived at Burghölzli. With the diagnosis of a psychosis.

He was a school teacher with a short temper, a really crazy fellow who could also be insolent and defiant. They wanted to put him in the "*Unruhigenabteilung*," the high-security ward where he would be extremely isolated.[3] "Anything but *that*," I said, "then the bridge to reality will be completely broken." I feared that an incurable hebephrenia[4] could arise. I was then given responsibility for this man, of course. The treatment was difficult. We knew nothing about psychology back then. But the man interested me and so I began talking with him and he gradually told me his story. We had long conversations, and I began to feel a bit ashamed about how many hours I was spending with this one single patient. I became a target of ridicule for the other doctors and nurses because of it. In the course of our conversations, however, I

3 *Unruhigenabteilung* = ward for disruptive patients. At the time C.G. Jung worked at the Burghölzli Psychiatric Clinic, there were two small separate wings for "disruptive female patients" and "disruptive male patients." [See also Rössler, W. and Danuser, H., eds., *Burg aus Holz – das Burghölzli*, 2013, Zürich, p. 8f.]

4 A subtype of schizophrenia which mainly affects the emotions and moods.

made it clear to the man that I enjoyed talking with him. We discussed a thousand-page manuscript he had written about his own visions. I gradually managed to go along with him so far that I could sincerely say I understood his ideas and even shared some of them. This gave him a connection to reality and made such a deep impression on him that he decided, from that moment on, to be normal. Over the next two or three months he progressed so much that he could be released. The boss[5] was impressed, but said: "He'll be back!" He never did return. Around twenty-five years later I received a letter from this man thanking me for my help. He had emigrated to California and was the general manager of a big hotel in San Francisco – while continuing to harbor some of his philosophical ideas.[6]

5 Eugen Bleuler was director of the Burghölzli clinic from 1898 to 1927; C.G. Jung worked at the clinic under Bleuler from 1900 to 1909 (with a break of several months from August 1902 to April 1903) as trainee, resident physician and then assistant medical director; from September 1904 to the end of 1908, C.G. Jung and his family lived in the on-site apartment above the Bleulers at Burghölzli. Jung later called the clinic a "monastery of the world," see Jaffé, A. (ed.), 1962, p. 112.

6 In a seminar given in English in 1925, Jung mentioned this case (with slight differences in the dates), to underscore the importance of understanding the ideas and fantasies of a mentally ill patient in order to build a bridge back to reality for the patient: "Sometimes, if it is in any way possible for a supposedly insane man to get his ideas understood, he can get well from the very strangest aberrations." Cf. C.G. Jung, *The Seminars, Vol. III, Analytical Psychology, Notes of the Seminar given in 1925*, McGuire, W. (ed.), 1989.

Recognition Through Empathy

November 21, 1958

I have an innate capacity for empathy which means I can identify with *n'importe qui*. I can feel what others are feeling along with them, as it were.[1] It always surprised me that other people cannot do this, and I thought it must be a lack of imagination on their part. Or that they were too imprisoned in their own way of thinking. It sometimes even shocks me how immediately I can enter into another person's perception of life. I simply find myself there, I do not do it deliberately. Then I know exactly how other people feel – especially, for example, those who are difficult to understand. With such people I might observe how they walk, for instance. In my head, I imitate how they walk or how they move their hands, and in this way I find out what feelings arise in me as I imagine moving like that.

Tathagata, a name for the Buddha, literally means "the one walking thus."[2] The one who moves in a very specific way. The way we move is actually an expression of our individuality. A person's gait is very idiosyncratic. Someone's current mood is mainly expressed through the way they move, and this affects me below the threshold of consciousness. Because I have a sufficient sense of self, I can allow myself to identify so strongly with others; I know I will emerge from the

---

1 On C.G. Jung's pronounced empathy and his associated unconventional therapeutic methods see also Jaffé, A., 1989, p. 120ff.

2 *Tathagata* in Sanskrit and Pali means "one who has thus come, one who has thus gone." It is one of the ten names of the Shakyamuni Buddha, and one which he used when referring to himself or other Buddhas.

identification. I identify with the other, and recognize him or her, but it does not take me over. Otherwise, it could overwhelm, and then you would be hurt. But with me, I can allow the wave to break over me and walk away unscathed.

On the Phenomenon of Suicide

June 13, 1958

> *Volume 16 of the Collected Works of C.G. Jung, The Practice of Psychotherapy, the first volume to be published in German, met with great interest when it came out in the spring of 1958. The following conversation took place in connection with Jung's memories of his psychiatric work and his experiences with suicidal patients.*

The majority of suicides are committed by people who are not under medical observation. Thus, we cannot speculate about the reasons for those suicides. In the observed cases, it seems these patients see no possible way out of their difficulties and are therefore plagued by suicidal thoughts.

As a doctor working with such cases, even if there appears to be no reasonable solution, one can observe the patient's dreams and manifestations of the unconscious in order to find out whether any stimulus will come from there, or whether the unconscious will reveal new possibilities for living. In general, it does. Suicidal tendencies can often be circumvented in this way, thank God; maybe the unconscious hints at a new possibility, opening a door that had not been considered before; or perhaps the patient can gain another perspective on the situation, bringing about a change in the conscious attitude. Then suicide is no longer mentioned. The attitude can change from one moment to the next – that happens quite often.

Then there are the cases of people – I am not talking about psychosis here, only about suicide due to neurotic disorders – to whom nothing can get through. But these people rarely seek out an analyst. If they do, then one really has to try hard to find an approach and a way out. But in some cases, these patients simply do not take anything on board, and then they leave therapy or analysis again. It is pointless to try something if the patient does not want it – that would be giving treatment against the person's will and you cannot do that.

Occasionally it can be effective if the doctor identifies with the patient to a certain extent and together they fight for the patient's life. That could lead to a dramatic, but ultimately helpful, confrontation. But if the patient refuses to take part in this joint struggle, the doctor also cannot go down that road. And then it may end in suicide.

I once had such a case: a young woman, twenty-six or twenty-seven years old, with a compulsion neurosis. An incident which in itself was insignificant led, after a long time of fruitless effort, to the therapy being broken off. She brought a dream one time which she had just scribbled on a torn-off scrap of newspaper. That provoked my anger: "Listen to me! This will never happen again! If you come again with such a sloppy mess, you can go to another doctor!" The next time she came again with the same scrappy mess. This time I threw her out. But I prudently waited behind the door for a little while. Then I heard a quiet knocking. After letting her knock for a while, I opened the door: "Well, where are *you* coming from?" "I have brought my notebook."

But she was a case in which simply nothing worked. One might as well have been talking to a stone. I knew there was a possible suicide risk, but I simply was not able to identify with her. I could not summon up any belief in her, and I had to let her go. Six months later, I learned that she had committed suicide.

There was another case which also gave me great concern. The patient was a gifted, rather well-known person of outstanding character. She showed certain signs of last-minute panic about being "left on the shelf." She suffered from anxiety and deep depression and was genetically burdened. She was a very respectable woman. I really fought for her life and tried in every way to help her feel something that would make life worth living. But I needed the unconscious to work with me. As a doctor one cannot simply say: "Now I will give you a reason to live!" That would be completely ridiculous. I just said: "*I* cannot offer you a way of living, but maybe the unconscious can." She sensibly agreed to try it. But the dreams, by God, brought only indications of suicide. There seemed to be a certain inevitability about it. I even tried to deceive her a little with my interpretations. But the dreams insisted more and more on suicide as the only possibility. I was extremely alarmed. In the end I said: "According to what I know, I must honestly say that your dreams point to the inevitability of suicide. So we need to try to go along with the unconscious in the quiet hope that it will then eventually bring another possibility."

We then looked together at the problem of suicide from all angles: the religious aspect, the ethical aspect. What it meant for her, what it would mean for her relatives – and the dreams continued to insist on suicide. I saw her three to four times a week over the course of a good six weeks, but the dreams continued with the suicide theme. We even discussed the various ways in which one can commit suicide, and she told me precisely how she intended to do it. Which is exactly how it did happen.

Now, I should really have told the family; then she would have been locked up in Burghölzli. But she was terribly afraid of that. And also she did not have any symptoms of melancholia. It was simply that she could not accept life. She saw her life as completely meaningless, and the unconscious had not helped her at all. "I cannot help you any more, I do not know what to advise you." "No, you have given me the best advice and help." She was grateful for our conversations. Then she went to another doctor for two months so that in the case of a suicide, the shadow would fall on the other doctor and not on me!

That really was one of the worst cases I ever had, because this woman on the one hand was such an ethical and worthy person, and on the other hand was so possessed by a death wish. And the unconscious did not help her. "God" did not intervene!

There are cases in which no amount of identification succeeds and neither God nor nature helps; where a tendency to end life is present and no well-meaning doctor or anything else helps, not even a sacrifice. It comes from inside – a death wish.[1] I know from my own experience what it is like. The death wish once got into me, when I was desperate following my dream about the murder of Siegfried, because I could not see the meaning or purpose of it at all. I knew it would take just one move of my hand and I would be dead. The loaded revolver was lying in my bedside table. I was forced to get up in the middle of the night and analyze the dream until I had worked out its meaning.[2] From outside it seems absurd that I had to rack my brains so. But I knew: if I did not do my utmost, I would lose the battle. I could go on and on, telling myself it was only a dream – nevertheless, I would know I had failed. So I did all I could to find the solution.[3] The death wish can arise in a totally normal life. That is why there are suicides which seem to have no explanation.

Suicide is still murder. It is murder of oneself, and the person who commits suicide is a murderer. Family murders have to be seen in the same way: the self-murderer takes the family to their deaths too. But we are all potential murderers, and it is only thanks to the favorable conditions in which we live that our murderer or self-murderer does not assert itself in reality.

Think of the countless Jews who committed suicide before they were taken to the concentration camps! I too would have wanted to shoot myself first in that situation. It is clear: life would no longer have appeared to me worth living under such conditions. But perhaps one cannot predict how things will be?

1 On Jung's view of suicide cf. also C.G. Jung, *Letters II*, p. 25 and 279.

2 Cf. Jaffé, A. (ed.), 1962, p. 180. In the dream (at the end of 1913), Siegfried – a Germanic mythical figure, in particular in the Nibelungen saga – is shot by Jung. Jung interpreted the dream as showing the need to sacrifice his identification with the archetypal figure of the hero – a problem that did not affect Jung alone, but which was collectively constellated in the period before the First World War.

3 Jung recognized that he had to give up his identification with the ideal hero, with the hero's courage, strength of will, and pride: "(...) suddenly the meaning of the dream dawned on me. 'Why, that is the problem that is being played out in the world.' Siegfried (...) represents what the Germans want to achieve, heroically to impose their will, have their own way. [...] I had wanted to do the same. But now that was no longer possible. The dream showed that the attitude embodied by Siegfried, the hero, no longer suited me. Therefore it had to be killed." Jaffé, A. (ed.), 1962, p. 180. "Siegfried" was also the name Sabina Spielrein called the son she imagined having with Jung – it is possible that the dream that Jung found so emotionally disturbing could also relate to this. [Cf. also Shamdasani, S., ed., C.G. Jung, *Introduction to Jungian Psychology, Notes of the Seminar given in 1925*, 2012, p. 61f.]

My patients – it was *they* who made me question things. The original questions came from the patients. Their neuroses arose because they had so far managed with fragmentary answers to life's questions: they had sought a position in society, marriage, a good reputation, and had believed they would be happy when they had achieved all this, or something similar. But they were not happy, even if they had heaps of money. And so they came to me and wanted to find out what else could fulfill them. Then it emerged that their current lives had no *meaning*. They are neurotic because they have no purpose, because their lives are meaningless.

Of course it is possible to walk with only *one* foot, or to live with only *one* hand, but it is not the ideal state of affairs. It is a kind of resignation. But such resignation is not necessarily what is needed. Resignation is not the ideal solution here. Under certain circumstances one has no other choice, then it is right to resign oneself to the situation. But when there is a possibility of progression without resignation, a possibility of development, then it is one's duty, even, to tread this path. At least for the doctor. If patients can bear to simply resign from life at age forty, then no one can stop them. But whether they are happy with it, or "normal," whether it is experienced as meaningful, is another matter.

My therapy has no rules. Each patient is a new proposition, no matter how much experience or expertise one has. Of course one has to master the "tools of the trade." But when it comes to the essential questions, the conventional tools no longer suffice. If one wants it or not: when one has analysis for long enough, the essential questions will naturally emerge. There is no other possibility.

Psychology and Experience

June 27, 1958

This conversation took place around the time I was editing the chapter about C.G. Jung's psychiatric activities and asked him to clarify certain aspects again.

In psychology one has not really understood something until one has lived it. Just having a *term* for something means nothing. It needs to touch the heart or affect one's life. A word has to get under our skin, sink in deep, so that it becomes part of us, that we live in it. Only when *this* is the case, when it is about more than words, does one know what the heart says and what the spirit thinks.

When the word enters deeply into one's psyche rather than remaining at the intellectual level, only then is one faced with the problem of a conscious individuation process – a very difficult and often painful task. Everyone who *experiences* psychology in this way is isolated from others to a certain extent. Not just from the hardheaded fools, but also from intelligent people who have a different attitude and usually also have prejudices.

All those who consciously undergo and want to pursue the process of individuation should be aware that this path can be isolating and that there is a certain danger when coming into contact with the huge inner world. But it is only when you allow yourself to be touched directly that deep life-changing consequences arise, and only then can one's totality unfold. This is the true effect of psychology. Until then, it is mainly limiting.

But you do not become yourself until you are prepared to defend yourself in the real world. The demands and insights of my psychology make one unwelcome out there in the world. The world is very different from how we try to imagine it. If people were more conscious, the world would now be in quite a different state.

Emptiness and Intuition

June 25, 1959

All intuitives must learn to bear a high degree of emptiness. Otherwise they are not able to grasp something with their intuition. As soon as their consciousness is filled with content, intuitions cannot get through or are weakened. Actually it would be better for intuitives to see nothing and hear nothing. Then their perceptions could emerge via the unconscious and their intuitions could achieve a high degree of accuracy. But then they would immediately be at risk of suffering hubris and inflation, after previously having been tortured by feelings of non-existence, i.e. by the state of emptiness. There is hardly an intuitive who is not familiar with this feeling.

Because it is difficult to withstand the emptiness, intuitives very often have feelings of inferiority. If they realized that the emptiness is fullness, it would be easier to bear. They would not have these feelings of inferiority and accordingly would avoid the compensatory inflation. The emptiness is an unperceived abundance – a fullness – of possibilities. But it creates an unpleasant feeling, and then intuitives often overfill life with activity in order to numb that feeling. They might overeat to compensate for the inner emptiness. Sometimes they have a concrete feeling of physical emptiness. It belongs to this type. When they feel empty, they ought to say to themselves: I float like a lotus blossom on the surface of the water's depths. But they fear the possibilities that lie in the depths. The intuitive is often too afraid of the possibilities.

Destruction and Evil in Illness

June 18, 1958

> *At this time Jung received an invitation to a conference on the theme "Good and Evil in Psychotherapy"; his contribution was published in 1959.*

The mentally ill are often more deeply immersed in the essence of the world than other people, and as a result have different and more extreme attitudes. They identify with extra-personal archetypal contents, sometimes even with evil. "I am the Anti-Christ," wrote Nietzsche during his period of mental illness.

I was once asked to give a consultation for a patient in England. She was psychotic and a suicide risk. She said to me: "I am identical with evil. I am the evil one." She believed she was the incarnation of evil itself. This was a dangerous inflation.

I gave instructions that she was not to be left alone for a moment. But one evening she asked the nurse to make her a hot-water bottle – and the instant the nurse left the room, she jumped out of the window. I will never forget the expression on her face – it was the expression of evil triumph because she had managed against the odds to leap out of the window. Life did not matter to her. As the incarnation of evil, she was prepared to sacrifice her life.

November 12, 1959

Working with a patient who has a predominantly evil character can be damaging for the therapist. If the patient is naturally destructive, an analysis can on occasion have a very negative effect. There is a danger that it bores a hole, as it were, through which the evil can uncontrollably break out of the unconscious and take effect. That could affect not only the patient and immediate environment, but also the doctor.

We have long known that analysis can trigger a latent psychosis. For this reason one should refrain from undertaking an analysis in certain cases – one would only be doing the patient harm.

It cannot be repeated enough – you cannot fundamentally change or improve someone. You can only make them more conscious of who they are. In the best case, this leads to a change of attitude. In analysis, the shadow of course usually makes an appearance. But it alarms the patient or analysand, they are distressed by their darkness. In such cases, the analysis has a positive effect: the ego is more capable of confronting and asserting itself against a shadow made conscious than against an unconscious darkness.

The art of the doctor is to recognize in good time whether it is appropriate to undertake an analysis or not. After all, there are other therapeutic methods that do not involve confronting the unconscious.

Relationship, *Imago* and Projection

February 1959

It can happen that dreams hold on to the continuation of a relationship between two people even when it is long finished, whether because of estrangement or the death of one of the partners. The dreams may nevertheless continue to represent the relationship not only as still existing, but also, contrary to all actual experiences, as extremely positive, particularly if the dreamer had a close bond to the partner. Then it almost appears as though the unconscious were trying to mislead our conscious mind: one dream after another appears to be a wish fulfillment.

Of course one initially thinks of a compensation: nothing of the relationship remains on the outside, but in the dreams everything seems perfectly in order. How can this be explained? We get closer to the truth if we assume the relationship had only a limited basis in reality from the start, as it was primarily based on projections. This is often the case. Then the figure in the dream is not based on the actual partner, but on the image which had been projected onto them.

Every relationship goes through a critical moment when the projections need to be withdrawn. If this does not happen, the projection continues to be made, even if the partner is no longer there. Then it is possible that the dreams relate not to the other person, but to the projected image.

This phenomenon can also be seen in people's relations with their parents, not always in a positive sense. I had a patient whose parents had died more than ten years before I met him. But he still labored under the impression that his father was tyrannizing him. Here the negative father image lived on, and the patient experienced a relationship that was ostensibly about his father, but which in reality was based on the unconscious projection of this image.

Such cases are proof that the *imago relationship*[1] can be stronger than the relationship to the real person. After the outer relationship ends, our consciousness sadly notes that the person has gone, but the attachment to the *imago* remains, exactly as before. And then in the dreams it appears as if nothing at all had changed, nothing had been lost, everything had stayed the same. There is a complete denial of reality, because the projection holds on so firmly to the image. Once I had a patient who had a fantastic transference onto me. She became increasingly convinced that I was the right man for her, even though I told her I was already a grandfather and I had not the slightest inclination to love her or marry her. She responded urgently: "Do not disturb me. Please be quiet!" It seemed inexplicably fateful. I had to let her have her fantasies. It dragged on for a few weeks like this. She filled notebooks full of fantasies and dreams. Most of them were wish-fulfillment images.

Eventually she had the following dream: on a wonderful spring afternoon she was sailing down a river in a dinghy. She heard a voice say: "In fourteen days is the wedding." Then she suddenly heard a roll of thunder. The water was moving faster, the boat was caught in the rapids, she saw the spray of the waves around her and the boat capsized into the depths of the river. Then she awoke.

When she told me the dream, I tried to warn her. But she did not believe there was any danger. "In fourteen days is the wedding." She kept insisting on it. There was no other reality for her. After that she left town, and for a while I did not hear from her. One day, however, I received a letter in which she wrote: "God has forbidden me from ever coming to see you again." I would probably have disturbed her

1 *Imago*: Latin for image. In the psychological sense it is an inner image that is projected onto another person and distorts one's perception of the other: often too positively or too negatively.

wishful fantasies too much. Sometime later I learned that she had died of intestinal cancer.

Only after her death did I realize what it all meant: she had to experience a love story with me, even if it was only in the form of projections of the *imago*. Only then had something hitherto unlived been satisfied and could she die.

I had always understood her fantasies as inner realities and tried to explain this to her and to help her differentiate between inner and outer reality. When I saw that it was impossible to detach her from the concrete interpretation of her transference images, I initially thought she was mentally ill. But I was not able to diagnose schizophrenia. I lost the courage to say anything critical – and in hindsight this proved to have been exactly right. I just let it happen. I sat there without saying a word and let her fantasies pour over me like water.

It didn't become clear to me until afterward that she was experiencing a development which would normally take years compressed into a time of around six weeks, in the form of a relationship to an *imago* which she had projected onto me. In such cases, which thank God are very rare, one must take the *imago* into particular account. It conveys information about inner events that have an intensely real effect, even if they do not correspond with outer reality.

Small Children and the Pleroma

October 12, 1957

Yesterday one of my daughters told me about something my grandson said to his great-grandmother when he was a small boy. He had gotten into mischief and she scolded him. Then he looked at her crossly and said reproachfully: "You can't scold the dear Lord God!" That is child psychology!

Many years ago I observed something similar. I was sitting in the garden and my little daughter Marianne, who was then about five years old, was also nearby. I could hear her talking to her doll which she was pushing in her toy baby-buggy. She could not see me. I heard her say to her doll: "You know, we are the Royal Highnesses, the Jungs!"

An experience of my own: when I was three years old, one of my mother's younger brothers once came to visit. At the time I had a little wooden horse nailed on to a board with wheels. My uncle asked me: "Now then, little boy, are you going to play giddy-up horsey?" And I turned to my mother – she told me the whole story later – and asked: "Why is that man talking so dumb?" I don't know who I thought I was: God or His Majesty. How could this man talk to me in such an idiotic way, as if I were just a "little boy"?!

That is how children are. They still have some knowledge of the primordial and whole human. They still live in close proximity to the pleroma,[1] where the eternal images are alive; and they themselves are

1 Pleroma (Greek): in Gnosticism the fullness of divine wholeness. According to Jung, as young

still whole and therefore significant.[2] That is child psychology, but you will not find it in any text book.[3]

children are still very close to the collective unconscious, archetypal images and fantasies are in the foreground during this stage of life.

2 In the same vein, C.G. Jung also recalled his experience as a somewhat older boy of eleven, when he was suddenly propelled out of this universal consciousness and experienced the sense of an "I" for the first time; see Jaffé, A. (ed.), 1962, p. 32f.

3 On this topic, see also the four series of seminars on children's dreams given by C.G. Jung at the ETH in 1936/37, 1938/39, 1939/40 and 1940/41; the four winter semester seminars were published in German as an appendix to the *Gesammelte Werke* in 1987, and first published in English in 2008 (*Children's Dreams, Notes from the Seminar Given in 1936–1940 by C.G. Jung*, ed. Jung, L. and Meyer-Grass, M., trans. Falzeder, E. and Woolfson, T., Princeton University Press).

The Individuation Process and the Christmas Tree

December 1957

C.G. Jung expressed the following thoughts after receiving a letter from Georg Gerster asking for an interview on the subject of the Christmas tree. In the fifties, Jung had spontaneously spoken several times about this topic. The reflections expressed here formed the basis of his more comprehensive answers in the interview he later granted for a Swiss weekly magazine.[1]

If you ask people why they put up a Christmas tree, decorate it and light candles on it, you rarely get a proper answer. But it's hardly surprising, as we often do something first and only later think about what we were doing.

The tree is a symbol. To understand its meaning, we have to be clear about what a "tree" is: the tree is a living creation, a plant. It grows where it has put roots down into the ground. It cannot move from one place to another, but is fixed in one place, "*for better or worse.*" It has to live with the conditions in *that* location, has to obtain its nutrition from the very ground where it grows and can only get what is present in the earth there. It cannot walk away and look for better conditions

1 See "*C.G. Jung und der Weihnachtsbaum,*" interview with Georg Gerster, literature scholar and photographer, first published in the 1957 Christmas edition of the magazine *Weltwoche*; cf. "Jung and the Christmas Tree" in *C.G. Jung Speaking, Interviews and Encounters*, McGuire, W. and Hull R.F.C. (eds), 1987, Princeton University Press, pp. 353ff. On earlier occasions, C.G. Jung had spontaneously spoken about this custom and symbol during Christmas celebrations at the Psychology Club.

elsewhere; it is exposed to the elements, and does not always have an easy time of it.

I am not saying all this to edify, but in order to explain that the tree is a symbol and expresses a psychological fact. As a symbol, it refers to the situation of human beings, who have to live with the means and gifts they are given, and develop themselves within their own individual limits. If they accept themselves with their own limitations, they can develop as *the* personality that is inscribed within them, just as an oak tree grows from an acorn and a cherry tree from a cherry stone.

However, the human is more than and different from a plant. Only when we accept ourselves, without running away from or avoiding our true selves, can something new emerge within us. As reflective beings, people begin to realize that limitation is just one aspect of their existence, and that they are limited creatures living within a limitless realm. Then, as if a light has been switched on, they become aware of a supra-personal transcendence.[2] The stars and lights we decorate the tree with are an indication of this enlightenment, and of the limitless cosmic background of each individual life; they are symbols of a new inner light which brightens the darkest of days of the year.

There are alchemical representations of a tree – the alchemists called it the "Philosopher's Tree," *arbor philosophorum* – on which hang the large "luminaria" sun and moon; their child is found in the middle between them, like a Christ child.

The work of the alchemists represents the individuation process, which grows slowly like a tree. But only in rare cases were the old masters aware of the meaning of their actions and fantasies. This is why they tried to capture the meaning again and again with countless names and images – as with the image of the tree – without being able to fundamentally understand the analogy in their work.[3]

Similarly, we today are unconscious of the meaning of the Christmas tree, which we put up and decorate at the time of the winter solstice without really knowing what it represents. But there is some

2 Cf. Jaffé, A. (ed.), 1962, p. 325: "In knowing ourselves to be unique in our personal combination – that is, ultimately limited – we possess also the capacity for becoming conscious of the infinite. But only then."

3 Cf. C.G. Jung "The Philosophical Tree" in CW 13, 1967, para. 304ff.

*fore*knowledge in us – of which we are unconscious. This is what I mean by the Self. It forces us to perform certain meaningful acts and rituals. A psychological function is at work *ahead* of consciousness, before we have thought and reflected. That is difficult for us to accept.

On the Here and the Beyond

"I have never written expressly about a life after death; for then I would have had to document my ideas, and I have no way of doing that. Be that as it may, I would like to state my ideas now.
Even now I can do no more than tell stories – 'mythologize.' Perhaps one has to be close to death to acquire the necessary freedom to talk about it."

(*Memories, Dreams, Reflections by C.G. Jung*, p. 299)

Life After Death

February 15, 1958

I don't know how it will be, existence after death. What happens to consciousness? I don't know – and of course it is an urgent question.

The problem of conscious awareness is connected with the Godhead, which is why so many myths tell of the soul's spark – the light of consciousness – flying into the sun after death. After all, it is in the interest of the Godhead for humans to become conscious.[1]

So it is also conceivable, and well within the realm of possibility, that after death individual consciousness returns to a universal consciousness. But that is a great mystery. I feel quite certain, though, that the process of becoming conscious continues after death.

1 Cf. in this regard the chapter "On the Unconsciousness of God," p. 183ff.

An Existence in Psychic Images

November 14, 1958

The following ideas were voiced after Jung had read a draft of the chapter called "The Work" as well as the one with his reflections on the afterlife, but before he took up the writing of his contribution to "Late Thoughts," which he began to formulate in January 1959.

With increasing age, contemplation and reflection play an ever greater role. One begins to uncover and recognize the images behind events and experiences.

This world of images, which I am already experiencing, could be a precursor to a step beyond this earthly life to a mythical existence, an existence in psychic images. Life after death would then be like progressing into the world of images.

Because of our nature, however, we are unable to imagine this afterlife existence as anything other than a process, a happening in time. But actually, this temporality only appears to be so, in the same way as psychic images only appear to have a particular spatial location. We are simply unable to imagine a four-dimensional or multi-dimensional existence. And we are just as incapable of recognizing the ontological qualities of the psychic images.

My exploration of the inner images serves the same purpose for me as philosophy did for Plato: it is a preparation for death. In a way it helps me to avoid ending my life in retrospection. Some old people are completely caught up in reminiscence and retrospection. They are imprisoned in their memories, while for me it is rather a case of *reculer pour mieux sauter*: I am trying to see the thread that has led me into my life, into the world, and will lead me out again.

My work reflects this quite clearly: it was exactly at the mid-point of my life that the eternal images broke through.[1] Goethe wrote about these images – although at a much older age: "Ye wavering shapes, again ye do enfold me..."[2] For me, these figures were never wavering. They had substance, had a kind of solidity about them, although the expression they took varied. Contrary to expectations, one *knows* that the images are something definite, even though this cannot be precisely expressed, nor can it be proven.

1 Reference to the inner images that assailed Jung in the years 1912 to 1920. Cf. the chapter "Confrontation with the Unconscious" in Jaffé, A. (ed.), 1962, p. 170ff. [See also C.G. Jung, *The Red Book*, Shamdasani, S., (ed.), 2009].

2 Goethe, J. W. V., Goethe's Faust, part one. trans. A. Swanwick, Philadelphia, 1898

"Thy dead shall live"

November 21, 1958

When dealing with the unconscious I again and again think of the verse in Isaiah: "Thy dead shall live."[1]

If I regard the inner world of images as a precursor to a post-mortal existence, then I could also imagine that the dead for their part live on in certain involuntary fantasies of the living. Albeit not necessarily appearing as specific figures, but rather as their "arranger." They would thus perform the same function as the archetypes in the collective unconscious. The archetypes are not graspable, yet must be understood as "arrangers" of archetypal ideas, fantasies and images.

The dead appear to exist in a sphere to which we are connected through our inner world of images. In psychological terms, what we call events in the land of the dead may actually take place in the unconscious psyche.[2] In the traditions of many native peoples, the dream world is often the same as the land of the dead, and this connection or concordance should not be completely rejected out of hand. It would seem that the psyche, or rather the unconscious, could be the region in which the dead live on.

The unconscious is limitless, unknowable, without time or space, just as the so-called "hereafter" is described as limitless, unknowable, and outside of all notions of time and space.

1 Isaiah 26,19
2 Cf. in this regard also Jaffé, A. (ed.), 1962, p. 191ff.

Dreams of a Post-Mortal Existence of My Mother

June 23, 1958

Long after my mother died, I had a dream in which I paid her a visit at the place where she apparently now resided. She lived in a house from the 18th or 19th century, a small country cottage surrounded by roses. The house was located, I knew for certain in the dream, in the afterlife.

Later I had another long dream. The setting was Mendoza in Argentina, at the foot of the Aconcagua, the highest mountain in the South American Cordillera. In the dream, it was said that my mother lived there and was married to a pharmacist. Then I saw a younger woman – I was told she was the wife of a pharmacist – with bandages on her head and arms. She was injured.

A few days later I read in the newspaper that an earthquake had destroyed the city of Mendoza!

For lack of something better, one could connect this dream with a post-mortal existence of my mother and also make a connection between the earthquake and the wounded woman in the dream.

My mother had a powerful eros attraction to faraway places. But she projected it onto me and often voiced her fantasy that I would someday travel to the East and marry an Asian woman. "I do wonder what kind of woman you will marry one day, she will certainly be Japanese or Indian!" Such images are the expression of vivid expansive fantasies that could easily have been a catalyst for her own further development.

We usually regard ideas about an afterlife and apparent "experiences" of the beyond as "only psychological," i.e., subjective fantasies. But actually, we do not know what kind of reality psychic contents have, and we know even less about the extent to which images and apparitions of the deceased may have something like autonomy and an objective reality. It is not always possible to distinguish them from inner images and fantasies. I am of the opinion that our fantasies from the unconscious have a certain degree of independent validity. If I cannot come up with any evidence for an afterlife with my logical reasoning and intellect, I am dependent on intuitive hints and suggestions from the unconscious, including dreams, and feel justified in taking them more or less seriously. If the unconscious says "Mendoza," it initially sounds like nonsense. But when it then appears in the newspaper...!

I can say neither "yes" nor "no," but for the sake of my mental balance, it is important to consider the offerings from the unconscious as possibilities, even if they remain unprovable.

My mother, for all her inner expansiveness, naturalness and variety, lacked greatness. She was a country parson's wife. Nevertheless, in her unconscious there lived a more comprehensive personality who roamed across huge expanses and stumbled across exotic things – and this side of her personality she projected onto me. Thus, she thought I would one day bring home a wife from the East! That shows that there was such a woman inside her. This possible corresponding compensation was quite in line with her character.

Perhaps there is after all something to the idea that one chooses one's life before birth. In this case there would be a connection between previous fantasies and a specific life. You may harbor a yearning for something during your life and have fantasies about the unlived aspect right up until you die. People often regret not having done something or other. If there were a continuation, according to the laws of the psyche an impulse would arise to realize these compensatory fantasies.

I could imagine that I might compensate for my current life in the future by again being a pioneer, but in a different field, perhaps in the natural sciences. I can well understand why Buddha finally, after however many incarnations, no longer wanted to return to life. I am not claiming that I would like to disappear into Nirvana forever. And

I can certainly conceive of a world situation coming about in which I could not but say: "*Encore une fois!*"

At the moment, I do not feel that way. Now I have had enough. The only thing that could tempt me would be the natural sciences – further insight into the nature of things. Research in the natural sciences, yes, I could imagine myself doing that! But I don't know whether *this* motive would be enough.

My burning interest now is of course the situation after death, and what one can experience there. Are time and space necessary conditions? To experience something, two elements are required: the one having the experience – the I – and the object being experienced. We don't know whether this distinction between subject and object is also present after death.

This raises the question of whether we have consciousness after death and if so, how much. That is the big question: whether one dies with a developed consciousness or not. Or whether one then simply *is*, and is blown out into existence again by the great universal wind. Although the question of reincarnation seems reasonable to me, I cannot rationally understand how it would be possible.

What excites me the most is insight. From my point of view, I do not need to experience another earthly existence for that. It is conceivable that in the "beyond," after death, one will have unlimited access to insights. That is certainly possible, if we descend into a universal consciousness after death, into an existence beyond opposites, where the division between the subject having the experience and the object being experienced no longer exists.

But such insights would still not be comprehensive. Because they would give information about facts and connections: i.e., breadth rather than depth. It would be a direct knowledge of things, without the limitations of space and time. Conversely, I see the recognition of that which gives one's own life meaning, and insights that one has gained from this life, as knowledge attaining depth. Increased breadth of knowledge and acquisition of information would simply be an aid for such insights in the realm of the depths.

Dream of My Late Sister's Wedding in the Hereafter

November 15, 1957

Yesterday I had a dream that I would like to tell you:[1]

In the dream I am on a journey or at a railway station. It was an impression, I couldn't really pin it down. Anyway – I am somehow in a foreign country. There is a large building. Maybe it is a station concourse or a hangar at the edge of an airfield. But there are no airplanes there. A wide field stretches before me as far as the horizon, to a distant darkness, to infinity. And I am aware that I am on a journey, returning from far far away.

The next part of the dream I remember very clearly... No, actually it is just as unclear. It was like this: in the background is a train on a track. We are standing by the engine – I and a crowd of people. I am there with Father and Mother. It was more that I knew they were there than actually seeing them. So I was on a journey with Father and Mother, and we were wearing formal attire. I knew we were on our way back from a wedding that had taken place abroad, far away. Father was wearing a top hat. In the dream I also have a top hat, but I am holding it in the same hand as my suitcase. It's rather uncomfortable. I think: how foolish, why did I not bring a *hat box*? I look at the top hat; in fact it does look rather "*ruffled*" and crumpled. Mother was somewhat more recognizable than my father, and we were, as I said, returning

1 The style of the narration here reflects the great pains Jung was taking to remember his dream, which was already threatening to slip back into the unconscious.

home from a wedding. In the dream, I am the son of my parents. I was an adult, middle aged, around forty years old.

Suddenly I realize: my sister is missing! Of course: *she* is the one whose wedding was celebrated! The country from which we were returning must therefore have been the hereafter – whatever that means.

My sister died in the thirties. I was going back and forth tonight thinking about this dream. My sister Gertrud was a curious person: I was never very close to her. And now my sister appears as the anima in my dream. I have told you about her and her marvelous attitude.[2] I always admired her. She died of an operation that was supposed to have been a minor procedure – but she clearly knew that it was a matter of life or death. I only went to the hospital when she died, as I had no idea about the seriousness of the situation – it all happened rather quickly.

While it already became clear in the first part of the dream that this journey was a return from great cosmic distance and that we had landed on the airfield, the motif of return is taken further in the second part of the dream. We were standing on the platform next to a locomotive. Had we disembarked from the train? I don't know. We walked from the engine along the length of the train, as though looking for a carriage in which to sit. It was as if we were catching a train in Vienna or Paris to travel home, but had already traveled from much further away.

The top hat is a strange detail which didn't mean anything to me at first. Of course a top hat makes people bigger, enables them to appear taller. That is its purpose. Then one is more important because one is taller. That makes sense "there," in what one might call "the hereafter." But here it is a hindrance, an *impedimentum*. It reminds me of an earlier dream about trousers I had received that were far too big for me. To return from this greatness back to earthly proportions is a very awkward affair!

Oh, and there was also something else that was very odd: Father was on my left, and he was, or was walking, much higher up than me, as if his feet were at the level of my head. Mother was on my right, and

2 Gertrud Jung (1884–1935), cf. Jaffé, A. (ed.), 1962, p. 112.

her feet were half as high up as Father's. I had the feeling that I had a short stocky form. I was the only one with my feet on the platform, *au niveau*.

The huge space of the airfield had something frightening about it. It was dark, evening, or rather nighttime, and it was a space of enormous range, of emptiness – a colossal emptiness. There was this hall, this hangar, very wide and tall. I stood on the outermost edge of the field, with this colossal expanse before me. I was concerned with "departure" or "arrival."

Now, the sister in the dream I interpret as quasi the personification of my unconscious or my anima. She had married. Thus, she must have somehow entered into a vital connection with a masculine element. What this means for me personally, I do not yet know.

I have the feeling that my fatigue of the last few days has something to do with this dream experience, that it is connected with this colossal distance from whence I had to return. I felt like one might feel after some huge achievement: I had to return, reduce the scale back down, take off the top hat, set my feet back on the ground. My father had his feet at the level of my head. But it did not look like he was hanging in the air, for him it was simply in order to be like that.

Two Dreams of a Deceased Friend

January 10, 1958

When I was working on the book Death Dreams and Ghosts, Jung and I often discussed the phenomena of precognitive experiences and dreams occurring shortly before or after the death of a person close to the dreamer, in which the deceased appeared.

On January 9, 1927, my friend H. died.[1] Half a year before in June 1926, I had the following dream: I am traveling with H. by car around Lake Geneva. We are driving from Lausanne in the direction of Vevey. But I know in the dream that "Vevey" is actually Luxor; we are therefore not on the shore of Lake Geneva, but on the bank of the Nile.[2] When we arrive at the *Place de la Ville* in "Vevey," H. says to me: "I need to get something on the car repaired. It will take about an hour. You can go for a walk in the meantime. We'll meet on the eastern road out of town in the direction of Montreux." I agree and go for a walk around the town, and after an hour I go to meet H. at the appointed place. But he does not come. So I start walking along the highway on foot in the

1 Hermann Sigg-Böddinghaus was one of C.G. Jung's neighbors in Küsnacht; the two men were the same age and soon established a close friendship. When Sigg, a businessman with international ventures, married Martha Böddinghaus who was part of the early circle around C.G. Jung and the Psychology Club, contact between the two men increased. In 1920, after recovering from the Spanish flu, C.G. Jung accompanied his friend on a business trip to Tunisia and Algeria; cf. p. 136f. Jung was greatly affected by the relatively early and sudden death of Herman Sigg after a "paralytic stroke."

2 Jung visited Luxor on the return journey from the Bugishu Psychological Expedition in the winter of 1926.

direction of Montreux, to see if he is perhaps waiting further along. Suddenly a car stops behind me. It is H. He is angry: "Honestly, you could have waited for me instead of walking off!" Curiously, this bit of the dream was then repeated. Then the dream ended.

When I thought about it, I realized that Luxor is on the left bank of the Nile and not like Vevey, which is on the right shore of Lake Geneva if you follow the direction of the Rhone. On the right bank of the Nile, opposite Luxor, is the City of the Dead! After H.'s death, it seemed to me that the dream had a precognitive aspect.

About two to three weeks after the death of H. – his funeral had already taken place – I had another strange and uncanny dream about him: we were now actually in Luxor, in a restaurant with small white marble tables and plush armchairs. We sat on a sofa in a corner. I knew I was with H. in Luxor – and it was very significant because of the other dream about H. Somehow I had been waiting for him before. He hurried up to me and said to me with great emotion: "You know that I'm alive. There's no need for you to imagine I am dead. I am as alive as you!" This scene repeated itself. In the previous dream, our encounter on the road from Vevey to Montreux had also been repeated. He then got threateningly close to me, and I was suddenly overwhelmed by the stench of rotting cadaver. I knew: "Now something dangerous is going to happen!" I took my machete, a kind of dagger, out of the case and waved it about in the air and sliced it up and down between him and me, as if I wanted to keep him at a distance.

That was the last dream I had of H. I cannot explain the threatening atmosphere. Maybe the vehemence on my part was needed to cut his bond to me and to transform the relationship?[3]

3 In connection with the two dreams Jung also told of how he saw an "inner image" of his friend on the day after the funeral. He saw H. standing at the foot of his bed and had the feeling H. wanted Jung to follow him. Jung denied that it was an apparition; he perceived it as a fantasy, but respected the reality of the fantasy. H. then led him to his study and pointed to several books with red covers on a high bookshelf. When Jung a few days later asked H.'s widow if he could look in his study, he saw that the books were a set of Émile Zola novels in German translation, one volume of which bore the title *The Legacy of the Dead*. See also Jaffé, A. (ed.), 1962, p. 312f.

On the Idea of Rebirth as a Mythical Concept

September 23, 1957

I dreamed that Toni came back. Her death had only occurred due to a sort of mix-up – as if she had died through some misunderstanding.[1] And so now she was here again, in order to somehow live a further part of her life.

I can only understand this dream figure as the anima.

When I asked if he thought the dream could relate to a possible rebirth because of something left unlived, undone, C.G. Jung answered:

With my wife I have the feeling of a much greater detachment or distance than with Toni Wolff. With Toni I have noticed that she still seems to be nearby. My wife has attained something that Toni has not.

The idea or concept of rebirth is an incredibly useful way of enlivening reality. But even if something inspires us profoundly in reality, this does not indicate or prove that it really exists. However, we also cannot prove that rebirth does not exist. We could call it a "healthy belief" or a "therapeutic myth." Its positive effect does not work for everyone, however, and neither can it be seen as evidence for its existence. But such a belief about the continuation of life after death can have a kind of revitalizing effect or healing value, and maybe we have this fantasy for precisely that reason. A fitting image or thought can lift

1 Toni Wolff; her sudden death on March 21, 1953 at the age of 64 had come as a complete shock to C.G. Jung.

one's spirits in certain circumstances. Whether rebirth can be proven is another question. We cannot exclude the possibility that there are metaphysical processes that we are totally incapable of grasping.

I have always had the conscious and distinct impression that Toni is still closer to earth, which is why she manifests herself to me more easily than my wife. My wife is as if on another level, beyond my reach. Toni seems to me to be close enough that one could possibly reach her. She seems to have remained much closer to the sphere of our three-dimensional existence and would thus have the opportunity to slip back in – at any rate, this was the conclusion I drew from my dreams.

With her, I feel strongly, or even know, that she has not reached a state in which a continuation of three-dimensional life would no longer make sense – on the presupposition that certain stages of insights would liberate us from the urge to return to earth. That is, if increased insight would prevent a spirit wishing to be reincarnated. Leaving the three-dimensional world is referred to as Nirvana. But if there is any remaining karma[2] to be dealt with, one is lured back to one's desires; one returns to life on earth in order to live the missing part, maybe even in the belief that something needs to be completed.

At a later time, Jung added:

I was not able to put aside the question about reincarnation, I was tormented from within to give an answer. I could not find the answer using my intellect, it goes beyond human understanding. That is why from an early age I began to listen to what the unconscious has to say. But even when one takes the answers of the unconscious seriously – because the problem is presented convincingly in dreams – there is the niggling doubt: "Is it really so?" I have nothing to say to that. I cannot answer the question. These are mythical ideas.

2 Karma refers to a law of cause and effect in Indian philosophy. This effect need not necessarily manifest itself in the current life, but could also be carried over into a future life.

Further Dreams About Toni Wolff and Emma Jung After Their Deaths

November 14, 1958

If one believes in the possibility of reincarnation, the idea logically follows that those people who are reincarnated did not complete something in their life that they were meant to do.

That was very impressive for me with Toni. Basically her natural tendency was to be very down-to-earth. But for all her great humanity, she became very intellectual. Her manner was often forced and unnatural. I saw clearly how she resisted her own character, her own earthy nature. Had she acknowledged it, she would have had to admit: I have neglected a part of life. But she denied it during her lifetime. Only gradually, but too late, could she admit it to herself; and that required a high degree of honesty and courage. But by that time, she was no longer able to accomplish that missing part of life. That was her tragedy.

If there is a possibility of reincarnation, then in Toni's case it would be in order for her to be more in an earthly here and now, and closer to nature. And that was evident in my dreams about her after her death.

In those dreams of her, I always had the distinct feeling of reality and liveliness. My wife was much further away in my dreams. Toni remained absolutely alive and close to reality. Once I had a dream which made a deep impression: she was a farmer in the Umbrian countryside in Italy, working the land. It was exactly what one might have wished for her – you could imagine her getting well there. She was tanned from the sun and had a tremendous vitality, which she never had in reality. Her whole visceral, chthonic side came to the fore. She felt natural and simple, was very earthy, very chthonic; she even had that pagan influence one sees in farming folk in the south. The people there are very much in contact with the earth.

At first it did not occur to me to think it might have a connection with the possibility of reincarnation. But bit by bit, the idea began to appear completely logical.

With my wife I have a very different impression. I had dreams after her death from which I suddenly awoke and knew that I had been with her, and that we had been together the whole day in Provence, where she was working on her Grail studies.[1]

It seemed just as natural as the development of Toni after her death, but on another level. In Umbria there is so much sun and so much earth that a person's chthonic side gets more chance to ripen than in the north. With my wife, this step was not emphasized at all: she seemed to be developing further along the spiritual path. I had the feeling my wife was in a spiritual realm, while Toni was in a chthonic world. No one ever told me that my wife had appeared in their dreams. Even with me, she did not appear again – except as an image she presented to me.[2] But here I did not feel that she was really present.

The dreams recounted by C.G. Jung in our conversations about Toni Wolff and the repeated comparison with his wife show how much the challenges of his relationship with these two women occupied him, even years after their deaths. As a young woman, Toni Wolff had accompanied Jung on his research into the unconscious, into the inner world, with her "high natural intelligence and genial psychological

1 Emma Jung spent many years studying the Grail legend, but was not able to finish writing the manuscript before her death. It was subsequently completed by Dr. Marie-Louise von Franz. Cf. Jung, E./von Franz, M.-L., 1960. In spring 1958, Jung recounted that he had heard his wife tell him in a dream that she now accepted his views. He wondered whether her post-mortal development was also having an effect in him. In contrast to the assertions in this chapter, a few months earlier Jung claimed he was in constant contact with his wife Emma, while the connection to Toni Wolff was lacking and "empty."

2 Cf. chapter "The Afterlife and Sexuality," p. 169ff.

sensitivity."[3] *She played a similar role to the "soror mystica" in the alchemical opus. His wife Emma was for Jung the foundation of the house, and as mother of their five children and grandmother to a flock of grandchildren also the bedrock of the family. Thanks to her psychological strength and independent spirit, she gave him "a point of support in this world" during the most difficult of times.*[4]

The creative solution to the difficult personal constellation is implied in the following words of Emma Jung: "He never took anything from me to give to Toni, but the more he gave her, the more he seemed able to give me."[5]

In the decades-long mutual relationship, all three demonstrated, in my opinion, great achievement in the service of individuation.

3 C.G. Jung, "Introduction to Wolff's 'Studies in Jungian Psychology,'" CW 10, 1970, para. 889. Jung had written the foreword to this selection of essays by Wolff a few weeks before this conversation in August 1958. Cf. Wolff, T., 1959.

4 Cf. Jaffé, A. (ed.), 1962, p. 189.

5 Hannah, B., 1976, p. 119f.

The Dead Appearing as Animals

December 6, 1957

In some of the reports which comprised research material for the book Death Dreams and Ghosts, animals appeared to have the ability to live in a space-time continuum in which there was no separation between this world and the beyond. C.G. Jung made the following remarks after reading what I had written on the subject.

The dead seem to choose the most curious forms for manifesting themselves. Even as animals!

I once had a dog, a boxer, called Pascha. Whenever I was digging in the garden, he would sit next to me and eagerly devour the grubs that were dug up. After he died, I was very sad. Then I was once again digging in the garden when a little robin flew across, alighted nearby, and began eating the grubs, just as Pascha had always done. Eventually the bird even perched on the spade and waited to see if grubs would appear. I was very touched and thought, that is my Pascha who has come back in the soul of a bird, eating the grubs. But then I was annoyed with myself for having such an idea and thought: now you're hallucinating! So I called my wife over to get me in check. "Come here for a moment and look at this!" She came immediately, but when she was about fifteen meters away, the robin flew off. She did see the bird, however. That was about twenty years ago.

And then: two years ago on the anniversary of Toni Wolff's death, I was in Bollingen, and Hans[1] had brought a load of dry wood down to the house. So there was a big pile of wood and scrubs lying there. Then he came over to me and said somewhat sheepishly, it was odd but there was a bird there on the pile. It remained there the entire time and simply would not go away. He could not make sense of it. I went straight away to look. And there was a little robin again. It sat on a branch and – very surprisingly – let me get very close. It was not at all disturbed by our presence. It sat there for over an hour. When it began to get dark, the little bird came into the courtyard and perched on the pile of dry sticks. Hans knew it was the anniversary of Toni Wolff's death and asked if the robin might not be her soul? I had already noticed his reaction and the same thought had also crossed my mind.

Pascha was always a remarkable dog. Once I came down the steps into the garden and he was standing at the bottom looking at me quite expectantly. His eyes had exactly the same expression my father used to have. I immediately thought: that is my father looking at me! I was completely bowled over by this impression. I cannot explain it. But, you know, Native people believe the spirits of the dead can appear as all different kinds of animals near their graves and houses. Unfortunately I don't recall what happened in reality in connection with this experience.

I had apparently reacted in the way a primitive might, without reflecting on the objectivity of the impression. The primitive soul lives on in modern educated people, who can have such experiences.

1 Hans Kuhn was a young man from Bollingen who acted as a gardener, driver and general handyman and was Jung's close and trusted helper for many years.

Animals and the Fullness

November 7, 1958

The older I grow and the more I observe animals, the greater my admiration for them. The way an animal experiences the world must be of an unsurpassable abundance and originality.

December 17, 1959

What we can acquire in old age goes back to the animal soul which doesn't speak. I try to go along with the instinct, and it leads to a place without language, a self-contained world. A world in which one only has inklings or hunches. There I feel alive.

It is particularly difficult for me to get an objective view of myself. I have no desire to talk about things or explain myself. I do it, as far as I can, but I have a need for this stillness. The silencing of language. The essence, the act of simply being, is otherwise disturbed. By talking about it, you push it away. It is as though something falls out of the fullness of being, lost through chatter.

The Afterlife and Sexuality

November 21, 1958

At the time of this conversation I was working on the "Visions" chapter of Memories, and Jung and I talked again about his experiences during the time he was close to death and lost consciousness. We also spoke about the chapter "On Life after Death," which was just being written. In connection with the chapter about C.G. Jung's relationship with Freud, which was also in progress, the significance of sexuality in the psychology of both pioneers had arisen as well.[1]

When I was very ill and had an out-of-body experience,[2] a feeling of great relief came over me. It was no longer about age or youth; what counted was the unfolding of meaning. I experienced how the element of meaning took up its rightful space, which here in this material life is only dimly perceived or hardly recognized because of so much superficiality. It had freed itself from the bonds of matter and of developed existence and could fully reveal itself. Space ceased to exist, there were no more collisions between entities. "There" it takes no time to get from one end to the other. It is one great image. This is the *visio dei*.[3] To experience *that*! With the feeling: *yes, this is it*! There is nothing else

1 See the chapter "Visions" in Jaffé, A. (ed.), 1962, p. 289ff. and the chapter "On Life after Death," ibid., p. 299ff., in which Jung reflects on experiences and dreams which contained images suggesting a possible connection between a "here" and a "hereafter." See also the chapter "Sigmund Freud," ibid., p. 146ff.

2 Jung refers to his experiences after his heart attack of 1944.

3 *visio dei*: vision of God

– it is so beautiful and grand that a deep all-satisfying peace unfolds. No one with such an experience can be convinced that this is invalid or nonsense.

Ultimately, we cannot know whether we will experience anything after death. But it seems highly probable that to a considerable extent, the psyche continues to exist, since the unconscious extends beyond limitations of time and space. It transcends our reality of here and now.

For me, the image that my wife is now in the South of France working on the Grail legend is very calming.[4] Or that my late friend Oeri is being taught by his daughter about psychology.[5] Or that Toni Wolff, colored by the sun, is vigorously and happily tilling the land in Umbria.[6]

"Over there" separation does not exist: everything is being-in-one. But this we are unable to grasp. It is something penetrating one's entire being. It was emphasized to me that this is not devoid of eros. Nor of what we sense as sexuality. Rather, they are major components. Think of the *houris* in paradise: Muslims are unable to imagine paradise without love.[7] And why is Christ in the *thalamus* with his bride?[8]

After the death of my wife, I had a dream: I saw her in an image that seemed to have been made for me.[9] In this dream I experienced a feeling of congruence reaching as far down as the depths of sexuality. A complete unity.

The depth of sensation is represented through sexuality. It is the strongest experience of union found in nature. Only two people joining together completely in spirit to become one comes close to this experience. That however is almost other-worldly. In our three-dimensional world, the potential of union is implied in sexuality. But only as potential. In actuality, it is extremely rare to experience spiritual unity.

4 Cf. p. 164 and Jaffé, A. (ed.), 1962, p. 309ff.

5 Cf. ibid., p. 309; the dream occurred two weeks after Albert Oeri's death.

6 Cf. p. 163f.

7 *Houri* is an Arabic word referring to a beautiful maiden in the images of paradise in Islam.

8 *Thalamos* or *thalamus* designates the heavenly bridal chamber. C.G. Jung reflected deeply on the role of sexuality as an expression of psychological wholeness, its spiritual aspect, and its numinous meaning in "The Psychology of the Transference" in CW 16, 1966, para. 353ff. and in *Mysterium Coniunctionis*, CW 14, 1970.

9 After the death of his wife, Jung had a dream or vision of her: "I knew that it was not she, but a portrait she had made or commissioned for me. It contained the beginning of our relationship, the events of fifty-three years of marriage, and the end of her life also." See Jaffé, A. (ed.), 1962, p. 296.

In our earthly existence, this is ephemeral and fragile. There, in the "beyond," it is apparently fully present.

Many experience sexuality as a cause of enslavement and suffering, believing they will become more spiritual if they repress it. That is not true at all, quite the contrary! But they want to prove that they are different from animals. If you can tolerate your own shadow, you can also accept your sexuality. But if you fall into uninhibited sexuality, you are lost – the shadow has you in its grip.

On an Indian Conception of Life After Death

1956

Shortly before making these observations, Jung had again read Die Reden des Gotamo Buddhos *by Karl Eugen Neumann and written an introduction for a new edition.*[1]

In the Indian myths, one finds the idea of eternal stretches of time, the "*kalpas*" or ages of universal time in which correspondingly slow changes take place in the world.[2] According to this concept, the soul does not live on after death for eternity, but only for a very long time.

The following legend tells of this:

Buddha was sitting in a grove and meditating. Suddenly he perceived that one of the highest Brahma gods had a false thought. He immediately made his way to the highest Brahma world and found the god in the enormous paradisaical garden of his palace, which was on a high peak of the Himalayas. The god was enjoying himself with the ladies of the court. They had climbed a tree and were throwing down petals and fruits. The god thought it was wonderful and said to

1 German scholar and Indologist Karl Eugen Neumann was the first translator of many of the Buddhist scriptures from Pali into a European language. *Die Reden Gotamo Buddhos* [The Speeches of Gotama Buddha] was first published in 1911; C.G. Jung wrote a text for the new edition of 1956 for the publishing houses Artemis, Zürich and Zsolnay, Vienna; see CW 18, 1976, para. 1576. In the winter of 1960 he again addressed this text.

2 Kalpa in Sanskrit means a universal time period, an eon of mythological time, i.e., a very long period of time and the longest unit of time in the cyclical cosmology system of Hinduism and Buddhism.

Buddha: "The scene you see here, this joy and resplendence, will last for eternity, for I am immortal."

Buddha said "You are mistaken. It's true that your life will last for many *kalpas*, but eventually it will end." The Brahma god refused to believe him. At that moment all became totally silent. No more petals or fruits fell from the tree, and the laughter of the court ladies was no longer heard. The Brahma god was astounded and asked Buddha to explain. Buddha said: "You see, at this moment the karma of your court ladies expired – and they are no longer. This will also happen to you one day." Then the Brahma god converted to Lord Buddha and vowed his allegiance.

This is the story. It expresses the natural intuition in India that time is relative. In the "hereafter," and this means also in the unconscious, time approaches timelessness. But between our time and an absolute timelessness there are countless stages. According to Indian tradition, the soul can survive through many *kalpas*, but it does not live forever.

C.G. Jung 1958 in Bollingen; photo © Aniela Jaffé.

Human Image, God Image, Worldview

"Epistemologically I take my stand on Kant, which means that an assertion doesn't posit its object. So when I say 'God' I am speaking exclusively of assertions that don't posit their object. All such assertions refer to the psychology of the God-image. Their validity is therefore never metaphysical but only psychological."

C.G. Jung, *Letters I*, p. 294

God Revealed

September 21, 1956/February 1959

Jung and I spoke extensively in the autumn of 1956 about the aims of Eastern meditation practices. This was in connection with a planned paperback edition of some of Jung's essays. In the winter of 1959, as he was writing about a further development of the Christian myth, Jung returned to his remarks of 1956.[1]

In India, the aspiration is to get *behind* the world of images, to kind of extinguish the world of images and nature through meditation. My approach is a different one. I wish to remain in the world of images and of nature, as a way to see God. I couldn't wish for more! The world, nature, is after all the manifestation of God. The Chinese approach also is rooted in a humble means of harmonious contemplation of nature – *in modest harmony with nature.*[2]

I do not desire to free myself from humankind, nor from myself, nor from nature. For me, all of this is part of an indescribable wonder – including, naturally, the inevitable accompanying abyss. Without

1 A paperback volume of four essays by C.G. Jung was in preparation with Fischer Bücherei, conceived with the intention of introducing a wider public to his work and I had been charged with its editing. Jung had suggested the inclusion of his article "The Psychology of Eastern Meditation", explaining his choice with the above remarks. In January 1959, he had written his contribution to the final chapter of *Memories*, "Late Thoughts"; cf. Jaffé, A. (ed.), 1962, p. 327–354. Cf. C.G. Jung, *Bewusstes und Unbewusstes*, 1957.

2 Rascher Verlag had just informed Jung that a fifth edition of the book he had produced together with Richard Wilhelm, *The Secret of the Golden Flower. A Chinese Book of Life*, was planned. Wilhelm, R./Jung, C.G., first German edition 1929; first English edition, trans. Cary Baynes, 1931, London, Kegan Paul.

it, there would be no texture, no contours and depths, no concrete vitality. The highest sense of being can only exist because it *is* – not because it is *not*.

Because nature is the manifestation of God, God is also manifested in us. However, we long had no way to express it. It is about wholeness. And it actually is not important who speaks of it, and where this knowledge comes from. Where the knowledge or insights come from is basically irrelevant. And who says it is also unimportant. At first, insight may come to one indirectly – through seeing, books, newspapers, people or events. And then it can also happen that we receive knowledge directly from within. At one time an insight occurs to *me*, at another, to *someone else*. That is completely irrelevant. It is always the same God who speaks in all of us. The fish, the birds, the plants also tell us of God. And the mountain is God, the tree is also God. In them, God speaks.

The human being is the organ of reception, the perceiver. If the Tao is in nature or not, we do not know.[3] But it is the individual who makes the Tao, who makes God – existing and present in our existence – *conscious*. That is why God alone is not enough. We human beings are also necessary, an individual is needed for the experience of wholeness. *Deus et homo.*[4]

3 *Tao* or *Dào* in Chinese means "way" or "path." However, contemporary Sinologists prefer using the term *Tao* without translation, as no English expression can capture the complete meaning. In the work *Tao Te Ching* by Lao-Tze, the term is used to refer to a transcendental highest reality and truth, as well as an eternal creative principle.

4 God *and* human.

On Our Conscious Knowledge

October 24, 1957

On this day, Jung spoke about experiencing a kind of fateful inner knowing, once when he first set eyes on his future wife, and again when he visited Freud in Vienna in 1909. He was convinced that this knowledge was already present in his unconscious. It was "knowledge that belongs to the future, knowledge that is there but that I do not know." His subsequent reflections led him to explore the idea that human consciousness developed in order for humans to be able to recognize and reflect upon the world and thus in a certain sense confirm the existence to its creator. Jung would take up this topic again in early 1959 in his text "Late Thoughts."[1]

When I say there is an absolute knowledge present in the unconscious – in religious terms, that God is all-knowing[2] – it is not a contradiction when I add that only humans or their consciousness can possess this knowledge. As a human being, I am a creature knowing that I know. We are aware of our knowledge, while this all-knowing universal being is not aware of its knowledge.[3] The knowledge is simply there, it exists, presumably even in the smallest parts of the cosmos and of nature.

1 Cf. Jaffé, A. (ed.), 1962, p. 327ff., in particular p. 338f. See also the following chapter in this book.
2 For Jung the terms "Godhead" and "unconscious" are not identical, but are probably synonyms for an ultimately unrecognizable power. Cf. Jaffé, A. (ed.), 1962, p. 336f. On "absolute knowledge" in the unconscious see also CW 8, 1969, para. 912ff.
3 Cf. next chapter "On the Unconsciousness of God," p. 183ff.

In nature some things appear to arise from and are arranged according to some kind of knowledge. In, for example, the symbiosis between two animals, or between animals and plants, there must be some "knowing" present that brings them together. Or think of the *hydrocephalus* virus: it behaves as though it knew human anatomy.[4] If you cut out the lens of a salamander's eye, it can form again from the adjacent tissue, even though this tissue is of another sort. A certain type of wasp needs the flesh of a caterpillar for its eggs. So, what does this wasp do? It stings a caterpillar in a ganglion in its spine containing the motoric nerve center, thus paralyzing it. How does the wasp know to do this? Bees can even express their "knowledge": they communicate with each other by indicating the direction of nectar-rich plants with their dances.[5] These are decisions of a sort, acts of judgment. But whether the animals themselves *know* what they are doing, we cannot say. It is the same with migratory birds: we do not know whether they are aware of their mysterious orientation knowledge.

We humans know that we know, or rather, that we know to a certain extent. Beyond that, precognitive phenomena can appear – what we refer to as catalytic exteriorization, as happened during my first encounter with Freud, and with my future wife. At that time I knew nothing about the psychology of such phenomena, but on both occasions I knew that something fateful would occur and that within me there was knowledge belonging to the future – a knowledge, so to speak, that is already in me without my being consciously aware of it. There is knowledge present in my unconscious. Synchronicity is a direct manifestation of the absolute knowledge in the unconscious.[6]

4 Jung speaks here erroneously of a hydrocephalus virus, which does not exist per se, although viruses can be a cause of hydrocephalus (also known as "water on the brain"). He is actually referring to the findings of biologist Adolf Portmann published in 1956 on the rabies virus and its effects on a completely different organism. On the complex interaction of the rabies virus and the organisms infected with it cf. Portmann, A., *Biologie und Geist* [Biology and Spirit], 1956, p. 203ff. There the author writes, i.a.: in observing these "terribly meaningfully" coordinated processes, "we get into the realm of mystery." And: "The virus behaves in a way that must be ascribed to an 'extraneous knowledge.' ... The powers at work here are ultimately hidden from us."

5 Here Jung refers to the research findings published by ethologist and Nobel laureate Karl von Frisch in his 1927 work *The Dancing Bees*.

6 Both in his first encounter with his wife and during a conversation with Freud in Vienna in 1909, a cracking sound was heard in the furniture, which Jung identified as catalytic exteriorization phenomena; cf. Jaffé, A. (ed.), 1962, p. 155. Jung used the term synchronicity to describe the coincidence in time of two or more meaningfully linked but acausal events, i.e. a psychological state

Eros belongs to our conscious knowledge. The feeling of obligation toward the insights obtained through logos is actually eros. Eros always wants to combine two things in one, it is a force that brings together what has been separate. Logos discriminates and differentiates, separates and creates duality; eros creates unity from the many. These two phenomena are, however, only possible within a three-dimensional space, that is within time.

Because I originally came from a state of unity, there is still knowledge of unity inside me. Eros comes to the aid of this dark knowledge. Thus one's unconscious knowledge is brought into the light by love. *Qui amat cognoscit.*[7] Human cognition is a *re*cognition, as Plato said. That is why it is quite accurate to say that humankind is the crowning glory of creation: because we have the ability to know what is. The human knows: this is the world. With its capacity for cognition, the human psyche is equivalent to the world. We are able to wrest things from eternally reigning darkness. The world only really becomes world when we become conscious of it. The soul, then, is not just a personal problem, but a problem of the greatest scope and importance.[8]

Consciousness really knowing about its knowledge has cosmic significance: a world that is known is different from a world that is not known, i.e., a world that merely comes into being, passes, and is not acknowledged or perceived by any form of consciousness. The knowledge is *in* it, but it does not know that it knows. I saw this type of knowledge in primitive peoples. They do not know that they know, they do not reflect, they are completely unconscious. The Old-Testament God is another example of a power that has knowledge but does not know it. Even the New-Testament God as a loving God still does

coinciding with external events which are perceived as meaningful parallels to the momentary subjective condition. Jung had been interested in the phenomenon of synchronicity for a long time, having had doubts from an early stage about the universal application of a causal principle in psychology. Following an Eranos lecture on synchronicity in 1951, C.G. Jung published his paper "Synchronicity: An Acausal Connecting Principle" together with Wolfgang Pauli's monograph "The Influence of Archetypal Ideas on the Scientific Theories of Kepler," see Jung/Pauli, 1952; Fröbe-Kapteyn (ed.), 1952; CW 8, 1969, para. 816–968.

7 The one who loves, knows.

8 Cf. CW 16, 1966, para. 201: "For without consciousness it would never have become known that there is such a thing as a world, and without the psyche there would be absolutely no possibility of knowledge, (...) This [psychic] image alone is the immediate object of knowledge. The existence of the world has two conditions: it to exist and us to know it."

not express knowledge about this knowledge. This is why I believe that we humans are the ones that bring with us at the end of our lives our knowledge about this knowledge. The knowledge of humans means that we virtually "tell" God *what* the world is.

And this is why I also believe that the Godhead periodically must vacate the Godhead, as it were, and take on human form in order to experience this recognizing consciousness. One has to be separated from something in order to be able to perceive it. As long as God is the totality, God cannot know anything. Everything is God. Only that which is detached from or separate from God can really see and know. If I *am* this world, I cannot perceive it.

This explains the significance of the mystical distance from God – a lost state, but also a Lucifer, a light-bearer. No-one sees the glory of God more clearly than the devil. The devil's fire is the fire of the passionate yearning for God, which God is unable to satisfy alone.

On the Unconsciousness of God

March 6, 1959

In early February 1959, a first draft of the text C.G. Jung had written in January, and which later became the "Late Thoughts" chapter of Memories, was sent to Erich Neumann. He responded with a long letter written on February 18, 1959. Jung expressed the following thoughts to me as he considered how to formulate his reply. A short time later, on March 10, 1959, his letter to Neumann followed.[1]

People do not understand me when I say God is unconscious and requires the human being in order to become conscious. This process of becoming conscious can only take place within humans, because here God touches his other side.

One could also hypothesize that God is conscious. But why would he need to create humans and their consciousness if he already knew everything? For what? If he did not need to undergo the painful human process of becoming conscious?[2]

1 Both letters are published as an appendix in Jaffé, A., *Der Mythus vom Sinn im Werk von C.G. Jung*, 1967, p. 179ff (the letters do not appear in the English version, *The Myth of Meaning*). [Cf. Liebscher, M. (ed.), *Analytical Psychology in Exile, The Correspondence of C.G. Jung and Erich Neumann*, trans. McCartney, H., 2015, Princeton University Press, p. 361ff.]

2 Following a lecture given by Rivkah Schärf at the Psychology Club on December 1, 1945, "The Figure of Satan in the Old Testament," Jung responded at length to a statement of Schärf about the depiction of a God figure in the Bible's Book of Job as having an "egotistical interest" in humans gaining insight. Jung found her idea of human insight being a need of God extremely thought-provoking. From a theological point of view it would be condemned as highly heretical, he said. During the post-lecture discussion, Jung postulated the hypothesis of an unconscious God who, owing to a dissociation of consciousness, needed human consciousness. He said that if one took a serious look at the "Deus creator," one saw a strangely fumbling creature at work, making thousands of

It caused me the most terrible conflict to have to accept that the Godhead is unconscious.[3] As is stated in Hebrews: "It is a fearful thing to fall into the hands of the living God."[4] I felt deep terror and shaken to the core as I was forced to comprehend the unconsciousness of God. It was the realization of one's very worst fears, to think of the power that gives us life as a *tremendum*.[5] What then is the meaning of the human relationship to God? What has been handed out to you? What agony it was to admit it to myself! It was an experience that seized the ground from beneath my feet.[6] I had to become ill, just to be able to say a word.[7]

I wrote it down as a confession. What does it mean for people to experience God? There is no greater experience. Struggling with writing my book on *Job* was a glowing-hot iron for me, a battle of passion. But what does it mean for others? Most cannot comprehend me. They do not understand the nature of the problem. What it means when Jacob wrestles with the angel. I was frightened to death of this confrontation. Pure torment forced me to say that God was unconscious. Because if he had not been unconscious, I would have had to curse him.

Why would God create humans with an inferior consciousness if God himself were conscious? The notion of a divine incarnation in Christ essentially expresses the idea that the Godhead enters into the human being who is capable of consciousness. But first it took the story of Job – of the man who realized that he, with his cognizance, his consciousness, stood against God, opposite God, in contradiction to

---

attempts and failures – a power that lacked consciousness. The idea of "God becoming human" could be justified by God's longing for one who sees and recognizes. How strangely ambivalent it was, however, to plant a tree of knowledge and then to prohibit it. Did this creator perhaps not realize that he wanted the perception and recognition of humans? Jung went on to develop his ideas on this subject further in *Aion* and "Answer to Job," and toward the end of his life with his late thoughts about the further development of the Christian myth. The paper of Rivkah Schärf was included by Jung in *Symbolik des Geistes*, Psychologische Abhandlungen, Vol. 6, 1948, Zürich.

3 In Jung, C.G., "Answer to Job," in CW 11, 1969, para. 560ff.

4 Hebrews 10, 31

5 *Tremendum* lat.: causing trembling and fear.

6 Here Jung is vehemently rejecting a formulation Erich Neumann used in his letter of February 18, 1959, in which he said the idea of God becoming conscious was a favorite thesis of C.G. Jung's. Jung emphatically responded that it was anything other than a "pet idea," but rather an "exceedingly painful experience," which had forced him, agonizing and shaken, to make this statement.

7 Jung wrote "Answer to Job" while he was sick with a very high fever.

God. He had recognized God in his dark aspect.[8] In his consciousness and insight, he was thus superior to God.

Thus a process begins with Job which is later continued with the idea of Christ, about whom it is said that God established himself in Christ as in the human. That is the result, the consequence of the superior consciousness that was expressed in Job. When Job thought he needed an advocate in the wrathful God, then this is the first stage of creating an image of such an advocate.[9] This advocate then comes in the figure of the Human Son, God's grace in human form.

---

8 Job 42, 5

9 Despite the misery inflicted on him by God, Job is certain that he will ultimately find an advocate against God within God (cf. Job 16, 19 and 19, 25). He is not throwing overboard the image of the unity of God, but has become aware of the antinomy of God. That is the source of his superiority as a human, which for its part had to lead to God himself becoming human. "This is what happens in Job: *The creator sees himself through the eyes of man's consciousness* and this is the reason why God had to become man." Jaffé, A./Adler, G., *Letters II*, 1971, p. 436. Cf. also "Answer to Job," CW 11, 1969, paras. 553f.

God and Humans

May 23, 1958

Asked about his own myth about the meaning of life this afternoon in Bollingen, C.G. Jung mentioned his idea of God being compelled to attain consciousness in the existence of humans in order to be able to recognize the unconscious creation as meaningful. At that time, he did not want to integrate these "hypothetical" thoughts into the biography, but after the chapter "Late Thoughts" had been written in January 1959, we again discussed his remarks from the previous May. He expanded on some points and said he considered them essential for the development of his ideas, attesting to the passionate nature of his inner struggles. When Jung uses the words "God" or "Godhead," it is in the sense of an image, idea or symbol.[1]

Our life is so important because it demands that we become conscious. We are not making a mistake when we take our own lives very seriously. Otherwise, the Godhead suffers from the stagnation of consciousness. God's crisis leads to a crisis in the world – if the Godhead were complete in itself, it would not need the suffering of the world. It causes great distress to the Old Testament's Yahweh that his people might not obey in the end, because then he would have played his game in vain.

---

1 "Psychologically, the God-concept includes every idea of the ultimate, of the first or last, of the highest or lowest." C.G. Jung in CW 11, 1969, para. 738, fn. 1.

The opinion is repeatedly stated that God wants to test the human being. No – he wants to convince himself that humans have consciousness. The human *must* resist the angel, that is why Jacob fights him.[2] God wants to be convinced. If God wanted to deliver us completely from this world, its existence would have absolutely no point! And such a God could be compared to a potter who makes bad pots and then complains that the pots are poorly made.

Being able to bear life and its trials by continuously battling to remain conscious ultimately means being able to bear the presence of God. But that is in the distant future. If, however, we consciously lead a very simple life, like living in the forest and thereby reducing life to the simplest formula, then consciousness has won. When the evening of humankind approaches, then the highest culture lies in the greatest simplicity. Because then one has recognized the meaning of existence and knows that everything is illusion, apart from living in what *is*.

But were I to consider emigrating to Polynesia à la Gauguin,[3] in the hope that I would find some perfection, or withdraw from the world like a hermit, to cut myself off from the world in order to contemplate its meaningless, the result would be neither meaning nor value. Rather, it would be like a reproach to the creator for making such a nonsense of this earthly existence.

Life, nature, poses a deep problem. We would need to know an unimaginable amount more in order to comprehend the meaning of it all. This requires not just great scientific progress, but also a deepening of consciousness scarcely imaginable today – a distant goal, but one that gives dignity and hope to our existence.

Apparently, we need to battle for our lives with all the fibers of our being, with the aim of achieving as much consciousness and knowledge as possible – knowledge about ourselves, about the world, about eternity. That is what gives meaning to life. Without consciousness, the existence of this world would be only a stupid incident of a silly demiurge.[4]

2 Genesis 32, verses 23–31; see also Jaffé, A. (ed.), 1962, p. 344; see also Jaffé, A./Adler, G., ed., *Letters* II, 1971, p. 239 and CW 5, 1967, para. 524.

3 French artist Paul Gauguin (1848–1903) moved to Polynesia in 1891 in an attempt to get closer to a primeval and unspoiled life far from civilization.

4 While in Platonic philosophy the demiurge is a sublime being who only wants and creates the best,

This reminds me of the Gnostic belief that the true God is a god of goodness who does not care about the imperfect world. It is solely the fault of the demiurge that there is a world of suffering, in which humans live like animals. As the "master builder" of this world, the demiurge is responsible for it.

All I can imagine is *this*: a continuously unfolding world, and a human whose consciousness develops within this created natural world. A consciousness is required in order to give the unconscious creation meaning. Humans can accomplish this, however, only if they understand the language of nature, the language of animals and plants. Then a higher culture of consciousness could develop. In this culture humans would not always think they know better than nature. But we are still far from there today. However, we are only around one million years old. That is really nothing.

But there is one thing we must not forget: the more we know, and the further consciousness extends or the more it develops, the more dangerous it becomes. This Earth could end one day, a final catastrophe is a possibility. Why not? It is also conceivable that humankind will be destroyed and another experiment will begin elsewhere. There are probably such experiments underway all over the universe which could culminate in the emergence of a continuously regenerating and deepening consciousness. The mysterious intention of the creator appears to me to be that existence is transfigured by the fact of knowing about itself. Otherwise, nothing would be gained. A creation does not exist if no one *knows* about it.

It made a deep impression on me when I read in Schreber's work[5] that the Godhead longs for people in order to experience itself in them. Schreber saw something, but it drove him crazy. It is not certain that humans can withstand this divine experiment. Schreber exploded just from thinking about it.

In nature, there is an enormous waste of seeds – of potential. Look at this pear tree: how many blossoms and how many seeds go to waste!

the demiurge in Gnosticism is a dubious figure who created a defective, evil-filled world.

5 Daniel Paul Schreber, see chapter "Transference, Willingness to Follow and Responsibility," p. 36 in this book.

It is just the same with humans – what a ridiculous number of humans there are, and so few who are really conscious! The overwhelming abundance of life forms is evidence of an enormous creative power. God had to create the world in order for there to be an object for his consciousness.

This idea is expressed in the Indian myth where for an eternal time-span there was nothing apart from God. Then one day God noticed that he was all alone. That gave him the idea of an "other," a counterpart, an object. And so he split himself and generated an other from himself. This is how the world came to be.

Usually the reflections of the philosophers stop at this point, because now the world has been created and one gets lost in that. No-one asks: "And what happened to God after he divided himself?"

One must make everything of life of which one is capable. This is why people regret what they did *not* do, despite being called to do it. "If I could start my life over again, I would..."

Being able to withstand the suffering is what gives life meaning. It means one can bear God. For God himself is in doubt about whether he can be withstood, or can become so. That is why he provides humans and animals with the most unbelievable weapons to defend their lives, and why all living things have such a survival instinct. What the creature has to assert itself against is actually a God who is split: one wanted to, the other did not. One creates, the other destroys.

Incarnation

November 10, 1956

The following remarks were made by Jung during a talk with a small group of theologians. It must be emphasized once again that he is of course speaking of ideas and images of incarnation. Incarnation is understood by Jung here as an image for a supra-personal will residing within us. This will is both good and evil, creative and destructive. In order to cope, a high degree of consciousness is necessary.

What does the incarnation of God in the human mean? It is like a second will within the human, and this has far-reaching moral consequences.

It is often difficult, because this second will differs from the will of the ego. I do not want what this other will wants, and it does not want what I (the ego-will) want. Paul experienced this.[1] It is a question of determining which will is valid. Perhaps this second will wants something that I believe is immoral. But I must do it because I believe it is the will of God. That is an enormous conflict!

I am answerable not only to my ego-morality, but also and in equal measure to this second will. The incarnation, however, means exactly this: God's will occurs through me. This I must endure to the end.

We can think of the incarnation as a determination living within us that we are obliged to follow. It is mentioned already in the Old

1 Romans 7, 18–21

Testament, for example in Abraham's sacrificing of Isaac,[2] or in the calling of the prophets, who followed only reluctantly.[3] Or in the New Testament: "Nevertheless not what I will, but what thou wilt"; "Father... take away this cup from me"[4] – these statements express the humblest acknowledgment of a second will that is perceived as the incarnation of something divine.

It is the strange and inexplicable will of God in us that wants to be realized. When one says: "Christ in us," it means nothing other than "God in us." God wants to become human – i.e., God, and also God's will, enters the empirical human. This can lead to heavy ethical problems.

The difficulty lies in the fact that for Christians, God is pure goodness. But this overlooks that God, or what we call "God," is also not-good, is also evil, and that with the incarnation of God, this negative will is also incarnated. God burdens humans with this good-bad essence, so that actually we would have to say that the human is afflicted by God. That is what people find so deeply discouraging.

The relationship of humans to God is polyvalent. It would be easier to live with an unequivocal God-image like the following: God is a loving father, whose intentions I put into practice. But this does not correspond with the reality of our experience. God and his works appear to be ambivalent, and this ambivalence burdens us.

One of the tragic consequences is the atomic bomb. To acknowledge this is no trivial matter. Human intellect has discovered how to split atoms – the building blocks of the world. Humans are capable of destroying life on earth. Humanity thus now has power over world-forming forces. Thus, the image of our God-likeness emerges.

When Robert Oppenheimer[5] watched the first test of an atomic bomb, the words in the *Bhagavadgita* that refer to the Godhead came

2 Genesis 22
3 Jonah 1, 1
4 Mark 14, 36
5 Robert Oppenheimer (1904–1697), American physicist. The first atomic bomb was produced in Los Alamos in 1943 under his direction, after he overcame great moral doubts about it. Nevertheless, he was later accused of political unreliability and in 1954 was dismissed as Director of the Institute for Advanced Studies in Princeton.

to mind: "Brighter than a thousand suns."[6] We cannot know what might occur next. Developments march inevitably onward. The forces that hold the world together are falling into the hands of humans. Primordial forces are now in our hands, in our frail human hands. In the hands of humans, such forces pose a terrible danger. Unthinkable, what might happen! Humankind must learn how to deal with it. God is an incredibly explosive force that we must learn to deal with. Our entire human rationality, insight, critical reasoning and love will be required.

It would be a mistake, however, to believe that one cannot pray to such a God. The Old Testament repeatedly tells us how to pray to a God who is also wrathful. We can learn from Judaism how to pray to an ambivalent God.

The terms "good" and "evil" mirror human limitations. We are incapable of thinking other than in antinomies, in statements that contradict one another – otherwise nothing can be defined. We cannot express it other than to say that there are light and dark sides of God.[7] That is human thought and human language.

Basically we are talking about a *numinosum*, about something intangible, which *appears* to us in this way or that – we simply cannot express it any other way. The subject of religious experience itself, God or the Divine per se, is and remains a *mysterium*, an *ineffabile*,[8] about which I cannot say anything. It remains a mystery.

---

6 Cf. *Bhagavadgita*, chap. 11, verse 12. Shortly before this conversation, Robert Jungk's well-regarded book *Brighter than a Thousand Suns* had just been published (Bern, 1956). The book is based on conversations with nuclear physicists examining the development of the atomic bomb. Jung was also working at that time on his essay "The Undiscovered Self (Present and Future)."

7 C.G. Jung often quoted in this regard: Isaiah 45, 6–7: "I am the Lord, and there is none else. I form the light and create darkness, I make peace, and create evil: I, the Lord, do all these things."

8 *Ineffabile*: in Latin, the unsayable and incomprehensible.

Doing What One Is Capable Of

December 5, 1958

We only can do that of which we are capable. Our achievements will be measured by our karma – by whether or not it has been sufficiently answered. Everyone has the possibility of achieving something particular. A shepherd who dedicates his life to caring for his sheep deserves credit, as does a pastor who carries out his duties with commitment and devotion. We must not make the mistake of thinking there is a specific panacea, one remedy for all. It is not about something defined for all. It is about doing one's best in *the* position one is in, with *those* means one has. And not trying something exceeding one's means. Someone who does something small to the best of their ability also helps humanity to progress. It is not about this or that, but rather whether my existence here in this three-dimensional system has answered the individual call. Whether I have engaged myself with whatever was meant for me, in order to fulfill my life's purpose and complete the task that was assigned to me. And not just thinking or talking about it, without then actually doing it.

Life's meaning is fulfilled according to the full unfolding of one's disposition, when one becomes what one already was in one's basic structure – in the way the chicken hatches from the egg, the oak tree grows from the acorn, or the tiger cub becomes the tiger. Then one has the feeling: now *it* has come about, *that* has been achieved, for which this life was actually meant. Whatever it happens to be. Probably this internally prescribed task or demand is something inexorable. It must be fate.

I am not convinced that the creator intended to create this world as an ideal, but rather that a world *becomes*. This, in my opinion, is the purpose. But not with the idea that then everyone will be wise or happy. Some are destined to continue, some to die, some to ascend, some to decline. These are the conditions of existence. So it is, and so it always shall be. What humanity will be like when it eventually perishes, we do not know. It might be just as it is now. Hypothetically one could claim we are at the highest point of human understanding. But we will always think that. The early Christians believed this. Nevertheless, it continues, further and further. As long as humanity does not wipe itself out with a nuclear war, or by blowing up the planet, we continue.

Last Note, Three Weeks Before Jung's Death

May 16, 1961

Nothing can be created without indebtedness, and only one who bears the cost can create.

The person without indebtedness who renounces the world and refuses to pay life's dues does not achieve individuation, because the dark God would find no place in him.

Many paths lead to the central experience. Those who have descended to their own depths also recognize the value and legitimacy of other paths leading to the center. Knowledge of the manifold paths gives life its fullness and meaning.

After a brief illness, C.G. Jung died at his home in Küsnacht on June 6, 1961.

Historical Commentary by Elena Fischli

Introduction

Sixty loosely connected recollections, reflections and anecdotes from C.G. Jung's world of experiences and thoughts, based on notes made by his closest collaborator from her conversations with Jung in his final years. They are the thoughts of a man looking back over his life, attempting not only to understand himself, but also to prepare for the approaching unknown, hinted at through intuitions and inner images. Presented here in written form, the gathered material is arranged in short chapters – from several pages to only one paragraph – placed in context and complemented with Aniela Jaffé's helpful annotations.

This fascinating kaleidoscope was drawn from records made by Aniela Jaffé between 1956 and 1961. What was the reason for and background to these conversations and Jaffé's resulting notes? What kind of relationship existed between her and C.G. Jung and how did they actually work together? Who was this woman whom Jung accepted as his biographer? Why were these additional insights and illuminations not published before Jaffé's death, as she planned? How did others handle Jaffé's notes, the base material for a major biographical work? The following historical appraisal not only provides insight into Jung's ideas, work, personality and life, but also documents the convoluted history behind the germination process of the biographical work – described by Jaffé as both enriching and painful.

The questions above cannot be answered without examining Jung's ambivalent and slowly evolving attitude to the idea of a biography and the story behind the creation of the "memory book," as Jaffé often referred to it. *Memories, Dreams, Reflections by C.G. Jung* (*MDR*), published in 1962 with the byline "recorded and edited by Aniela Jaffé", introduced Jung's work and life to a wide readership, and offers for many readers still today a first encounter with Jungian ideas. This historical analysis not only explores the role of Aniela Jaffé – i.e., what her task of recording and editing precisely entailed – but also examines the circumstances that led to the project being undertaken in the first place. C.G. Jung's collaborative role with *MDR* and with a previous failed project are investigated, along with the nature of the cooperation and relationship between C.G. Jung and Aniela Jaffé.

The basis for this research has been the considerable archival material that is now available: letters and papers of C.G. Jung and numerous documents preserved by Aniela Jaffé; detailed correspondence and notes about the work and progress on the book from Jaffé, Jung, and publisher Kurt Wolff and his colleagues; further notes, documents and manuscript drafts from the developmental phase; other valuable personal information from Jaffé's papers as well as written contributions by C.G. Jung.[1] This rich and extensive source material facilitated the research into the multifaceted and manifold aspects of a literary project that was not devoid of considerable conflict, but ultimately became a great success.

The present analysis can be understood as a first step towards a historical revisioning based on primary sources. With a focus on the presentation and evaluation of original documents and accounts of the

1 Aniela Jaffé's papers are stored in the Archive Aniela Jaffé Daimon Verlag (hereinafter AAJD); the correspondence between publisher Kurt Wolff, his wife Helene Wolff, Aniela Jaffé and C.G. Jung is inter alia in the Helen and Kurt Wolff Papers, Beinecke Rare Books and Manuscript Library, Yale University, New Haven (hereinafter YBL); further letters of C.G. Jung and Aniela Jaffé are in the C.G. Jung-Arbeitsarchiv, Eidgenössische Technische Hochschule Zürich (hereinafter ETH); documents and notes of Aniela Jaffé and related correspondence between the Bollingen Foundation, Princeton University Press and Aniela Jaffé are in the Library of Congress, Washington (hereinafter LoC); Lucy Heyer-Grote's correspondence and manuscript drafts are in the *Universitätsbibliothek Basel*, NL 335 (hereinafter UBB).

protagonists, a light is shone on the complex story of how *MDR* and *Reflections* came into being, as well as the intense dynamic that played out among the various parties involved.[2] In addition, this literary-historical investigation presents and contextualizes the fascinating life story of a woman whose significance has often been underestimated or even disregarded: author and analyst Aniela Jaffé.

2 In her book Jung – A Biography, Deirdre Bair, disregarding basic academic research criteria, wrote much on this subject that was false or inaccurate. The present historical commentary sets the record straight on several points. Cf. also the criticisms of Bair's work by Shamdasani, S., *Jung Stripped Bare by his Biographers, even*, 2005, p. 87ff. and by Lammers, A., "Correctio Fatuorum re. the Jung-White Letters" in *Journal of Analytical Psychology*, no. 49, 2004.

"This monstrous Gordian knot of fatality, denseness, and aspirations."

"The idiotic business of a biography," as Jung referred to it in the early fifties, was directly connected with the publication of his Collected Works. The first concrete steps toward such a collection were taken after the end of the Second World War, thanks to the economic backing of American banker Paul Mellon, majority owner of the Gulf Oil Company and one of the richest men in the United States. His first wife Mary was so enthusiastic about C.G. Jung's work that a few years before her death in 1946, she founded the Bollingen Foundation, with the aim of publishing the primary writings of the revered psychiatrist. Because of the war, the project was initially suspended. With the copyright for the UK already in the hands of the British publishing house Routledge & Kegan Paul and the German rights belonging to Rascher Verlag in Zürich, the Bollingen Foundation acquired the American copyright in 1947. The foundation then funded the lion's share of the editorial work for the publication of the Collected Works on both sides of the Atlantic for several decades.[1] As a result, the first volumes

1 Paul Mellon (1907–1999), also a major shareholder in British Petroleum and owner of large aluminum and steel companies and the Mellon Bank, was a lifelong generous philanthropist. He and his first wife Mary (1904–1946) became personally acquainted with C.G. Jung in Zürich in 1938. Shortly before his retirement, William McGuire, whose work had been financed by Mellon for many decades, wrote a comprehensive history of and tribute to the Bollingen Foundation: *Bollingen – An Adventure in Collecting the Past*, 1982. On Paul Mellon, see also Mellon, Paul/Baskett, John, *Reflections in a Silver Spoon – A Memoir*, 1992; Schoenl, William, *C.G. Jung: His Friendship with Mary Mellon and J.B. Priestley*, 1998; Hoffmann, William S., *Paul Mellon – Portrait of an Oil Baron*, 1974.

of the comprehensive collection of C.G. Jung's work initially appeared in English translation.[2]

From 1938 on, Paul and Mary Mellon also provided financial support to Olga Fröbe-Kapteyn – founder and organizer of the Eranos conferences in Ascona – for the publication of the Eranos yearbooks and other personal research projects. Fröbe-Kapteyn was to play a mediating role in an initial biography project. It was at a conference in Ascona at the end of the forties that the wish for a biography of C.G. Jung was first expressed by representatives of the Bollingen Foundation's *Bollingen Series*, in particular by its director, John Barrett.[3] They believed that such a book would increase awareness of Jung and generate more interest in his work. Naturally the preferred option was an autobiography written by C.G. Jung, a possibility Barrett broached with Cary Baynes, a long-time confidante of Jung. However, in two early conversations in 1950 and 1952, in which Baynes' daughter Ximena de Angulo tested the waters, Jung rejected the idea.[4]

According to a message from Jung to Jaffé, the initial proposal for a biography stemmed from Cary Baynes as far back as the mid-twenties. "This idiotic business of a biography comes from Cary Baynes' time (seminar 1926)[sic]. First she wanted to do it, then together with Mrs H[eyer-Grote]."[5] Jung did nevertheless agree to think it over should

2 In 1953, the first volumes to be published, in accordance with the wishes of C.G. Jung, were *Psychology and Alchemy*, Collected Works (CW) Vol. 12, and *Two Essays on Analytical Psychology*, CW Vol. 7; in 1976, the final volume in the series, *The Symbolic Life*, CW Vol. 18, was published. The German *Gesammelte Werke* (GW) followed between 1958 and 1981.

3 The editorial committee consisted of Sir Herbert Read, C.G. Jung and John Barrett; under the editorial committee and responsible for the practical implementation was the "executive sub-committee," composed of Michael Fordham, Gerhard Adler and Sir Herbert Read; William McGuire acted as the "Bollingen house editor" in the U.S.

4 Ximena de Angulo to Cary Baynes, 5.9.1952, cited in Shamdasani, S., 2005, p. 13f. Cary Baynes, 1883–1977, traveled to Zürich and met C.G. Jung in 1921 at the recommendation of New York analyst Kristine Mann. In 1924 and 1925, she transcribed parts of Jung's edited text from *The Red Book*, as well as recording Jung's 1925 seminar which was held in English – both of which contained much autobiographical content (cf. Shamdasani, S., ed., 2009, pp. 212ff.). From 1927 to 1931, she was married to English psychiatrist H. Godwin Baynes, who was also a close colleague of Jung. For over two decades, she worked on the English translation of Richard Wilhelm's *I Ching*, published by the Bollingen Foundation in 1950. Her daughter from her first marriage, Ximena de Angulo, worked briefly for the Bollingen Foundation from its first editorial office in her mother's house, before later moving to Switzerland. For a few years Cary Baynes was also a member of the Foundation's editorial committee. Mary Mellon had suggested that Cary Baynes might act as the translator of Jung's work, a request that Baynes firmly turned down in 1946 due to "a whole *host* of fears and misgivings" (McGuire, 1982, p. 109).

5 C.G. Jung to Aniela Jaffé, 20.1.1954, ETH. (Name added in brackets, ed.). The seminar in question

the Bollingen Foundation deem a biography necessary. His categorical opinion on writing about his own life came already in 1948: "An autobiography is the one thing I will never write."[6] He had already read enough books of this sort that were never completely accurate, and basically never could come close to the truth – the essential was missing throughout.

A similar sentiment was voiced four years later (1952) in response to a colleague's letter suggesting an autobiography: Jung wrote that he disliked biographies because they were seldom true, and only of interest if experiences from life were described that one could understand. There was not only a lack of understanding of his contributions to psychology, felt Jung, but also little interest in his discoveries about the unconscious.

From a further statement, one could infer that he actually also pondered a possible narrative form of a biography, without convincing results: he said he felt no desire to write an autobiography "because quite apart from the lack of motive I wouldn't know *how to set about it*." It also appeared unlikely that someone else could master the task: "Much less can I see how anybody else could disentangle this monstrous Gordian knot of fatality, denseness, and aspirations and whatnot! Anybody who would try such an adventure ought to analyse me far beyond my own head if he wants to make a real job of it."[7]

Despite this resolute refusal, C.G. Jung's resistance to a biography would soon begin to soften somewhat. Several factors contributed to this change of heart. After his seventy-fifth birthday and the related interviews and articles in the press, but also upon increasing insistence from among his circle of friends, it became clear to him that, despite his ongoing ambivalence, a biography about him would inevitably be published sooner or later. Before such an ever more likely project might be undertaken by an incompetent or even completely unauthorized party, he wanted to have at least some measure of control over it.

did not take place in 1926 as indicated by Jung here, but in 1925. On Lucy Heyer-Grote see the next page.

6 C.G. Jung to Prof. Antonio Savides, 13.1.1948, in *Letters I*, p. 489. See also his letter to Jürg Fierz in *Letters I*, p. 404.

7 C.G. Jung in a letter to John Thorburn, 16.2.1952, *Letters II*, p. 38f (editor's emphasis).

Another factor might have been Jung's awareness that Ernest Jones was working on a major biography of Freud. In early 1952, Jones had asked Jung's permission to consult his letters from Freud. This request saw him once again confronted with the decades-old correspondence. He asked Aniela Jaffé, then responsible for the administration of the recently founded C.G. Jung Institute, to look over Freud's letters and assess whether they might be of historical value or public interest. Jaffé informed Jung that the letters from Freud contained, in addition to psychoanalytic or scientific topics, many "very personal remarks" and comments about other people, as well as organizational matters.[8] The question for Jung was how to deal with these documents, which were doubtless of significance for academic scholarship – what should he disclose, and what not?

As Emma Jung was also involved in the correspondence and had exchanged letters with Freud, the couple discussed the matter and together decided that the letters did have a certain historical value. In Jung's opinion, however, their contents were "not significant."[9] He informed Jones that he did not want the letters to be published, saying they were "not particularly important" and mostly contained information about publications or organizational matters, some were too personal, and overall, they would contribute little to Freud's biography. The request for personal recollections was also declined: "Since there is no witness but myself I prefer to refrain from unsubstantiated tales about the dead."[10]

The Bollingen Foundation editors, aware of Jones' work on Freud, were no longer willing to wait for a biography of C.G. Jung. Following Cary Baynes, Lucy Heyer-Grote now also entered the picture as a potential biographer. Like Jung, she hailed from Basel; her brother Fritz Grote, a student friend of Jung's, was medical director of the Sonnmatt Clinic near Lucerne for many years. Lucy, born in 1891, spent her childhood years in Riga where her father managed a paint factory, before moving to Germany to complete high school in Karlsruhe. She became one of the first women in Germany to enroll at a universi-

8 Aniela Jaffé to W. McGuire, *The Freud/Jung Letters*, Introduction, p. xxi
9 C.G. Jung to the Curatorium of the Jung Institute, 22.3.1952, ETH.
10 C.G. Jung, *Letters* II, p. 40f.

ty, studying classical philology and ancient history in Munich and Heidelberg. In 1917, she married Gustav Richard Heyer, a physician. The couple took part in a group established by neurologists Rudolf Laudenheimer and Leonhard Seif to study the writings of C.G. Jung, and from 1928 came into personal contact with the Swiss psychiatrist Jung. In the years 1930 to 1932, Lucy Heyer-Grote underwent analysis, primarily with Toni Wolff, but also with Jung and with Eva Moritz, chair of the C.G. Jung Society in Berlin. During the thirties, her reviews of several of C.G. Jung's works appeared in German newspapers and journals. Around the time of Jung's sixtieth birthday, the idea arose for a monograph in order to increase knowledge of Jung's psychology in the German-speaking world and contextualize Jung and his work in the Western philosophical tradition. However, the project planned by Lucy Heyer-Grote and her husband never came to fruition. A practicing psychotherapist in Munich from the mid-twenties, she also became a pioneer in psychotherapeutic body work, after training with dancer Mary Wigman, movement therapist Elsa Gindler and breath therapists Clara Schlaffhorst and Hedwig Andersen.[11]

In spring 1931, Heyer-Grote was invited by Jung to present her innovative methods to the Psychology Club in Zürich. After lecturing on gymnastics in cases of neurosis and psychosis, she subsequently worked with patients referred to her by Jung and H.G. Baynes. In 1934, she divorced her husband, and C.G. Jung too later distanced himself from Gustav R. Heyer, due to the latter's National Socialist sympathies. Lucy Heyer-Grote attended the Eranos conferences regularly until the outbreak of the war in 1939. Closely connected since her youth with the editors of the Eranos yearbooks, Daniel and Daisy Brody of Rhein Verlag, she also had a longstanding friendship with the founder of the Eranos conferences, Olga Fröbe-Kapteyn. In 1949, Fröbe-Kapteyn defended Heyer-Grote to the Bollingen Foundation, emphasizing that Heyer-Grote had always rejected National Socialism.[12]

11 The archive of Lucy Heyer-Grote (1891–1991) is housed at the *Universitätsbibliothek Basel, Handschriften Abteilung* (UBB, NL 335). Cf. also the Master's thesis by Gsell, Yael, "*Lucy Heyer-Grote Biografie. Eine emanzipierte Frau im Wandel der Zeit*", 2019; some of the assertions made therein are incorrect, however, for example regarding a lecture given by Lucy Heyer-Grote at the Eranos conference of 1950. Heyer-Grote was a participant in the conference but did not lecture there.

12 Olga Fröbe Kapteyn to John Barrett, 20.7.1949, LoC, Bollingen Archive.

Upon Daniel Brody's recommendation, on August 24, 1952 Heyer-Grote sent a book concept to the Bollingen Foundation with the title "*Gesichtspunkte einer Biographie C.G. Jungs*" [considerations for a biography of C.G. Jung].[13] From her introductory remarks, it was clear that the focus of the biography would be on the evolution of Jung's work and ideas, with outer events mentioned only in connection with the unfolding of his psychology and oeuvre. The aim was to illuminate the character of a man who had taken up and addressed the collective currents of the age.[14] She expressed her willingness to work with Cary Baynes on the project, a collaboration also favored by Jung, who saw the differing perspectives of the two women as complementary.[15] The text would be based on comprehensive personal interviews with C.G. Jung "on all important questions."[16] Heyer-Grote's exposé was apparently well-received by the Bollingen Foundation.

Jung was now also showing the first signs of agreement, as can be gleaned from a letter of February 1953 informing Henri Flournoy of his assent to a suggestion from America for "an attempt at biography in interview form."[17] While the letter shows more willingness than previously, it also reveals Jung's view of the project only as an "attempt" with uncertain outcome. He said he had no wish personally to "write any fiction or poetry about the bizarre experience called life." It was enough for him to have lived it.[18] He could hardly have spelled out more clearly how little interest he had in *bio-graphia* – i.e., putting a life into written form – and how skeptical his attitude toward the endeavor was, despite his acquiescence.

Heyer-Grote proposed as a title "*C.G. Jung – Werden und Wirken seiner Ideen*" [C.G. Jung – the Emergence and Workings of His Ideas], with the material grouped into nine chapters: "Background

13 Lucy Heyer-Grote, 24.8.1952, ETH.

14 Ibid. In her draft, Heyer-Grote stressed that she wanted to present C.G. Jung as a personality who had reacted in a particularly sensitive and creative way to a collective "need" of his epoch: "We believe that the most natural and fruitful access to the work is through learning about it as the manifestation of a personality who to a great extent tackled and still tackles the problems of the age."

15 Cf. C.G. Jung to Cary Baynes, 7.10.1953, cited in Shamdasani, S., 2005, p. 15.

16 Lucy Heyer-Grote to C.G. Jung, 16.9.1952, ETH.

17 C.G. Jung to Henri Flournoy – son of Théodore Flournoy – on 12.2.1953, see C.G. Jung, *Letters II*, p. 106.

18 Ibid.

and Beginnings" [*Voraussetzungen*], "Psychiatry," "Psychoanalysis," "The Path Inward," "Complex Psychology," "Light from the East," "Transfer to the West," "Questions of Time," and "Jung's Successors and his School." Jung's ideas and work were to be placed in the context of a large arc from the Presocratics to the poets and scientists of the modern era.[19]

The conceptual outline suggests that Heyer-Grote was informed, or at least aware, of Jung's views and preferences. Her proposed structure for the contents reveals not only the serious thought that went into the project, but also the planned scholarly and historical approach, with everything of a private or personal nature taking secondary importance.

Paul Mellon subsequently pledged to finance the project from his own pocket. The idea was to publish it first in German with the publisher of the Eranos yearbooks Rhein Verlag, whose director Daniel Brody was a longstanding friend of Jung.[20] While Jung had now explicitly consented to Heyer-Grote's authorship and concept, he was also assuming that Cary Baynes, given her previous overtures, would lend her support. But Baynes felt passed over with the appointment of Heyer-Grote, for which she held Daniel Brody responsible. Annoyed, she approached Jung's wife Emma, whereupon Jung promptly addressed the situation personally. He was under the impression that the biography project had been her idea, he told her, and therefore expected that she would wish to contribute. Although convinced that Lucy Heyer-Grote was the right person for the overall project, he had insisted from the start on Baynes' involvement due to the valuable alternative perspective she would bring. He advised her to begin seriously collaborating with Heyer-Grote and quickly, "before I am getting altogether too senile!"[21] Baynes, finding Heyer-Grote's concept

19 Lucy Heyer-Grote Archive, undated typescript, UBB.
20 Daniel Brody (1883–1969), together with Olga Fröbe-Kapteyn, published the yearbooks of the Eranos conferences from 1933 until his death in 1969. Jung and other speakers at the Eranos conferences had published other works with Rhein Verlag through Brody; he was also closely connected to the writer Hermann Broch, and published a ten-volume series of his work. Brody, his wife Daisy, and Lucy Heyer-Grote had a longstanding mutual friendship. The choice of Heyer-Grote as biographer could conceivably also be traced back to Daniel Brody.
21 Extract of letter from C.G. Jung to Cary Baynes, 7.10.1953, cited in Shamdasani, S., 2005, p. 15.

too philosophical, declined. Nevertheless, she was to play an ongoing role in the realization of the biography project.

"I have found no rounded answer to myself"

In January 1953, Olga Fröbe-Kapteyn informed the Bollingen Foundation that C.G. Jung was willing to conduct biographical interviews with Lucy Heyer-Grote, who subsequently (1953 through 1955) received several payments from Paul Mellon for her work.[22] It was several months into 1953, however, before Jung and Heyer-Grote really began working together in earnest. Jung's participation was most likely a practical decision as a result of external pressure. Until shortly before, he was intensively occupied with the publication and reception of three new books: *Aion*, completed in 1951 with the subtitle, "Researches into the History of Symbols" – a comprehensive study of the archetype of the Self including many symbolic amplifications of the Christ figure; "Answer to Job," the passionate essay arising out of his work on *Aion* in spring 1951, which provoked extremely strong reactions and a high volume of correspondence; and a text on synchronicity, the term Jung used to describe meaningful coincidences of certain causally unrelated events.[23] In addition, in 1953 he wrote "The Philosophical Tree," a long manuscript on the significance of tree symbolism in alchemical texts.[24] These weighty projects demonstrate Jung's continued creative and intellectual productivity, despite his advanced age and poor health. His interests at that time clearly lay more in exploring major universal themes and contemporary issues than in self-reflective retrospection and navel-gazing.

In the autumn of 1953, Lucy Heyer-Grote moved from Germany to Basel to conduct the biographical interviews. Interestingly, at the

22 Cf. Paul Mellon to Lucy Heyer-Grote, 14.4.1953; John Barrett to Lucy Heyer-Grote, 1.4.1953; John Barrett to Lucy Heyer-Grote, 25.1.1955; LoC.

23 Aion, Researches into the Phenomenology of the Self, CW 9/II; "Answer to Job" in CW 11, para. 553ff., originally Rascher Verlag, 1952; "Synchronicity: An Acausal Connecting Principle," originally in collaboration with Wolfgang Pauli in *Naturerklärung und Psyche*, Rascher, 1952, "On Synchronicity," Eranos lecture 1951, Rhein Verlag, 1952, both in CW 8, para. 816ff.

24 First published in C.G. Jung, *Von den Wurzeln des Bewusstseins*, Psychologische Abhandlungen Vol. IX, 1954; CW 13, para. 304–482.

start of their work, Jung presented her with the first volume of Ernest Jones' biography of Freud, saying it would give her an idea of the sort of hearsay that was spread about him.[25] Despite having turned down Jones' request for recollections about Freud, Jung now complained that no-one had asked for *his* side of the story. Jones' depiction of the relationship with Freud was one-sided and distorted, he claimed, writing to him reprovingly: "It would have been advisable to consult me for certain facts."[26] Jung provided Heyer-Grote with additional general biographical information.

At the same time, he was having to come to terms with another relationship that had played an essential part in his life. Although he seldom spoke of it, the unexpected death of Toni Wolff in March, 1953, affected him greatly. He tried to continue cooperating on the biography, but along with his reservations about the project itself, he felt growing self-doubt. Difficult questions were emerging: What should be disclosed to Heyer-Grote and what not? What was so significant that it must be mentioned? How might certain moves and developments be explained and put in their proper places? He was trying to find some coherent narrative for his life, as he explained to Jaffé in a letter (cited further below). But the more he tried to find such a form, the further he got from it. Again he voiced his opinion that biographies did not really present the truth – they only pretended to do so.

In March 1954, Heyer-Grote wrote enthusiastically to Paul Mellon: "Professor Jung has shown great interest in the work and is most willing to give me all the information I need." Jung's perception of the situation, however, was quite different. Barely a week later, he told Cary Baynes that he could no longer carry on with "this funny kind of playing at a biography."[27] An earlier letter to Baynes evoked the same idea in even more vivid imagery: "I still don't see exactly how she is planning to catch the bird."[28] In casting himself as a bird flitting

25 Ernest Jones, *The Life and Work of Sigmund Freud. 1856–1900: The Formative Years and the Great Discoveries*, 1953. Jung referred to chapter 13, "The Fliess Period," and declared Jones' description of Freud's fainting attack in his presence to be incorrect.

26 Cf. C.G. Jung, *Letters II*, p. 133 and p. 144.

27 First quotation Lucy Heyer-Grote to Paul Mellon, 28.3.1954, LoC; second quotation C.G. Jung to Cary Baynes, 4.4.1954, cited in Shamdasani, S., 2005, p. 18.

28 C.G. Jung to Cary Baynes, 28.3.1954, cit. ibid.

away from his biographer, Jung apparently saw it as her task to catch an elusive protagonist, and regarded it as a challenge she was almost certain to fail.

In a more serious and self-critical tone, he disclosed to Aniela Jaffé a few days later the deeper reason for his unease:

"I observe myself in the stillness of Bollingen and with all my experience of nearly eight decades must admit that I have found no rounded answer to myself. I am just as much in doubt about myself as before, the more so the more I try to say something definite. It is as though familiarity with oneself alienated one from oneself still further."[29]

This confession is revealing in several respects. Open, unresolved questions relating to his life and work were clearly playing on Jung's mind during this phase. The "rounded answer" he sought would require a cogent, expository frame: a cohesive model revealing a kind of "circle of life." Presumably he was trying to hew a coherent and convincing life picture from a very heterogeneous set of experiences and body of work. To accomplish this, it would be necessary to make connections, to link events and present them as developmental stages, and finally to combine it all into one whole. Or, a basic underlying structure would need to be found in order to arrive at something like a "rounded answer." Despite intensive engagement and soul-searching, the endeavor was unsuccessful. Attempts to state anything about his character or life with any measure of certainty brought him no closer to himself, leading rather to a sense of alienation and estrangement. Unequivocal formulations were seen as too one-sided and simplistic[30] – the questions about his own history and person were greater than any answers that could be formulated. All of his own pronouncements about himself struck him as brittle and inaccurate.

Jung's doubts likely did not diminish when his wife was diagnosed with cancer in the late summer of 1954, leading to an operation and subsequent radiotherapy. Emma and C.G. Jung were clearly very wor-

29 C.G. Jung to Aniela Jaffé, 6.4.1954, *Letters II*, p. 163.

30 Cf. in this regard C.G. Jung's letter of 17.6.1952 to Zwi Werblowsky, *Letters II*, p. 70: "The language I speak must be ambiguous, must have two meanings, in order to do justice to the dual nature of our psychic nature. I strive quite consciously and deliberately for ambiguity of expression, because it is superior to unequivocalness and reflects the nature of life. My whole temperament inclines me to be very unequivocal indeed. That is not difficult, but it would be at the cost of truth."

ried and initially kept these events to themselves, not even telling their own children. Meanwhile, surprising news from London in March brought further grounds for reflection: Anna Freud had come across the lost letters from Jung to her father. The Freud Archive in New York, wishing to make copies, contacted C.A. Meier, president of the Jung Institute Zürich, to discuss the possibility of publishing the correspondence. Before making any decision, Jung wanted to review the letters, so in November 1954 Meier traveled to New York to obtain copies. The discovery of the letters meant that Jung was again confronted with this significant phase of his life that had also included conflict. His ultimate decision was once again dismissive: in January 1955, Meier was to inform Kurt Eissler, secretary of the Freud Archive, that Jung had now decided not to reread his letters to Freud and would on no account agree to their publication in his lifetime.[31]

In the meantime, Jung expressed his growing skepticism about the biography project to several parties, a skepticism that had less to do with the work of Heyer-Grote and more with his conventional bourgeois life, as he saw it. Here we see another of Jung's reasons for reluctance: he doubted there was sufficiently widespread interest in him and his work, believing that a wholly undramatic, unspectacular life, as he now claimed to have led, would be of no particular interest to anyone. He sarcastically pointed to the much greater public appeal of the life of Albert Schweitzer, who had, in Jung's opinion, run away from the challenges in Europe to become a lauded 'savior' for poor Africans.[32] At this stage, Jung was evidently not yet clearly thinking of focusing on his inner processes – which were at times certainly dramatic – and his innovative analytic work; rather, he was concerned about a lack of interest or even hostile reactions to him and his work. In the postwar years, public criticism and controversy about his attitude toward National Socialism had not abated, leaving him feeling embittered and at times resigned. Furthermore, he had been painfully affected by the harsh critical reactions to *Answer to Job* after 1952. He often referred to himself in the aftermath as a victim of "the weirdest misunderstand-

31 See *The Freud/Jung Letters*, 1974, introduction by W. McGuire, p. xxii ff.
32 C.G. Jung, *Letters II*, p. 40, p. 140f.

ings" and a "battering" against which he had to "armor" himself.[33] A similar sentiment was expressed in his rhetorical question to Aniela Jaffé in the letter cited earlier: "What is it in me that the world finds so offensive?"[34]

In November 1954, Jung asked to see Lucy Heyer-Grote's work-in-progress for the first time.[35] She therefore sent him a draft of her foreword and a few chapters in early December.[36] Believing that the project would continue for quite some time, she had a few weeks earlier requested a continuation of the "grant" from the USA. However, she was finding the biography work increasingly challenging: Jung's ambivalence had become all too clear and her own inner "resistance against the work as conceived of by Bollingen and Brody" conflicted with her sense of how to respond to the task.[37] Emma Jung (who was also involved in some of the biographical conversations) had promised to make her own correspondence with Freud available to Heyer-Grote, but then neglected to do so, without explanation.[38] In the preceding months, reservations about the choice of biographer had been ventured from some quarters in Zürich: according to Lucy Heyer-Grote's detractors, it would damage Jung's reputation if a former German Nazi supporter were to write about him. Jung strongly refuted the

33 C.G. Jung, *Letters II*, p. 79; cf. also C.G. Jung to Erich Neumann, 5.1.1952, p. 32.

34 C.G. Jung, *Letters II*, p. 162f.

35 According to Jung, by the beginning of 1954 about seven biographical conversations had taken place with Heyer-Grote, but he doubted whether anything would come of them; C.G. Jung to Aniela Jaffé, 20.1.1954, ETH. For her part, Lucy Heyer-Grote wrote to Paul Mellon that she was visiting Jung almost every week to talk about the biography; Lucy Heyer-Grote to Paul Mellon, 28.3.1954, LoC. From another letter to Jaffé four months later, it would seem that Jung was still involved with the biography project right up until the summer and that on July 22, 1954 he had visited his birthplace with Heyer-Grote: "Yesterday I was at the house where I was born in Kesswyl in Canton Thurgau – Cassiovilla is the Roman name." It seems that he was also revisiting early dreams, writing in the same letter to Jaffé of his "third dream before the First World War" about a "tree, full of grapes, meant for humanity"; C.G. Jung to Aniela Jaffé, 23.7.1954, ETH. On the dream cf. Jaffé, A. (ed.), 1962, p. 176.

36 Lucy Heyer-Grote's manuscripts in her archive, UBB.

37 Lucy Heyer-Grote to Gustav R. Heyer, 29.3.1955, UBB. This comment suggests that both the Bollingen Foundation and the publisher Daniel Brody had apparently issued instructions regarding the content and form of Lucy Heyer-Grote's work on Jung. Unfortunately, further information about the differing goals of the author, the publishing house and the sponsors could not be found. From the available manuscripts by Heyer-Grote, it can be assumed that the publisher and the Bollingen Foundation wanted a book aimed at a wide readership, which perhaps contradicted the academic intentions of the author.

38 Ibid.

allegations.[39] Nevertheless, he too made some disparaging comments to his American contacts Barrett and Baynes regarding his increasing lack of enthusiasm and doubts about Lucy Heyer-Grote's abilities – he regretted the valuable time he had to devote to the "sad lady", saying she lacked the necessary drive and had no results to show from her interviews. Such comments were for Jung initially perhaps a way of saving face and concealing his own conflict and self-doubt. Mainly, however, they introduced to the initiators and the sponsor of the project the idea that the undertaking might yet be broken off.

At the beginning of 1955, Emma Jung was hospitalized again. Her serious illness, Jung wrote, was consuming all of his spare time.[40] After completing the essay "Mandalas"[41], the following months were taken up with the final phase of a work that had taken more than ten years to write, *Mysterium Coniunctionis*. Exhausted, he insisted that it would be his final book. Much of the first half of 1955 was spent correcting the galley proofs for part 1.[42] The English editions of the *Collected Works* also entailed a considerable amount of work: planning, reading and correcting the translations, and responding to the editors' questions. Jung claimed to be quite overwhelmed at times, feeling the "burden of age."

Disappointed by the draft manuscript pages, Jung finally wrote to Heyer-Grote on February 2, 1955, terminating the project. By way of justification, he primarily cited his many other duties and obligations. He added one other crucial reason: his inability to address everything that needed to be said. He could not presume to be able to get above his own head. The termination, he assured her, was no criticism of her comprehension or abilities: he believed the undertaking itself was an impossible task.[43] For Heyer-Grote, it was both a shock and a relief,

39 In a letter to Aniela Jaffé on 20.1.1954, Jung wrote that Heyer-Grote had never been a National Socialist, her brother had studied with him in Basel, and she was Swiss by birth. ETH.

40 C.G. Jung, *Letters II*, p. 251.

41 First published in the Swiss monthly magazine *DU*, XV/4, April 1955, p. 16ff. The theme of the issue was the Eranos conferences. See also CW 9/1, para. 713ff.

42 Part 1 with the chapters "The Components of the Coniunctio," "The Paradoxa" and "The Personification of the Opposites" first appeared in summer 1955 as volume X of the series published by Rascher, *Psychologische Abhandlungen*; cf. CW 14, part 1. *Mysterium Coniunctionis* was produced in collaboration with Marie-Louise von Franz.

43 C.G. Jung to Lucy Heyer-Grote, 2.2.1955, ETH.

for which she was "deep down prepared."[44] In a letter to Daniel Brody, Jung again posited the argument that his life was too uneventful for a biography. Reading the manuscript had unfortunately confirmed the impression that his life offered none of the stuff that made a story worth reading, he said. That had been his fear from the start, and he could not imagine how a convincing, publishable portrait could be formed from a long series of banalities and unspectacular events.[45]

44 Lucy Heyer-Grote to Gustav R. Heyer, 29.3.1955, UBB; Lucy Heyer-Grote to Lida, 12.2.1957, UBB. She resumed work on the project sometime later, but then left it unfinished.
45 Undated letter from C.G. Jung to Daniel Brody, ETH.

"A creative resonance which seems like a revelation of the feminine being"

While the aforementioned events were unfolding in February 1955, Aniela Jaffé was working on a portrait of C.G. Jung for the renowned Swiss cultural magazine, *DU*.[1] Little did she know that within two years, she would be tasked with a further biographical project. Her introductory remarks in the *DU* portrait suggest that she knew Jung had broken off the work with Heyer-Grote and was aware of his fundamental reservations about the very idea of a biography. She also forestalled possible attempts by third parties to undertake a biography, describing such a venture as impossible and presumptuous: "The greatness of this life does not lie on the outside. The personal details – studies, career, professional milestones, honors, travels and encounters – are only clues, outer markers, between and behind which the fullness of human experience plays out and the great arc of psychological development extends. The discrepancy between the relative inconspicuousness of the life of a researcher and the inner abundance and density of that life is enough to discourage any biographer. Only the person himself who lives such a life, who has shaped it and been shaped by it, would be entitled to report on his experiences. Only he would know what of the most intimate to reveal or conceal, what he would possibly share with his contemporaries and with posterity."[2] Jaffé's use of the subjunctive in German – "*nur dem Menschen selber käme es zu*" ("only he would be entitled to") – indicates on the one hand her opinion that only an

1 Aniela Jaffé, "Carl Gustav Jung," in Swiss monthly magazine *DU*, XV/4, April 1955, p. 22ff.
2 Ibid. p. 22.

*auto*biography could legitimately, appropriately capture Jung's life and work, and on the other, expresses her skepticism if such a book would ever be written. It is interesting to note that she places equal value on both revelation and concealment in autobiographical writing. Jung was very taken with Jaffé's portrait, in which she included biographical information only in connection with his scientific research and findings, and characterized his work as a lifelong process combining inner experiences and external research, at the same time as concisely conveying the complexity of his work.

Aniela Jaffé was at this time working as the administrative secretary of the C.G. Jung Institute (founded in 1948), alongside her activities as a psychologist and author. Among her previous publications was a detailed study of the imagery and symbols in E.T.A. Hoffmann's *The Golden Pot*, which was published in a volume together with Jung's 1947 work, *Gestaltungen des Unbewussten.*[3] In addition, she reviewed many of Jung's publications for major German-language newspapers and scientific journals during the early fifties.[4] A friend of physicist Wolfgang Pauli, she also wrote a review of his and Jung's joint publication *The Interpretation of Nature and the Psyche.*[5] In conjunction with Jung's eightieth birthday, the C.G. Jung Institute prepared a two-volume celebratory *Festschrift* publication with contributions by

3 "Bilder und Symbole aus E.T.A. Hoffmanns Märchen ‚Der Goldne Topf'" in C.G. Jung *Gestaltungen des Unbewussten*, Psychologische Abhandlungen, Vol. VII, 1950, Zürich. Jung and Rascher Verlag presented the book as the sole work of Jung. However, Jaffé's section, which is only mentioned as a "contribution" on the inner title page, makes up about two thirds of the publication. In the Foreword of January, 1949, Jung writes of Jaffé's work: "This book by Hoffmann has long been on my list of those literary creations demanding, as it were, interpretation and deeper understanding. I am therefore particularly grateful to Aniela Jaffé for taking on the no-small amount of effort and work required to comprehensively illustrate the psychological background of *The Golden Pot* and thereby relieving me of a task that I had felt duty-bound to complete." (Op.cit., p. 2). It is strikingly clear here that, despite the appreciation, there is an asymmetry in the treatment of the authors both by Jung and the publisher, with Jaffé listed merely as a secondary contributor working to order. But Jaffé's interest in E.T.A. Hoffmann's work actually came from her own initiative, following a dream in 1942. In 1945, she penned an additional chapter on German Romanticism and its fatal effect on the recent history of National Socialism. The expanded version later appeared as a book in its own right; 4th edition, Daimon Verlag, 1990.

4 For example, reviews of *Aion, Answer to Job, Psychology and Alchemy, Von den Wurzeln des Bewusstseins.* Cf. C.G. Jung to Aniela Jaffé, 2.9.1953, ETH: "The review has turned out excellently, something that has not happened for more than eight years in the NZZ!", or a letter of 6.4.1954: "Best thanks for your excellent review! After all the rubbish that gets delivered to my house on my work, it is such a pleasure to find something understanding and friendly for once." *Letters II*, p. 162.

5 C.G. Jung/Wolfgang Pauli, *The Interpretation of Nature and the Psyche*, Zürich, 1952.

its lecturers; the first volume was dedicated to the theory and practice of analytical psychology, the second to its relevance for cultural history and the humanities.[6] Emma Jung was a member of the small editorial committee and also one of the authors, along with Aniela Jaffé. Impressed by Jaffé's intellectual abilities and sensitivity, in late 1954, Emma Jung asked her younger colleague to lend editorial support to the project when her own capacities became limited due to illness. On reading Jaffé's draft contribution, C.G. Jung again expressed – as on many previous occasions – his admiration of her gift for writing and her sense of the essential.[7] Jaffé's earlier career and her relationship with C.G. Jung will be explored in more detail later in this chapter.

By spring 1955, it was becoming ever more urgent to find someone to fill the role of Jung's private secretary, no suitable replacement having been found for Marie-Jeanne Schmid, who had retired after decades of service. Emma Jung, keen to relieve the burden on her husband and trusting Jaffé's competence and character, pushed for Jaffé to transfer from the Institute to Jung's home office in Küsnacht. Jung then asked Jaffé if she might do so and organize a handover plan for her position at the Institute. As Jaffé wrote later, she hesitated about whether to accept, but due to the amount of urgent business helped out by working in the private office in Küsnacht as a kind of emergency solution from the early summer of 1955. Until then, the relationship between her and Jung had, in her own words, taken place in a more or less protected space for many years: "The imminent confrontation with external reality was reason enough for two introverts to consider the situation thoroughly and to make the necessary preparations."[8] She would remain his personal secretary to the end of his life.

A short time before, Jung had asked her to edit a paperback edition with S. Fischer Verlag of some essays on the relationship between consciousness and the unconscious,[9] following her collaboration in 1953 with Gerhard Zacharias on a compilation of essays for *Welt der Psyche.*

6 C.G. Jung Institute, Ed., *Studien zur analytischen Psychologie C.G. Jungs, Festschrift* for the eightieth birthday of C.G. Jung, 2 Vol., Zürich, 1955.
7 C.G. Jung, *Letters II*, December 26, 1954, p. 200.
8 Aniela Jaffé, "From Jung's Last Years," in *From the Life and Work of C.G. Jung*, 1989, p. 117.
9 *C.G. Jung, Bewusstes und Unbewusstes*, edited and with a postscript by Aniela Jaffé, 1957.

Eine Auswahl zur Einführung.[10] She also had the task of transcribing the complete handwritten correspondence between Freud and Jung for the archives in Zürich and New York.

As expected, Jung's eightieth birthday in the summer of 1955 brought a barrage of interviews and visitors. In October, Emma Jung asked Aniela Jaffé, who by then had been working as Jung's private secretary for several months, to join the editorial team of the *Collected Works.* In view of her already heavy workload, Jaffé turned down the request. Nevertheless, a year later Jung brought her onto the committee for the German edition in an advisory role, together with Gerhard Adler.[11] It was later a source of considerable regret for Jaffé that she had turned down one of Emma Jung's last requests.[12] Despite her initial refusal, Jaffé subsequently gave unstinting practical and intellectual support to the preparation of the *Collected Works*, as well as being one of the main points of contact with the Bollingen Foundation.

It also fell to Jaffé, in early October 1955, to inform Kurt Eissler, secretary of the Freud Archive, that C.G. and Emma Jung would not agree to publication of the letters at that time. Torn between his desire to ignore the letters and the external pressure to act, however, Jung's sense of obligation to academic research ultimately prevailed: he now declared for the first time his willingness to re-read them. Furthermore, he was prepared to allow someone with the necessary expertise, a contemporary of him and Freud, to prepare selected letters for eventual publication as the Freud Archive wished, while stipulating that publication could only happen "in the distant future, for the generation of the grandchildren."[13] Meanwhile the second volume of Jones' Freud biography had been published and, like the first, had sold exceedingly well. During discussions about the Freud-Jung correspondence and the biography project, an idea arose to collate and potentially publish

10 Published in 1954 with Rascher in Zürich/Stuttgart.

11 In a final directive regarding the German edition of his collected works, Jung specified on 26.10.1956 that the committee include Aniela Jaffé alongside Gerhard Adler in an advisory role, and that her name was to be listed wherever she had had significant input in the editing and printing of the text. ETH.

12 Aniela Jaffé to Herbert van Erkelens and Robert Hinshaw, 22.12.1989, unpublished interview, AAJD.

13 Aniela Jaffé on behalf of C.A. Meier to Kurt Eissler, 1.10.1955, AAJD; *The Freud/Jung Letters*, Introduction, p. xxv.

a carefully curated selection of Jung's letters to various correspondents. The information such letters contained would not just be of scientific relevance, but also give biographical insights. In the face of Jung's ambivalence, the question was left open and not pursued until spring 1956.[14]

Later in the year, Jung suffered another great loss: on November 27, 1955, his wife Emma died. With her passing and the death of Toni Wolff in 1953, Jung had lost his two most significant female companions within the space of less than three years. He subsequently withdrew for several months, and Aniela Jaffé tried to manage his correspondence and relieve him of as many tasks as she could. In February 1956, she wrote to their mutual friend, author Laurens van der Post: "He carries the loneliness most courageously. Sculpting a stone with Chinese motives and a text was his help in the darkest days. But now he seems to come back from where he has been."[15] During 1956, preparations for the publication of the second volume of *Mysterium Coniunctionis* took up much of Jung's time. He had been working on the two volumes for more than ten years and at one point, tired and feeling his age, referred to it as his "last work."[16] Further manuscripts would soon follow, however. In May of that year, a "Letters Committee" was established, to which Jung appointed his daughter Marianne Niehus-Jung along with Aniela Jaffé and Gerhard Adler as the editors of a selection of his correspondence, from which the letters to Freud were expressly excluded.[17]

In the meantime, the publisher Kurt Wolff had learned from Cary Baynes that the previous biography project of his competitor, Daniel Brody of Rhein Verlag, had been abandoned.[18] Baynes still did not

14 With regard to the Freud-Jung correspondence, Anna Freud, the Freud Archive, C.G. Jung, and Aniela Jaffé as representative of the Jung Institute determined, after preparation of the transcripts in March 1956, to provide copies of the same to Anna Freud, Heinz Hartmann, Ernst Kris, Ernest Jones and Hermann Nunberg, for the purpose of evaluation and commentary with the utmost confidentiality. Cf. also op. cit. p. xxv. As Kris died in February 1957 and Jones in February 1958, this plan was never realized.

15 Aniela Jaffé to Sir Laurens van der Post, 16.2.1956, AAJD (original in English).

16 C.G. Jung, *Mysterium Coniunctionis*, Foreword, p. xiii.

17 Cf. C.G. Jung to Gerhard Adler, 24.3.1956, in C.G. Jung, *Briefe I*, p. 9f (cited in the Foreword of Aniela Jaffé, which was not included in the English-language edition).

18 Kurt Wolff, born in Germany in 1887, studied German literature for a few semesters before starting work in publishing under Ernst Rowohlt at the age of 21. Supported by an inheritance from his pre-

want to risk burning her fingers by becoming overly involved, and suspected that resurrecting the project would be difficult. She would nevertheless continue to play a background advisory role at the Bollingen Foundation throughout the project's evolution. Kurt Wolff was eager to seize this opportunity for his publishing house, and discussed the matter with Jolande Jacobi at the Eranos conference of August 1956.[19] While agreeing that such a book was urgently needed, Jacobi doubted that Jung would enter into such a sensitive project again with her. In her view, there was only one person who was close enough to Jung and had both his trust and the necessary writing abilities: she suggested Aniela Jaffé for the task and offered to try to convince both Jung and Jaffé of the idea.

It was now more clear than ever to Jung that a biography would only make sense if his scientific and academic development, i.e., the formation and evolution of his ideas, were at its core. In order for him to have confidence in a biographer, it was essential that this person have an in-depth understanding of his work. He was furthermore beginning to feel that such an endeavor would best be approached by several biographers from various angles – theological, medical, etc. – understanding himself as a phenomenon which could only be presented through a variety of disciplines.[20] In addition, the inclusion of significant dreams and their part in his development, i.e., unconscious manifestations and attitudes, would be essential. This idea had long

maturely deceased mother and money from his wife, Elisabeth Merck, he founded the Kurt Wolff Verlag in 1913 and successively acquired three other publishing houses, Verlag der Weissen Bücher, Hyperion Verlag and Der Neue Geist, all of which were closed in 1930. In 1941 he fled to the USA, where he founded Pantheon Books, Inc. with his second wife, Helene. A shrewd businessman, he had negotiated a contract with the Bollingen Foundation for the production and distribution of their publications, which provided him and his publishing house with a solid financial basis (cf. McGuire, W., 1982, p. 60ff.).

19 Jolande Jacobi, 1890–1973, associated with C.G. Jung since 1927, played a leading role in the founding of the C.G. Jung Institute and was a member of its Curatorium for twenty years. She was responsible for editing the series "Studien aus dem C.G. Jung-Institut" for many years. In 1940, Jacobi published *The Psychology of C.G. Jung* with Rascher Verlag, followed by *Psychologische Betrachtungen. Eine Auswahl aus den Schriften von C.G. Jung* in 1945, also with Rascher, and in 1952 she collaborated with C.G. Jung on the publication of *Symbols of Transformation*. In 1951, as volume 28 of the Bollingen Series, the Bollingen Foundation published an English version of her anthology of the work of Paracelsus (the German edition had come out in 1942): *Paracelsus: Selected Writings*. She gained widespread recognition in 1969 for her book *Vom Bilderreich der Seele*. Jolande Jacobi played an active role in propagating the work of C.G. Jung until her death in 1973.

20 Cf. fn. 23, p. 220

been simmering under the surface, as evidenced in a letter written in the winter of 1949 to the analyst Alwine von Keller:

"I too am in a retrospective phase and am occupying myself, for the first time in 25 years, thoroughly with myself, collecting my old dreams and putting them together. There are all sorts of strange things among them. How little one still knows of the 'unconscious'!"[21]

In a conversation with British physician E.A. Bennet in August 1956, Jung shared his dream about the murder of the Germanic hero Siegfried. He wanted to impress upon Bennet the preeminent role he felt dreams must take in a biographical work – for Jung, this dream represented an important turning point in his life, which could not really be understood without knowledge of his subsequent psychological work. He explained that the dream images had released long-restrained forces that inspired him to follow his own path.[22] The mainspring from which his work originated ought to be seen in the unconscious images, he told Bennet. When Bennet later wrote to Jung in September 1956 requesting authorization to write his biography, Jung's response shows that he had already spoken with Aniela Jaffé about a possible biographical work by her. He replied that, because he was such a complicated phenomenon, a full portrayal could not be given by one single biographer. Bennet should write about him from the medical perspective, if he really were to decide to engage himself.[23]

21 C.G. Jung to Alwine von Keller, *Letters I*, p. 516. (A. v. Keller, 1878–1965, educator and long-time colleague of social reformer Paul Geheeb at the Odenwald school, was a pupil of C.G. Jung. In her later years, she lived next door to Eranos in Moscia.) Jung is referring here to his English seminar of 1925, in which he looked more deeply into his own development by reexamining his dreams from the year 1913. The seminar gave an insight into his own reflective processing of personal dream material to inform his innovative theoretical-conceptional psychology. See in this regard the chapter "Confrontation with the Unconscious" in Jaffé, A. (ed.), 1962, p. 170ff.

22 For a more detailed explanation and interpretation of the Siegfried dream, see Jaffé, A. (ed.), 1962, p. 180f.

23 C.G. Jung on 10.10.1956 to E.A. Bennet: "As you know, I am a somewhat complicated phenomenon which hardly can be covered by one biographer only... Therefore I should like to make you a similar proposition, namely that you proceed along your line as a medical man like Philp has done on his part as a theologian. ....A biography written by specialists in their field has the best chance of being accurate, although not comprehensive in as much as the specific psychological synthesis would demand somebody equally at home in primitive psychology, mythology, history, parapsychology and science – and even in the field of artistic experience." ETH (original in English); cf. Shamdasani, S., 2005, p. 41f. H.L. Philp, an acquaintance of Bennet, was planning a book about Jung and religious beliefs, which led to an extensive correspondence; cf. CW 18, para. 1584–1624. In 1958, Philp published *Jung and the Problem of Evil*, but Jung was not in agreement with the content.

Jung evidently believed that his collaborator and private secretary Aniela Jaffé was capable of creating a synthesis of his various developmental strands from a psychological point of view. She, however, required time to think about the proposal. In the following weeks, she and Jung discussed the matter repeatedly. On the one hand, she saw it as a great challenge and enriching endeavor that would give her the opportunity for in-depth reflection with Jung on his life story. On the other, she anticipated a wide variety of reactions from others, many of whom might be envious of her privileged position and Jung's trust in her. Jung had rejected Jacobi for the task, then held a few conversations with Liliane Frey-Rohn before breaking them off and explicitly choosing Jaffé.[24] It was clear to her that she would be taking on a difficult legacy and that this attempt could likewise end in failure. She was also well aware of Jung's continuing doubts, and wanted in no way to force something that did not correspond with his sense and will. Although Jaffé began keeping notes of various conversations from September 1956, she was not yet willing to commit herself. To the insistent Kurt Wolff, she therefore responded reservedly that C.G. Jung was "in principle not against the idea, but he wants to approach the whole thing as an *experiment* about which one does not know *whether it will succeed or not, whether something will come of it or not.*"[25]

Jaffé pointed out Jung's full schedule to the American publisher and wrote that she, as the biographer, did not wish to work under pressure. Neither she nor Jung considered themselves to be under contract with Pantheon, she continued. To Wolff's request for a provisional list of contents, she gave no response. At this time, Jung was working on preparations for the German and English editions of *The Undiscovered Self (Present and Future),*[26] while Jaffé, in addition to her analytic practice, her work on the Fischer paperback, and her usual office tasks (which included the typing of revised manuscripts as well

24 Aniela Jaffé to Robert Hinshaw, 14.6.1991, AAJD.
25 Aniela Jaffé to Kurt Wolff, 9.11.1956, YBL. Italics Elena Fischli.
26 "Gegenwart und Zukunft" first appeared as a special supplement to number XXXVI:12, March 1957, of the *Schweizer Monatshefte*, then as a separate paperback volume with Rascher in autumn of 1957; see CW 10, paras. 488–588. Following a conversation with Carleton Smith, the then director of the National Arts Foundation in the United States, Jung discussed in this work the necessity of addressing the destructive, the shadow, which was essential in a time after two devastating world wars and after the development of "monstrous agents of destruction" such as atomic weapons.

as dealing with correspondence), was occupied with her own book, *Death Dreams and Ghosts.*[27] She therefore informed Wolff that they would not be able to begin before the spring of 1957. She was, she said, looking forward to the task and hoped it would come to something.[28]

By this time, Jaffé had been intensively involved with C.G. Jung's psychology for around twenty years – her personal analysis with him had begun in 1937. But who was Aniela Jaffé, what was her background, and what made Jung feel he could entrust her with this thorniest of projects?

Biography of Aniela Jaffé

Aniela Jaffé, daughter of prosperous industrialist, jurist and passionate art collector Alfons Jaffé (1861–1948) and his wife Hedwig (1878–1963), was born on February 20, 1903, in the elegant residence of her grandparents, the Fürstenbergs, on Viktoriastrasse in Berlin. The name Aniela came from her maternal grandmother, whom she also took after in character, as Jaffé later recounted. Her grandmother Aniela Fürstenberg, whose husband Carl was head of the *Berliner Handels-Gesellschaft*, was an emancipated woman who held a leading cultural and social position in Germany's capital city. She conducted an extremely liberal salon which became one of the leading cultural establishments of the aspirational metropolis that was Berlin at the start of the twentieth century.[29] An illustrious circle of industrialists, ambassadors, senior civil servants and politicians, artists and intel-

27 *Geistererscheinungen und Vorzeichen* by Aniela Jaffé first appeared with a foreword by C.G. Jung in 1958; first English edition with the title *Apparitions and Precognition* first published 1963 by University Books; revised English edition published by Daimon, Einsiedeln, 1999, with the title *Death Dreams and Ghosts*. In the book, tales of ghost sightings are treated as psychological facts arising from images from the collective unconscious, are examined from a psychological viewpoint and interpreted as synchronistic phenomena.

28 Aniela Jaffé to Kurt Wolff, 9.11.1956, YBL.

29 See Bilsky, Emily D., *Berlin Metropolis: Jews and the New Culture, 1890–1918*; Wilhelmy, Petra, *Der Berliner Salon 1780–1914*. Under Carl Fürstenberg, the *Berliner Handels-Gesellschaft* had become one of the leading financers of the industrial revolution and had close ties with the electricity company AEG, of which Carl Fürstenberg was chairman of the board. Cf. Hans Fürstenberg, *Carl Fürstenberg. Die Lebensgeschichte eines deutschen Bankiers*, 1931.

Aniela Fürstenberg, prominent figure in Berlin at the turn of the century: oil painting by Leopold Horowitz around 1890.

Frau E. Vogelsang
FIRMA (GESCHW. PAULY)
BERLIN,
LEIPZIGER-STR. 1
vis-à-vis der Reichspost.

lectuals were among the guests, including prominent female writers, musicians and women's rights activists.[30]

Young Aniela and her two sisters Gabriele and Käthe grew up in a progressive upper class milieu, and their childhood and youth were shaped by the diverse ideas and modern dynamic attitudes they experienced. Their father, an ardent music-lover, had the means to create a significant art collection.[31] He and his best friend Max J. Friedländer, director of the Berlin *Kupferstichkabinett* (Museum of Prints and Drawings), often took Aniela with them to see exhibitions, plays, concerts and films. The family belonged to a burgeoning and very committed assimilated Jewish upper class in Berlin, which saw itself first and foremost as German. Aniela's mother, who had converted to Christianity as a young woman, had all three daughters christened in the Protestant church and raised them as Christians. Nevertheless, their social environment was dominated by Jewish representatives of a cultural and economic elite.

After the *Berliner Handels-Gesellschaft* became one of the leading German banks, Aniela's grandfather was involved in developing the new villa quarter in Berlin-Grunewald, and the family subsequently spent summers in their newly built residence at Königsallee 51-55. He also played an active role in the extension of the Kurfürstendamm, where the young Jaffé family soon moved into an elegant city-center apartment directly opposite the *Gedächtniskirche* (Kaiser Wilhelm Memorial Church).[32] The three Jaffé daughters received a classical

30 Hedwig Dohm, Gabriele Reuter, Nobel Peace Prize laureate Bertha von Suttner, Richard Strauss, Max Reinhardt, Gerhart Hauptmann, Henry Van de Velde, Max Liebermann, literature and theater critic Alfred Kerr, publisher and art dealer Paul Cassirer, scientists such as Robert Koch, leading Berlin physicians including Otto Heubner and Adalbert Czerny, and international ambassadors and prominent politicians such as Walther Rathenau were among the regular guests of the Thursday soirées. Aniela Fürstenberg was also a friend of Auguste Rodin, whom she visited in Paris several times.

31 Alfons Jaffé was managing director of Lenz & Co. GmbH, a railroad construction company with activities in Germany as well as in North America and the German colonies in Africa. When he fled from Germany, Alfons Jaffé donated, in hopes of securing their safety, the majority of his art collection to the Leiden Municipal Museum in the Netherlands; the artworks were seized by the Nazis in 1941. Cf. H.C. Löhr, *Das Braune Haus der Kunst. Hitler und der Sonderauftrag Linz – Visionen, Verbrechen, Verluste*, 2005 and G. Aalders, *Nazi Looting. The Plunder of Dutch Jewry During the Second World War*, 2004.

32 These and the previous biographical details are based on conversations with Aniela Jaffé and Frank Herrmann, and on an unpublished manuscript of the diary of Gabriele Jaffé, annotated in 2013 by

Aniela Jaffé around 1906.

education at the nearby private girls' high school *Wellmann von Elpons* in Berlin-Charlottenburg.

At school, Aniela and Gabriele found a role model and close confidante in their young teacher Agnes von Zahn-Harnack.[33] The educator and writer was the first woman in Germany to enroll as a student in Humboldt University's faculty of arts, following a new regulation for girls' education issued by the Prussian ministry of culture. Prior to that, women had only been allowed to attend lectures as guest auditors at the discretion of the respective professor. Von Zahn-Harnack played an instrumental role in the establishment of educational institutions for girls leading to the *Abitur* (graduation certificate permitting university entrance), a step which met with resistance even in the forward-thinking Berlin of the early 20th century. She not only actively supported Aniela Jaffé's university ambitions, but also awakened her awareness of social issues.

It was the First World War, many men were away in the military, the majority of women had to work and do their best to feed their families with scarce provisions. As a young high-school student, Aniela Jaffé organized outings to the theater and the zoo for working-class children and provided them access to books. To raise money for buying her charges Christmas presents, she offered tutoring in Latin and mathematics to children from wealthier homes – her father deliberately did not contribute to the financing of the operation, in order to let his daughter take responsibility for her undertaking.[34]

Thomas Föhl, Klassik Stiftung Weimar; see also Hans Fürstenberg, *Carl Fürstenberg: Die Lebensgeschichte eines deutschen Bankiers*, 1931.

33 Agnes von Zahn-Harnack, 1884–1950, great-granddaughter of the chemist Justus von Liebig, earned a doctorate in German, English and philosophy and contributed to the founding of the Deutscher Akademikerinnenbund (German Academic Women's Association) for the promotion of women's university education and professorships for women. In Prussia, women were permitted to study at university only from 1908, seven years after they first won the right to sit the *Abitur*. Von Zahn-Harnack represented the middle-class, liberal-protestant wing of the first wave of the German women's movement. Cf. von Zahn-Harnack, Agnes, *Die Frauenbewegung: Geschichte, Probleme, Ziele*, 1928. She was friends with the theologian Dietrich Bonhoeffer and like him, was part of the internal Christian resistance against Hitler and his regime during the Third Reich; before and during the Second World War she gave private tuition to children from Jewish families who were officially prohibited from attending school. Her brother, president of the Prussian provincial government Ernst von Harnack, was executed by the Nazis in 1942.

34 Aniela Jaffé in conversation with Werner Wieck and Robert Hinshaw, 8.5.1991, AAJD.

While it was von Zahn-Harnack's support that encouraged Aniela Jaffé to pursue a university education, her choice of subject and future career were again influenced by her grandmother. Aniela Fürstenberg, together with leading pediatricians Otto Heubner and Adalbert Czerny, had founded and financed the mother and baby home in Berlin-Westend.[35] During her medical studies at the Friedrich Wilhelm University Berlin, Aniela Jaffé interned under Professor Czerny at the Berlin Charité hospital, where she was assigned to look after babies with feeding problems. She carried the babies around with her and played with them until they relaxed and finally began to drink normally. In her old age, she commented on this early love of babies as an instinct or archetypal impulse, adding: "Maybe *it* inside me already knew that I would not have children and therefore had me live out my maternal nature in that way."[36]

Aniela Jaffé fell in love at a young age with Jean Dreyfus, the son of an art historian from an old Basel banking family. This relationship enabled her to escape National Socialism by emigrating to Switzerland a few years later.[37] For the first twenty years of her life, Jaffé enjoyed a protected and secure existence within her circle of family and friends as part of an influential, liberal upper class which actively contributed to the welfare of society. She was thus shielded from the growing anti-Semitism in the country. This security came to a shocking end in 1922

35 Today the Clinic for Child and Youth Psychology Berlin-Charlottenburg. Aniela Fürstenberg, like her father, the well-known Warsaw doctor and philanthropist Dr. Ludwig Natanson, was committed to charitable and social causes throughout her life. Under Prof. Otto Heubner, 1843–1926, who held one of the first professorial chairs in Germany for children's medicine and was head of the children's clinic at the Charité Hospital, Berlin became a leading center for pediatrics. Heubner's work led to a massive reduction in infant mortality. His successor Prof. Adalbert Czerny, 1863–1941, ran the children's clinic from 1913 to 1932 and contributed to the foremost reputation of Berlin pediatrics in the early part of the twentieth century; he also founded the international school of pediatrics at the Berlin Charité. A medic with a great interest in painting and music, Czerny's research focus was on nutritional physiology and metabolism pathology in infants, in particular the psychosomatic aspects of early childhood eating disorders. Aniela Jaffé's interest in psychological aspects of non-functional disorders began with her activities under Professor Czerny.

36 Information about medical studies from the family archives of Herrmann/Jaffé in Pretzfeld; correspondence from Thomas Föhl, Klassik Stiftung Weimar, interview by W. Weick and R. Hinshaw with Aniela Jaffé, 8.5.1991, AAJD (audio file). Following a miscarriage in 1932, Jaffé discovered she would not be able to have children.

37 Jean Albert Dreyfus, 1904–1985, son of the art historian, publicist and translator Albert Emil Dreyfus, long-standing friend of the sculptor Aristide Maillol. His grandfather Isaac Dreyfus-Jeidels of the Basel bank Dreyfus & Söhne had opened a bank in Berlin in 1891. Though born in Paris, Jean Dreyfus was a Swiss citizen.

with the murder of Walter Rathenau, a close friend and colleague of her grandfather Carl Fürstenberg.[38] A quote of Rathenau's from 1917 describes this kind of fateful moment, which for Jaffé occurred when she heard of his violent death: "In the years of his youth there is a painful moment for every German Jew that he remembers his whole life: when he is struck for the first time by the realization that he has entered the world as a second-class citizen and that no ability or merit can liberate him from this situation."[39]

The famous/infamous surname of her great love – Dreyfus – revealed his Jewish origins instantly.[40] Jean studied national economics and electrical engineering at the Swiss federal technical university (ETH) in Zürich. The childhood sweethearts, teased for years by family and friends about their unmarried state, finally tied the knot in 1929 in Paris, where Jean's parents lived. Aniela's young husband first worked in a Paris branch of the AEG (the company led by Walther Rathenau), before later finding a position as an electrical engineer in Berlin, thanks to the close relationship between Rathenau and Carl Fürstenberg.

Aniela Dreyfus-Jaffé had in the meantime realized that her interests lay more in psychological development and processes than in organic disorders, and turned her attention to the work of a pioneer in child psychology: William Stern. The Hamburg professor was known for his differential psychology and his philosophical-psychological approach of critical personalism.[41] His publication *Psychology of Early*

38 The industrialist, writer and liberal politician Walther Rathenau, born in Berlin in 1867, was the victim of a politically motivated assassination in Berlin-Grunewald in 1922. He had held leading positions at the AEG and the *Berliner Handels-Gesellschaft*, and in 1919 co-founded the German Democratic Party, which was also supported by the Jaffé family. Shortly after his appointment as foreign minister, he was killed by a radical right-wing populist group, which led to him later being described as the first victim of the Third Reich.

39 Walther Rathenau, "Staat und Judentum. Eine Polemik," in *Zur Kritik der Zeit. Mahnung und Warnung*. Berlin, 1918, p. 188f. See also the essay by Hans Fürstenberg about his personal memories and the economic and literary achievements of the murdered industrialist and politician, "Erinnerungen an Walther Rathenau," in: Harry Graf Kessler, *Walther Rathenau. Sein Leben und Werk*, 1962. Emil Rathenau, Walther's father, was founder of the AEG, and deputized for Carl Fürstenberg as chair of the AEG board.

40 The family of Jean Dreyfus was, however, not related to the French officer Alfred Dreyfus.

41 William Stern, 1871–1938. In *Über Psychologie der individuellen Differenzen* (1900) and *Die differentielle Psychologie in ihren methodischen Grundlagen* (1911), he distanced himself from the investigation of general principles of mental functioning and was one of the first in the field to posit that psychology in the future would be mainly concerned with scientifically exploring

With her husband, Aniela Dreyfus-Jaffé discovers the Swiss mountains, skiing and even the "Schwyzerörgeli"; photo © Jean Dreyfus/Aniela Jaffé.

Childhood made him a significant figure in the field, with his renown extending far beyond national borders. This textbook for developmental psychology became a kind of groundbreaking "basic handbook of the child."[42] Stern had scientific and professional links with Binet and Janet, and also with the US center for child research established by Stanley Hall at Clark University in Worcester, Massachusetts. This connection led Stern into personal contact with C.G. Jung, who was impressed with Stern's research into the psychology of testimony in relation to his own association experiments.

In 1909, William Stern, Sigmund Freud and C.G. Jung were invited, through Stanley Hall, to the United States to receive honorary doctorates from Clark University. On the voyage to New York, Stern and Jung established a good rapport – which Freud did not greatly appreciate, given the reservations Stern had voiced about certain theories of psychoanalysis with regard to child development.[43] A few decades later, this contact would have a decisive influence on the course of Aniela Jaffé's professional life.

In 1919, when she was just sixteen, Jaffé heard that Stern was involved in the founding of the University of Hamburg and was planning to appoint the philosopher Ernst Cassirer, a family friend of the Jaffés, as a professor.[44] Under Stern's leadership, the University of Hamburg's Institute of Psychology soon became one of the most important research institutes of the Weimar Republic. Together with Ernst Cassirer, Stern also led the Hamburg Institute of Philosophy.[45]

individual dissimilitudes. In his theory of personalism with a focus on the dynamic interrelations between subject and environment, "person" was understood as a unique and intrinsically valuable *unitas multiplex*, a diverse unit. Cf. William Stern, *Person und Sache. System der philosophischen Weltanschauung*. Vol. 1. Ableitung und Grundlehre, Vol. 2: Die menschliche Persönlichkeit, Vol. 3: Die Wertphilosophie, 1906, 1918, 1924.

42 Günther Stern-Anders, Foreword to 7th edition, 1952, p. IX. The book, based on the meticulous diaries of Clara and William Stern observing their own children's development, was first published in 1914 and by 1928 was in its fifth edition; it first appeared in English in 1924.

43 C.G. Jung in conversation with Kurt Eissler, 29.8.1953, Manuscript Division of the Library of Congress, Washington (audio recording, unpublished transcript); cf. also Rebecca Heinemann, *Das Kind als Person. William Stern als Wegbereiter der Kinder- und Jugendforschung 1900 – 1933,* 2016, p. 56, p. 108–113 and Angela Graf-Nold, "Stern versus Freud. Die Kontroverse um die Kinder–Psychoanalyse" in Werner Deutsch, ed., *Über die verborgene Aktualität von William Stern,* 1991.

44 Ernst Cassirer, 1874–1945, lectured at the University of Berlin until his professorial appointment in Hamburg.

45 Cassirer's three-volume major work *The Philosophy of Symbolic Forms* was written in Hamburg.

After her wedding, Aniela Dreyfus-Jaffé enrolled to study philosophy and the new discipline of child psychology in Hamburg, where Ernst Cassirer was now rector of the university. At the time Jaffé began her studies, Stern was broadening the scope of developmental psychology, which had hitherto focused predominantly on child and youth development processes. Stern now emphasized the exploration of the "childhood world" as a research goal. "The focus of the Hamburg Institute's work should not just be the personalistic-holistic perception of the child, but also the environment of the child, because we will only understand children if we understand their world."[46] For him, the important question was less about the influence of the environment or the family situation, and more about how children make the world their own and how they imagine and describe it.[47] This approach shaped Aniela Jaffé's studies and research interests, as is clear from the topic of her later dissertation.

During her time in Hamburg, she also immersed herself in the cultural philosophy of Ernst Cassirer and his theory of symbolic forms, and attended lectures by the young Erwin Panofsky[48] on the visual arts, which had interested her since childhood. A short time earlier, Panofsky had founded the Hamburg School of Art History, along with Fritz Saxl, Ernst Cassirer and Aby Warburg, to whom Aniela Jaffé was related on her father's side.[49] The group believed that visual contents, forms and motifs should be interpreted from an interdisciplinary perspective. According to this view, as a contemporary document of

46 William Stern, third Hamburg Institute report, 1931, cit. in Rebecca Heinemann, *Das Kind als Person. William Stern als Wegbereiter der Kinder- und Jugendforschung 1900–1933*, 2016.

47 Cf. William Stern, "Das Kind und die Welt," lecture of 12.2.1932, in: *Geschichte der Psychologie*, Nachrichten Blatt deutschsprachiger Psychologen, vol. 4, 1987, p. 19.

48 Erwin Panofsky, 1892–1968, professor of art history at the University of Hamburg from 1928, became a leading figure in the young discipline, supported by the rich collection of the *Warburg-Bibliothek für Kulturwissenschaft* (cultural studies library), see footnote below. A first draft of the book *Saturn and Melancholy* was written during Panofsky's time in Hamburg. Aniela Jaffé came into contact with him again after the Second World War via Wolfgang Pauli, when Panofsky was working at Princeton University.

49 Aby Warburg, 1866–1929, art historian and cultural studies scholar, founder of one of the foremost libraries for cultural studies, today called the Warburg Institute and affiliated with the library of the Courtauld Institute of Arts in London. Fritz Saxl, 1890–1948, art historian and pupil of Warburg, was the institute's head librarian and largely responsible for saving the collection during the Second World War. In the twenties, Saxl was a private lecturer and then adjunct professor of art history at the University of Hamburg until spring 1933; Aniela Jaffé also attended his lectures.

a historical context, a piece of art displays symbolic values addressing and incorporating cultural, political, religious and philosophical contents. As a student at the University of Hamburg, Aniela Dreyfus-Jaffé not only received rigorous training in scientific research with the day's leading proponent of child psychology, but also had the opportunity to deepen her understanding of cultural philosophy and art history under great minds such as Cassirer and Panofsky. The knowledge and skills she acquired no doubt later facilitated her grasp of analytical psychology, and certainly won her the respect of C.G. Jung.

While Jaffé was immersed in the world of academia and scholarship, the 1929 global economic crisis, triggered by the New York Stock Exchange's Black Friday, caused upheaval to the social and political landscape around the world. In Germany, it led to mass layoffs, widespread unemployment and political instability. With the rise to power of the National Socialists – something deemed unthinkable by most – the now twenty-seven-year-old Jaffé became aware of much more widespread anti-Semitic behavior among her compatriots.

Although the leadership and professorial staff of the University of Hamburg were liberal and inclusive, an aggressive right-wing group, the *Hochschulgruppe Hamburg des Nationalsozialistischen Deutschen Studentenbundes*, had been agitating for some years within the university. Aniela Dreyfus-Jaffé's Protestant baptism and upbringing did not prevent her from being the target of anti-Jewish discrimination on account of her name – she was excluded from student excursions, for example. From the rare comments she later made about her pre-exile life, it seems that her closest friends were upset about this and stuck by her. Although at that time no-one in her family or academic circle imagined the extent to which anti-Semitism would escalate under Adolf Hitler, the latent and increasingly manifest aggression simmering at all levels of society was painfully clear to her. The general malicious and tense atmosphere was reflected in the research findings presented in Jaffé's dissertation on the social behavior of children in kindergarten. A significant degree of the interactions observed were disturbed, irritable, aggressive and anxious; children's play was dominated by warlike games. That "the world as seen by the pre-school child" would be a world of war had heretofore been unthinkable for Stern, and even less had he imagined that, by the spring of 1933, this world would put an abrupt end to the Hamburg Institute with its stellar staff and students. Stern was not alone in underestimating the threat.

When, a few days after the National Socialists seized power in February 1933 and issued the decree "*Recht ist, was dem Führer dient*" [the law is what serves the *Führer*], Ernst Cassirer was one of the first to realistically predict the consequences of this political development: "If tomorrow all German lawyers do not rise up as one man and protest against these paragraphs, then Germany is lost."[50] Shortly after the *Reichstag* elections in March 1933, the University of Hamburg officially supported, despite a few dissenting voices on the executive board, the politics of Adolf Hitler and the momentous "*Gesetz zur Wiederherstellung des Berufsbeamtentums*" [law for the restoration of the professional civil service], which forced all non-Aryan civil servants out of their jobs. According to Goebbels' statement after the burning of books in May 1933, the Nazis' aim now was to "end the age of extreme Jewish intellectualism" in order to "clear the path" for the "German spirit." Anyone who had at least one Jewish parent or grandparent was considered to be non-Aryan.[51]

In Hamburg, some fifty Jewish academics, including William Stern, Ernst Cassirer, Erwin Panofsky and Fritz Saxl, were immediately suspended from the university. Aniela Dreyfus-Jaffé was one of many young students who thus suddenly lost their doctoral supervisor. In spite of having written her thesis, which had been accepted, she was not allowed to graduate: Stern, banned from setting foot in his own institute from one day to the next, was no longer permitted to conduct

50 Toni Cassirer, *Mein Leben mit Ernst Cassirer*, 2003, new edition of 1948, p. 195

51 Joseph Walk, ed., *Das Sonderrecht für die Juden im NS-Staat: Eine Sammlung der gesetzlichen Massnahmen und Richtlinien, Inhalt und Bedeutung*, Heidelberg, 1981, p. 12f. The aim of the so-called "restoration of the civil service" law, which entered into force on April 7, 1933, as well as excluding Jews, was to "cleanse" public offices of communists and other opponents of National Socialism. The licenses enabling lawyers, judges, medical doctors and university teachers to practice their professions could thus be immediately withdrawn. The law forced at least two million civil servants and ten thousand people in academic and cultural roles to provide proof of their Aryan heritage; see S. Friedländer, 2010, p. 31ff. On April 25, 1933, a law was passed restricting the acceptance of "non-Aryan students" to 1.5 percent of the student body; furthermore in 1937, a law that had already been in discussion since 1935 was passed forbidding Jewish students from gaining doctorates.

her final examination. When Aniela Dreyfus-Jaffé refused to give the Hitler salute, she too was peremptorily removed from the university roll.[52]

In the light of Stern's contact with developmental psychologist Jean Piaget in Geneva and with C.G. Jung in Zürich, Jaffé was advised to emigrate to Switzerland – not least because of her Swiss citizenship through marriage. The extent of the risk of remaining in Germany became shockingly clear when her brother-in-law, the conductor Efrem Kurtz, was sought by the Gestapo and had to flee immediately to Paris with Aniela's youngest sister Käthe.[53]

After a stopover in Heidelberg, Aniela Dreyfus-Jaffé crossed the Swiss border in September 1933. In 1935, William Stern, urged to emigrate without delay by his son Günther and daughter-in-law Hannah Arendt, went briefly to the Netherlands before being offered a professorship in the United States at Duke University in Durham, North Carolina, thanks to his former student Gordon Allport who was by then dean of the faculty of psychology at Harvard University. Letters show that in 1937, Aniela Dreyfus-Jaffé was still considering following Stern to the USA – a plan that she abandoned after Stern's sudden heart attack and death in March 1938.[54]

52 William Stern, shaken to the core, said his world view had collapsed. After retreating to his darkened apartment, he made the difficult decision to emigrate. His colleagues of many years, Otto Lipmann and Martha von Muchow, both committed suicide. In her memoirs, Cassirer's wife described Stern's disbelief and the dramatic situation at Hamburg University: "Ernst's closest colleague, the kind-hearted psychologist Stern, who was already over sixty, could not bear the thought that he had to leave his students before they had completed their final examinations. Saxl was the quickest to realize what needed to be done: he asked Ernst to convince the well-known banker Max Warburg, younger brother of the deceased scholar Aby, that the Warburg library collection needed to be relocated, which then took place. But had the library not happened to be American property, it would have been subject to a 'German historical preservation' order and its relocation to England would have been impossible..." op. cit., p. 205f. Cf. also conversation of R. Hinshaw with A. Jaffé, 22.12.1989.

53 Efrem Kurtz, 1900–1995, came from St. Petersburg and from 1924 led the Stuttgart Philharmonic and was occasional deputy for the legendary conductor of the Berlin Philharmonic, Arthur Nikisch. Kurtz married Käthe Jaffé shortly before they had to flee. He was presumably on the Gestapo's wanted list due to his contacts with Russian émigrés. Fame or prominence offered no protection for Jewish artists and intellectuals, and even conductors such as Otto Klemperer and Bruno Walter were forced to flee.

54 In summer 1936, Stern gave the famous William James lectures at Harvard University. After Stern's death, Gordon Allport ensured that his papers were kept, initially in the archives and manuscripts department of Harvard University Library; in November 1970, they were transferred to the Jewish National and University Library of the Hebrew University in Jerusalem. William Stern

In Switzerland, Dreyfus-Jaffé initially enrolled at the *Institut Jean-Jacques Rousseau* in Geneva under Jean Piaget. But she soon realized that for her, Piaget's approach took too little account of individual differences and barely looked at depth-psychological aspects. In November 1933, she therefore decided to move to Zürich, a city she knew from previous visits with her husband. His uncle Georg Ludwig Dreyfus, previously professor of neurology at Goethe University Frankfurt, had also emigrated to Zürich following the Nazis' April law.[55]

Aniela Dreyfus-Jaffé attempted to have her German doctoral studies recognized in Switzerland, but she was far from alone in this regard: as a result of the mass dismissals of university lecturers and professors from German universities, a multitude of students suddenly had to find new professors, and the German-speaking countries of Switzerland and Austria were the obvious first ports of call. The Swiss government soon introduced restrictive conditions for admission to Swiss universities with the issuing of new federal decrees at the end of 1933.[56] Dreyfus-Jaffé unsuccessfully tried to get her dissertation approved by Professor Heinrich Hanselmann, who was known to her through his early work in Frankfurt under Georg Ludwig Dreyfus. Since 1931, he had held the first professorial chair for special education at the University of Zürich.[57] Her efforts were in vain, but as a result of this connection, she was offered an opportunity to work with disabled children at the Balgrist Clinic, and then later in the psychiatric chil-

had managed to take his scientific book collection with him when he left Germany, and this is now also located in Jerusalem.

55 The "*Wiederherstellung des Berufsbeamtentums*" law, see fn. 51, p. 233.

56 Cf. Bolliger, Silvia, 2019, "Im Zeichen der Nationalisierung. Die Haltung der Universität Zürich gegenüber ausländischen Studierenden in der Zwischenkriegszeit." Zürcher Beiträge zur Geschichtswissenschaft, Bd. 11, Böhlau, Wien/Köln and Hengartner, Michael in UZH News, 24.10.2019: "The University's admissions policy during the interwar period was defined by anti-Semitic motivations, and humanitarian considerations were not paid heed to."

57 Heinrich Hanselmann, 1885–1960, founded the institute for special education in Zürich in spring 1924 after having worked at the Frankfurt department of psychology and as head of an establishment for young people with learning disabilities and mental disorders. He directed the institute until 1940. His professorial chair for special education established in 1931 was the first of its kind in Europe; cf. Rudolf Castell, ed., *Geschichte der Kinder- und Jugendpsychiatrie in Deutschland von 1937 bis 1961*, 2003 and Aniela Jaffé in conversation with Roswitha Schmalenbach, Schweizer Radio Beromünster, July 1975.

dren's ward of the University Hospital of Psychiatry Burghölzli under the leadership of the dynamic young psychiatrist Jakob Lutz.[58]

Like many émigrés, the challenges Aniela Dreyfus-Jaffé encountered were not just professional but also personal. She and her husband had planned to have a large family, but after suffering a miscarriage, she discovered that she would not be able to have children. Life for her family back in Germany became more and more difficult and humiliating: the architect husband of her older sister Gabriele had his professional license revoked in 1935, and when their son dared to contradict the teacher's anti-Semitic remarks in class in defense of his Jewish grandfather, the boy was immediately expelled. Lengthy efforts to arrange emigration to England followed, and Aniela meanwhile organized a place for her two small nephews in a children's home in the Swiss Engadine mountains and did her best to comfort them during the separation from their mother and father. The three sisters' elderly parents were still in Berlin, and for the time being, nothing could convince them of the magnitude of danger.

During their marriage, Jean Dreyfus and Aniela Jaffé had often been separated by work and study commitments, and although they would go on to maintain a lifelong close friendship, in February 1937 the pair divorced. Thereafter, the young woman who had grown up in a highly privileged and protected milieu urgently needed to earn her own money. Her living situation amid the backdrop of the tense political climate was so stressful that she did not feel strong enough to undertake another doctoral dissertation. Many Swiss universities had in any case imposed admission limits for students of Jewish descent in the meantime.[59] In addition to her posts in child psychology and psychiatry mentioned above, she also found work as an academic secretary for various professors, most notably the psychiatrist Jakob Lutz, whom she assisted with a book on child psychiatry, the art historian

58 Jakob Lutz, 1903–1998, was from 1930 head of the "Stephansburg" psychiatric children's ward of the University Hospital of Psychiatry Burghölzli, which became the child psychiatric service of the Canton of Zürich from 1947.

59 Aniela Jaffé in an interview with Roswitha Schmalenbach, Schweizer Radio Beromünster, July 1975; cf. also many personal remarks to Robert Hinshaw, and see Frank Herrmann, *Low Profile*, 2002, p. 3ff. See also Sibold, Noemi, *Bewegte Zeiten. Zur Geschichte der Juden in Basel 1930–1950*, 2010.

Carola Giedion Welcker, the Sinologist Eduard von Tscharner and the Indologist Emil Abegg.

In the midst of those dark times, Jaffé began immersing herself in the psychology of C.G. Jung. This led to a profound personal turning point during the destructive pre-war and war years. In the winter semester of 1936/37, a fellow Jewish woman who would become a friend for life, Rivkah Schärf,[60] took Jaffé as a guest auditor to C.G. Jung's seminars on children's dreams at the ETH Zürich.[61] By arrangement with Cornelia Brunner,[62] Jaffé then began to study privately in the library of the Psychology Club, devoting every free morning or afternoon she had to reading C.G. Jung's seminar notes and published books. Feeling in need of psychological support due to the personal, financial and political difficulties she was facing, Jaffé began an analysis with Liliane Frey-Rohn,[63] with whom she later also formed a lifelong friendship. Then in the late fall of 1937, she started a personal analysis with C.G. Jung, shortly before his trip to India. Later she would say that during those war years, it was like receiving "private tuition" in analytical psychology from Jung himself.[64]

Following William Stern's death in spring 1938, with Hitler's ever more aggressive actions after the annexation of Austria, it became clear to Jaffé that, given her Swiss passport, the relatively secure best option for her future was to stay in Switzerland. However, remaining

60 Rivkah Schärf (following her marriage in 1955 Rivkah Kluger-Schärf), 1907–1987, received her doctorate in Semitic languages and religious studies from the University of Zürich and became a Jungian analyst. See also p. 183, fn. 2.

61 C.G. Jung, *Children's Dreams*, ed. Lorenz Jung/Maria Meyer-Grass, trans. Ernst Falzeder with Tony Woolfson, 2008, for the winter semester 1936/37 see p. 32–103; the manuscript was based on notes by Rivkah Schärf, Liliane Frey-Rohn, Hans Baumann, Kurt Binswanger and Marie-Louise von Franz, ibid., p. xii.

62 Cornelia Brunner, 1905–1998, an early pupil of C.G. Jung, was already a "statutarischer Gast" (statutory guest) of the Psychology Club, of which she was later president from 1952 to 1977. Aniela Jaffé provided her with valuable assistance in the early seventies with the organization of an exhibition at the Helmhaus in Zürich held in 1975 for the centenary of C.G. Jung's birth.

63 Liliane Frey-Rohn, 1901–1991, made the acquaintance of C.G. Jung as a young woman through her father, who at the time was rector of the ETH Zürich. Her dissertation completed in 1933 at the University of Zürich was a comparison of the theories of Freud and Jung. In 1936 she began working as an analyst under the supervision of Jung.

64 Aniela Jaffé in conversation with Robert Hinshaw, 1.2.1988, 22.12.1989, AAJD. In a conversation on 26.1.1989 with Steve Martin, Aryeh Maidenbaum and Robert Hinshaw, recorded by Peter Ammann, she said that Jung had been so impressed by her images and dreams in reaction to their first session together, that he had offered her regular analysis. AAJD.

in this neutral country was also perilous, and not just because of the growing threat of war. For many years, Jews in Switzerland experienced hostility and ostracism: despite the extremely low proportion of Jewish citizens (only 0.5 percent of the population) and foreign nationals (only around 5.5 percent), at the end of the thirties fears of "foreign infiltration and over-Jewification" were continually stoked by politicians and journalists. Since 1933, there had been a steady increase in regulations aimed at excluding Jews. Beginning in 1934, foreign Jews could only transit Switzerland if they held a visa for another destination country. The fight against all that the "spiritual defense of the nation" movement deemed "*unschweizerisch*" (un-Swiss) was also directed specifically at Swiss Jews, who were portrayed as dangerous, unpatriotic "pseudo-Swiss." Even within the circle around C.G. Jung, Jaffé, while tolerated, was nevertheless one of the "undesirables." Swiss refugee policies were so restrictive that at the end of 1938, only 123 political refugees were granted leave to remain in Switzerland; for the entire period from 1933 to 1945, the figure is a shockingly low 644 individuals.[65] For over a decade, then, Jaffé faced an ongoing existential threat.

The support she found through her contact with Jung was crucial to helping her deal with the anxiety and insecurity caused by the political situation. He soon waived the fee for her analysis and when she refrained from accepting the offer, he responded that he had no doubt that she would make a significant contribution to analytical psychology. Jung was impressed not just by the scientific background she had obtained with Stern and her in-depth cultural and philosophical understanding of symbols in mythology, religion and art, but also by her calm nature and maturity beyond her years. In the summer of 1939, amidst the upheaval of the outbreak of war in Europe, he asked her to analyze and comment upon a dream of a young boy and to

65 Independent Commission of Experts Switzerland – Second World War. *Die Schweiz und die Flüchtlinge zur Zeit des Nationalsozialismus,* Zürich, 2001; Ludwig, C., *Die Flüchtlingspolitik der Schweiz seit 1933 bis zur Gegenwart,* Bern, 1966; Heinrich Rothmund, chief of aliens police on 27.1.1939: "We have not fought particularly against the Jewification of Switzerland for twenty years to allow ourselves to be forced to accept emigrants today." Diplomatic Documents of Switzerland, dodis.ch/46769, in Holenstein, A., Kury P., Schulz, K. *Schweizer Migrationsgeschichte,* Baden, 2018.

Aniela Jaffé around 1938.

present her contribution in his seminar on children's dreams given at the ETH.[66] Beginning in 1938, she also attended the annual Eranos conferences, never imagining that a few decades later, she would be lecturing there herself. During the war years when finding work became ever more difficult, Jung helped her to survive financially by assigning her research tasks, large and small. She expressed her gratitude by giving him, for Christmas or birthdays, the meat ration stamps that she saved from her own meager supply. The quiet young woman's great courage became clear in 1939 when she helped her elderly parents to flee Germany and save their art collection: just a few weeks after the terrible pogroms of "*Kristallnacht*" she traveled to Berlin, despite the urgent entreaties of her Zürich friends and of Jung not to do so, and organized her parents' last-minute escape to England.[67] She would not again set foot on German soil for more than three decades.

After the capitulation of France in early summer 1940, when it was feared that Switzerland would be the target of bombing raids by the Germans, Aniela Jaffé was included in a small group that joined the Jung family at a privately organized refuge in a remote village in the Valais region.[68] After her personal experience with Jung and the support she received from him during this period, she found the later repeated accusations of anti-Semitic behavior leveled against Jung most upsetting. She wrote to Kurt Wolff in 1958, for example, in response to his request that Jung write an "apology" in the memoir book: "I began my analysis with him during the worst Nazi period, and at the beginning the Jewish problem was in the foreground. If I, so highly sensitive as I was in this regard, had sensed even the slightest whiff of such a tendency, I would have run out of there immediately.

66 See contribution by Aniela Jaffé in: C.G. Jung, *Children's Dreams*, p. 236ff. She and Liliane Frey-Rohn were asked by Jung to edit the entire seminar series of 1939/1940, in order to make a written manuscript available for participants and members of the Psychology Club. "Liliane Frey and Aniela Jaffé edited the third seminar, given in 1939/40, on the basis of the notes of Rivkah Schärf," C.G. Jung, *Children's Dreams*, 2008 p.xv

67 An extensive collection of letters of the Jaffé and Fürstenberg families from 1937–1939 reveal the drama of the situation, the active role of Aniela Jaffé, and the efforts made to save part of Alfons Jaffé's art collection. Unpublished documents, AAJD. In the night of November 9/10, 1938, thousands of synagogues, Jewish-owned business, apartments and Jewish cemeteries were destroyed, and tens of thousands of Jews were arrested and deported to the concentration camps of Dachau, Buchenwald and Sachsenhausen.

68 Aniela Jaffé to Frank Herrmann, 13.5.1982, AAJD.

But in fact, those conversations gradually healed my Jewish complex or feelings of inferiority."[69] A few years after Jung's death, she wrote a long essay on the subject, in which she examined "facts which present favorable, as well as unfavorable, evidence about Jung."[70]

But even in analytical psychology circles there was anti-Semitic discrimination during the war years: in 1943 Toni Wolff informed Jaffé that her membership of the Psychology Club had been refused, allegedly to "protect" C.G. Jung from possible German sanctions. An outraged Jung subsequently campaigned energetically on Jaffé's behalf, threatening his resignation from the Club if she were not to be accepted.[71] In doing so, he publicly sided with Jaffé against the board, of which Toni Wolff was president. Aniela Jaffé and Rivkah Schärf were also excluded from participating in the club members' Christmas dinner in December 1944, with the justification that "we want to be among ourselves" – even by that time, being Jewish was still a reason for exclusion. It was not until after the end of the war, in mid-June 1945, that Jaffé was granted membership, with Jung and C.A. Meier as her sponsors. The vote was unanimous.[72] Seven years later, Jaffé would herself become a board member.[73] The anti-Semitic restrictive clause that had been secretly introduced in December 1944 was not removed until an intervention by Siegmund Hurwitz in 1950.[74]

69 Aniela Jaffé to Kurt Wolff, 16.5.1958, YBL. Aniela Jaffé described how at the end of an analysis session in which they had discussed the differences between Jews and non-Jews, Jung had made a moving gesture: he had placed his left hand palm-up on the table, taken her hand and laid it next to his with the words "Just look, how many similar lines there are!"; he wanted to stress the commonalities rather than the differences. A. Jaffé, Radio Bremen, 1.9.1988. Cf. also Jaffé, A., *From the Life and Work of C.G. Jung*, 1989, p. 86 "At the time Jung gave me as well as many other Jews both financial and moral support."

70 Jaffé, A. (ed.), 1989, p. 78. At the urging of Sir Laurens van der Post, in 1967 she wrote the essay "C.G. Jung and National Socialism," first published 1968 in Aniela Jaffé, *Aus Leben und Werkstatt C.G. Jungs*; in English 1971 in *From the Life and Work of C.G. Jung*, trans. R.F.C. Hull, revised edition 1989. Cf. p. 336ff of this book.

71 Jaffé, A., unpublished, undated manuscript on the Psychology Club, AAJD. "Jung protected me. It was a horrible and depressing business, but I felt Jung's goodwill. This exclusion was not right to him." A. Jaffé in conversation with Robert Hinshaw, 1.2.1988, AAJD, cf. also Radio Bremen program, 1.9.1988. Cf. also *Lingering Shadows – Jungians, Freudians, and Anti-Semitism*, ed. A. Maidenbaum/S. A. Martin, 1991 and *Jung and the Shadow of Anti-Semitism*, ed. A. Maidenbaum, 2002.

72 Minutes of the extraordinary assembly of members, 16.6.1945.

73 Annual report 1951/52, Psychology Club Zürich.

74 On anti-Semitic discrimination and ostracism in Switzerland after the end of the war see Aram Mattioli, *Antisemitismus in der Schweiz 1848–1960*, Zürich, 1998 and Alfred A. Häsler, *Das Boot ist voll*, Zürich 2008. Although after the Second World War, the undesirability of Jews in govern-

If it had not already been clear, Jung's public stand on her behalf demonstrated how much he appreciated Aniela Jaffé. A collection of some eighty letters written by C.G. Jung to Aniela Jaffé over a period of twenty years give a valuable insight into their relationship.[75] After reading her comprehensive manuscript on E.T.A. Hoffmann, he wrote to her in 1946 that he had "wholehearted admiration for the way in which you understand the inner connections of my intellectual production and with what clarity you present them," and that it was "amazing, what you have achieved."[76] Jung decided to publish this "magnificent essay" together with four shorter pieces of his own.[77]

A few months earlier he had written wryly to another correspondent that "a considerable effort of imagination" was needed to envision a connecting thread from the "zigzag track" of his essays – they seemed to him rather like random signs of "a grasshopper with lead type on its feet jumping through the world of ideas, leaving occasional traces behind it." To detect therein the nature of the author was recognized by him as an unenviable task – one that he himself would not take on due to his "distaste for autobiography."[78] That Jaffé had succeeded in capturing and elucidating the inner connections behind his work surprised and pleased him in equal measure. The analysand and pupil of C.G. Jung had, by the mid-forties, become a respected colleague and author.

After the war, which had torn apart her family and claimed the lives of several close relatives and friends, Jaffé's economic situation at last

ment authorities, associations, political parties and decision-making bodies was not discussed, in practice Jews were still excluded.

75 After initial letters commenting primarily on Jaffé's dream images, he soon began to write to her about his own dreams and the things he was currently working on, as well as giving details of his daily life in Bollingen, where many of the letters were written. Sometimes he wrote simply from the impulse to give her a sign of life from him (cf. letter of 29.4.1942), or in reaction to her essays, research and lectures, or to her comments on his manuscripts and publications. Some of Jung's letters to Aniela Jaffé were published in C.G. Jung, *Letters I, II*, 1973, while others are located in the ETH archive.

76 C.G. Jung to Aniela Jaffé, 9.4.1946 and 20.7.1946, ETH.

77 C.G. Jung to Erich Neumann, 19.7.1947, C.G. Jung, *Letters I*, p. 473. An interesting point in this regard is that the first contributions by third parties that Jung included in his "*Psychologische Abhandlungen*" were written by two female Jewish authors: Rivkah Schärf and Aniela Jaffé (in volumes VI and VII, published in 1948 and 1950).

78 C.G. Jung to Jürg Fierz, 21.12.1945, C.G. Jung, *Letters I*, p. 403f. Fierz had prepared a bound volume of essays by Jung, and had asked him to write some lines about the connections between them.

became more stable. As preparations were beginning at the Psychology Club for the founding of the Jung Institute, Aniela Jaffé was employed to handle the administration and secretarial work. This part-time position left her openings to continue her own research activities and analytic practice. In addition, Jung was regularly giving her his latest manuscripts for feedback and editing. His appreciation, however, appeared to be not restricted to Jaffé's competence and qualified expertise alone, but also revealed a marked positive counter-transference on his part.

This is vividly illustrated in a letter from Jung to Jaffé after she had commented on his revised draft of "A Psychological Approach to the Dogma of the Trinity" [79] in summer 1947:

"Dear Aniela,

I thank you with all my heart for your response to my 'Trinity': I couldn't imagine a more beautiful one. It is a 'total' reaction, and it had a 'total' effect on me too. You have shown true recognition of the images I embedded in my work. It again becomes clear to me from your letter how much one misses when one receives no response or a mere fragment, and what a joy it is to experience the opposite – a creative resonance which is at the same time like a revelation of the feminine being. It is as though a wine, which by dint of toil and sweat, worry and care has finally become mature and good, were being poured into a precious beaker. Without this receptacle and acceptance the masculine work remains a delicate child, followed with doubting eyes and released into the world with inner anxiety. But when a soul opens to the work, it is as though a seed were lodged in good earth, or the gates of a city were closed in the evening, so that it can enjoy surer repose. I thank you. Warmest wishes, Your C.G." [80]

Deeply moved, Jung's words are filled with enthusiasm and one cannot help but note the libidinous nature of the metaphors chosen.

79 Expanded and revised version of a lecture given in Eranos in 1940, published in C.G. Jung, *Symbolik des Geistes*, Psychologische Abhandlungen VI, 1948; cf. CW 11, para. 169–295.
80 C.G. Jung to Aniela Jaffé, 10.8.1947, ETH, C.G. Jung, *Letters I*, p. 474f. [translation modified].

In the light of of Jaffé's Hamburg training in experimental and scientific research, Jung recommended her to his Basel colleague Dr. Adolf L. Vischer for a multi-disciplinary medical, sociological and psychological study of old people in care homes.[81] Jaffé was responsible for the psychological part, which was conducted using Rorschach tests and individual conversations.[82] At the same time, she wrote a comprehensive interpretation of Honoré de Balzac's gender-diverse literary figure *Séraphita*,[83] followed soon after (with Jung's encouragement) by a book about the English physician Anna Kingsford, a woman who could not resist the "terrible reality of evil" and fell victim to it.[84] Before and during her time at the Institute, Jung often delegated research and other tasks to her – "letters, research in libraries, reports on offprints and manuscripts that were sent to him for criticism and which were piled mountain-high in his library" – and asked her for editorial assistance with his writings.[85] In 1954, she wrote an extended essay on Hermann Broch's novel *The Death of Virgil*, which was published in Jung's eightieth birthday *Festschrift*.[86] Jaffé also had a longstanding friendship with physicist Wolfgang Pauli, documented in a large collection of letters between the two with frequent exchanges on depth-psychological and personal matters. Pauli often visited Jaffé and sometimes also asked her to do historical research or secretarial tasks for him. From 1953, she also at times acted as his connection to C.G. Jung.[87]

81 Adolf Lukas Vischer, 1884–1974, chief physician of the Basel retirement home at the Bürgerspital, appointment as honorary lecturer for gerontology at the University of Basel in 1954.

82 Aniela Jaffé, "Untersuchungen im Altersheim über die Psychologie des alten Menschen" in Jaffé et al., *Alte Menschen im Altersheim*, 1951, p. 81-131.

83 Honoré de Balzac published his fantastical tale about the androgynous figure of Séraphita in 1835. Aniela Jaffé gave two lectures on the subject at the Psychology Club, on November 5 and 19, 1949; unpublished manuscript, AAJD.

84 Aniela Jaffé, *Anna Kingsford – Religiöser Wahn und Magie*, 1980; 2nd edition, *Religiöser Wahn und schwarze Magie – das tragische Leben der Anna Kingsford*, 1986. Jaffé lectured on the subject at the Psychology Club on June 16 and 30, 1951. Jung had come across the story of Anna Kingsford and her extensive dream material when working on his commentary for *The Secret of the Golden Flower*. See also p. 355.

85 Jaffé, A., 1989, p. 117.

86 Aniela Jaffé, "Hermann Broch: Der Tod des Vergil" in *Studien zur Analytischen Psychologie C.G. Jungs*, vol. II, 1955. Jung wrote to her in a letter of 26.12.1954 reacting to her essay: "I don't know what I admire more: your patience, your feeling for essentials and your descriptive powers, or Broch's astonishingly profound insight into the mystery of transformation, his pertinacity and consistency, and finally his linguistic artistry." C.G. Jung, *Letters II*, p. 200. Jaffé's essay also appeared in her book *Mystik und Grenzen der Erkenntnis*, 1988.

87 Letters from Wolfgang Pauli to Aniela Jaffé, 1948–1958, ETH. The correspondence includes

C.G. Jung and Aniela Jaffé;
Liliane Frey-Rohn, C.G. Jung, Aniela Jaffé in Eranos 1942;
photos © Margarethe Fellerer.

In the winter of 1952, Jung gave her the Freud letters to evaluate – a further sign that he trusted her judgment.[88] For her part, Jaffé had a deep appreciation for Jung's work in developing a psychology which did not shy away from acknowledging and confronting the dark side of the God image and the real existence of evil. This had helped her to recognize, accept and bear her own suffering during a destructive time of war as a necessary experience and part of the totality of existence. She described Jung personally as a good-natured, kindly man with a sense of humor and great respect for "any genuine knowledge and ability of others," who would gladly allow himself to be taught by those who knew more about something. She found his authority not intimidating, but profoundly human – an expression of the fact that he had "engaged in a life-and-death struggle with the creative daemon." Thus, she said, his presence was not felt as "crushing, it does not embarrass or make you feel small," but was transformative, commanding veneration.[89]

Her corrections and criticisms of Jung's draft chapter "The Conjunction" in summer 1954 indicate her having become an independent thinker who was able to challenge the "dear Herr Professor." However, she was not yet quite without the scruples of a loyal pupil, as one of her letters shows: she writes that she is presenting her objections after much hesitation, wary of provoking annoyance or criticism from Jung for her lack of understanding.[90] She described Jung's visits to her or hers to Bollingen and Küsnacht during these years, whether for work or analytical sessions, as "islands of peace in the flux of time," adding "our relationship [was] quiet and harmonious."[91] A sign of Jung's fond-

poems and prose writings by Pauli which he sent to Jaffé. Jaffé donated a total of 97 letters to the ETH archive, comprising 72 from Pauli to Jaffé and 25 from Jaffé to Pauli. For further letters between the two, cf. *Atom and Archetype: The Pauli/Jung Letters, 1932–1958*, Meier, C.A., ed., trans. David Roscoe, Princeton, 2001. On the friendship between Pauli and Jaffé see also *Psychological Perspectives*, no. 19, 1988; the letters from Pauli show that Jaffé meant much more to him than merely a bridge to Jung.

88 William McGuire/Wolfgang Sauerländer, ed., 1974, Introduction, p. xxi. Cf. also this book, p. 203.

89 Jaffé, A., 1989, p. 116.

90 Imprecisely dated, four-page letter from Aniela Jaffé to C.G. Jung, ETH. Unfortunately, other letters from Aniela Jaffé to C.G. Jung could not be found. The chapter on the conjunction was published in *Mysterium Coniunctionis*, vol. 2, first in *Psychologische Abhandlungen*, vol. 11, 1956. See CW 14, para. 654–789.

91 Aniela Jaffé, 1989, p. 116.

ness and concern for Jaffé is that he twice paid for her to take extended cures in the mountains due to her delicate physical health.[92] On the other hand, he also placed large amounts of work on her desk when the sheer volume or his age limited his capacity to deal with it. In his words, Jaffé displayed so much "psychological tact, understanding and insight," that he could not have placed the material about ghost sightings in "worthier hands," and referred to her "valuable contributions to the literature of analytical psychology."[93]

When she became his personal secretary in 1955, resulting in almost daily contact, the nature of the relationship changed, as Jaffé later recalled. Their mutual idealization gave way to a more realistic picture and a "more complete relationship" that now included the realities of daily life in all its aspects. Jung's demanding nature and occasional flares of temper soon displayed themselves. To combat the bouts of irritable grumbling – not seldom as a result of the heavy mailbag – Jaffé learned "to turn the tables and use the weapon which never failed": getting Jung to laugh.[94] Along with his patience, she now experienced his impatience and sensitivity, the reverse side of which, however, was his strong empathy and caring nature. For example, if she arrived at Bollingen feeling tired and carting a basket full of letters, files, manuscripts and books, he would first have her lie down on a deck chair under a blanket and rest.

Well aware of the privileged nature of the position of private secretary, Jaffé was unwilling to accept this new position unless Emma Jung was agreeable to her being so present in the house. Only after Jung assured her that his wife had been the one to suggest her for the role did Jaffé agree.[95] While Jaffé years later spoke of Toni Wolff with reserved respect, she was much less restrained regarding Emma: she adored her. Emma Jung was evidently also taken by Jaffé's way of being and her competence.[96]

In view of this overall context, it is hardly surprising that Jolande Jacobi proposed Aniela Jaffé as the person best suited to become

92 Interview Werner Weick with Aniela Jaffé, 8.5.1991, AAJD.
93 C.G. Jung's Foreword to Jaffé, A., 1963, p. 7.
94 Jaffé, A., 1989, p. 130.
95 C.G. Jung to Aniela Jaffé, 14.6.1955, ETH.
96 Aniela Jaffé to Herbert van Erkelens and Robert Hinshaw, 22.12.1989, AAJD.

Jung's biographer – and that Jung agreed with this choice. Not only was Jaffé already in almost daily contact with Jung, with a profound understanding of his character, his work and ideas, but she had by then become a well-established author and independent researcher in her own right. In the fall of 1956, Jaffé thus wrote to Kurt Wolff agreeing to attempt the biographical project with Jung.

C.G. Jung and Aniela Jaffé in the circle of participants at the Eranos conference in 1948; photos © Margarethe Fellerer.

"Find a way through the jungle of my memories"

Jaffé and Jung began turning their attention to the new project in September 1956. Kurt Wolff, in his very first letter to Jaffé that autumn, instructed her to "present the material in a very direct way" and suggested an approach modeled on Eckermann's conversations with Goethe. He wanted her to give "Jung's memories of people, places and events in his own words in the first person singular."[1] In a subsequent letter in January 1957 inquiring whether work had begun, Wolff repeated this request. Jaffé acquiesced, a decision which would have far-reaching consequences. The use of the first-person narration led to an assumption by a majority of readers that it was actually an "autobiography" in the usual sense – a misconception which has persisted to this day – and caused unclarity about its authorship.[2] The themes Wolff proposed for the content indicate that his understanding of biography was rather conventional, and his knowledge of Jung and the history of psychiatry and psychology relatively limited.[3] The topics he wished to see covered included Jung's thoughts about animals, children, man and woman, people of different nationalities, "primitives," and famous

1 Kurt Wolff to Aniela Jaffé, 24.10.1956. Wolff refers to Johann Peter Eckermann, *Conversations with Goethe in the Last Years of His Life*, trans. S.M. Fuller, Boston and Cambridge, 1852 (first published in German as *Gespräche mit Goethe in den letzten Jahren seines Lebens*, Leipzig, 1836). On 16.1.1957 Wolff wrote to Jaffé: "The whole idea of the book is that it should not be a biography, but as nearly as possible an autobiography. What I am aiming at for the whole book is as much direct speech by Jung as possible." YBL (original letters in English). Although Wolff was a German native speaker and had only lived in the USA since the early forties, until the end of 1957 he wrote to Jaffé primarily in English. Unless otherwise stated, quotations from letters written until the end of October 1957 are in the original English. After November 1957, he mostly corresponded in German.

2 On the reception of the book, see p. 326ff. In recent times, Sonu Shamdasani in particular has pointed out that the book is not C.G. Jung's autobiography; cf. Shamdasani, S., 2005, p. 22ff.

3 For example, he did not know that Charcot had died when Jung was still at school.

names such as Charcot and Freud – like so many others, Wolff seemed fascinated by Jung's relationship with the latter. Jaffé immediately replied that one could hardly ask Jung such "normal questions." Jung wanted her to focus primarily on the influence of the interior world (psychological material, dreams and fantasies) on his development – the inner experiences and their effects. She wished to leave the topics of Charcot and Freud to Bennet, and surprisingly declared: "Frankly, these questions do not hold a particular interest for me. When Jung speaks about them, he always adopts a solemn demeanor, so to speak, and is not quite himself."[4]

Knowing that Jung much preferred to talk freely, Jaffé had already decided to directly ask him as little as possible.[5] When Bennet sent him a list of questions in November 1956, Jung was characteristically reluctant to answer them and instead invited his colleague to Küsnacht with the following words: "I have been exposed to so many misunderstandings that I am rather scared to tell the truth about my biography, as I see it. I should therefore prefer you should first try to find your way through the jungle of my memories."[6]

Jung apparently believed it was the biographer's task to dive in and find paths through the forest. The message to Bennet is noteworthy in two respects. Along with revealing his anxiety about telling the "truth" about his life, it suggests that Jung was drawn to the more fragmentary structure offered by the genre of memoir. While biographies implicitly claim to present a factually accurate and complete picture, memoirs, with their explicitly subjective, anecdotal character, have much fewer constraints. A year later, this preference would be reflected in Jaffé's suggestion of a title highlighting the "memories" aspect of the book.[7]

Returning to the initial situation in the autumn of 1956, Jung at that time expressly welcomed the idea of having his life and reminiscences portrayed by various people from different angles. Although Jaffé had assumed that they would wait until spring to start work in the seclusion of Bollingen, on January 18, 1957, Jung surprised her by

4 Aniela Jaffé to Kurt Wolff, 11.1.1957, AAJD, YBL. Her letters were written in German and here translated into English.
5 Cf. Aniela Jaffé to Kurt Wolff, 20.1.1957, YBL.
6 C.G. Jung to E. A. Bennet, 10.12.1956, ETH (original in English); cf. Shamdasani, S., 2005, p. 41f.
7 Cf. p. 266ff.

announcing that he was ready to tell her about his earliest childhood memories.[8] The biographical conversations between the two thus began. Those conversations were to continue for several years and would ultimately lead to the book *Memories, Dreams, Reflections by C.G. Jung*, and now, many decades later, to this volume, *Reflections*.

On the Friday afternoons set aside for the biography work, Jung would describe the experiences and dreams that had shaped him, often in connection with reflections about his personal development and the evolution of the ensuing works. Jaffé later said it sometimes felt as if Jung were "talking to himself in my presence," and recalled how he told of his life and ideas in an associative, meandering, circular way, at times hopping from one thought to another. She experienced Jung as quite motivated to speak about his experiences, "although God knows not systematically, but always whatever occurs to him at that moment." This approach pleased Jaffé greatly, as she felt that "only in this way does one get the vital *prima materia*."[9] All too often had she observed Jung being interviewed in recent years and heard his tired and irritated responses to the same old uninspiring questions. She therefore knew how important it was to remain open and patient, and to strike the right vein with unobtrusive questioning. In this first phase, she took the role of an active listener, like an anthropologist doing field research, occasionally inserting brief encouraging queries such as "Isn't that when the vision of the 'cactus' occurred?" or "What did your mother say about the experience?" She deliberately held herself back, as she wrote to Wolff: "Jung is a great storyteller by nature, continually transforming the stream of inner images into words. I refrain from interrupting him, even if he digresses – which happens often – because these detours are full of surprises."[10]

Before further exploring Jaffé's role in this process, it is worthwhile to take a closer look at the course of Jung's "stream of inner images."

8 Aniela Jaffé to Kurt Wolff, 20.1.1957. YBL. (of note: Jung had shortly before received Bennet in Küsnacht) 8A The published translation of the German title in English is *Memories, Dreams, Reflections by C.G. Jung*, but it actually should be *Memories, Dreams, Reflections of C.G. Jung*. The word 'by' was adopted by the publisher to give the appearance of it being an autobiography, a misconception that has endured to this day. See also pp. 330.

9 Aniela Jaffé to Kurt Wolff, 20.1.1957, YBL.

10 Aniela Jaffé to Kurt Wolff, 2.3.1957, AAJD, YBL.

Interestingly, in the conversations that took place with Jaffé up until the autumn of 1957, and later in his autobiographical texts about his childhood and youth, he chose to follow a more-or-less chronological narrative structure, albeit with repeated detours. The main themes are Jung's childhood, school days and youth, his student years, his experiences as a young doctor, the influence of important figures such as Théodore Flournoy, William James, Sigmund Freud and Richard Wilhelm, and his confrontation with the unconscious after leaving Burghölzli. He begins by describing his earliest sensory perceptions as a small child, then the first dream he could remember clearly, and the associated feelings from subsequent childhood experiences.

Equally characteristic of his narrative style are the hints and connections to themes that he later took up in his psychology, such as the idea of the anima and his relationship to it. Thus, the seeds of his later works, already germinating in those early experiences, can be discerned. We witness a retrospective interpretation of past occurrences and images from the perspective of old age, an attempt to attribute meaning and to place them within the context of a whole life. The idea and conception are expressed that, already as a child, he carried in him an intrinsic task or duty determined by fate. One inevitably thinks here of the words of Heraclitus, *ethos anthropoi daimon* – "a man's character is fate."[11]

Jung was not seeking to retrieve some individual outward details of his earlier life, but rather to identify an underlying "basic truth" that had determined the course of his life. In similar ways, Goethe had described his attempts at retrospection at the end of his life: "It was my most serious intention to describe and express as far as possible the deeper basic truth that, as far as I was able to recognize it, had presided over my life. But if such is not possible without allowing reminiscence and thus imagination to have an influence, so that one always ends up utilizing a certain poetry, then it is clear that what is assembled and highlighted are the results of how we think of the past now, rather than relating the individual details as they happened at the time."[12]

11 Diels/Kranz, *The Pre-Socratics*, Fragment 119.
12 J. W. Goethe, *Sämtliche Werke*, ed. Horst Fleig, Vol. II/11, 1993, letter to King Ludwig of Bavaria, December 1829, p. 209. (Trans. CS)

Jaffé informed Kurt Wolff on several occasions that Jung could recall matters he had perceived as soulfully significant, but was unable or not motivated to retrieve factual details.[13] Jung later formulated the interesting hypothesis that the external manifestations of his existence had largely disappeared from his memory because he had taken part in them with all his powers. Almost without exception, they had therefore become "phantasms which I barely recollect, for they no longer lend wings to my imagination. On the other hand, my memories of the 'inner' experiences have grown all the more vivid and colourful."[14] Like Goethe, he also realized that reminiscence is coupled not only with fantasy and imagination, but also with a creative energy – a poetic ability.

The fertile "detours" alluded to by Jaffé, as well as circumambulations of biographically relevant topics, also included long chains of associations, often prompted by something Jung was occupied with at the time – lecture preparations, correspondence, books he was working on or reading, or conversations between Jung and Jaffé about other shared interests.

Jung took it for granted that Jaffé would recognize even implicit references to his later work within his descriptions of early dream images or experiences. "Jung does not spell out these connections, he assumes that I understand them, as he explicitly told me."[15] When he recounted his earliest dreams to Jaffé, he thus relied on her knowing his views on childhood dreams, namely their early prefigurative, fateful character: "Children's dreams can be a preview of a whole human life, setting out a basic pattern of a life."[16] He was also able to count on her intimate knowledge of his *Red Book* and therefore her understanding of his in-

13 James Hillman explored this phenomenon years later in the context of case histories and observed: "The biography of the soul concerns experience. It seems not to follow the one-way direction of the flow of time, and it is reported best by emotions, dreams, and fantasies... The experiences arising from major dreams, crises, and insights give definition to the personality. [...] they are like boundary-stones which mark out one's own individual ground. These marks can be less denied than can the outer facts of life [...]" *Healing Fiction*, 1983, p. 24 (ref. to *Suicide and the Soul*, Dallas: Spring Publications, 1978, pp. 77-79).

14 C.G. Jung to Gustav Steiner, 30.12.1957, *Letters II*, p. 407.

15 Aniela Jaffé to Kurt Wolff, 20.1.1957, YBL.

16 Cf. C.G. Jung, *Children's Dreams*, ed. Lorenz Jung/Maria Meyer-Grass, trans. Ernst Falzeder with Tony Woolfson, 2008; quote taken from unpublished notes of a conversation between C.G. Jung and analysts (in German), 29.6.1957, ETH.

ner journey in midlife, something he had shared with few others. Jaffé therefore seriously considered playing a bridging role for the reader by providing explanatory comments "in a quiet voice".[17] It later emerged that Jung would not only have agreed to her suggestion, but would have expressly welcomed a second voice. The publisher, however, was at first ambivalent, and as time passed, came to reject this idea with increasing vehemence, preferring a text that would lead the reader to believe that author and protagonist were one and the same.

Jung also provided Jaffé with other autobiographical material, including private correspondence, as well as the 1925 seminar[18] in which he discussed his relationship and conflict with Freud. In October 1957, he additionally entrusted her with six volumes of the *Black Books*,[19] a series of very personal diary-like notebooks, from which she was permitted to extract relevant information for her biographical work. He had already gifted her a copy of *The Red Book* on an earlier occasion.

During their conversations, Jaffé noted down those remarks that she wanted to remember, sometimes in detail, at other times using abbreviations and fragmentary key words.[20] The written protocols show that she herself decided when and what to record, meaning that in many cases the complete conversation was not documented, with the beginning often missing.[21] She emphasized on several occasions that Jung had given her complete freedom in making her notes. He had simply spoken freely and spontaneously following his own associations and recollections; it had never been a "dictation" in any sense of the word. For her part, she granted Jung the liberty to follow the trails his thoughts took him along by playing the role of a knowledgeable and interested but discreet listener, who could also accept long periods of silence.

17 Aniela Jaffé to Kurt Wolff, 20.1.1957, YBL.

18 Cf. C.G. Jung, *Analytical Psychology, Notes of the Seminar Given in 1925*; ed. McGuire, W., 1995.

19 Aniela Jaffé described these black notebooks as a kind of precursor to *The Red Book*, writing in a letter to Kurt Wolff that "they contain the whole of Jung's person." She also wrote that they contained the "Urstoff" (original material), in which "the personal in relationship with the impersonal (...) is shockingly clear," and said that they described no outer events, but only the "confrontation with the inner world." (Letter to Kurt Wolff, 29.10.1957, YBL). C.G. Jung, *The Black Books*, ed. Shamdasani, S., 2020.

20 Jung spoke standard German with Jaffé; occasional idiomatic expressions in Swiss German or in other languages were recorded as spoken in her notes.

21 See also Aniela Jaffé to Kurt Wolff, 1.1.1958, YBL.

Certain chapters of this volume bear testimony that Jung was not "talking to himself" as Jaffé suggests in her introduction, but was addressing her as a close confidante who was often personally involved in the conversation. As the addressee and conversation partner, she had an influence on both the direction and content of their talks. Although regular meetings of one-and-a-half hours a week had initially been agreed upon, the regularity and length of the sessions soon began to vary greatly. If they were discussing a topic which very much interested or inspired Jung, the session could last much longer, be it because he spent more time circling around a topic, or because it fired his imagination, awakened memories or elicited further reflections.[22]

The information-gathering process also differed starkly from conventional interviews in other ways. Jung had already conveyed many biographical particulars to Jaffé in years past, there was a comfortable familiarity between them and both shared an introverted side, greatly facilitating the process. It was not difficult for Jaffé to create a receptive, accepting space in which Jung could speak openly, with only limited interventions and sparing questions from her. Well aware as she was of the ambivalence Jung had previously felt about looking back over his life, she also respected without question his unwillingness to talk about certain topics and experiences. When, thanks to their trusting relationship, he nevertheless did open up about such matters, she either refrained from taking notes or indicated that the comments were not intended for publication. "Of course Jung also talked to me about Toni Wolff. But before we began work on the book he had written to me that he did not want to have anything personal about his private relationships in it."[23] She thus largely respected Jung's self-censorship and wishes, and not only in terms of biographical concealment and privacy. A telling example is a set of notes with a comment in Jaffé's handwriting that it was "an extremely introverted day full of inner

22 An example of the free form the conversations could take is provided by Jaffé when she describes the afternoon on which Jung told her of his visions of 1944: "It was an unforgettable afternoon when Jung told me about the visions: we sat in the garden and he kept talking even after the sun had gone down. It one was of those fall evenings when the sun strays into autumn. That for me was the real, most authentic Jung." Aniela Jaffé to Kurt Wolff, 2.11.1957, YBL.

23 Aniela Jaffé in conversation with Robert Hinshaw, 15.3.1991, AAJD.

In Bollingen, the conversations were often accompanied by good food and drink, and often it was evening before you knew it. Even in old age, Jung had lost none of his affection and humor. Photo © Aniela Jaffé.

images"; the images, however, were not recorded.[24] She and Jung were of the same mind about the psychological significance of mystery. They also shared an interest in synchronistic and parapsychological phenomena, due in part to other projects they were both working on at the time. Such common interests and viewpoints of course also influenced the content of their conversations.[25] By nine months into the process, Jung was so deeply involved that even at times of great exhaustion he wanted to meet Jaffé for the conversations. Thus he told her in November 1957: "When I talk about myself, I am also doing it for my own sake."[26]

Jaffé's editing process consisted of a first phase in which she would revise, transcribe and complete her shorthand notes. This involved typing up the fragments and abbreviations as full sentences, while maintaining as much as possible the original form in which Jung expressed himself – the "raw material."[27] From her correspondence with the publisher, it appears that this initial transfer and editing process did not always take place immediately after the sessions, and sometimes not until several days, weeks or even months later, contrary to an assertion of Jaffé's twenty years later.[28] For example, in one of her letters to Wolff, it is evident that notes taken during two conversations with Jung at the beginning of December were not transcribed and typed up until mid-January 1958 or even later. This process she described as "*Ausarbeitung*," a kind of working out or elaboration.[29] Thus, although her stated intention was to reproduce Jung's testimony as faithfully as possible, it cannot be assumed that Jung's original speech was literally reproduced word-for-word. Similarly to Eckermann's conversations with Goethe, in which Eckermann's shaping hand must be taken into

24 Cf. Conversation notes of 21.3.1958, p. 2, LoC/ETH.

25 In 1957, shortly after finishing the book *The Undiscovered Self (Present and Future)*, Jung began writing *Flying Saucers: A Modern Myth of Things Seen in the Sky* – a psychological examination of the phenomenon of UFOs, see CW 10, para. 589–824. As previously mentioned, Jaffé was working at the same time on the publication *Death Dreams and Ghosts*, for which Jung wrote a foreword in August 1957.

26 Aniela Jaffé quotes a sentence of Jung in a letter to Kurt Wolff, 15.11.1957, YBL

27 Aniela Jaffé to Kurt Wolff, 20.1.1957, YBL.

28 Cf. Aniela Jaffé to Kurt Wolff, 1.1.1958, 10.1.1958, 1.5.1958, YBL.

29 Cf. Aniela Jaffé to Kurt Wolff. 10.1.1958, YBL.

account, the notes should be read as Jung as perceived and reproduced by Jaffé.[30]

The typed-up copies were marked with the date the conversation had taken place, and Jaffé referred to them variously as "manuscripts," "protocols" or "reports."[31] These notes were at times less comprehensive than others. Transferring her shorthand fragments into standard text sometimes proved difficult, as she mentioned in a letter to Wolff about a pending write-up. For example: "I just hope that from my cursory notes I can still make sense of the intricate ideas – the protocol will follow later."[32] In this case, the protocol finally written by Jaffé several weeks after the conversation is so coherent, fluent and clearly formulated in terms of both the content and language, however, that it must be assumed that considerable editing had taken place.[33] A comparison of the many protocols suggests significant differences in the degree of editing: some appear to be very close reproductions of direct speech while others have clearly been extensively worked upon editorially during the writing process. In addition, some of the protocols follow a perfectly seamless chain of associations while in others, certain remarks have apparently been left out – therefore neither the direct narrative style nor the complete protocols can be taken as a one-to-one rendering of Jung's words. Jaffé considered the protocols her personal initial base material from which to later develop a manuscript – at first dubbed *Mémoires Improvisées* à la Paul Claudel[34] – meaning that her own questions or comments are rarely included. Later remarks and letters to Wolff revealed that she or Jung often chose focal topics for each conversation.[35]

30 Johann Peter Eckermann, *Conversations with Goethe in the Last Years of His Life*, trans. S.M. Fuller, Boston and Cambridge, 1852. Regarding the authenticity of the conversations, Eckermann stressed explicitly in his foreword that the book presented "his Goethe." Both C.G. Jung and Aniela Jaffé distanced themselves, however, from the "Goethe and Eckermann" model in their project.

31 Aniela Jaffé to Kurt Wolff, 9.6.1957, 13.10,1957, 27.10.1957, YBL.

32 Aniela Jaffé to Kurt Wolff, 1.1.1958, cf. also Aniela Jaffé to Kurt Wolff, 9.6.1957, YBL.

33 Protocol of 13.12.1957, LoC/ETH.

34 Kurt Wolff recommended to Aniela Jaffé in a letter of 7.1.1957, YBL, that she use the form of the conversations of Jean Amrouche with Paul Claudel as a model (Claudel/Amrouche, *Mémoires Improvisées*, Paris, 1954). Unlike the conversations between Jung and Jaffé, these were recorded in a radio studio and transcribed, and contained long passages by Amrouche. Jaffé answered Wolff immediately that she did not want to appear in the text to the extent that Amrouche did. The publisher was in agreement.

35 Cf. Aniela Jaffé to Kurt Wolff, 9.6.1957, YBL: "The topic for the next 'session' with Jung is his

Jaffé's biographical research was not restricted to the conversations. With Jung's permission, she added to her records communications and comments about his experiences and ideas revealed on other occasions, such as lectures or seminars. For example, for the later chapter about Jung's clinical work as a psychiatrist, she drew on her notes from a talk Jung held with psychiatrists at the Burghölzli on January 27, 1956. Her introductory comment describes what she understood by "protocol": "Record based on keywords. Not a literal protocol, only intended as an *aide mémoire*."[36] As Jung's private secretary, Jaffé was in almost daily contact with him. Thus, if memories, reflections or additional thoughts on previously mentioned topics came up in the course of their day-to-day work – for example when dealing with correspondence or during talks with theologians or analysts – Jaffé would add them to her base material for the biography project.[37]

For eight months, Jung and Jaffé enjoyed an undisturbed process of reminiscence and taking stock together. This ended in the fall of 1957, when Kurt Wolff traveled to Zürich to discuss the project with them both. Along with content-related discussions, contractual matters were now put on the agenda. Wolff had already previously attempted to impose binding obligations on Jaffé by offering her advance payments, which she, however, had refused. When he now saw her notes and realized how much additional personal material Jung had provided her with, he wanted to draw up a contract without delay. He was anxious to avoid any possibility of Jung withdrawing from the project again, as had happened with Brody. C.G. Jung thereupon formally transferred specific rights to Jaffé:

"I hereby authorize you to use your records of conversations with me at your discretion; I permit you to complement and complete these records with extracts and selections from autobiographical writings of

encounters with R. Wilhelm, Flournoy, Keyserling." Certain conversations also began with Jung introducing a topic – saying that today he wanted to talk about his father or his mother, for example.

36 Aniela Jaffé's typescript of "C.G. Jung's answers to psychiatrists' questions," January 27, 1956, ETH.

37 E.g. Conversations with theologians, 10.11.1956 and 26.1.1957, question-and-answer session with members of the Curatorium of the C.G. Jung Institute, 22.6.1957, LoC, ETH; Jung's verbal reactions to correspondence, see Aniela Jaffé to Helene Wolff, 18.3.1958, AAJD.

my own which I do not wish to publish in my *Collected Works*, as they are not of a scholarly nature."[38]

The document specifies in detail the autobiographical material from which Jaffé was permitted to use extracts of her choice: *The Red Book*, the English seminar of 1925, the African diary, the report "Impressions from a Trip through India," and the 1916 essay "Septem Sermones ad Mortuos," which Jung saw as being closely connected with the "Liber Novus" and "Liber Secundus" of his *Red Book*.[39]

In the same document, Jung further explicitly transferred to Jaffé not only the copyright to her records of conversations, but also to any extracts from the aforementioned autobiographical texts used as additional or complementary material.[40] However, in view of the fact that he was contributing valuable material to the project, he requested a fifty percent share of Jaffé's author royalties for the published book. She had already proposed to the publisher that her fee should be shared with Jung and was in agreement with the fifty percent split. Jung reiterated, however, that Jaffé was responsible for the compilation of the entirety of the biographical material, the drafting of the text, and the editing and publication of the planned book, and rejected Wolff's request that he write an introduction.[41]

While Jung's letter of authorization and transfer of copyright to Jaffé is clear and unambiguous, the wording and royalty arrange-

38 C.G. Jung to Aniela Jaffé, 21.10.1957, AAJD.

39 On *The Red Book* see fn. 3, p. 90; C.G. Jung, *The Red Book*, Shamdasani, S. (ed.), 2009; the English seminar of 1925 was published in *C.G. Jung, The Seminars. Vol. III, Analytical Psychology. Notes of the Seminar given in 1925*, McGuire, W. (ed.), 1989, revised edition by Shamdasani, S. (ed.), *Introduction to Jungian Psychology; Notes of the Seminar on Analytical Psychology given in 1925 by C.G. Jung*, 2012; "Impressions from a Trip through India" and the African diary are unpublished texts from the C.G. Jung private archive; "Septem Sermones ad Mortuos" Jung described as sermons to the dead, more specifically to the "voices of the Unanswered, Unresolved, and Unredeemed." He saw them as answers to questions from the inner world. The text was a kind of prelude to his later, decades-long work on the world of the unconscious. From 1916, only a private printing of this text had been in circulation. Jaffé managed to convince Jung to allow her integrate the whole text as an appendix to *MDR* by emphasizing to him the significance of the contents with regard to his subsequent work and the poetic style of the text that made it unique among his writings; cf. Jaffé, A. (ed.), 1962, p. 191f., p. 378ff., see also this volume p. 91, fn. 6. And C.G. Jung *The Red Book*, op. cit., p. 344ff.

40 C.G. Jung to Aniela Jaffé, 21.10.1957, AAJD.

41 Agreement of 25.10.1957 between "AUTHOR" and "PUBLISHER" issued by Pantheon Books, signed by Kurt Wolff "for a work tentatively entitled 'Carl Georg Jung's Improvised Memories'"; upon Jaffé's intervention, the spelling of Jung's name was subsequently corrected. AAJD (original in English).

ments in the publisher's contract are unusual: Aniela Jaffé is listed as the sole author, but one who is also acting "in the name of Jung."[42] The contract grants Jung half of Jaffé's author fee on account of his providing significant material for use in a biographical project with a large print-run.[43] Jung, however, expressly does not wish to appear as the author of the said book, which at this stage is referred to as a "so-called autobiography." One detects different interests among the various parties involved: Jaffé's concern was to secure a clear legal basis for her use of the biographical material; Jung wanted an unequivocal transfer of responsibility for the project to Jaffé; and Kurt Wolff's goal was to indirectly bring Jung into the Pantheon stable with a project that promised to become a considerable success.

Both Jaffé and Jung insisted on clarity and transparency: they required explicit prior agreement from the English and American publishers of the *Collected Works* that no claim would be made to the above-mentioned writings which Jung did not consider to be a part of his scientific work. They also made clear to Wolff that Jaffé was granted only the right to use *extracts* from these diary-like writings of Jung. Jaffé again expressly asserted that she granted Pantheon the publication rights solely for the volume she had been asked to produce, not for the records and notes used for such purpose or other source materials *in toto*.[44] The British publisher of the *Collected Works*, Sir Herbert Read of Routledge, indicated in his response for the first time that he would be interested in releasing the English translation of the planned book in the UK; two years later, this would lead to a bitter struggle with Wolff. With the agreement of October 1957, Wolff had claimed the exclusive world rights for Pantheon – subsequently to be amended following an intervention by Jung in 1960.[45]

Despite the extremely polite tone of the exchanges between Jaffé and Wolff during this period, the divergence in their conception of the project's content and form were already in evidence. The publisher continued to request material about Jung's personal life, such as his

42 "acting in her own name as well as in the name of Professor Dr. C.G. Jung" [...] "The work shall be based on the interviews given by Dr. Jung to the author." Ibid., p. 1 (original in English).
43 Aniela Jaffé to Kurt Wolff, 4.10.1957, YBL.
44 Aniela Jaffé to Kurt Wolff, 2.11.1957, 9.11.1957, YBL. C.G. Jung to Aniela Jaffé, 6.11.1957, AAJD
45 See p. 309f.

love life, his role as a family man and father, relationships with his wife and children, as well as general themes such as "house, food, money," his thoughts on literature, music and art, and his impressions of "famous people" such as Einstein, Freud, Charcot, Bachofen, Burckhardt, William James and Richard Wilhelm.[46] Wolff's preparatory notes for his meeting with Jaffé and Jung reveal that his knowledge of Jung and his work was at best sketchy and in some cases simply incorrect.[47]

After Jaffé had allowed Wolff to look at her conversation notes, he reacted enthusiastically. He anxiously requested copies of them, along with the chapter "Refinding the Soul" from *The Red Book*. Jaffé had shown him the protocols merely in order to give him an impression of the associative and meandering nature of Jung's stream of thoughts. She thought that by showing Wolff her notes, she would be able to convince him of her plan to edit them as little as possible. At most, she planned at that time to group them thematically and publish them as momentary reminiscences and reflections with specific dates. Wolff, however, continued to insist on a linear, chronological narrative structure. Because Jaffé felt that the process of gathering data was not yet complete, and because she also needed time to thoroughly examine the substantial additional source material provided by Jung, she requested that they leave the question of the book's form open for the time being.[48] She told Wolff that she needed peace and quiet to do the necessary work, which she could only do alone. Wolff, however, did not desist. Arguing that he simply wanted to read the notes again in more detail, so as to be able to accompany her more competently, as well as to decide if the information could potentially be ordered chronologically, he finally convinced her to give him copies of her notes.[49]

46 Kurt Wolff's notes from late September/early October 1957, partially handwritten on notepaper from the Hotel Storchen, Zürich, where he stayed during his visit, YBL.

47 For example, he wanted to know whether Jung's "resistance to religion" was due to his being the son of a pastor, and believed that Jung hated Russian writers – "hates the Russian writers, Dostoevsky," undated handwritten notes of Kurt Wolff, probably end of September 1957, YBL.

48 "I think it is not yet time to compile the material" and "I would like to listen to Jung for as long as he still has something to say." "I am not in favor of too much ordering: it is part of Jung that he 'talks in circles' as it were. He always comes back to things, returns to them in more depth, or circles around a topic and finally arrives (...) at what he was looking for." Aniela Jaffé to Kurt Wolff, 29.10.1957, YBL.

49 One year later, Jaffé would reiterate that she had in vain tried to set boundaries at that time: cf. Aniela Jaffé to Kurt Wolff, 13.11.1958, YBL.

The effect of these negotiations between Wolff, Jaffé and Jung was to intensify the whole undertaking. In the month of October 1957 alone, Jaffé and Jung held nine further biography sessions – Jung was apparently now taking a great interest in the project and, having submitted his German manuscript for "Flying Saucers" to Rascher for printing, had a lot more time for it.[50] Wolff's reaction to Jaffé's notes was euphoric – he said he was "extremely happy about the wonderful things you were good enough to hand over to me" and told her that on his return to New York, he had immersed himself in the material. He submitted a list of questions and informed Jaffé that he was eagerly waiting for more copies.[51]

He also pressed her to let him see Jung's diary from Africa, his impressions from India, and further excerpts from *The Red Book*. In addition, Wolff approached Cary Baynes to ask for a copy of the 1925 seminar, from which he transcribed much of the information relating to Freud and to Jung's inner experiences following their split. In further correspondence with Jaffé, Wolff now referred to the project as "our book," and said it was all he could think about, day and night. Unfortunately, however, as he saw it, there were still large gaps in the life story which he wished to reduce to a minimum, and he enclosed another list of pending questions and topics.[52] Jaffé did not accede to Wolff's requests for copies of Jung's texts, and emphasized that the entire process must be allowed to unfold and emerge undisturbed at its own pace. She begged Wolff to show restraint and wished to wait until summer 1958 before having any discussion about the book's content and form.

Wolff ignored this plea and had not the slightest intention of returning Jaffé's notes to her after reading them. In fact, by this time he had brought on board Wolfgang Sauerländer, who worked for both Pantheon Books and for the Bollingen Foundation, to edit the material and order it thematically and chronologically, and also to obtain

50 Aniela Jaffé to Kurt Wolff, 4.10.1957, AAJD

51 "I am eagerly looking forward to getting a carbon of your notes." This and the quote above from letter of Kurt Wolff to Aniela Jaffé, 24.10.1957, YBL .

52 He wrote that one could hardly expect to get a seamless life story from Jung, but "it would certainly be very desirable to reduce the most obvious gaps to a minimum," Kurt Wolff to Aniela Jaffé, 1.11.1957, YBL (original in English).

additional information and structure the first few chapters.[53] From the copies of the protocols that were preserved, it can be seen that they were edited by both Wolff and Sauerländer shortly after receipt. Alongside the few additions made by Jaffé after drafting them, there were many comments of an editorial and stylistic nature inserted in New York. Wolff noted in the margins of Jaffé's "base material" the passages he found relevant and those which he considered repetitive or superfluous, crossed out many sections and made "corrections," indicated parts that could be grouped together, and moved text around. He unfortunately also often did away with several pages at once, so that the copies now available do not represent the complete set of materials sent by Jaffé.[54]

By the end of November, Wolff had already collated material from the protocol copies he had received thus far into several chapters in chronological order – "Early Years", "Freud", "Contemporaries", "Visions 1944" – and had given these to Wolfgang Sauerländer for further editing. Documents and notes dating from that time show that Sauerländer clearly had more knowledge than Wolff of C.G. Jung's work from a historical and psychological perspective, and thus he played an important role in the arranging of the material. A few weeks later, Wolff sent Cary Baynes a copy of the compiled chapters and asked her to come to New York to discuss them. Jaffé remained in the dark about this interference in her work. Nor was she informed that the chapters "Early Years" and "Visions 1944" had already been sent to an English translator in early December.[55]

Wolff and Sauerländer also compiled a chapter on Freud, based primarily on extracts from Jung's 1925 seminar, but put it on hold after new protocols on the topic arrived from Jaffé.[56] Without any consul-

53 Wolfgang Sauerländer came to New York from Germany as a young man in 1939. His parents knew Kurt Wolff from his time in Munich. Sauerländer became the first employee of Pantheon Books in 1943, initially acting as accountant and warehouse clerk.

54 Cf. Protocols of Jaffé based on conversations with C.G. Jung, 21.9.1956–19.9.1958, LoC/ETH.

55 Handwritten note by Kurt Wolff, "Chapter Early Years and Visions 1944 to Richard Wilbur on Dec 3, 1957," YBL (in English). Wolff presumably was confused about the name of the translator: it was Richard Winston who was officially commissioned by Pantheon for the translation; the poet Richard Wilbur moreover translated only from French into English.

56 C.G. Jung did not begin telling Aniela Jaffé in more detail about his relation to Freud and his theories until after Wolff's visit; as mentioned, Jaffé had previously wanted to leave this subject to E.A. Bennet.

tation on the matter with Jaffé or Jung, Wolff was already thinking of selling this Freud chapter to certain journals and magazines (e.g., *The Atlantic Monthly*) as a promotional advance publication. The extent to which he disrespected Jaffé's role as author and editor and passed over her explicit requests for restraint, while continuing to be dishonest about the work being done on her material, is documented in a letter he wrote to her during this period: "I agree with you completely that we should not try to order things too much. We are in agreement that it is still too early to start talking about grouping the material etc."[57]

When Jaffé discovered that Wolff had been contacting other people in Zürich asking for information about Jung, and the publisher himself then informed her that he had taken the liberty of "showing your records" to Cary Baynes in New York,[58] she wrote to him in mid-December insisting that she wanted, indeed *needed*, to "be alone" with the task. She asked him again to grant her peace and said that she did not want any further involvement of third parties at that point. In time she would provide him with the framework of a manuscript, but until then he should trust her as Jung trusted her. "Your enthusiasm and interest in the protocols did me good. But now you should – and this is my innermost wish – forget all about them or even return them to me." She repeated her request that Wolff show respectful restraint, not just for her own sake, but also for the sake of Jung: "With a creative spirit like his, one may know to a certain extent where and when to start, but one has no idea – him least of all – where it will lead." In order to "give this unpredictable stream a chance," one needed, according to Jung's own words, the courage to bear a certain amount of decent ignorance. "And what emerges may not be touched from the outside," wrote Jaffé.[59] Because it had long been clear to Jaffé that this would not be a biography or even a memoir in the usual sense, she proposed to Jung a title that would reflect the project's very particular nature: *Erinnerungen, Träume, Gedanken* [Memories, Dreams, Reflections]. This title would offer greater freedom, the content could remain frag-

57 Kurt Wolff to Aniela Jaffé, 2.11.1957, YBL.

58 Kurt Wolff to Aniela Jaffé, 10.12.1957; he did not disclose that Cary Baynes had already read and commented on a manuscript which he had composed from Jaffé's notes, and he also concealed Sauerländer's involvement: "by the way, I have shown the material to nobody at all (...)"; YBL.

59 All quotes from the letter of Aniela Jaffé to Kurt Wolff, 15.12.1957, YBL.

mentary, and there would be ample space for reflective thoughts – Jung immediately agreed.[60]

In two subsequent ingratiating letters, Wolff extolled the personal contact and cooperation with Jaffé as the best and most wonderful gift of 1957, but failed to acknowledge the boundaries she had set and also ignored Jaffé's "deepest wish" that he return her protocols.[61]

In the meantime, Jung's intensive occupation with his memories had taken a surprising turn: in a letter to an old schoolfriend from Basel, Jung wrote that he had decided "to take up at least the very first beginnings of my life and consider them in an objective fashion."[62] Jaffé was one of the first to know of this decision.

60 Cf. Aniela Jaffé to Kurt Wolff, 1.1.1958, YBL.

61 It is thanks to this circumstance that copies of the protocols up to 19.9.1958 are available today. After this date. Jaffé no longer sent protocols to Kurt Wolff. For details regarding what happened to Jaffé's protocol copies in the USA after 1961, see p. 324 and p. 347ff. No further copies were found in the papers of Aniela Jaffé.

62 C.G. Jung to Gustav Steiner, 30.12.1957, *Letters II*, p. 406f. See also p. 68ff of this volume.

“Entering into a collaborative relationship”

Jaffé had been aware from the end of November 1957 that Jung was debating whether to write something autobiographical himself. He let her know that in the course of their conversations so much became clearer to him, in particular “the significance of his life, the full scope of which he had not previously grasped,” as she wrote to Kurt Wolff. At the end of the year, Jung made an important decision: he began writing about his early memories, because now he was seeing “*how* he must frame them.”[1] These words reveal that the retelling of the past, whatever approach is used to elucidate, explore and relive it, is not simply a matter of acknowledging or recognizing what has been lived – it is also a process of framing and interpretation. Telling one’s story involves far more than merely reconstructing life’s events: often it becomes a process of identifying, consolidating and creating a narrative, of finding a structuring pattern of one’s life. The hand of Jung as composer and interpreter of his life story can clearly be seen in his process of describing the subject of himself. In the act of reminiscence, meaning is attributed and a particular form for telling one’s story is chosen, a particular way in which the memories are presented.[2] Jung was greatly relieved to have finally found a satisfying solution for this problem of *how* to frame and link together his memories.

In contrast to a conventional developmental narrative, he had devised the model of a dual personality – number 1 and number 2. No longer was he seeking the “rounded answer,” but had placed dynamic inner confrontations and connections in the foreground.

1 Aniela Jaffé to Kurt Wolff, 10.1.1958, YBL. Editor’s italics.
2 On biographical storytelling and narrative constructs, see also Hillman, J., 1983.

This approach now enabled him to write from a dual perspective. He presented personality number 2 as being closely connected, from his earliest years, with the collective unconscious and with the timeless, archetypal background and creative daemon. This part of him had also – unlike the outer personality number 1, which lived in the present – a "knowledge that belongs to the future."[3] Here we see once more the influence of Schopenhauer, who postulated that the choices people believe they make freely are actually based on an inevitable contingency: "He already *is* what he wills: for from that which he *is*, there follows of necessity everything that he, at any time, *does*."[4] Jung saw his personality number 2 as inevitable and decisive in terms of shaping his future life path, as well as being connected with the past, with the depths, even with eternity. This particular narrative form gave him the possibility to place significant isolated experiences, dreams and feelings from his childhood and youth in the context of a meaningful, fateful dynamic, and allowed him to draw connections between his early years and the direction of his later life and work. Not surprisingly, when Jaffé read the text, she saw it as "the confession of a man shaped by and 'chosen' by the spirit, even as a child."[5]

Jung, while clearly acknowledging that the conversations with Jaffé had prepared the ground for him to write about the beginnings of his life, described the task as an inner command: "an order from within to write up my earliest recollections."[6] This inner call required him to adopt a new attitude, namely to accept an autobiographical interest that he had previously resisted. He withdrew for several weeks to his tower at Bollingen to write, with the proviso that what he was working on would not be published until after his death: "Such a promise seemed essential to me in order to assure for myself the necessary detachment and calm."[7] The text was entitled "From the Earliest Occurrences of My Life," but Jung did not yet precisely delimit the time period, informing the publisher at the beginning of February 1958

3 See p. 180.
4 Arthur Schopenhauer, *Essay on the Freedom of the Will*, trans. Konstantin Kolenda, Indianapolis, 1960, p. 98f.
5 Aniela Jaffé to Kurt Wolff, 31.1.1958, YBL.
6 C.G. Jung to an unknown addressee, 9.1.1958, *Letters II*, p. 408 (original in English).
7 C.G. Jung to Gustav Steiner, 30.12.1957, *Letters II*, p. 406.

that "I myself don't know how far my preoccupation with my early memories will lead me." Initially he thought of ending his account "at the point where I begin with my scientific work."[8] He later considered continuing up to the point when he first came into contact with Freud, although he excluded writing about their relationship. In mid-March, he decided to end the text with his passing of the state examination for medicine, subsequently extending it as far as his marriage in 1903. His justification for ending here was one of discretion.[9]

Jung's text does follow the more or less chronological pattern of a classic biography, beginning with his birth and first memories, describing in more detail what he had told Jaffé the previous year. The earliest dream is the same as the first one recounted to her a year before, but now he reflects further and interprets the inner images as a shattering initiation.[10] The close coupling of memories from childhood and adolescence with reflections and interpretations from the perspective of old age, in which the experiences are implicitly linked with his later work and questionings, is characteristic of the entire text.

The last line by Jung, after his signature at the end of the manuscript, shows how concerned he was to make it clear to the future reader that this was a retrospective view of the past from his present perspective of old age: "Aet.s. a.82 m.8" – a Latin abbreviation giving his exact age, namely 82 years and 8 months.[11] Upon reading the first part of the manuscript, the publisher found this text to have a greater "coherence and continuity"[12] than the conversations recorded by Jaffé, where Jung's associative trains of thought and the fragmentary spontaneous nature of his reflections were much more evident.

Jaffé was very pleased that Jung himself was now writing about his early years. She informed the publisher that Jung was formulating the

8 C.G. Jung to Kurt Wolff, 1.2.1958, YBL/*Letters II*, p. 414.

9 "The reason he gave seemed to me valid for the first time (...). He said that if he continued writing beyond that point and wished to be truthful, he would have to write things that for reasons of discretion he could not reveal"; Aniela Jaffé to Kurt Wolff, 25.3.1958, AAJD.

10 Cf. Jaffé, A. (ed.), 1962, p. 15.

11 Aetatis suae anno 82, mensibus 8; at the end of March 1958, Jung was 82 years and 8 months old, he completed the text on 7 April 1958; typescript "Von den anfänglichen Ereignissen meines Lebens," ETH.

12 Handwritten note by Kurt Wolff, 19.2.1958. YBL

text completely afresh, not wishing to use the notes she had compiled in the meantime.[13] To Jung she proposed withdrawing from the biography project. But he did not agree. Later, she disclosed more of her position during this phase: "When I began working on this project, emotions ran high from the very start. A lot of people were envious and jealous of me. I also realized early on that there would be certain reservations on the part of Jung's family about the publication of a biography. So, at that point, I would have been more than willing to stop. But Jung insisted that he wanted to continue the work with me."[14] Her sense of loyalty toward Jung and her contract with Pantheon compelled her to feel obliged to carry on. She therefore told the publisher that she would continue for the time being, as Jung did not know where his text would lead. Jaffé had "urged him to write as much and for as long as possible. He knows that I would be most delighted if he were to write about the whole of his life, even if there were then hardly any use for the protocols." That, however, she deemed a highly unlikely "extreme case."[15] The form the two manuscripts would finally take and how they ultimately might be combined, remained open. Mindful of the unpredictable further developments, Jaffé at this point was working only on writing up the protocols of previous conversations. She therefore asked Wolff to suspend the advance payments which had begun some months before. She continued to see the entire endeavor as an experiment with an uncertain outcome. Furthermore, she regarded the creative process behind her contribution as incompatible with material obligation and had therefore not touched any of the money transferred from New York, so as to be able to return it if necessary.

During her visits to Bollingen, Jung allowed Jaffé to read his handwritten text as it progressed. He was writing almost without interruption, and she described him as "absorbed, fulfilled and satisfied" by the work,[16] but also beset by doubts about its worth. Repeatedly

13 Jaffé said on various occasions that Jung had not read her protocols; in her letter to Kurt Wolff on 27.10.1957, however, she indicated that Jung had checked and possibly expanded on or corrected some of her notes before they were written up as a complete conversation record: "The last 3 or 4 pages are somewhat messy, but Jg. has taken them along to Bollingen and wants to look through them again." YBL.

14 Aniela Jaffé in conversation with Robert Hinshaw, 14.6.1991, AAJD.

15 Aniela Jaffé to Kurt Wolff, 10.1.1958, 29.1.1958. YBL.

16 Ibid.

he told her that he pictured his children as his readers, whom he had explicitly addressed in his introduction. The text was written in "a nice leather-bound folio," Jaffé wrote to Wolff. Later Jung would say that this process of looking back was connected with looking ahead to death, as in a movement of drawing back in order to get a better start before a jump: "I am trying to see the thread that has led me into my life, into the world, and will lead me out again."[17]

Accustomed to Jung's surprising changes of heart, Jaffé was fairly optimistic that he would ultimately agree to publication in his lifetime. She feared, however, that the project could encounter opposition from the family, as Jung's children saw their father primarily as a private individual and not as a figure of public interest.[18] Her fears were not entirely unfounded. The project had heretofore not received much attention from those closest to him, but with Jung's obvious increasing enthusiasm for his autobiographical writing, they could no longer overlook it. However, the resistance came less from his daughters, as feared by Jaffé, but rather from his son and daughter-in-law. Jung was understandably "somewhat disturbed" by this, but continued to hold fast to the project.[19]

In the meantime, there was uproar on the other side of the Atlantic: the publisher was extremely alarmed at the surprising turn of events – both with regard to Jung's actual autobiographical writing and to the resistance against allowing anything to be published before his death. Worse, Wolff feared that Jung would give his text to Rascher while Jaffé edited the protocols for an English edition with Pantheon, an idea which Jung had recently voiced. If "two autobiographies were to be published in parallel,"[20] he wrote to Jung and Jaffé, the autobiography by C.G. Jung would have much more commercial success

17 See p. 151. Jung's text about the first twenty-five years of his life ultimately spans the arc toward death. Jung originally wrote a dedication for the text, which to Jaffé's regret was deleted due to the objections of Kurt Wolff, Cary Baynes and translator R.F.C. Hull. In the dedication, Jung stressed that everything he wrote was to a certain extent a letter to the world and was consciously or unconsciously directed at an audience. Here, he said, he imagined his children in the front row of the auditorium and he wished to tell them about his dimly recalled beginnings and the course his life had taken; cf. C.G. Jung, typescript "*Von den anfänglichen Ereignissen meines Lebens,*" p. 1, ETH.

18 Aniela Jaffé to Kurt Wolff, 29.1.1958, YBL.

19 Aniela Jaffé to Kurt Wolff, 7.3.1958, YBL. See also p. 77f.

20 Kurt Wolff to C.G. Jung enclosed with a letter to Aniela Jaffé, 26.1.1958. YBL, AAJD.

than a work by the as-yet unknown author Aniela Jaffé. Moreover, Wolff knew that Rascher, Routledge & Kegan Paul, and the Bollingen Foundation had contractual rights to works written by Jung. Jaffé and Jung had repeatedly expressed just a few months previously that they were wary of contravening any legitimate claims of other publishing houses by entering into contractual agreements with Pantheon.[21]

Later, Wolff would refer to the news about these plans of Jung as a "catastrophe" to be averted at all costs. In order to protect his interests, the publisher felt an urgent need to intervene in the creation and formation process, and even to control and define it. He wanted Jung's text to be seen as an extension of Jaffé's project to be combined with the protocols of the conversations. This had to be contractually settled as quickly as possible. Wolff now emphasized to Jung the value of the "revelations that you entrusted to Aniela Jaffé."[22] "Nothing you have written in books or said in lectures goes so directly to the heart, to the innermost center" as these conversation records, and they could not be "more purely or lucidly expressed."[23] Although some additions and smoothing out would be desirable, Wolff at this point regarded the conversations as already forming a successful whole. He expected and hoped that Jung was planning a "*conjunctio* of the written and spoken word."

Jung replied that it was indeed the conversations with Jaffé that had given him the impetus to look more closely at his early memories. He saw his text as a kind of support for her work, in which he and she would "enter into a collaborative relationship. I contribute my bit, so to speak."[24] As long as everything was still in flux and in a formative state, however, he refused to speculate about its future use in any possible book, and of course also rejected the request for a corresponding contractual agreement.

Despite Jung having thus made his position clear, Wolff immediately penned an addition to the contract in which "the autobiographical

21 Aniela Jaffé to Kurt Wolff, 28.10.1957, 2.11.1957, 6.11.1957, C.G. Jung to John Barrett, Bollingen Foundation, 6.11.1957, with copy to Sir Herbert Read, Routledge & Kegan Paul, YBL; see also p. 262.
22 Kurt Wolff to C.G. Jung, 26.1.1958, AAJD.
23 Ibid.
24 C.G. Jung to Kurt Wolff, 1.2.1958, YBL.

material is to be combined with the information shared verbally with Frau Aniela Jaffé in such a way that a complete book is produced under the editorial responsibility of Frau Jaffé, who will proceed according to the instructions of Professor Jung."[25] In his drafted addition to the contract, the publisher also stipulated that all requests regarding autobiographical material addressed to Jung, in writing or verbally, from other publishers, magazines, journalists or agents must be forwarded to Kurt Wolff "to be dealt with." Even though he had been suffering severe health problems since the beginning of the year, Kurt Wolff promptly booked a flight to Zürich for himself and his wife Helene, innocuously describing the trip as a "short vacation" in a telegram to Jaffé.[26] Jaffé's initial reaction to Wolff's insistence on a fusion of both manuscripts was reticent, and she again reminded him how important it was for the creative process to unfold without interference. Jung required complete freedom to decide what would happen with his newly written text. When she furthermore pointed out that Rascher might have rights to Jung's essay, Helene Wolff countered that her husband had always gotten what he wanted – and he would get his way this time, too.[27] Upon arriving in Zürich and finding that Jung was about to take a break in Minusio, Ticino, the Wolffs proceeded southward posthaste.

Jung had authorized Jaffé to transcribe his manuscript and to give a copy to Wolff.[28] Ahead of their meeting in Ticino, Wolff read the first thirty-nine pages of Jung's text,[29] along with a few more of Jaffé's conversation protocols. In the publisher's opinion, the inner life was fully present in Jung's text, but he saw many gaps in the description of the outer life. He found it imperative that Jung write and say more about personality number 1. Wolff now sang Jaffé's praises to Jung, applauding her sensitivity in carrying out and recording the conversations. He considered Jaffé to be quite free of personal ambition. With her modest manner, he attributed a *grandeur d'âme to her* that had

25 Draft contract by Kurt Wolff, dated 8.2.1958, YBL.
26 Telegram from Kurt Wolff to Aniela Jaffé, 12.2.1958, AAJD.
27 Cf. Aniela Jaffé to Kurt Wolff, 17.1.1961, AAJD.
28 Aniela Jaffé to Kurt Wolff, 31.1.1958, YBL.
29 "Von den anfänglichen Ereignissen meines Lebens," C.G. Jung, typescript ETH.

been missing with an "Eckermann."[30] Wolff moreover again emphasized what a fascinating treasure trove of material was contained in the protocols. He told Jung that the direct tone of the conversation records would provide a lively complement to Jung's own text, and that it was therefore essential to weave both parts together.

Wolff was successful in persuading Jung to agree to combine the protocols with the autobiographical text. However, he had to accept that Jung was determined to postpone publication in German indefinitely and would only permit publication in English. Also, Jung wanted to leave in place the original publishing contract between Aniela Jaffé and Pantheon along with his assignment of rights to her of October 1957, but he put a limit of ten years on Pantheon's right to use extracts from his earlier autobiographical texts. Wolff then employed all his powers of persuasion to obtain Jung's authorization for advance publication of selected chapters of Jaffé's book in magazines. In return, he offered Jung an unusually high advance of ten thousand Swiss francs. Before his return to the USA, the publisher sent Jung a case of wine, "in veneration" and as "strength and solace for the demands placed on number 1."[31]

Once back in New York, he sent a "Memo for Prof. Dr. C.G. Jung and Frau Aniela Jaffé" containing a list of the outcomes of his discussions with Jung. The central point of the memo was Wolff's assertion that Pantheon owned the exclusive world copyright for the book project commissioned by the publishing house, including "the spoken communications to Frau Jaffé as well as whatever Dr. Jung is putting down in autobiographical writing himself."[32] As neither the conversation records nor Jung's text belonged to Jung's "Works,"[33] all rights claimed by other publishers were invalid, according to Wolff. He was aware of the audacity of this formulation, in particular the contention that Jung was working under commission to Pantheon – Jung wrote only in response to his own inner drive and in no way

30 Handwritten note from Kurt Wolff, 19.2.1958, YBL.
31 Handwritten note from Kurt Wolff, 25.2.1958, YBL. On Wolff's demand for more material on Jung's personality number 1, see also his letter to C.G. Jung of 3.6.1958, YBL. The sum of 10,000 Swiss francs then corresponds to an amount today of close to 50,000 Swiss Francs.
32 Memo from Kurt Wolff, Pantheon Books, 4.3.1958, YBL (original in English).
33 "not belonging to Dr. Jung's 'Works'"., ibid.

because of a commission by Wolff or Pantheon.[34] Neither Jaffé nor Jung was willing to sign this memo without legal advice. Jung's lawyer Hans Karrer was of the opinion that the agreement would infringe Rascher Verlag's rights. Jaffé therefore, with the agreement of Jung, proposed to submit this issue to an independent lawyer from the Swiss Society of Authors so as to check the validity of Wolff's formulation.[35] In addition, she sent this lawyer copies of five contracts agreed upon between Rascher and Jung from the years 1953 to 1957. Wolff thus found himself having to meet with lawyer Beidler to discuss the matter during his planned summer vacation in Switzerland. Before the legal issues had been settled, however, and heedless of Jung's veto on a publication of the material in German, shortly after his return to America, Wolff negotiated a contractual agreement with S. Fischer Verlag in New York. The agreement granted the German publishing rights to S. Fischer and obliged the latter to produce a print-run of 50,000 paperbacks with a minimum selling price of 10 Deutschmarks per copy.[36]

With Jung himself taking a chronological approach in his text, Wolff gained a strong argument against the proposed structure hitherto favored by Jaffé, which had been to present excerpts from the protocols according to specific topics and their respective dates. This approach would provide readers with a valuable insight into Jung's associative style of thinking, she believed, and would show how his reflections varied on different days. Wolff, on the other hand, had long been advocating a linear chronological structure with thematically organized chapters.[37] In a conversation at the end of February, he

34 In an accompanying letter of 4.3.1958 to Aniela Jaffé, Kurt Wolff wrote, "I hate to use the word 'commissioned' but I don't know another one to make this point clear and avoid the danger in question." YBL (original in English).

35 Cf. Aniela Jaffé to Kurt Wolff, 17.3.1958, AAJD, YBL. On doubts about the legal validity, see "Memo for Prof. Dr. C.G. Jung and Frau Aniela Jaffé" from Pantheon Books, 4.3.1958, according to the correspondence apparently not signed by Jung and Jaffé until 31.3.1958; cf. Aniela Jaffé to Kurt Wolff, 31.3.1958, YBL, AAJD.

36 Agreement between S. Fischer Corporation and Pantheon Books Inc., 12.3.1958, YBL.

37 In a note to Wolff a short time before, Wolfgang Sauerländer had supported Jaffé's approach, but in vain: "It is probably wrong to force this material into something resembling chronological sequence. [...] Jung's method of circling around cardinal preoccupations rather than following a straight line, a method that involves repetition and elaboration, makes it impossible or undesirable to edit the material to conform to one-dimensional logics." His recommendation: "Leave everything basically

presented Jaffé with the provisional titles of eight chapters.[38] He also asked her to as soon as possible create a draft manuscript combining the contents from the protocols with Jung's text, an "amalgamation" as he called it. In his opinion, Jung's text also needed stylistic editing.

Wolff continued to keep Jaffé in the dark with regard to the involvement of Wolfgang Sauerländer and Cary Baynes, but he did at this point inform her about "his" draft of a chapter on Freud. Jaffé thereupon pointed out that Théodore Flournoy and William James had also been significant influences on Jung at that time and would therefore also need to be taken into account in such a chapter. Her intervention, it would soon become clear, fell on deaf ears. On March 10, Wolff sent her his "nicely rounded off" chapter on Freud, which incorporated excerpts from the 1925 seminar, but wrote that "adding the pages about Flournoy and William James would seem very disturbing to me."[39] He was, however, very much hoping for "some statements from CGJ that will let readers know what he has to say about *sex*."[40] This request illustrates how the publisher pushed the boundaries of his role further and further in an editorial direction. The contents and topics he chose to focus upon took little or no account of Jung's actual experiences and statements, or of the historically relevant factors. Jaffé was repeatedly reassured that she would have full freedom in shaping the material, and yet he continually interfered in the process.

Wolff's haste to finalize a chapter on Freud, while obviously for economic and publicity related reasons, also revealed that he considered the relationship with Freud to be a key part of Jung's biography. That view, however, did not correspond with Jung's own assessment

as it is (A.J. original recommendation)." Memo of 6.2.1958 from Wolfgang Sauerländer to Kurt Wolff, YBL (original in English).

38 Handwritten notes by Kurt Wolff, 22.2.1958, listing the following chapters: "Prologue?, I Early Years, II Freud and Break with Freud, III 1912–1931, IV Contemporaries, V Africa (North and East), VI India, VII Visions 1944, VIII Late Insights and Dreams," YBL.

39 Kurt Wolff to Aniela Jaffé, 6.3.1958, YBL. Without waiting for Jaffé's and Jung's reactions to his chapter draft, Wolff commissioned Richard Winston with the translation, which Winston supplied at the beginning of May. Cf. Richard Winston to Kurt Wolff, 4.5.1958, YBL.

40 Kurt Wolff to Aniela Jaffé, 6.3.1958, YBL. In a letter from Kurt Wolff to C.G. Jung a short while later, Wolff's preoccupation with selling advance publication rights to periodicals with print-run figures in the millions such as *Life* and *Saturday Evening Post* becomes evident. Such deals would potentially bring in around 250,000 Swiss francs, but he needed to be able to offer light and easy-to-read excerpts on appealing topics, wrote Wolff; cf. Kurt Wolff to C.G. Jung, 3.6.1958, YBL.

of its significance for his life and work. Even in old age, Jung often repeated that he found it difficult to write about the period during which he and Freud were in close contact. When informing Jaffé at the start of March 1958 that he would perhaps integrate the encounter into his autobiographical text, he described it as "a challenging task." Jaffé wished that the relationship should be dealt with in a "conciliatory" – though not uncritical – manner.[41] In the end, it was up to her to describe the relationship, and she did so without omitting the conflicts and divergent opinions, while maintaining an honoring and respectful attitude towards Freud.

In the meantime, Jung continued working on his text. Jaffé attempted to combine Jung's initial pages with comments from their conversations. In so doing, she also rearranged his text slightly for chronological reasons, and tentatively shortened or lengthened some sections. She submitted this draft to Jung for his critical appraisal at the beginning of March 1958, along with the full body of her notes. In a letter to the publisher, she mentioned that Jung was very satisfied with her "'amalgamation' attempts."[42] In the continuation of his text, Jung now referred to the talks with Jaffé and shortened descriptions of dreams, commenting that he had already told them to Jaffé – a clear indication that he was expecting her notes to be incorporated into a final version.[43] Jaffé, for her part, began to order her material thematically, identifying sections from the protocols that would fit under provisional chapter headings or themes. With Jung's permission, she added material from further sources, in particular regarding his psychiatric work. While filling certain gaps to accommodate some demands of Wolff, she took a critical stance toward other concerns of his, e.g., the wish for more material on "sex." She maintained that Jung had written "comprehensively and effectively" on the subject in his most recent book *Flying Saucers: A Modern Myth*, and "the things he has told me sound very meager in comparison."[44]

41 Aniela Jaffé to Kurt Wolff, 7.3.1958, YBL.
42 Ibid. The draft consisted of the first fifteen typescript pages of Jung's text with editorial changes. Jaffé later divided the complete text of "From the Earliest Experiences of My Life" into three chapters: First Years, School Years, Student Years.
43 Cf. typescript, p. 70, ETH; see Jaffé, A. (ed.), p. 84f.
44 Aniela Jaffé to Kurt Wolff, 12.3.1958, YBL. For C.G. Jung's discussion of sex in *Flying Saucers: A*

The following months saw her working intensively on the challenging biography project, after having completed her book *Geistererscheinungen und Vorzeichen* [*Death Dreams and Ghosts*]. It had been published by Rascher in the spring and met with great interest and acclaim in the press. Wolff and his wife also praised the book effusively in a letter to her: "I cannot tell you how impressed we both are: the organization of the material, the clarity of the interpretation, the beautiful language and the readable style are outstanding." He was astonished at her familiarity with "every idea from all of Jung's work" and how completely *au fait* she was with the immense body of literature.[45] At this point, Wolff was in need of Jaffé's cooperation more than ever if the fusion of Jung's text with her material was to be successful. He furthermore wanted to be able to rely upon her as an important ally in securing the rights and making the Pantheon project a reality. These fulsome words of admiration would, however, be the last such positive sentiments for a long time, as the relationship became increasingly conflictual.

From Jaffé's notes, it seems that the conversations between Jung and her in the first half of 1958 consisted less of free and spontaneous talking by Jung; rather they involved questions and answers concerning specific topics and renewed circumambulations of early experiences, fueled by his own writing in the winter months. A good example of the tone and the dynamic between them during this phase is Jaffé's description of a conversation on May 16, 1958. She had asked Jung to tell her more about his travel experiences: "My method of questioning has changed quite a lot recently. (...) I explain to him what I want to know, more or less, and then I wait. He usually starts reluctantly. And then he goes silent, and I wait. It is not easy to refrain from saying something or asking again, but I can sense very clearly that he is sinking into himself, and then it comes: a memory or an emotion. And then again, silence. Sometimes, a long silence. And then toward the end of the afternoon things sometimes become very lively when a vein

Modern Myth, see CW 10, para. 631–655.

45 Kurt Wolff to Aniela Jaffé, 9.4.1958, YBL. The tone of the correspondence in the spring of 1958 is markedly warm on both sides, probably not least due to the fact that Helene Wolff had informed Aniela Jaffé in confidence of her husband's fragile state of health.

has been struck and it flows. At the start, when there was still so much to tell, it was very different. Now he enjoyed talking about Africa, and the next morning he told me he remembered some letters he had written to his wife from India and Africa that I could use."[46]

It was a time of intense work for Jaffé – in addition to conducting the conversations, writing them up and researching biographical source material, she also produced the first drafts of several chapters. One of those was devoted to Jung's confrontation with the unconscious after his break with Freud, another to his body of work, and a third to Bollingen as his place of retreat. Going over her draft of the chapter "The Work" with Jung on May 9, 1958,[47] she elicited additional input from him. One month before – on April 7 – Jung had finished his autobiographical text. After describing his departure from Basel and initial work at Burghölzli in Zürich, he ended his narrative with a philosophical reflection about autobiography: neither did he intend to weave an illusion about how his life ought to have been, nor did he wish to attempt a justification for it. No one, he believed, was capable of judging themselves – and any judgment must therefore be left to others.[48] As soon as a copy of Jung's text arrived in New York, the publisher, without authorization and without informing Jung or Jaffé, commissioned Richard Winston with its translation.

Wolff's insistence that Jung owed it to his readers to also write about his activities as a medical doctor and his relationship to William James was rejected by Jung. He argued that he had written extensively about psychotherapy in his other books, and as he had only met William James briefly on two occasions, he considered it an "unpardonable exercise in superficiality" to sketch a man of James' stature in a few words.[49] Having been so often misunderstood, as he explained, there

46 Aniela Jaffé to Kurt Wolff, 18.5.1958, YBL.

47 Cf. Aniela Jaffé to Kurt Wolff, 12.5.1958, YBL: "I gave over my Friday afternoon session to reading part of the chapter 'The Work' with Jung. He added some important points (...)." AAJD. At the end of May, C.G. Jung took Jaffé's three draft chapters to Bollingen to read and evaluate.

48 Cf. Jaffé, A. (ed.), 1962, p. 113.

49 Kurt Wolff now had complained about the lack of material on William James as, alongside Freud, he was "the most important one to the Anglo-Saxon, specifically the American reader," while Richard Wilhelm, about whom Jung had talked more, was scarcely known in the US; cf. Kurt Wolff to Aniela Jaffé, 28.5.1958, YBL (original in English). On 3.6.1958, Wolff wrote to Jung about the planned advance publication of excerpts and said that it was important to provide for this purpose

was no desire to recall significant conversations – "for me life was something that had to be lived and not talked about."[50] It fell to Jaffé, therefore, to compile a chapter about Jung's clinical practice from a variety of sources. In so doing, she returned to her original plan of presenting Jung's remarks according to the dates when they had taken place. "In this way it feels like a spoken diary. And it means I can avoid the necessity of formulating transitional phrases which feel artificial."[51] Although Jaffé was unaware of it, this approach was in line with the narrative style now also favored by Sauerländer. Since November 1957, Wolff had been providing Sauerländer with all of the notes sent by Jaffé to New York. Sauerländer made editorial comments regarding how to structure the material, inserted corrections and added bibliographical information. He also evaluated the contents and, like Wolff, marked the parts he found interesting and those he thought should be cut or shortened. Clearly he, like Wolff, did not respect Jaffé as the author or editor of the book, but rather considered her as a supplier of data that was to be evaluated, arranged and edited in New York.[52]

Renewed criticisms of Jung for alleged National Socialist sympathies appearing in the American and British press in May 1958[53] irritated Wolff. Although he had originally not been considering inclusion of this topic in the biography, he now, after consulting with Cary Baynes, went a step further in his content-related instructions to Jaffé and Jung. Wolff now not only designated what Jung should write *about*, but *what* he should actually say in order to end the controversy once and for all. He suggested that it would be a "wonderful solution" if, with regard to his official function within the *Allgemeinen*

chapters on Freud, on psychiatric case studies, and on William James, but not about Bollingen, for example. YBL.

50 C.G. Jung to Kurt Wolff, 17.6.1958, *Letters II*, p. 452f.

51 Aniela Jaffé to Kurt Wolff, 25.6.1958, YBL

52 In addition to a large number of handwritten comments and questions from Wolff, Sauerländer's editorial notes, handwritten or typed, can be seen on or between the copies sent by Jaffé. Cf. protocols 1956–1958, LoC.

53 American psychoanalyst A.D. Parellhof in *The New York Times Book Review*, 11.5.1958, and *The New Statesman*, 17.5.1958. Cf. also C.G. Jung, *Letters II*, p. 443f. Jung told Jaffé that the accusations would not be silenced despite many attempts to set the record straight and said he was no longer willing to go into it again. His daughter Marianne Niehus-Jung was also of the opinion that the topic should not be taken up again. On 16.5.1958, Jaffé wrote to Kurt Wolff on the subject: "Jung never saw Nazism as anything other than diabolical." YBL.

ärztlichen Gesellschaft für Psychotherapie [General Medical Society for Psychotherapy] in the early thirties, Jung would simply state: "I made a mistake."[54] Neither Jung nor Jaffé agreed.[55]

Wolff's focus on a broad American reading public was becoming more and more apparent. He increased the pressure on Jaffé regarding his content demands. For example, because Charcot was for Americans "the most popular name" in European psychiatry, and as Janet was better known than Flournoy, it was imperative that Jung should say something about the first two.[56] After discussing three of Jaffé's draft chapters with Cary Baynes and Wolfgang Sauerländer, Wolff finally revealed their editorial involvement to her at the end of May.[57] Backed by Baynes and Sauerländer, he now recommended deleting all general reflections of a philosophical or mythological nature from the manuscript whenever they were not directly related to the context.[58] Such reflections could possibly be gathered in a chapter about "Religion, Death and the Hereafter" or "Religious Thoughts," Wolff proposed. Not surprisingly, Jaffé and Jung did not concur.

Jaffé did not immediately comment upon the involvement of Sauerländer and Baynes. She did, however, express her radically different viewpoint regarding the presentation of the material, all the while maintaining her customary polite and conciliatory tone: "[…] You and I have two completely different conceptions of the book's final form […]. As I was thinking over your comments, I actually returned once again to my original plan, which I never defended strongly enough, namely a presentation of the biographical material ordered by date à

54 Kurt Wolff to Aniela Jaffé, 21.5.1958, YBL (original in English). He was referring to Jung's acceptance of the presidency of the abovementioned society in 1933 and his editorship of the "*Zentralblatt für Psychotherapie.*" Cf. C.G. Jung, CW 10, para. 1016ff.

55 Jung told Jaffé that in hindsight and based upon what was later known, it had been wrong to take over the leadership of the society. At the time, however, he had been concerned with saving the society with the aim of creating an international status for excluded German-Jewish colleagues, and of maintaining cultural exchange through the "*Zentralblatt.*" C.G. Jung in conversation with Aniela Jaffé, 4.6.1958, AAJD. Cf. also Jaffé, A., 1985, "C.G. Jung and National Socialism."

56 Kurt Wolff to Aniela Jaffé, 12.5.1958, AAJD, YBL (original in English).

57 Kurt Wolff to Aniela Jaffé, 28.5.1958, YBL.

58 It would much improve the text "if one would take out of the chapters radically all general remarks, mythological and others (…)"; Wolff added a handwritten note citing Cary Baynes' assessment of the dedication to Jung's children: "dedication to the family wrong," as the book "belongs to the world"; Kurt Wolff to Aniela Jaffé, 28.5.1958, YBL (original in English).

la Eckermann [...]."[59] Jaffé had developed her own initial concept for the complete structure of the book's contents in the spring of 1958. According to her, the greatest challenge was the task of "small ordering," i.e., of joining together remarks on the same topic from different conversations and times, while also rendering a coherent flowing text. She compared the individual sections from different protocols to "mosaic stones" or "jigsaw pieces" with which she was trying to compose a bigger picture. She informed the publisher that the bulk of her work was taken up with attempting to combine the various sections and sentences, bridge the gaps and turn "the spoken word into the written form without completely changing the style."[60] Whenever she added something of her own, she showed it to Jung at an early stage, such as a section of the Bollingen chapter: "I 'composed' one section myself, and was pleased when Jung approved of it."[61] After Jung's refusal to write about William James, Wolff suggested that Jaffé should write a few pages about Jung's thoughts on James in a simple and readable style,[62] a suggestion she rejected. They agreed to spend two weeks discussing various editorial issues in more depth during Wolff's planned visit in the summer. In the meantime, Jaffé continued with a plan of structuring the book in two parts: the first half composed of the slightly expanded and edited autobiographical text by Jung, and the second half consisting of the chapters written by Jaffé based on the protocols and other sources. Wolff now supported this approach thanks to Sauerländer, who after an initial reading of Jung's text, recommended that it be kept as intact as possible, followed by thematically grouped fragments based on Jaffé's conversation notes.[63]

At the end of July 1958, Kurt Wolff arrived in Switzerland for a stay of several weeks. In direct discussions with Jaffé, the conflicts that had been simmering between them now came to the surface. Jaffé

59 Aniela Jaffé to Kurt Wolff, 3.6.1958, YBL.
60 Aniela Jaffé to Kurt Wolff, 2.6.1958, AAJD
61 Aniela Jaffé to Kurt Wolff, 1.5.1958, YBL.
62 "... try to put in a simple and colloquial way Jung's main thoughts about James' ideology," Kurt Wolff to Aniela Jaffé, 28.5.1958, YBL (original in English).
63 Note from Wolfgang Sauerländer to Kurt Wolff, 18.4.1958, YBL, Kurt Wolff to Aniela Jaffé, 20.4.1958, YBL.

made it clear that she would be open to critical reactions once she had delivered a complete manuscript, but that at the current stage of the process, she did not appreciate the interference of other parties. While respecting Wolff's suggestions, she insisted that she alone must decide about the text for which she and Jung were ultimately responsible. After all, Wolff had entrusted her with the role of author and editor and Jung had agreed to have her as biographer, and she was claiming her right to work on the challenging project in peace. She saw herself as the author of the second part and felt alienated by the considerable editorial interference in her base material that had taken place in New York without her permission.[64] In the interest of maintaining a good working relationship, she expressed appreciation for Wolff's "continuing efforts to represent the viewpoint of the average American reader." However, the "inferred, often even explicit, pressure" from him was putting a strain on her and inhibiting her work. The process of creating this book was a unique one, as she saw it – composing and editing the chapters was challenging and time-consuming. New and valuable material was still coming from Jung. "The work is a process and it grows like a tree which cannot be forced to flower or bear fruit. It requires the cold nights as well as the rain and sun."[65]

When Kurt Wolff's wife Helene wrote to her at the end of August attempting to persuade her to turn over additional chapters to her husband for mutual discussion, Jaffé responded: "At the moment I must continue working alone, as no chapter is far enough along for us to look through it together."[66] A prologue written by Kurt Wolff as an alternative to hers was not favorably received. Despite the continuing decidedly courteous and friendly tone of the correspondence, Jaffé's independent and resolute character was becoming more and more evident. In order to obtain constructive feedback from an expert in the field, she asked her friend Erich Neumann, who was in Europe for

64 A short time before, she had already told Wolff in a more subtle and humorous way that she perceived his actions as a violation and invasion: alluding to the voracious fairy-tale wolf, she signed off a letter from "Little Red Riding-Hood's Grandmother"; Aniela Jaffé to Kurt Wolff, 12.6.1958, YBL.

65 Aniela Jaffé to Kurt Wolff, 8.8.1958, YBL.

66 Aniela Jaffé to Helene Wolff, 25.8.1958, YBL.

an extended stay during the summer of 1958, to read and evaluate her chapter on Jung's psychiatric and clinical activities.

Jaffé and Wolff were able to resolve the content-related questions for the chapters drafted in the spring quite compatibly, even though Wolff continued to request more material on Jung's worldly personality number 1. When it came to discussing corrections that Wolff and Annemarie von Puttkamer[67] had made to Jung's text, however, their opinions diverged greatly. Jaffé could not accept the "casual attitude with which you correct Jung's text," to make it "more understandable" for an imagined average American reader.[68] Responding to an attempt by Helene Wolff to smooth things over, Jaffé explained: "I stood in for old Jung, or at least tried to do so, after he had shown such trust in me – for him a very rare thing – by putting this manuscript in my hands. (...) My aim was to preserve Jung's character – which I admit is at times idiosyncratic – in the text as far as possible. Here two worlds collided and it became a power struggle."[69] Jaffé managed to reverse many of Wolff's changes. She also succeeded in saving the final section of Jung, which the publisher wanted to cut completely. But she was shocked to learn that Kurt Wolff had already sent the text of "From the Earliest Experiences of My Life" to the English translator in mid-May 1958, without obtaining Jung's authorization or waiting for Jaffé's manuscript combining his written text with her protocol excerpts.[70] She refused to hand over her draft chapters for a translation, insisting that she did not yet regard them as completed. In a letter two months later, she would remind him how clearly she had "both quietly

67 The writer Annemarie von Puttkamer, 1891–1983, had been a close associate and colleague of Kurt Wolff since the twenties and translated the works of Anne Morrow Lindbergh into German for Pantheon Books. She spent the summer of 1958 with Kurt Wolff during his wife's absence. See also Kurt Wolff to Aniela Jaffé, 9.8.1958 and 10.9.1958, as well as six pages of undated handwritten notes by Jaffé pertaining to Kurt Wolff's correction suggestions, YBL. During that summer, Puttkamer also helped Wolff transcribe the correspondence between Freud and Jung, which he was considering for publication. However, after consulting with Kurt Eissler of the Freud Archive, Jung retracted his agreement. Cf. C.G. Jung to Kurt Eissler, 20.7.1958, Aniela Jaffé to Kurt Wolff, 4.8.1958, Kurt Eissler to C.G. Jung, 13.8.1958, Aniela Jaffé to John Barrett, copies to Sir Herbert Read, Kurt Wolff, 27.8.1958, YBL.

68 Aniela Jaffé to Kurt Wolff, 8.9.1958, AAJD.

69 Aniela Jaffé to Helene Wolff, 18.9.1958, AAJD, YBL.

70 Kurt Wolff had already commissioned Richard Winston to translate Jung's text on 15.5.1958.

and loudly, up to the limits of politeness, warned and warned him. (...) All my warnings, my objections, my pleas (...) were thrown to the wind, with the result that I finally despaired, resigned, and could no longer muster up the spirit to prevent you taking concrete measures whose dire consequences I foresaw."[71]

The repeated use of the word "amalgamation" to describe Jaffé's work on editing Jung's text and combining it with the protocols is misleading. An amalgamation implies a commingling or fusion, which is not at all what actually occurred. First, Jaffé added to Jung's text by inserting sections from the notes of their previous conversations. The three chapters produced in this way were then edited together with Jung during 1959 and 1960. The two of them completed, amended, deleted or rearranged text, and also made use of further source material. For the most part, however, Jung's original text was kept almost untouched, except for adapting the orthography to contemporary spelling. In spring 1960, further changes were suggested by the translator R.F.C. Hull.

Jung later described his original text for the first three chapters as a "sketch" or "draft" that he had provided to Jaffé.[72] He personally checked the English translation of the German text that had been edited by him and Jaffé, and a few weeks before Jung's death, a manuscript was ready which both Jung and Jaffé believed was the final one. Neither of them anticipated that shortly after his death, some family members would demand drastic changes to the "School Years" chapter. This conflict and its consequences will be described in detail on page 320ff.

Meanwhile, toward the end of his extended trip in summer 1958, Wolff had also encountered a legal stumbling block. At a meeting on September 3, the lawyer for the Swiss Society of Authors, Beidler, agreed with the opinion of Jung's lawyer Hans Karrer that Rascher Verlag had a valid right of first refusal for the publication of all further written works by C.G. Jung on the basis of existing contracts.[73] The

71 Aniela Jaffé to Kurt Wolff, 13.11.1958, YBL.

72 Cf. C.G. Jung to Jolande Jacobi, 25.8.1960, *Letters II*, p. 585, and Walther Niehus, representing C.G. Jung, to Rascher, 11.5.1960, to Cecil Franklin, 12.5.1960, Zentralbibliothek Zürich.

73 Four contracts from the years 1953, 1954 and 1957 between Rascher Verlag and C.G. Jung stipulated that Rascher had priority over other publishers to the rights to further works by C.G. Jung.

copyright transferred by Jung to Jaffé in the Pantheon contract was seen to be affecting prior agreements with Rascher. Beidler therefore strongly advised that Max Rascher should be informed about the current project and the arrangement with Pantheon as soon as possible. He recommended that Jung meet with Rascher senior personally to explain the situation "in good faith."[74] Jung's lawyer Karrer additionally advised that the English-language publisher of the *Collected Works* should also be informed about Jung's now substantial contribution to the present book, as their contracts also granted a right of first refusal on all future texts by Jung, and that a declaration of renouncement might be necessary.[75]

On September 19, 1958, before Wolff's departure, he and Jaffé visited Jung at Bollingen to discuss the provisional outline of the book's contents. At this meeting, Jung explained his determination to keep the Latin and Greek expressions in the text, regardless of the American readership. The protocol of this conversation was the last Wolff received from Jaffé,[76] as the conflict between the two of them soon escalated further. At this point, however, relations were still friendly enough that Jaffé gave Wolff a departure gift on the occasion of Yom Kippur, the Jewish Day of Atonement. She offered him a phonograph record of compositions by J.S. Bach with an accompanying note: "In memory of the Zürich summer of 1958, our work together, our conversations, our quarrels and fights, and your old AJ."[77] A note from Kurt Wolff in his wife Helene's handwriting thanked Jaffé for her time, patience and understanding for the "impatience of the old publisher who is eagerly awaiting YOUR book."[78] On the return voyage to America by ship, Wolff reflected on the reasons for their "great difficulties in working together," even though his "feeling, regard and respect" for Jaffé had grown constantly over the course of the summer. Jaffé, claimed Wolff, considered Jung "a great thinker and great writer"

74 Report by lawyer Beidler, dated 5.9.1958, based on the meeting of 3.9.1958, YBL.

75 Cf. Hans Karrer to Kurt Wolff, 16.6.1958, YBL.

76 Jaffé wrote at the top of the protocol "With K.W. in Bollingen, 19.10.1958" – on this date Kurt Wolff was already back in the USA. The conversation actually took place on September 18 or 19, 1958.

77 Handwritten note from Aniela Jaffé to Kurt Wolff, 24.9.1958, YBL.

78 Handwritten note from Helene Wolff on behalf of Kurt Wolff to Aniela Jaffé, 26.9.1958, YBL.

and thus defended his every word, whereas for Wolff, Jung was a great mind, but no writer: "*Il n'est pas du métier.*" He thus wanted "to take on, as the most modest of servants, the delicate task of editing" to improve "jumbled formulations" and "balance the unbalanced."[79]

In mid-October 1958, Jung and Jaffé discussed at length the form and structure of several draft chapters. On his first reading of the text in the summer, Jung had concentrated primarily on the content; this time, he focused on language and style. For Jaffé, the complex question now arose of how to satisfactorily combine the publisher's, Jung's and her own goals. It concerned Jung that she had inserted several phrases of her own in his name, i.e., using the first person singular, when joining together disparate protocol fragments. Even though the content of these formulations was correct, Jung felt that their style and tone was "too feminine" and he therefore could not entirely recognize himself in them.[80] He now wished – exactly as Jaffé had originally proposed to the publisher and had enacted in her draft of the chapter on psychiatric activities – to have sections ordered by date without any transitional or connecting sentences. He also pondered eliminating chapter headings altogether, which Jaffé agreed would certainly be a possibility: "The result would be longer or shorter statements that do not need to be connected in any way, like in a diary, appearing as fragmentary notes."[81] Notably, Jaffé later chose to use such a form for the present volume, *Reflections*. Jung also preferred having Jaffé become more visible in the text, and for her to insert her own questions and reflections on his remarks, even her own dreams. Furthermore, he found it essential to render the joint authorship and the unusual genesis of the book transparent.[82] Jung's desire for Jaffé to have greater

79 Kurt Wolff to Aniela Jaffé, 8.10.1958, YBL. See also p. 80.

80 Aniela Jaffé to Helene Wolff, 14.10.1958: "What bothers him is the fact that I have taken his comments about a particular topic from a variety of protocols of different dates and fused them together into a complete chapter. He is disturbed by it because in this 'welding work' I had to add quite some words of my own in the first person. And also some of the things he said himself had to be rearranged to make the whole thing fit together. He says that he no longer fully recognizes himself in it, that it contains a feminine influence." YBL

81 Ibid.

82 "It is incredibly important to Jung that the situation is clear to the reader. For this reason he asks you [...] to use my postscript as a foreword, as I will use it to orient the reader about the book's genesis. He also asks you (I also raised this question myself as I was always, as you know, unsure about

presence in the text corresponded with her original suggestion that she include her explanatory voice or commentary in the background. Thus, much of what Jung was now suggesting was in line with Jaffé's original ideas for the book's structure. Jaffé wrote to Wolff about the proposed changes and, anticipating a strong reaction, asked him to try not to see it in terms of a battle with a winner and a loser: "If Jung is now wanting to do things the way I had suggested, it only means that I knew him better."[83]

A few days later, Jaffé showed Jung her draft of a chapter about Freud, taking into account his new instructions, to which he reacted positively.[84] She disregarded the Freud chapter compiled by Wolff (and Sauerländer). Jung and Jaffé subsequently agreed that, rather than including her questions, she would add only occasional commentaries or explanations in her own voice. By this time, Erich Neumann had also read several of Jaffé's chapters as well as Jung's autobiographical text with her editorial additions. On October 26, 1958, he visited Jung at Bollingen and expressed enthusiasm about the project in general. His feedback regarding the drafts and Jaffé's style was very positive. Jung, convinced and reassured by Neumann's reaction, therefore no longer insisted on a fundamental change of form and linguistic structure. He did, however, still wish for the voices and reactions of others toward him to have a greater presence. During their conversation, Jung suggested that Neumann and Jaffé might jointly write a commentary to expand on what he had said about Freud.[85] After initial doubts, Jaffé accepted Jung's wish that she should make herself more visible, as she now saw the possibility of explaining factual material in her own

---

it) to keep the concluding section of his 'From the Earliest Experiences…', including his signature. This caesura in the middle of the book is important to him as it indicates the true situation. He is skeptical about the prologue. He finds the style too feminine, the whole thing too aesthetic." Jung was referring to a draft of a prologue written by Kurt Wolff. Aniela Jaffé to Kurt Wolff, 19.10.1958, YBL.

83 Aniela Jaffé to Kurt Wolff, 20.10.1958, YBL

84 Aniela Jaffé to Kurt Wolff, 19.10.1958: "Jung finds it fitting and I have to admit it is livelier than it could have been in its original form." YBL

85 Aniela Jaffé to Helene Wolff, 28.10.1958: "The conversation between Neumann and Jung (…) has bolstered my hope that the question of style is now resolved, and that I will not have to rewrite everything yet again." Neumann's judgment "obviously did Jung good. He needed to hear it from a man, and one who is not involved in the process." AAJD

words, without having to translate it "into Jung's style, which I have anyway not mastered."[86]

Wolff's reaction was not just one of disappointment, as Jaffé had expected, but of hurt and reproach, and with no understanding for Jung's standpoint. His wife had in the meantime asked Wolfgang Sauerländer for his opinion on Jung's idea for the structure, and she informed Jaffé in dramatic tones: "The new plan would sound the death knell, as it were, for Kurt and for the book itself in terms of its effect on the readership."[87] Based on Sauerländer's assessment, the idea of publishing the protocols ordered by conversation dates was categorically rejected: "It would be foolhardy to immortalize this raw material,"[88] in so doing one would return that which had currently been freed "from the rubble of chance" to a form which would be "truly meaningless and destructive." Helene Wolff continued: "The new plan seems to me as if someone had just cleared a wonderful garden of all the rampant climbing plants so that the plot as a whole (...) could be clearly appreciated – and along comes a Rousseau fanatic demanding a 'return to nature' and scatters great handfuls of weeds all over the place."[89]

Wolff, completely disregarding Jung's arguments, saw the proposal as an "atomization of the organically constructed book."[90] He was also irritated by Neumann's involvement – first, he said, "any day an old man" [*Altmann*] could come along and throw everything overboard again, and second of all, he, Wolff, knew more than a Neumann about how to structure and organize a book. "I am no *book merchandiser*, but a publisher, which (...) is a creative profession."[91] He disclosed that, immediately after returning to the USA, he had intended to send six chapters to the translator, a plan that had now been thwarted at the last minute.

86 Aniela Jaffé to Helene Wolff, 23.10.1958, YBL

87 Helene Wolff to Aniela Jaffé, 17.10.1958, YBL. Helene Wolff had already used emotional arguments to put pressure on Jaffé earlier that year in March, when Kurt Wolff was bedridden due to heart problems: only Jaffé's letters and protocols could enliven him and cheer him up, she wrote, they were the "best medicine"; Helene Wolff to Aniela Jaffé, 22.3.1958, 31.3.1958, YBL.

88 Cf. memo from Wolfgang Sauerländer to Helene Wolff, October 1958, YBL.

89 Helene Wolff to Aniela Jaffé, 25.10.1958, YBL.

90 Kurt Wolff to Aniela Jaffé, 9.11.1958, YBL.

91 Ibid.

Jung immediately sent a strongly worded reply. It ought to have been obvious that he, as the main protagonist, had the right to check every text of this project before it was passed on to third parties. He emphasized his appreciation for Jaffé's work: he had complete trust in her abilities, and her excellent knowledge enabled her to write about a subject that was "not exactly the simplest of propositions." [92] Nevertheless, there were still "shaky parts" which he was now correcting and augmenting. He wished to keep control of the whole project to ensure that nothing would be published which he did not feel to be "authentic."[93] Jaffé, for her part, repeated that no material could be released for translation without her and Jung's agreement. Wolff's actions in forwarding the earlier material – the chapters on childhood, school and student years, and the 1944 visions – in December 1957 had been completely impermissible and unauthorized.

In previous correspondence, Jaffé had often given the impression that she was assiduously trying to balance the conflicting demands of both Jung and Wolff, but now there was no doubt that her loyalties lay primarily with Jung. She categorically rejected, in stronger terms than ever, Wolff's considerable interference in the editorial process: "As for our collaboration, you know how much I resisted it at the start and from the very beginning." Out of sympathy and a wish to please him, she had allowed herself to be persuaded. Had she known that it would not be "a friendly exchange of ideas as I imagined, but a monitoring of my work in which I would lose the freedom to decide when something is 'finished' and 'unfinished'," she would never have agreed to it.[94] Drawing now on her analytic as well as editorial skills, she endeavored to move the discussion from an emotional back to a more objective level, for the sake of the future book. She well understood why her connecting sentences in the first person had "terribly irritated" Jung, and she was of course prepared to change the manuscript. This book, she wrote to Wolff, was the work of Jung's *daimon*. As a woman, she conceded, it was perhaps easier for her to adapt to the vagaries of this *daimon*, whereas Wolff's masculine ambition and desire to take the

92 C.G. Jung to Helene Wolff, 11.11.1958, copy in AAJD.
93 Ibid.
94 Aniela Jaffé to Kurt Wolff, 13.11.1958, AAJD, YBL.

lead meant he reacted with bitterness when his plans were thwarted and had to be subordinated. If Wolff in fifty years of publishing had never experienced the like, as he claimed, then it was probably because he had never before "meddled in the creative process of a 'master' from the very start."[95] Such involvement was only admissible if one were also prepared to step out of the process at any second, wrote Jaffé.

As a result of this decisive rupture, after October 1958 Jaffé no longer sent Wolff any copies of her conversation notes. Many further conversations did take place between Jaffé and Jung in connection with the project as a whole, Jaffé's draft chapters and the structure of the book, right up until Jung's death in 1961.

Helene Wolff made one more attempt to smooth things over toward the end of 1958, a "friendly peace offering" which Jaffé accepted: Pantheon promised not to reproduce or send any more material for translation without prior approval.[96] A *rapprochement* was all the more important to the Wolffs as the couple had decided, following a major dispute with the managing director and board of Pantheon Books, to move to Switzerland in the spring of 1959. They cited work on the project as an important reason for their decision.

A brief report sent by Jaffé to Kurt Wolff at the end of December 1958 reveals that by then she had written, in addition to the chapter on Jung's relationship with Freud, a chapter on Bollingen and on Jung's ancestry, and had revised the chapter on the visions of 1944. She had also completed a draft of the chapter "On Life after Death" and compiled another entitled "*Besinnung*" [contemplation] which included her own comments, introductory paragraphs and explanations. Jung had already corrected the part on Bollingen and the chapters "Psychiatric Activities" and "The Work" by the end of 1958, but he wished to add a little more to the chapter "Confrontation with the Unconscious."[97] At the end of that year, Jung took Jaffé's drafts of the chapters on Freud, the 1944 visions, and life after death to Bollingen to read and review. As had happened a year earlier, this absorption was to give Jung the impetus to put pen to paper himself once more.

95 Aniela Jaffé to Kurt Wolff, 15.11.1958, YBL.
96 Cf. Aniela Jaffé to Helene and Kurt Wolff, 14.12.1958, YBL.
97 Cf. report by Aniela Jaffé to Kurt Wolff about progress since October 1958, 28.12.1958, YBL.

"I have therefore encouraged A.J. to contribute as much material as possible in order that the text remains her book."

Throughout their previous conversations, there was one question Aniela Jaffé continued to address without getting an answer. Through Jung's early encounters with unconscious images, he had come to realize that he no longer lived in the Christian myth – Jaffé wanted to know whether, in his later decades of seeking, he had found a new myth that held meaning for him.[1] Now he spent the first three weeks of the new year 1959 in Bollingen attempting to formulate his thoughts and ideas about a myth going further than the Christian one.[2] These ideas went beyond the image of a creator-god and a human incarnation of the son of God. In the Christian God-image, which Jung understood as representing a fundamental vision of the human psyche, evil had been split off and repressed, something that was more evident than ever before in the global political situation of the day. For Jung, our potential to become conscious meant we were called upon to critically and creatively examine and come to terms with the opposing forces of good and evil present in the God-image. Without a thorough awareness of one's whole self, including evil aspects, there was no way of responding to the destructive forces that were all-too clearly activated.

1 Cf. Jaffé, A. (ed.), 1962, p. 170f.

2 For Jaffé, these thoughts were of particular biographical relevance as they could be read as the answer to a question that Jung had asked himself nearly half a century before. According to Jaffé, this question had presented him with his life's task and marked the beginning of his long quest. See in this regard her introductory commentary in the second version of the manuscript, which was deleted by Kurt Wolff; YBL. Cf. Aniela Jaffé to Kurt Wolff, 29.1.1959, YBL.

To truly have self-knowledge, to recognize the whole, Jung believed it was necessary to be thoroughly honest not only about the goodness, but also the shocking evil of which human beings are capable.

According to Jung, human existence could be seen as having one eminent purpose: to recognize the existence of the world. Only when its existence is acknowledged does the world become "the phenomenal world, for without conscious reflection it would not be. If the Creator were conscious of Himself, He would not need conscious creatures."[3] In this view, humans, thanks to their ability to perceive the world, could become not just "second creators," but also preservers of the Creation. Jung described his thoughts as an explanatory myth about the *raison d'être* of human existence which had taken form within him over decades. In a letter to Erich Neumann, he explicitly referred to his idea about this latent purpose and meaning of human existence as "a hypothesis."[4]

Jaffé ultimately incorporated Jung's new contribution into the book as part I of the chapter "Late Thoughts." She thought the text was "so brilliantly" formulated that "one ceases to breathe while reading it."[5] With Jung's permission, she sent a copy of the text and of the chapter "On Life After Death" to Neumann. He too – aside from a few content-related objections – found the text deeply moving. "For me it is the most beautiful thing you have written," he told Jung.[6] In her introductory commentary – later removed by Wolff – Jaffé described the thoughts Jung formulated here as the fruit of an almost fifty-year process of examination and reflection. They were, she wrote, in a way the conclusion of ideas explored in his later works *Aion*, *Answer to Job*, *The Undiscovered Self*, *Flying Saucers* and "A Psychological View

3 Jaffé, A. (ed.), 1962, p. 339.

4 Ibid., p. 338, C.G. Jung to Erich Neumann, 10.3.1959, *Letters II*, p. 495. In the letter, Jung refers to his text as a first unrevised draft and an attempt to pin down his volatile thoughts, suggesting that he later revised it further.

5 Aniela Jaffé to Kurt Wolff, 24.1.1959, YBL. Wolff's reaction was that some passages were incomprehensible to him and to his wife. Jaffé responded that the text was "of the greatest significance. It is a typical mature style: looking from afar from whence things become clear because they are no longer in sharp focus. (...) These pages are an essential part of that. They refer to the ideas in *Flying Saucers*." Aniela Jaffé to Kurt Wolff, 11.2.1960, YBL.

6 Erich Neumann to C.G. Jung, 18.2.1959, first published in Aniela Jaffé, *Der Mythus vom Sinn*, 1967, p. 179ff. (German publication only); cf. also Martin Liebscher, ed., *Analytical Psychology in Exile: The Correspondence of C.G. Jung and Erich Neumann*. 2015, p. 343ff.

of Conscience."[7] The various chapters arranged under the heading "Human Image, God-Image, *Weltanschauung*" in the present volume *Reflections* give further insight into Jung's development and circumambulation of these late thoughts.

All the while, Jaffé was continuing to work on chapters she had put together based on the conversation notes and other primary sources, now also inserting her own thoughts, connecting paragraphs and explanations into the text which was otherwise mostly presented as monologue. She regularly discussed this process with Jung, who found that reading the drafts was affecting him emotionally.[8] The corrections and amendments he brought were "extremely valuable," Jaffé told Wolff. At this point, Jung considered sending the edited chapters, including the text about his childhood, youth and student years, to Cary Baynes for a second opinion. Jaffé understood this as an expression of the insecurity he still was harboring about the value of the text – he continued to doubt if it should be published – and of a lingering "shyness about exposing himself to the world."[9]

The chapter about Jung's experiences in North America, Africa and India and the one about encounters with prominent figures were still in the initial rough stages. Early on, Jaffé was having doubts about the latter topic, and concentrated mainly on the travel chapter. Jung had made clear from the start that he did not want to publish anything about important relationships such as those with his wife, his children, or Toni Wolff, a proviso Jaffé had accepted without question.[10] One of Jung's motivations in agreeing to the biographical projects of Jaffé and Bennet was certainly the fact that with those two authors, he would have control over the contents. For the chapter about encounters with others, Wolff wanted primarily anecdotal material from Jung's

7 See CW 9/II, CW 10 and CW 11.

8 Aniela Jaffé to Kurt Wolff, 7.2.1959, YBL.

9 Aniela Jaffé to Kurt Wolff, 16.1.1959, YBL. Jung was unable to overcome this "shyness" until a year and a half later, only nine months before his death. After Jolande Jacobi had read and given her reaction to the German manuscript of *Memories, Dreams, Reflections by C.G. Jung*, he answered that he was "pleased to hear that my autobiographical sketches have conveyed to you something of what my outer side has hitherto kept hidden. It had to remain hidden because it could not have survived the brutalities of the outside world. But now I am grown so old that I can let go my grip on the world, and its raucous cries fade in the distance." C.G. Jung, *Letters II*, p. 585.

10 Cf. Aniela Jaffé to Kurt Wolff, 11.1.1957, YBL

encounters with "famous people." Because of Wolff's lack of expertise in the history of medicine, he undervalued the significance of certain contemporaries for the development of Jung's psychology, believing they would be unfamiliar or unknown to American readers.[11] When Jung did speak with Jaffé about public figures he had met or people he was close to, it was almost always in connection with a background that transcended the personal. The chapter about Jung's meetings with contemporaries was ultimately omitted from the book *Memories, Dreams, Reflections by C.G. Jung*. Jaffé later decided that some of Jung's comments on these relationships were worthy of publication, and now these can be found in the present book.

In March 1959, the meeting with Swiss publisher Max Rascher and his son Albert, as recommended by the lawyer Beidler, finally took place. Jung was represented by his lawyer Hans Karrer and son-in-law Walther Niehus. Karrer informed the Raschers that Jaffé had been commissioned by Wolff to write a biography of Jung, but that Jung had over the course of time shifted from being "an object of observation" to a kind of "co-worker" and had written a few contributions for the book. Niehus, on behalf of Jung, insisted that Jung absolutely did not want to have the term "autobiography" used for the book. Max Rascher nevertheless invoked the right of his publishing house to Jung's future work, referring to previous contractual agreements. On April 1, 1959, Rascher sent an unequivocal telegram to Pantheon Books and Kurt Wolff: "German and World Rights of all works and publications of C.G. Jung – also in collaboration with other authors – in our hands. This concerns biographical book Jaffé/Jung as well."[12] Pantheon could only claim the rights for an American edition upon approval of the Bollingen Foundation, and negotiations with S. Fischer Verlag must also be ceased immediately.

11 An example was Théodore Flournoy, professor of philosophy and psychology at the University of Geneva, who was a very important figure for Jung at the time of his conflict with Freud, forming a kind of counter-balance to Freud for Jung. Jung adopted the term "imagination créatrice" from Flournoy. Jaffé had wanted to integrate the information about Jung's relationship with Flournoy into the Freud chapter, which would have been meaningful from a historical perspective, but the passages were deleted by Kurt Wolff and Wolfgang Sauerländer. The relationship between Jung and Flournoy is briefly depicted in an appendix, but only in the German edition.

12 Rascher Verlag to Pantheon Books, 1.4.1959, YBL (original in English).

Wolff deemed Rascher's claim "outrageous" and urgently told Jaffé: "Whatever finished or unfinished material you have must on no account fall into the hands of Rascher, either directly or indirectly."[13] A few months later, when Sir Herbert Read and Cecil Franklin of the British publishing house Routledge became aware of Jung's own written contributions, they too asserted their right to publish the project based on existing contracts as the publisher of the *Collected Works* in the United Kingdom.[14] Wolff, having already offered the British publication rights to Collins, proceeded to conduct a long and acrimonious battle against these claims. One of his arguments was that S. Fischer and Collins were both much larger, more dynamic publishing houses than Rascher and Routledge, and would therefore give the book a much greater likelihood of success.

At the end of May, Helene and Kurt Wolff arrived in Zürich and installed themselves at the Dolder Grand Hotel for three months, prior to their planned permanent move to the Hotel Esplanade in Minusio, Locarno, at the end of August. Although Jaffé had warned them that not all chapters were finished and that Jung had not yet approved the manuscript and did not wish at this time to hand it over, Wolff was adamant that he should read it. He appealed to Jung directly in a letter: the "autobiography as a whole" was now surely ready and only in need of the "finishing touch," he wrote. Not having seen any of the book since September 1958, he claimed to be a "fresh new reader." If Jung continued to refuse to let him see it, Wolff continued, he would wait patiently, but that would be unfair to Jaffé, "who has spent years putting her life and soul into this work."[15] Jung's response, in which he used the terms autobiography and biography interchangeably, disclosed not only his vacillation about how to classify the text, but also that he now saw himself as its co-producer. He wrote that "there are still a few significant contributions from my many-layered life to incorporate, which I became aware of through a very impressive

13 Kurt Wolff to Aniela Jaffé, 1.4.1959, YBL.

14 Routledge had already expressed interest in the publication in November 1957, even if the material did not form part of the Collected Works: "Routledge will want to publish the material even though it is not to form part of the *Collected Works*." John Barrett to C.G. Jung, 23.10.1957, quoted in a letter from Aniela Jaffé to Kurt Wolff, 6.11.1957, YBL.

15 Kurt Wolff to C.G. Jung, 30.5.1959, YBL.

dream," and said he had instructed Jaffé not to give Wolff the chapters until after this was done. He continued: "I am well aware that I need to hurry with the biography. I will do my best to finish the work as soon as possible."[16]

In July, Wolff had a second meeting with Beidler, the lawyer from the Swiss Society of Authors, to discuss Rascher's legal claims. Beidler said he would be willing to meet with Jung's lawyer and Max Rascher to reiterate Wolff's argument that the book had been initiated under commission to Pantheon Books. Nevertheless, he continued to assess the situation as being legally problematic, particularly since the scope of Jung's contributions had now increased. Whereas in spring of 1958, Wolff realized how daring it was to assert that Jung and Jaffé were working under commission to him, he now increasingly argued that such an arrangement did exist, in order to defend Pantheon against the claims of Rascher and Routledge.

When Wolff finally received the manuscript from Jaffé in the second half of July 1959, he was relieved to have a more-or-less finished text in his hands – but extremely upset with its new form. His criticism concerned above all Jaffé's more visible role, even though this actually lent weight to his justification of the legal situation. In the contract with Pantheon, only Jaffé was listed as author, since Jung, despite his contributions about his childhood, youth and student years, and late thoughts on meaning, had refused to be contractually named as co-author. In the meantime, Jung, having seen the extensive writing and editing of Jaffé, had also moved away from the idea of putting his signature after the first three chapters, instead agreeing to and approving the conjunction of his text with the comments from the conversation protocols. Wolff had initially tried to refute the legal claims of Rascher and Routledge by pointing out Jaffé's role and referring to the contract citing her as author and editor. At the same time, he wished her role as author to be as imperceptible as possible in the text itself. His intention to present the book as Jung's autobiography, by largely concealing Jaffé's work, was becoming ever more evident. While Jung wanted Jaffé and her role to be more visible in the text, Wolff wished her to

16 C.G. Jung to Kurt Wolff, 30.5.1959, AAJD.

be as unobtrusive and invisible as possible – in effect, a ghostwriter. Although Jung's contributions in the new version did help with that goal, the text was no longer written exclusively as a monologue in the first person, but rather with passages and longer commentaries from Jaffé written freely in her own style, or in collaboration with Erich Neumann. Recollections by Jung's old friend Albert Oeri were also included, adding the perspective of a third person.

Jung favored this form of presentation, as his goal was to create a three-dimensional picture of himself which would show the conscious and unconscious, personal and archetypal aspects of his life. He wanted the reader to see a "real body appearing in the cone of light of the observing consciousness," including the perceptions of others of the observed object.[17] In August 1959, after reading Jaffé's composition about his travels in Africa, Jung wrote some further autobiographical material on the subject in order to illustrate how "things happen on two levels simultaneously."[18] Wolff, however, was busy trying to forge alliances, with the intention of convincing Jung that Jaffé's "interventions" disrupted the flow and were completely superfluous and unnecessary. For several months, Wolff avoided openly telling Jaffé his opinion. But he and his wife were also critical of Jung's own recent contributions and considered his "late thoughts" to be "a very difficult proposition for the average reader."[19]

Rascher had meanwhile demanded to see the manuscript, after even Jaffé had used the term autobiography in a letter intended to clarify matters. Jung, not wishing to be involved in the legal conflict, delegated the matter to his lawyer Karrer and son-in-law Walther Niehus. Wolff found himself in a quandary: on the one hand, he was determined to present the book as Jung's autobiography, while on the other, he was trying to use the legal argument that Jaffé was the book's author and was merely supported by Jung. In terms of the legal conflict, his strategy proved unsuccessful. Forced to acknowledge that Jung felt a greater loyalty to Rascher[20] – his publisher of many years who in

17 Cf. also C.G. Jung to Kurt Wolff, 21.8.1959, YBL.
18 Ibid., cf. also Aniela Jaffé to Kurt Wolff, 11.8.1959, YBL.
19 Undated note from Helene or Kurt Wolff, YBL.
20 Max Rascher had been publishing C.G. Jung's work since 1917; despite several unprofitable publications, Rascher remained unswervingly faithful to his author for many decades.

Karrer's opinion had a valid claim – than to Pantheon, Wolff decided to change tack. He drafted a contract stating that Jung, as proposed and commissioned by Pantheon Books, was writing an autobiographical book with support from Aniela Jaffé: "Professor Dr. C.G. Jung, Küsnacht, and Frau Aniela Jaffé, Zürich, have declared themselves willing, at the proposal of and under commission to Pantheon Books [...], to produce an autobiographical book with the provisional title *C.G. Jung, Erinnerungen, Träume, Gedanken, herausgegeben von Aniela Jaffé*."[21] According to the contract, the authors had transferred all rights for all languages to Pantheon Books, but now wished Rascher to receive the rights for a hardback German edition. The document then states that Pantheon had acquiesced to this demand and granted Rascher the right to publish in German an "autobiographical book by C.G. Jung, written in collaboration with A. Jaffé." Wolff retained the option to sell the rights for a paperback edition to a German publishing house of his choice at the latest two years after Rascher's initial publication of the hardback. Neither Jung nor Karrer accepted this contract.

When Jaffé departed for a holiday, Wolff seized the opportunity to approach Jung directly about the structure of the manuscript. Asking Jung to keep the letter secret from Jaffé, he wrote of his "serious reservations: the way Frau Jaffé's comments are inserted in your text disrupt [...] the great flow of your speech." He said he wanted to "preserve the substance, coherence and uniqueness of your voice, your cadence and [...] the purity of the effect on the reader."[22] While he knew Jung had explicitly requested the presence of the second voice, Wolff thought it should appear only in a foreword or footnotes. He asked Jung to back him up and help avoid making Jaffé "feel that she is being pushed aside and offended by his interference" as, he said, "her achievement is so great that one almost feels embarrassed to venture any critical comment."[23]

Jung's rejoinder was comprehensive and categorical. He had never intended nor dared to write an autobiography himself, he said. Aware

21 Undated two-page typewritten document, YBL.
22 Kurt Wolff to C.G. Jung, 17.8.1959, YBL.
23 Ibid.

of how challenging the task facing Jaffé was, he had offered her support, from which "a collaboration" had arisen. As the book was about Jung's life and ideas, somewhat more weight had inevitably fallen on his side of the scales. In order to give more weight to Jaffé, he had asked her to bring more of her own voice into the book.[24] Moreover, he continued, this had the advantage of loosening up the whole thing and enlivening the flow. For readability in particular, the "results of A.J.'s collaboration" should certainly be maintained as far as possible. Often, wrote Jung, his statements assumed certain knowledge which the reader might lack. The only matter he was willing to discuss was the placement of Jaffé's insertions: some of them could possibly appear as introductions or conclusions to chapters. As soon as the chapter about his travels was satisfactorily finished, he told Wolff, he would read through the entire manuscript and assist Jaffé in her efforts to establish the book's definitive form.[25]

The contrasting way in which the two men refer to Jaffé in their respective letters is revealing. While acknowledging Jaffé's great achievement, "without which the manuscript would not exist at all today," Wolff names only Jung as the author and calls Jaffé his "self-sacrificing helper."[26] Jung, in his letter, reverses the order, claiming he is assisting with Jaffé's enterprise and that responsibility for the book's final form rests with her. He also, however, describes her definitions and explanations as the indispensable "duties of a midwife," suggesting that he saw her as playing a helping role in the birth of a book whose "father and mother" were not clearly defined. Jaffé on the other hand, saw herself "as author or co-author,"[27] based on both the contractual agreement with Pantheon and her responsibility for the written form – a responsibility Jung wanted to be made explicit in the publication.

Wolff seemed to take in only what suited him from the letter, and remained deaf to Jung's concern that Jaffé be present in the text. He replied to Jung: "It is reassuring to find out that you also see the problems and wish to eliminate them."[28] Wolff was in full agreement with

24 C.G. Jung to Kurt Wolff, 21.8.1959, YBL, AAJD
25 Ibid.
26 Kurt Wolff to C.G. Jung, 17.8.1959, YBL.
27 Aniela Jaffé to Dora and Ernst Bernhard, 15.6.1959, ETH.
28 Kurt Wolff to C.G. Jung, 27.8.1959, YBL.

Jung's decision to depart from his original plan of marking the change in authorship by placing his signature after the first three chapters. He now tactically asked his wife Helene to address Jaffé about the form of the manuscript, hoping that Jaffé would be won over more easily by another woman. Meanwhile, Wolff expressed his displeasure with the new version to R.F.C. Hull, the English translator of Jung's *Collected Works* who had been living in Ascona since 1953. He also complained to Cary Baynes that Jung's suggestion for Jaffé's "intrusion" had come far too late – the "monologue form" had already been firmly established.[29] To her, he described the new manuscript as "catastrophic." Furthermore, he claimed it was almost impossible to contact Jung without going through Jaffé.

Disregarding Wolff's plea for discretion, Jung informed Jaffé about Wolff's letter. In response, she asked Jung to once again unreservedly take a clear stance on the basic form the manuscript should take. He affirmed that in principle, he wanted to retain the text in its current state, but said that certain comments could possibly be moved to different places.[30] He also agreed with her that she should insert additional material from the conversation protocols about Africa.

Upon completing his contribution about Africa and following an ensuing period of illness, Jung returned to his inner conversations with Philemon, Salome and the snake which had also become a bird.[31] He told Jaffé that it was his last conversation with these figures. The impulse for it had come from several directions – the dream of the abandoned house, the thoughts he had formulated in January of that year about a continuing myth of the meaning and purpose of human existence, and his reading of the chapter "Confrontation with the

29 Handwritten note for the attention of Cary Baynes from Kurt Wolff; attached to a copy of the letter from C.G. Jung to Kurt Wolff, 21.8.1959, YBL.

30 "I presented this whole complex of questions about the form of the book to Jung with the request that he once again unreservedly set out his position. I myself do not identify so strongly with my words of wisdom as it might seem and am quite willing [...] to change, rewrite or move selected interjections or even to do away with them altogether [...]. Jung would also approve any corrections. In principle, however, he would like – and he asked me to write this to you – to retain the current form of the book with all of A.J.'s interjections." Aniela Jaffé to Kurt Wolff, 4.9.1959, YBL.

31 Significant figures in Jung's inner process, documented in *The Red Book*, see fn. 6, p. 72 of this volume.

Unconscious." Jaffé therefore added Jung's concluding remarks about his inner dialogue to this chapter.[32]

In Bollingen at the end of October 1959, Jung wrote his final contribution for Jaffé's biographical project under the title "*Besinnung*" [contemplation]. This section was later integrated into the chapters "Late Thoughts" and "Retrospect." The final chapter of the book was still in flux and Jung gave Jaffé free reign to order the concluding text in whatever way she thought best. Even though it seemed the bulk of the work was done, when James Hillman, the Director of Studies of the C.G. Jung Institute, asked Jaffé to give lectures at the institute in 1960, she declined. As it turned out, the demands of the book project were to continue unabated.

After discussing the manuscript in depth with Jaffé, Helene Wolff wrote a frustrated letter to Jung in mid-November, again asking him to keep it confidential. Helene Wolff claimed that she and Jaffé had understood each other perfectly in many matters of details, however regarding the "principal question, namely the structure of the whole," they were at a total impasse.[33] For Helene Wolff, the effect of the passages that were "not animated by Jung's spirit" was disruptive. Here, she cited not only Jaffé's explanatory insertions, but also Neumann's text about Jung's relationship with Freud, for example, calling it "a defensive Jewish contribution." The text by Albert Oeri recalling his youthful experiences with Jung was in her opinion out of place. All in all, she claimed, the insertions constituted a "glaring break" with the "great directness and effect of Jung's voice" and caused the reader to feel "increasingly irritated about being taken away from the 'I' tes-

32 On the dream of the abandoned house see p. 86ff. Cf. also Jaffé, A. (ed.), 1962, p. 199. NB. Page 387 of the German edition, titled "*Nachtrag zum 'Roten Buch'*" ["Addendum to the 'Red Book'"], is omitted entirely from the English version as it was deleted by Pantheon, Routledge and Collins. In 1959, Jung had tried again, but not managed, to complete the final unfinished picture in *The Red Book* (folio page 169) which, he told Jaffé, had to do with death. According to Jaffé, in August 1959 Jung had again worked on copying text passages from the *Black Books* into *The Red Book* using calligraphy. These may be the folio pages 168 to 189 which have a clearly different structure and calligraphy from the preceding pages. It seems likely that he broke off the process because it was too strenuous and time-consuming, and that he intended to complete the volume with the last lines on folio pages 190/191, which also remained unfinished. Jaffé typed up Jung's final additions to his inner dialogue. According to Jaffé, in a letter of August 1959 Jung referred to his final inner conversation: he had been drawn into the dream "which is oneself, and in which there is no longer an I and a You." Cf. *Letters II*, p. 514 [translation slightly modified].

33 Helene Wolff to C.G. Jung, 18.11.1959, YBL.

timony." Jaffé's argument that the new structure reflected the express wish of Jung was dismissed by Helene Wolff as an "unconscious power claim" by Jaffé. She could not accept Jaffé's defense of the several-voice format, and ended her letter by appealing to Jung with flattery: "Maintaining the effect of your spirit, the directness of your voice: that is at stake here." She was fighting for it, concluded Helene Wolff, due to her enormous admiration for Jung and for his "towering testimony."[34]

While Helene Wolff continued to call the book an "autobiography," Jung deliberately avoided the term in his response, which he openly showed to Jaffé, describing it as the "biography" he had never wanted to write. Not only, he said, because for a variety of reasons he would be incapable of completing it, but above all, because he could not climb above his own head to write about himself from a position of "conceited superiority."[35] He had only written his contributions, he repeated, to assist Jaffé in matters too complex for her to handle. This had led to the absurdity[36] now confronting them, he wrote with ironic humor. Although Jung had agreed to relocate some of Jaffé's longer commentaries into appendices or possibly footnotes, he continued to stand by his overall support for the manuscript in its current form. Apart from a few exceptions, his contributions consisted of fragments, he wrote, and all bridging and linking texts by Jaffé should therefore be left in. He declared once again, even more strongly, that he did not want a text that could be construed as *his* work. He moreover reiterated that he was not under commission or contractual obligation to Kurt Wolff and Pantheon, and stressed his loyalty to Rascher. He had encouraged Jaffé to contribute as much material as possible "in order that the text remains her book."[37] Kurt Wolff had suggested involving Cary Baynes to mediate in future conflicts, but Jung did not mention the idea in his reply. After Kurt Wolff continued to exert pressure regarding the manuscript, Jung one month later drew a clear boundary: "As I have done what I thought was necessary for the biography, I no longer wish to be occupied with questions regarding the publication."

34 Ibid. and memo by Helene Wolff, 15.11.1959, YBL.
35 C.G. Jung to Helene Wolff, 23.11.1959, copy in AAJD.
36 Trans. note: Jung used the German word "*Unding*", (literally "un-thing"), which means something preposterous or undefinable.
37 Ibid.

He left Jaffé responsible for editorial issues and his lawyer Karrer for legal matters.[38]

With dogged disregard for Jung's position, Kurt Wolff continued to refer to the project as an autobiography, a unique and sacrosanct monologue that could not be touched. Jaffé, for her part, had received great praise for the new version from both Erich Neumann and Rivkah Kluger-Schärf, but this served more to irritate than to impress Wolff. His relentless criticism, both direct and indirect, coupled with his unwillingness to take the repeated defense of Jaffé and Jung seriously, finally led Jaffé to cave in. She had again and again received contradictory double messages from Wolff: it was *her* book, he had told her – she should write the text, create the final version, introduce contents, explain things, make amendments, etc. – while simultaneously repeating at every opportunity that any evidence of her authorship was disruptive. The publisher did not relent with his demand that the entire text should appear to be direct testimony of Jung. He continued to insist that Jaffé's active role – both in terms of collecting and evaluating the information and in writing a coherent complete text – needed to be concealed as much as possible.

Ultimately, Jaffé's goal was to publish the book to which she and Jung had devoted so much time and effort within a foreseeable period of time. Realizing that the acrimonious and tenacious resistance put up by the Wolffs could not be overcome, she found herself forced to edit the manuscript yet again. The burden on her was even greater now that Jung wanted to have nothing more to do with the publisher. Thus, at the end of 1959, with Jung's approval, she agreed to change the main body of the text to render her authorship and editorial role so discreet that the book could largely be read as a direct testimony of the main protagonist. Only the foreword would refer to her part and to Jung's actual role in the book's creation.

In an explanation decades later for her two revisions of the manuscript, Jaffé wrote: "At Jung's request I had incorporated my questions, comments, etc. into the manuscript so that it took the form of a conversation, in the manner of the Goethe-Eckermann conversations.

38 C.G. Jung to Kurt Wolff, 24.12.1959, copy in AAJD.

Kurt Wolff, the publisher, did not agree at all with this structure – understandably – because from the start he had wanted a book that would be as close as possible to a book by C.G. Jung, i.e., I was to fade into the background. That was plausible to me and also to Jung. I therefore again revised the entire manuscript, in accordance with Wolff's wishes, to present solely Jung's side of the conversations. That may be how the legend arose that Jung 'dictated' it all to me!"[39] Not until near the end of the collaboration with Wolff, which Jaffé described as "exhausting and burdensome," did she admit to him how oppressive she had found his constant pressure, how difficult it had been for her to accept his interference, and how much of a sacrifice it was for her to make herself invisible and write herself out of the book in this way. At the outset, his wife Helene had described him as a man who achieved everything he set his mind to. That had turned out not to be the case with Routledge and Rascher, but in relation to "the more important matter, the form of the book," Jaffé concluded that Helene had been proven right. She made it clear that she herself had paid a high price for his determination.[40]

Jung, weary of the conflict, had ostensibly stepped back from the project and told others he had done so.[41] But despite this, he still wished to continue checking the text. Jaffé, to whom he had again explicitly transferred sole responsibility for the undertaking, stuck to the task. She took into account Jung's instructions and consulted him about portions of text which the publisher wanted to change.[42] She was pleased when she managed to put Jung's thoughts and remarks into writing, to combine notes from conversations with texts written

39 Aniela Jaffé, 7.8.1982, typed addendum to a copy of a letter from C.G. Jung to Kurt Wolff, 24.12.1959, AAJD.

40 Aniela Jaffé to Kurt Wolff, 17.1.1961, YBL. A letter from Jaffé to Rivkah and Yehezkel Kluger-Schärf written ten months earlier shows that the process of making her role invisible was a sacrifice that she wrestled with for a long time: "It looks as though I am going to be wiped out of the book entirely and it will be published solely as a 'book by C.G. Jung.' But I have not yet given up hope." Aniela Jaffé to Rivkah and Yehezkel Kluger-Schärf, 25.3.1960. AAJD.

41 C.G. Jung to Emma von Pelet, author, translator, partner of Alwine von Keller, on 6.1.1960: "It seems rumours have reached you that I am writing my biography. I have always vowed I would never write an autobiography and in this case have only wetted my feet a little; it is rather Frau Jaffé who is writing a biography to which I have made a few contributions. So I have nothing more to do with it and am in the fortunate position of leaving the headaches to others […]." C.G. Jung, *Letters II*, p. 531.

42 Cf. Aniela Jaffé to Kurt Wolff, 9.3.1960, YBL.

by him or to expand on his thoughts in ways that he deemed satisfactory. In the third version of the manuscript, on which she began work in December 1959, her role as author was hardly in evidence at all. All that remained of her were "faint traces of mist," she wrote to Wolff.[43] By the end of January 1960, she judged her work on the biography to be complete, and by mid-February, had sent Wolff the majority of the chapters. Jaffé now hoped finally to be able to work undisturbed on two new projects: the chapter "Symbolism in the Visual Arts" for the volume *Man and his Symbols*, and a paper on parapsychology.[44] It was a relief to have time to devote to her own projects at last, she wrote to Wolff – clearly, the work on the biography had made huge demands on her time and energy.[45]

However, the publisher and his wife then wanted yet again to make corrections that were not merely stylistic but also content-related and would distort the message – Jaffé and Jung refused. Wolff even attempted to move the explanation of the book's creation from the foreword to the end of the book. The foreword gave precise indications of the authorship of the individual chapters, information Wolff found irksome.[46] In this matter, Wolff was unsuccessful. Jaffé checked all the proposed corrections, competently defended sections of text to which Wolff objected, and insisted that the interference must now cease: "The nature of the manuscript meant its preparation required an enormous amount of effort – far more than writing one's own book! Jung and I have considered every individual part of the book so often and in such depth – often also with input and critique from countless others – that the manuscript should now be taken as definitively finished."[47] As will be seen further below, however, there were still to be further objections and interferences – in some cases substantial – from various sides.

43 Aniela Jaffé to Kurt Wolff, 26.1.1960, YBL. A few days later she wrote to James Kirsch "the work on the biography is finished," and said that although it had tired her greatly, she was already thinking about a new topic. Aniela Jaffé to James Kirsch, 3.2.1960, AAJD.

44 First published in English as "Symbolism in the Visual Arts" in *Man and his Symbols*, London, 1964, followed by a German version "Bildende Kunst als Symbol" in *Der Mensch und seine Symbole*, 1968; the paper on parapsychology first appeared in German in *Zeitschrift für Parapsychologie und ihre Grenzgebiete*, IV, Nr. 1, 1960, then in English in "Psychological Aspects of Spontaneous Cases" in the *International Journal of Parapsychology*, 1962.

45 Aniela Jaffé to Kurt Wolff, 26.1.1960, YBL.

46 Kurt Wolff to Aniela Jaffé, 4.5.1960, YBL.

47 Aniela Jaffé to R.F.C. Hull regarding the first three chapters, 8.5.1960, YBL.

The English translator R.F.C. Hull meanwhile entered the picture as the potential translator of the biography. Since moving to Ticino, Wolff had socialized several times with his new neighbor Hull. On February 29, 1960, Jung and Hull met in Ascona to discuss the English edition of *Mysterium Coniunctionis*. During this meeting, Hull mentioned Wolff's and Baynes' criticism and resentment with regard to Jaffe's presence in the second version of the biography text. In response, Jung vehemently defended his reasons for favoring the structure used in the second version: he said that in the first version it had irritated him to read about himself in the first person singular but in Jaffé's style; he had heard a feminine tone in the text but the person responsible for it was invisible. He had therefore asked her to write the text with two voices and to give herself more presence and transparency as author.

In a report of this conversation (not written until five months after the event), Hull falsely presented this explanation for the first changes to the manuscript during the autumn and winter of 1958/1959 as a criticism by Jung of the second version – see page 312. Hull's reason for compiling this report was to justify his involvement in the biography project to the editors of the *Collected Works*, shortly after they had blocked him from continuing work on translation of the biography. Hull's role will be discussed in more detail later in this chapter.

"Not an autobiography, but a joint creation"

With the new third version, in which Jaffé now (again) hardly featured and in which the text was mostly formulated as a direct testimony, it became more important than ever to Jung that Jaffé's authorial and editorial role be clearly stated. This emphasis was later interpreted by various third parties as a purely tactical move due to the legal situation – an interpretation which falls short in light of Jung's considered and well-documented position on the matter.[48] Jung had informed

48 C.G. Jung wrote to Walther Niehus on 5.4.1960 that the "so-called autobiography" was a work by Jaffé, had been written by her and must appear under her name. The parts of it written by him he regarded as "a contribution to Frau Jaffé's work"; cf. C.G. Jung, *Letters II*, p. 550.

Kurt Wolff and the *Collected Works* editorial committee of the book's definitive German title in July/August 1960: *"Erinnerungen, Träume, Gedanken von C.G. Jung* Aufgezeichnet und herausgegeben von Aniela Jaffé"[49] (the English translation of the title will be examined later in this book).

Prior to this, Rascher had commissioned a lawyer named Streuli to write an expert opinion on the copyright issue. This report, while acknowledging Aniela Jaffé as co-creator, was based on the assumption that Jung was also the co-author of the autobiographical text. Cecil Franklin of Routledge also assumed Jung's authorship: "It appears that a good deal of this book will be by Professor Jung although it is masked as being written by Mrs. Jaffé."[50] Jung's son-in-law Walther Niehus had already made a detailed examination of certain chapters written by Jaffé based on protocols and other source material, and had praised her work highly.[51] On behalf of Jung, Niehus wrote to Rascher and Routledge telling them that the book actually consisted of a text for which Jaffé was responsible, written in the style of a direct testimony of Jung. The contributions written by Jung were in the form of drafts which Jaffé had revised and expanded.[52] With his final choice of the above title, Jung chose to emphasize that the psychological contents, experiences and reflections were his, while the written formulation and editorial decisions were Jaffé's. By repeatedly referring to the project as Jaffé's undertaking, Jung also resolutely rejected any suggestion that he was the autobiographer. Kurt and Helene Wolff, seconded by

49 Note with handwritten comment by Kurt Wolff that Walther Niehus on behalf of C.G. Jung had said that this title was binding, dated 13.7.1960, YBL; meeting resolution of 26.8.1960 between C.G. Jung, Herbert Read, John Barrett, Walther Niehus, Marianne Niehus-Jung, Aniela Jaffé, Vaun Gillmor. "C.G. Jung has always maintained that he did not consider this book as his own enterprise but expressly as a book written by Mrs. Jaffé. The book was to be published in the name of Mrs. Jaffé and not in the name of C.G. Jung, because it did not represent an autobiography composed by C.G. Jung." AAJD (original in English). Prior to this meeting, the executive subcommittee of the *Collected Works*, of which Gerhard Adler, Michael Fordham and William McGuire were members, had requested to see the manuscript in order to assess Herbert Read's concern that the book should be seen as part of C.G. Jung's works, or with a view to publishing it through Routledge. Following the above meeting resolution, Herbert Read subsequently opted for a joint publication by Routledge and Collins.

50 Cecil Franklin to Walther Niehus, 20.3.1960.

51 Aniela Jaffé to Kurt Wolff, 1.4.1960, YBL

52 Walther Niehus to Rascher, 11.5.1960, Zentralbibliothek Zürich, Walther Niehus to Cecil Franklin, Routledge, 12.5.1960. C.G. Jung himself had referred to his contributions as "sketches"; cf. C.G. Jung to Jolande Jacobi, 25.8.1960, *Letters II*, p. 585.

Cary Baynes and R.F.C. Hull, were less than happy about this full title: they believed that the presence of the scarcely known name of Jaffé would reduce interest in the book, which if presented solely as the work of Jung would be a certain bestseller.[53]

Neither Jung nor Niehus, whom Jaffé described as a clever and talented negotiator, wished to burden the existing relationships with Rascher and Routledge with legal conflicts. With Barrett's support, they attempted to find a way for both publishing houses to be involved in the publication. After it emerged that Jung's lawyer of many years, Karrer, had long felt aggrieved about the involvement of another lawyer (Beidler) and continued to view the project as an autobiography, Walther Niehus engaged a third lawyer, Bernhard Peyer, to negotiate a compromise between the publishing houses. Finally, in the winter months of 1960/61, Peyer managed to contractually regulate the situation between Rascher, Pantheon and Routledge. As a result of Jung's contributions written specifically for the project, Peyer saw Jung as co-creator or co-author, a view which lent some validity to the claims of Rascher and Routledge. The new arrangement gave both publishers of the *Collected Works* the rights to publish an edition of the forthcoming book.[54] Pantheon was granted, in addition to the rights to the American edition, all further rights, thereby securing for Collins the rights offered by Pantheon for the paperback editions.

R.F.C. Hull had already translated Jaffé's manuscript containing the first three chapters in May 1960. His English version was based in many places on Richard Winston's 1958 translation of the manuscript "From the Earliest Experiences of My Life." Hull informed Wolff that he had deleted the opening lines of the text in which Jung addressed his children, and drafted a different opening, at Wolff's request.[55] In so

53 Helene Wolff agreed with Baynes: a book in Jaffé's name was sure to be "a dud." Helene Wolff to Cary Baynes, 9.6.1960, cited in Shamdasani, S., 2005, p. 37; R.F.C. Hull backed this assessment, 27.7.1960, cit. ibid, p. 34.

54 Aniela Jaffé to Helmut Hungerbühler: "Jung arranged matters so that Rascher Verlag kept the German rights and ancillary rights." 26.9.1982, AAJD.

55 R.F.C. Hull to Kurt Wolff, 22.5.1960, YBL. Hull said he would begin Jung's text as follows: "When I was six months old..." as "this would be the proper fairytale beginning." As already mentioned, Cary Baynes had previously objected to the dedication to Jung's children, which she evaluated as "wrong."

doing, he assumed an editorial role extending beyond that of a translator. Hull's editorial measures included the deletion of passages which were not to Wolff's liking. He also omitted important new sentences connecting the original text of "From the Earliest Experiences of My Life" with contents from the protocols – bridging passages which Jaffé and Jung had spent long hours working on together.

Jung, together with Jaffé, promptly set to work assessing, correcting and amending Hull's translation. Jung patiently examined the translator's "burdensome and complicated suggestions with regard to additions, rearrangements, etc." but was taken aback by his editorial incursions. Moreover, said Jung, he had been very satisfied with Winston's work, and there was no need for Hull to correct him.[56] He returned the re-edited text to Hull and shortly thereafter requested him to refrain from interfering in the contents. Hull continued long thereafter to claim to others that Jaffé had watered down Jung's direct and sometimes bawdy tone. Yet in his translation, Hull himself proceeded to polish and smooth the text. When Jaffé pointed out to him that his content changes were inadmissible and contradicted the meaning of Jung's statements, Hull was riled.[57] He now joined with Kurt Wolff, denouncing Jaffé with defamatory allegations, accusing her of having made adulterations, minimizations and omissions behind Jung's back.[58] Offended by Jaffé's criticism, Hull told Wolff she was a "Jungfrau on the warpath" whom only a steamroller or ruthless subterfuge could stop.[59] This bellicose attitude characterized the way he subsequently spoke about her to others for months to come.

56 Cf. Aniela Jaffé to Kurt Wolff, 16.1.1961, YBL.

57 "A sentence has been added in the English translation that is not present in the original. The German text is simple and strong, and bears the whole weight of the 'horrifying secret.' A sentence has been inserted in the English that testifies that everything is well and good after all! It has the effect of trivializing the overwhelming power." Aniela Jaffé to R.F.C. Hull, 8.5.1960, YBL. Cf. also Aniela Jaffé to Kurt Wolff, 16.1.1961, YBL. Hull's draft translation of the first three chapters, annotated with comments and corrections by C.G. Jung, Jaffé and a third person, is archived in the Library of Congress, Washington.

58 R.F.C. Hull to Kurt Wolff, 22.5.1960, YBL. Hull wrote that he believed Jung did not in the least realize how much Jaffé had tampered with, emasculated and castrated the original text. Her nonsense should really be thrown in the wastepaper basket, he said. Hull told third parties on several occasions that Jung had accused Jaffé of a "*Tantifizierung*" (aunt-ification, or old-maid-ification) of his words.

59 R.F.C.Hull to Kurt Wolff, 22.5.1960, YBL.

Both Barrett and Franklin, of the Bollingen Foundation and Routledge respectively, now objected to the appointment of Hull as translator, also because the English translation of the *Collected Works* was behind schedule. At Wolff's entreaties, Barrett conceded that Hull could do a final check of the completed translation. In an attempt to defend his involvement, Hull sent a report to Sir Herbert Read on September 2, 1960, as previously mentioned. In this document, which he predated to the end of July, Hull conveyed his impression that Jung was unhappy with Jaffé's style. As the translator, he had felt obliged to replace her feminine tone with a more direct masculine one that was closer to Jung's "original voice." The report was ostensibly written to justify to Hull's employers Routledge & Kegan Paul and the Bollingen Foundation the fact that he was also working for Wolff. But it also lent credence to the criticisms by Wolff and Baynes, who had been dismayed by Jung's staunch insistence that the book must be presented and published as a work by Jaffé.

Exactly who was responsible for bringing in Hull as translator is unclear, with contradictory sources of information. Wolff claimed on various occasions that Jung was the initiator. Jung refuted this claim, stating in his last letter to the responsible parties at Pantheon: "From the very beginning I was opposed to the involvement of Mr. Hull, whom Mr. Kurt Wolff had suggested."[60] Hull, Jung wrote, was indeed an outstanding translator of his *Collected Works*, but this project was not part of them. Jung professed himself very satisfied with Winston's work, and admired his lively, exceptionally elegant style and his unusual sensitivity.[61] Moreover, as Jung was certainly aware of how much work Hull still had to do on the *Collected Works*, it is unlikely that he would have asked him to translate "Jaffé's undertaking."[62] Barrett, too, would probably not have so forcefully demanded Hull's withdrawal if he believed Jung had requested him. There is strong evidence that Hull became involved in the project in early 1960 through Wolff's intervention. The wording of Hull's report drawn up several months after his

60 C.G. Jung to Gerold Gross, 6.5.1961, YBL

61 R.F.C.Hull to Kurt Wolff, 22.5.1960, YBL.

62 Handwritten note by C.G. Jung from the meeting of 26.8.1960 with Sir Herbert Read, John Barrett, Walther Niehus, Marianne Niehus-Jung, Aniela Jaffé, Vaun Gillmor, AAJD.

conversation with Jung at the end of February 1960 gives no indication of a request by Jung. Rather, it seems likely that Hull himself wanted to take on the task of making Jung appear more direct and "authentic" in an English version, and was supported in this endeavor by Wolff.[63] Various actions reveal Wolff as the party responsible for the contractual arrangements with Hull: in spring 1960 he paid a large advance to Hull and gave him material for translation and instructions for the text. Jaffé, who at first assumed that Winston was no longer available, was willing to work with Hull. It was not until a few months later, when she and Jung evaluated Hull's edited version of the Winston translation of the first three chapters, that she became aware of Jung's reservations about Hull's involvement.

Richard and Clara Winston were in fact two of the leading translators of German literature into English at that time. They had translated works by authors including Hannah Arendt, Thomas Mann, Hermann Hesse, Friedrich Dürrenmatt, Martin Buber and Franz Kafka, and received numerous awards for their work.[64] Both were also writers and often collaborated on translations. Jung and Jaffé were both greatly impressed by the high sensitivity and literary quality of their English version.

In summer 1960, during Erich Neumann's last visit to Switzerland, Jaffé was able to show him the revised third version of the German manuscript, which would now serve as the basis for the English translation. He was greatly impressed by it, as he had been with the earlier version. The two of them also discussed Jaffé's contribution on the visual arts to the forthcoming book *Man and his Symbols*.[65] Neither Jaffé nor Jung had an inkling that a mere three months later, their mutual friend and colleague Erich Neumann would suddenly pass away.

By the end of July, Jaffé had given Wolff the majority of the manuscript for Richard Winston, now back on the task, to translate. The remainder followed at the end of September. Jung had now approved

63 Cf. R.F.C. Hull, 27.7.1960, LoC.

64 Richard Winston, 1917–1979, Clara Winston Brussel, 1921–1983. The pair received the 1972 PEN translation prize for their translation of Thomas Mann's letters; they were also awarded the National Book Award for Translation in recognition of the high artistic quality of their translations of literary works.

65 Conversation between Aniela Jaffé and Robert Hinshaw, March 1991.

the entirety of the German manuscript; a chapter about recollections of famous personalities had been deleted as he and Jaffé deemed it unsatisfactory. Jaffé reiterated several times to Wolff that this manuscript was the final version for publication in German, and should also be used for the English translation. According to standard practice protecting authors' and editors' rights, no further changes could be made without explicit agreement. Jung continued to advise Jaffé on minor questions regarding the project, but during his final year of life was mainly occupied with his essay "Approaching the Unconscious."[66]

Due to an ongoing conflict with the executive board and directors of Pantheon Books, and possibly also reasons of health, Kurt and Helene Wolff decided to leave the publishing house in the summer of 1960. But because of their unwillingness to completely let go of the Jung/Jaffé project, their handover of responsibility at Pantheon was slow and unclear. At the beginning of October, Jung and Jaffé asked to see some of the translation for a first review, Wolff having assured them that Winston would begin work on it immediately in September. They requested to receive chapters of the English translation as soon as they would be ready, so that they could check it in stages.[67] With no response forthcoming, at the beginning of November Jung wrote a memo for Jaffé to pass on to Pantheon. In this handwritten document, he spoke of the "joint creation" (in line with the wording used by the lawyer Peyer), and declared that no further delays to the publication would be tolerated: "I hereby confirm my wish that the book produced as a joint creation '*Erinnerungen, Träume, Gedanken*' should now finally be published. I see no reason why it should be further delayed in going to press."[68] Two days later, Jung wrote directly to Sauerländer, reiterating that he would prefer to check the English text chapter by chapter, rather than being suddenly surprised by the entire translation.[69] Sauerländer replied that Winston had not yet begun, but that he would send some pages in a few weeks and planned to finish the English edition by the end of June 1961. In December 1960, Jaffé

66 Published in *Man and his Symbols*, 1964. See also CW 18.
67 Aniela Jaffé to Kurt Wolff, 25.9.1960, YBL
68 C.G. Jung to Aniela Jaffé for forwarding to the relevant parties at Pantheon Books, 1.11.1960, AAJD.
69 C.G. Jung to Wolfgang Sauerländer, 3.11.1960, AAJD.

and Jung received the translated chapters on Jung's psychiatric activity and on his relationship with Freud (which at that time had the title "*Begegnungen*" in German and "Meetings with People" in English). They were very pleased with the English version. Both Sauerländer and Wolff rejected Erich Neumann's text in the appendix to the Freud chapter as being too didactic and defensive. Jung made "a few small changes" to these chapters in English, and asked Jaffé to incorporate the changes into the German manuscript.[70] In view of the time pressure, Richard Winston now enlisted the help of his wife Clara. With an intensive effort, the couple then managed to translate the entire manuscript within a few weeks.

70 Aniela Jaffé to Kurt Wolff, 19 and 22.12.1960, YBL. Jaffé suggested making the German corrections in red or green ink to make them easier to follow.

"In case of my incapacity, I entrusted her with the responsibility for the final version of the whole manuscript."

Although Jaffé and Jung's main correspondence partner was now Sauerländer, who had taken over responsibility for the project at Pantheon Books in New York in October 1960, the Wolffs continued to play a significant role. At the beginning of January 1961, Kurt Wolff asked Jaffé to send him the English translation of the childhood text to present to Milton Waldman of Collins. At the same time he informed her that the entire Winston translation would be checked by Hull to correct certain specialist terms. When Jung heard about this, he wrote to Wolff immediately voicing his opposition: he and Jaffé were fully capable of correcting glaring errors themselves. Jung found Winston's fresh approach to certain terms very helpful in making them more understandable – for him the most important factor. In addition, despite appreciating Hull and his efforts, he foresaw from previous experience that Hull would not restrict himself to checking specific terminology, but would suggest numerous further additional changes, entailing unnecessary extra work and complications.[1] To Jaffé, Jung repeatedly expressed his admiration for the Winstons' work as it was.

Jung's reaction annoyed Wolff so much that he forwarded a copy of the letter to Cary Baynes with a brief note saying he was struggling to remain respectful. He composed a response to Jung, but had "reservations about sending it" – interestingly, he then decided to send his answer only to Jaffé. In it, he claimed that it was Jung himself who had once requested Hull as the "final reader responsible for the English

1 C.G. Jung to Kurt Wolff, 9.1.1961, YBL

version." Wolff had discussed the matter in these terms with Hull, and had informed Pantheon in New York and Collins in Glasgow accordingly. Wolff further claimed that also Winston was expecting his text to be read by Hull. Of course Hull would make only "the necessary linguistic and terminological corrections." The publisher warned Jaffé of the "catastrophic consequences" of using unconventional translations of specific terms, and appealed to her feelings of "responsibility, love, friendship and devotion for C.G. Jung."[2]

At the same time, Wolff was attempting to block Rascher from exercising the right to publish excerpts from the text in German newspapers or journals as pre-prints. Wolff asserted vis à vis Peyer that Jung and Jaffé had full confidence in the American publishers and therefore granted Pantheon unreserved freedom to make advance excerpts available in all countries. He also complained about the passage inserted in the agreement, at Rascher's instigation, specifying that the decision on final permission to print lay with Jung and Jaffé.

In mid-January, Jaffé returned the three chapters "Psychiatric Activities," "The Work" and "Sigmund Freud" (at that time still titled "Meetings with People") to Winston with a few corrections from her and Jung; in the meantime, Jung also checked the chapter about his travels. She let Wolff know that Hull sometimes made "serious factual mistakes," which the editors of the *Collected Works* in London had unfortunately also noticed. But that was not the core problem, she said – the difficulty with Hull was that he interfered too much regarding content by making "creative suggestions" for ideas he had misunderstood, requiring endless correspondence. With the first three chapters, Jung had been lenient and "patiently dealt with Hull's troublesome and complicated suggestions [...], but he had not forgotten it – Hull went too far." It was important to Jung that the style of the book was distinct from that of the *Collected Works*, Jaffé continued, and it need-

2 Kurt Wolff to Aniela Jaffé, 13.1.1961, YBL. Wolff's great frustration is clearly apparent in the letter, a frustration likely heightened by the contractual agreement that Peyer had reached with Rascher and Routledge, and the protracted battle over the rights. Wolff speaks of "repudiation and rebukes" and says that he cannot cope with further complications. In a letter of 25.1.1961, Sauerländer also approached Hull to do a final check, as "Winston's translation was done in the hope that Hull would see it." Wolfgang Sauerländer to Aniela Jaffé, 25.1.1961, YBL (original in English).

ed to be clear that the text was based on conversations.[3] Nevertheless, in view of Wolff's strong displeasure, Jaffé offered to approach Jung again on the subject of Hull's involvement. Jung thereupon agreed to Hull doing a final read-through on condition that his corrections would be restricted to the most necessary linguistic errors and incorrect terminology. Interestingly, Jung had begun referring to the book as a "so-called biography." Both he and Jaffé were by now more aware than ever that the manuscript was much closer to the genre of memoir, with anecdotal biographical material closely combined with, or even used in the service of, reflection.

In a supreme effort, by the end of January 1961 the team of Clara and Richard Winston had translated the entire manuscript in less than three months. Their co-working arrangements and their means of dividing the work are not known. Wolff now finally loosened his grip and put an end to the confusing overlap of responsibilities with Pantheon: he would henceforth "take no further part in the final editing of the book in either language."[4] Despite his professed relinquishing of control, he instructed Jaffé in the same letter not to give the German version to Rascher under any circumstances, regardless of the contractual agreement. It would be up to Pantheon to pass the manuscript on to Rascher in due course.

Hull, after his final check of the translation, reported that there were very few mistakes to change if he were really to limit himself to the most necessary corrections. The Jungian expressions were accurate; the Winstons were evidently familiar with Jung's clinical terminology. Like Wolff, Hull continued to call the book an autobiography and objected to Jaffé's "explanatory interpolations" within the text. These should be kept to a minimum or put into footnotes so as not to interrupt the narrative continuity, he wrote to the publisher.[5] Hull strongly resisted acknowledging Jaffé's co-author role, and as translator wished to expunge her presence in the text as much as possible. He found it

3 Aniela Jaffé to Kurt Wolff, 16.1.1961, YBL
4 Kurt Wolff to Aniela Jaffé, 26.1.1961, YBL.
5 R.F.C. Hull to Kurt Wolff, 24.1.1961, R.F.C. Hull to Aniela Jaffé, 27.1.1961, YBL, AAJD.

exasperating "to hear that proprietary voice in the background, constantly pointing out the obvious!"[6]

After takeover proceedings in the early months of the year, Pantheon Books was purchased by Random House in May 1961. Wolfgang Sauerländer passed responsibility for the final stages of the book's publication to Gerald Gross, and henceforth worked only for the Bollingen Foundation. In a subsequent letter to Gross, C.G. Jung again expressed his appreciation for the Winstons' work and his explicit reservations with regard to Hull's involvement. By this stage, difficulties had apparently arisen in coordinating the work of the different translators. Jung wrote that "from the very beginning" he had opposed Wolff's determination to involve Hull in this non-scientific project. Jung emphasized the Winstons' artistic and empathic style. He had acquiesced to Hull's involvement only reluctantly due to Wolff's insistence, but foreseeing complications.[7] From the further exchange of letters, it is possible to extrapolate which of the English-language chapters Jung probably did not manage to check before his death: the chapter entitled "The Tower at Bollingen", "The Visions of 1944", "Life after Death", "Late Thoughts", and the "Retrospect" section. Jung had wanted to approve the translation of these chapters as soon as possible so that the book "may go to print."[8] He requested that all chapters be sent from the U.S. to Jaffé, to whom Jung now explicitly transferred final responsibility in the event that he should no longer be able to check the English version: "In case of my incapacity I entrusted her with the responsibility for the final version of the whole manuscript."[9] This unequivocal sentence not only expresses explicit trust and clarification of responsibility, but also draws a clear boundary with regard to the role of Hull. One month later, on June 6, 1961, the life of C.G. Jung came to an end.

6 R.F.C. Hull to Kurt Wolff, 24.1.1961, YBL.

7 C.G. Jung to Gerald Gross, 6.5.1961, AAJD (original in English). "From the very beginning I was, as you may have heard, against the collaboration of Mr. Hull, proposed by Mr. Kurt Wolff. Mr. Hull is an excellent translator of my Collected Works, but I do not consider the so-called 'autobiography' to be a scientific book, and I liked Mr. Winston's artistic style based on real empathy. Only when Mr. Wolff insisted I reluctantly gave in, foreseeing all sorts of complications."

8 Ibid.

9 Ibid.

Despite his wish for an imminent publication, the English book would not actually appear in print until two years later. The publication continued to be delayed by disagreements – and in some cases major disputes – about the content from several parties. Hull doggedly persisted in trying to push through his translation suggestions, still calling for a less refined and more direct tone. For example, Hull insisted on translating the sentence about Jung's long-suppressed childhood vision of God letting an enormous excrement fall on the roof of the Basel Munster, as "God *shits* on the Basel Munster." Only most unwillingly did he finally accept Jaffé's explanation that the formulation in the German manuscript corresponded exactly to the wording used by Jung in "From the Earliest Experiences of My Life."[10] He repeatedly claimed to others that Jaffé had sanitized and diluted Jung's original formulations.

More serious, however, were the changes in the first two chapters that Marianne and Walther Niehus-Jung demanded after reading the English translation. They feared that certain passages about the adolescent Jung's experiences of and feelings about the church, God and the Eucharist were too provocative. Seen in context, it is clear that these thoughts are a kind of inner dialogue of the young man with himself. But some of the next generation in his family were concerned that readers might perceive these religious doubts and questions as blasphemous. Jaffé therefore offered to make minimal changes to emphasize the subjective and reflective character of the text and to clarify that such statements did not constitute any absolute judgments on the part of Jung.[11] She had also added some text about the phallus dream of

10 Trans. note: the German word used is "Exkrement," translated in the published English version of Memories, 1962, p. 39, as "turd."

11 The offending point for the Niehus-Jungs was a passage about Jung's disappointment at his confirmation and first communion, formulated thus: "*Ich wusste, dass ich nie mehr an dieser Ceremonie theilnehmen konnte. Es ist ja gar keine Religion. Es ist eine Abwesenheit Gottes, ein Ort wo man nicht hingehen soll. Dort ist kein Leben, sondern ein Tod.*" ["I knew that I would never again be able to participate in this ceremony. It is no religion at all. It is an absence of God, a place where one should not go. There is no life there, but a death."]. In order to emphasize the subjective nature of the experience, Jaffé edited it thus: "*Ich wusste, dass ich nie mehr an dieser Zeremonie teilnehmen konnte. Für mich war sie keine Religion und eine Abwesenheit Gottes. Die Kirche war ein Ort, an den ich nicht mehr gehen durfte. Dort war für mich kein Leben, sondern Tod.*" ["I knew that I would never again be able to participate in this ceremony. For me it was no religion, it was an absence of God. The church was a place I could no longer go. There was no life for me there, but death."]. Cf. typescript of "*Von den anfänglichen Ereignissen meines Lebens*", p. 38, ETH, and Jaffé, A. (ed.), 1962, p. 61

Jung's early childhood based on a letter written by Jung in 1922, found only after his death – Jung's daughter Marianne had no objections to this.[12]

Over time, Hull gradually revised his pejorative view of Jaffé and expressed growing admiration for her "objectivity and keen perception" in recognizing the resistance of some of Jung's heirs as a reflection of Jung's own ambivalence about the book. Regarding Jung's family circle, however, Hull now expressed contempt for what he deemed Swiss *petit-bourgeois* sensibilities behind their censorship wishes.[13] Jaffé's alterations of the passage about Jung's early religious thoughts did not satisfy Walther Niehus. Thus he demanded the removal of substantial passages from the School Years chapter.[14] What he saw as objectionable or offensive, however, Jaffé believed was of paramount importance in portraying the struggle of a doubting and questioning adolescent earnestly seeking answers. Furthermore, these were questions which would occupy Jung all his life – under no circumstances was she prepared to cut this important section. Fearing further interference in the text, she asked Gerald Gross to publish the book as soon as possible.[15] At the end of August, Gross traveled to Zürich to clear up remaining questions with her and to prepare a clean and final manuscript ready for print. This was quickly achieved by mutual agreement, and with the lawyer Peyer's assistance, it was confirmed in writing that the manuscript was now final and ready to print, with the exception of the pending queries in the School Years chapter. Jaffé, as well as Peyer, then tried to persuade Niehus – in vain. Resignedly, Jaffé was forced to report to New York that Jung's son-in-law still wanted to block the publication of twelve pages of the manuscript. As a concession to Walther and Marianne Niehus, she agreed to delete one further sentence

(German edition). [Trans. note: the translation in the English edition of *Memories*, 1962, p. 55, differs slightly from the above; the text is retranslated here more literally in order to demonstrate the difference between the passages.]

12 On the phallus dream cf. Jaffé, A. (ed.), 1962, p. 12f.

13 R.F.C. Hull to Gerald Gross, 11.8.1961, private Bollingen Foundation Archive; cit. in Bair, D., 2004, p. 631.

14 The passages he wanted to delete are found on pages 54 (mid) to 63 (top) of the English edition, Jaffé, A. (ed.), 1962 (p. 37 to 44 of the typescript "*Von den anfänglichen Ereignissen meines Lebens*," ETH).

15 Aniela Jaffé to Gerald Gross, 30.8.1961, AAJD

which could possibly have been misunderstood as blasphemous.[16] And as a result of the objections, two further formulations of Jung's were also toned down.[17] It is doubtful that Jung would have been in agreement with these amendments, but their adoption meant that blockage of the publication was finally withdrawn.

Yet another setback came at the end of September: Milton Waldman of British publishing house Collins demanded a shortening of the manuscript by more than two-hundred pages to save on printing costs. It is not known to what extent Kurt Wolff supported this abridgement. At the beginning of October, Waldman reiterated the demand and sent a long list of proposed cuts, including removal of the entire text of *Septem Sermones*. Gross then agreed, in early December, not only to this deletion, but also to leave out texts on Jung's relationship with friends of his youth Albert Oeri and Andreas Vischer, with his paternal mentor Théodore Flournoy (which Wolff had also wished to exclude) and with the Indologist Heinrich Zimmer, as well as sections on Jung's experiences at the Taj Mahal, in Sanchi and in other parts

16 The sentence in question is the last in the following sequence, shown here in italics: "God is not human, I thought; that is His greatness, that nothing human impinges on Him. He is kind and terrible – both at once – and is therefore a great peril from which everyone naturally tries to save himself. People cling one-sidedly to His love and goodness, for fear they will fall victim to the tempter and destroyer. Jesus, too, had noticed that, and had therefore taught: 'Lead us not into temptation.' *The true God has nothing to do with the communion, nothing to do with the church at all.*" Cf. Jaffé, A. (ed.), 1962, p. 56.

17 The contentious formulations concern Jung's fierce criticism of *Christliche Dogmatik* by Alois E. Biedermann and of Goethe's presentation of evil in *Faust*. Cf. typescript p. 43: "*Diese angebliche Dogmatik war offenbar nichts als Schönschwätzerei, ja schlimmer noch, ein absichtlicher Betrug oder eine ungewöhnliche Dummheit, welche nichts anderes bezweckte, als die Wahrheit verdunkeln.*" ["This alleged dogmatics was obviously nothing but fancy drivel, worse still it was a deliberate fraud or an uncommon stupidity whose sole aim was to obscure the truth."]. Jaffé edited it slightly as follows: "*Die Dogmatik war offensichtlich nichts als Schönschwätzerei, ja schlimmer noch, eine ungewöhnliche Dummheit, welche nichts anderes konnte, als die Wahrheit verdunkeln.*" Jaffé, A. (ed.), 1962, p. 65, German edition. [Trans. note: in the English edition, p. 59, the sentence is "This weighty tome on dogmatics was nothing but fancy drivel; worse still it was a fraud or a specimen of uncommon stupidity whose sole aim was to obscure the truth." Here we see that the deleted words "*ein absichtlicher Betrug*" are partially retained in the English ("fraud" is kept; "deliberate" is omitted).] Elsewhere on *Faust*, typescript p. 44f.: "*Ich bedauerte aufs Tiefste, dass auch Goethe, der theologischen – ach so betrügerischen – Verharmlosung des Bösen zum Opfer gefallen war.*" ["I was deeply sorry that Goethe too had fallen for those theological – oh so fraudulent – devices by which evil is rendered innocuous."] was changed to: "*Ich bedauerte es auf tiefste, dass auch Goethe der – oh so trügerischen – Verharmlosung des Bösen zum Opfer gefallen war.*" Jaffé A., 1962, p. 66; English edition p. 61. [Trans. note: as well as "theological" being omitted, there is a subtle difference in meaning between "betrügerisch" (fraudulent, deceitful) and "trügerisch" (illusory, duplicitous) – in the English published edition the word used is "cunning": "I was deeply sorry that Goethe too had fallen for those cunning devices by which evil is rendered innocuous."]

of India, information about *The Red Book*, and an extract from a text written by Richard Wilhelm, "My Encounter with C.G. Jung in China."[18]

Jaffé, loathe to delay the book's publication even longer with yet more battles, with a heavy heart reluctantly agreed to the cuts. She wrote to Gross: "One day you will regret it, of that I am certain."[19] Jung described so vividly how he had come to write *Septem Sermones* during his confrontation with the unconscious that readers would naturally be curious about it, claimed Jaffé. It was also one of the few poetic writings allowed by Jung to be published: "If you leave it out, a significant side of Jung is missing."[20] She also rued the omission of Jung's experiences at the Taj Mahal and in Sanchi. In the end, only around half of the cuts requested by Waldman for the English-language edition were authorized. Most importantly for Jaffé, Walther and Marianne Niehus-Jung had finally agreed to publication of the section they had wanted to delete. Jaffé informed Rascher and S. Fischer that she was not willing to undertake the same cuts in the German edition as had been made in the English.[21] Thus it came about that there were significant content differences between the English and German editions, with Waldman's cuts coming in addition to the previous excisions that Wolff had made to the Pantheon edition.

Included in the German but not in the English edition, therefore, in addition to *Septem Sermones*, were various references to *The Red Book*, the chapter about C.G. Jung's ancestry and family, letters to

18 An article by Richard Wilhelm which appeared in the *Neue Zürcher Zeitung*, 21.1.1929; Jung himself had wanted this text to appear in the book. In the article Wilhelm wrote about how he had been surprised and impressed by the congruence of ancient Chinese wisdom with Jung's research, and said that he had actually "encountered Jung's world of ideas in China." "Chinese wisdom and Dr. Jung have both descended independently of one another into the depths of man's collective psyche and have there come upon realities which look so alike because they are equally anchored in the truth. This would prove that the truth can be reached from any standpoint if only one digs deep enough for it, and the congruity between the Swiss scientist and the old Chinese sages only goes to show that both are right because both have found the truth." Cf. Jaffé, A., 1989, p. 52.

19 Aniela Jaffé to Gerald Gross, 5.12.1961, AAJD.

20 Ibid. Not until more than ten years later, in 1973, was "Septem Sermones" added as an appendix to the British edition.

21 She was prepared to leave out Jung's experiences in Paris and Oxford – which are now found in the present volume – as well as to shorten the passages about Africa (also now published in the present volume). Unlike Pantheon and Collins, Rascher agreed to publish the longer complete text. Memorandum of 22.1.1962, Rascher Archive, Zentralbibliothek Zürich.

Erich Neumann and Zwi Werblowski, sections on Théodore Flournoy and Heinrich Zimmer, and recollections of Albert Oeri and Andreas Vischer.[22]

At the end of 1961, when Jaffé gave Hull the now fixed final deadline for the English edition, she reminded him again that the final word rested with her, and that she could not completely disregard the family's wishes. In March 1962, she flew to Majorca (where Hull was now living) to discuss with him the last remaining open questions.

Thus, by summer 1962, the German and English manuscripts were finally ready for publication. After the English galley proofs had been corrected, Bernhard Peyer contacted Gerald Gross on behalf of Jaffé to ask him to return all of her protocols (a request Jaffé had already broached with Kurt Wolff several times, without success). Peyer also requested on behalf of Jung's family the return of all copies of manuscripts by C.G. Jung that had been given to the publisher to read. At the end of September, Gross left the Random-House owned Pantheon Books for Macmillan Publishers. Before leaving, he contacted Wolfgang Sauerländer, Kyrill Schabert and Kurt and Helene Wolff regarding the return of the documents requested by Peyer.

Despite Gross' enquiries, the only material that was ever returned to Jaffé or the family of Jung were the English-language galley proofs which she had corrected. Gross told Peyer that he had heard of the other documents, but upon his taking over of responsibility for the project, they were no longer on the premises of Pantheon and could not be found. The story of what actually happened to this material will become clear in one of the following chapters.

22 On the differences between the English and German editions, see also Shamdasani, S., "Memories, Dreams, Omissions," in *Spring, A Journal of Archetype and Culture*, 1995, and Muramoto, S., "Completing the Memoirs: The Passages Omitted or Transposed in the English or Japanese Versions of Jung's Autobiography," Spring, 1987, pp. 163ff.

Aniela Jaffé in 1962, after completing her work on *Memories, Dreams, Reflections by C.G. Jung*; photo © Barbara Kruck.

"A biography of Jung written in the form of an autobiography"

The German edition of *Erinnerungen, Träume, Gedanken von C.G. Jung* was published at the end of October 1962, enabling Max Rascher to see the fruit of his successful legal battle shortly before his death in December 1962. In Britain and the USA, the public would have to wait until the summer and fall of 1963 respectively to read the book. Shortly after the publication of the English versions, Kurt Wolff also died.[1]

In her introduction to the book, Jaffé made it clear that Wolff had asked her to write about Jung as his biographer, but with the explicit instruction that the book should be written "in the form of an autobiography."[2] In her preliminary remarks, she also outlined the collaborative process by which Jung made contributions to the text and added to and corrected her manuscript. At the same time, she made clear that she had also supplemented the texts provided by him with extracts from her records of their conversations, and that she had "expanded his sometimes terse allusions" and "eliminated repetitions." The further the work had progressed, she wrote, "the closer became the fusion between his work and mine."[3]

The degree to which this information was taken on board by critics and journalists varied greatly, as an evaluation of more than one hundred reviews and articles about the book in the German-language and English-language press reveals. About one quarter of all these

1 Deceased 21.10.1963 in Ludwigsburg.
2 Jaffé, A., 1962, p. vi.
3 Jaffé, A., 1962, p. vii.

reviewers had evidently read the introduction carefully – for example, one lauded Jaffé's "difficult and novel attempt to write a biography of Jung in the form of an autobiography,"[4] while another described Jaffé as "the biographer who was obliged to write an autobiography."[5] The chief features editor of *Die Zeit,* Walter Abendroth, himself the author of several biographies, attributed the main authorship of the book to Jaffé: "The book is largely written by Aniela Jaffé, who has put her notes of verbal conversations into autobiographical form."[6]

Another group of critics saw Jung and Jaffé as co-authors, with most of them acknowledging Jaffé as the responsible editor. Thus, for example, Jolande Jacobi wrote that the book was composed of autobiographical and biographical material that had been edited "so carefully and sensitively into *one* text" that it was not possible to distinguish which was which.[7] In *Acta Psychotherapeutica*, E.A. Carp wrote that Jaffé had taken on the difficult task of assembling Jung's memoirs and creating a concise unified text.[8] The co-authorship was also criticized by some, however. Hermann L. Goldschmidt, for instance, claimed that the "unreserved devotion" of Jaffé may have given Jung confidence that she would depict him as he saw himself, but that this devotion stood in the way of an objective representation of her subject. Another critic regretted that Jung's contributions and "Jaffé's additions" were never clearly distinguished, meaning that one was faced with an "impenetrable intermingling of personal statements and the testimony of a disciple."[9] In the English-speaking world especially, a leading role in the co-authorship was attributed to Jung. Reviewers emphasized

4 Friedrich-Carl Fischer, in *Buchbrief Kultur*, 19.12.1962, ETH (original: "*schwierigen und neuartigen Versuch, eine Biographie Jungs in Form einer Autobiographie gestaltet*").

5 Erich Randak, Radio Wien, 5.2.1963, ETH (original: "*Biographin, zur Gestalterin einer Autobiographie ausersehen*").

6 Walter Abendroth, *Die Zeit*, 12.4.1963, ETH (original: "*Zum grossen Teil entstammt es der Feder Aniela Jaffés, die ihre Aufzeichnungen mündlicher Mitteilungen in die autobiographische Form brachte*").

7 Jolande Jacobi, *Neue Zürcher Zeitung*, weekend supplement, Nov. 1962, ETH (original: "*so sorgfältig und einfühlsam zu einem Text gefügt*").

8 *Acta Psychotherapeutica*, 11.5.1963, ETH (original: "*Jaffé a entrepris la lourde tâche de rassembler ces mémoires et d'en faire une unité concise*").

9 First quote Hermann L. Goldschmidt, *Das Bücherblatt*, 16.11.1962 (original: "*vorbehaltlose Hingabe*"), second quote Karl Gerhard Steck, 1.4.1963, *Die Zeitwende*, ETH (original: "*undurchdringlichen Ineinander von Selbstaussage und Jünger Zeugnis*").

that Jung had supplemented, corrected and supervised Jaffé's work, and that he had written a considerable portion of the book himself.[10]

Finally, a large number of reviewers did not refer to the book as a work *about* Jung, but as a book *by* him – i.e., they read it as an autobiography, as Kurt Wolff had intended. In these reviews, Jaffé was either not mentioned at all, or if she was, relegated to the role of an assistant. She had "encouraged and accompanied" the work, for example.[11] Elsewhere she was even described as the recipient of Jung's "dictation." One representative example in this regard is the review by Germain Bazin: "It was first dictated by Jung to his loyal secretary, who wrote a summary which he then revised and completed himself."[12] Even the psychiatrist and medical historian Henri F. Ellenberger, who read and compared the German and English editions for his review, wrote of an "unusual autobiography," the most interesting chapters of which were those about Jung's confrontation with the unconscious after his split from Freud, and the discoveries made at that time. Like many others, Ellenberger also praised the book's focus on Jung's deepening of soul with evolving and broadening of consciousness through the inclusion of the unconscious.[13]

As early as the summer of 1962, Bernhard Peyer had to combat false statements about the work and authorship with the threat of legal action on behalf of Aniela Jaffé and the heirs of C.G. Jung jointly. The very first advance publication of large sections of the book appeared in the Swiss weekly magazine *Die Weltwoche*, which serialized the text in seventeen parts from mid-August 1962 to February 1963 as part of a special subscription offer. In the first announcement of the serialization, Jaffé and her role were not mentioned at all – the book was described as a "self-biography of the great physician of the soul,

10 Cf. Ninian Smart, *Birmingham Post*, 9.7.1963: "*Jung undertook it to supervise an attempt by Aniela Jaffé to write a biography. (...) He took over the work and so a substantial portion is actually written by him.*" See also reviews of 7.7.1963, *The Observer*, and 11.7.1963, *The Times*. All reviews, ETH. One of the few English articles that clearly rejected the use of the term "autobiography" was by E.A. Bennet, *British Medical Journal*, 23.9.1963.

11 W.L., *Glarner Nachrichten*, 10.1.1962, ETH (original: "*sie durfte das Werk fördern und begleiten*").

12 *Critique*, 1.9.1964, ETH (original: "*Il fut d'abord dicté par Jung à sa fidèle secrétaire qui en fit un abrégé, après quoi il le revisa et le compléta lui-même*").

13 Published in *Sage Journal* in the section "Book Reviews", page 272; undated, review signed: H.F. Ellenberger, M.D., Montreal.

Carl Gustav Jung" and as "a description of his life written by him." Incorrect claims were also made about the book's inception: "Upon his death the pages were ready: Jung wrote the first part himself, the later chapters were completely dictated by him or outlined and then checked by him."[14] The second announcement described it as a "unique self-testimony" and again failed to name Jaffé or to give the correct title and bibliographic information. The headline for the first installment, in large type, was "*Die Autobiographie von C.G. Jung.*"[15]

Following a sharp rebuke by the attorney Peyer, the title of the book was finally printed correctly in the edition of September 14, 1962, where Jaffé was named as editor and the correct bibliographic details listed. For Peyer, the weekly paper had played a "dirty trick" in violation of the authors' rights purely in order to increase the number of subscribers.[16] Unfortunately, this incident was the prelude to many years of misconceptions, with Jaffé's role as author, her rights and acknowledgment of her work continually overlooked or disregarded altogether. The reason, in Jaffé's view, for publishers to conceal her name and role came down to marketing: "in order to sell more."[17]

The "*Erinnerungsbuch*" or memory book, as Jaffé preferred to call it, having long since ceased using the word biography, was ultimately a great success. It continues today for many people around the world to be the first introduction to C.G. Jung's psychology and ideas. At the same time as the Rascher edition was published, an inexpensive licensed edition was made available through the Swiss book club, *Ex Libris*. Translations into numerous other languages quickly followed. Before long, even publishing companies that had purchased the foreign-language rights were presenting the book as an autobiography. Gallimard of Paris, for example, made a completely unauthorized change to the title in French, calling it *Ma vie* (my life) with C.G. Jung as the author. In the foreword, Roland Cahen called the book

14 *Die Weltwoche*, 17.8.1962, Zentralbibliothek Zürich (original quotes: "*Selbstbiographie des grossen Seelenarztes Carl Gustav Jung*"; "*eine von ihm selbst verfasste Darstellung des eigenen Lebens*"; "*Bei seinem Tod lagen die Blätter bereit: den ersten Teil hatte Jung selbst geschrieben, die späteren Kapitel hatte er vollständig diktiert oder dann skizziert und die Reinschrift durchgesehen.*")

15 Ibid., additionally issues of *Weltwoche* of 24.8.1962, 31.8.1962, 7.9.1962 and 14.9.1962, Zentralbibliothek Zürich.

16 Cf. Bernhard Peyer to Biilman & Eriksen, 11.10.1965, AAJD.

17 Aniela Jaffé to Helmut Hungerbühler, 26.9.1982, AAJD.

the "*édition française de l'autobiographie de C.G. Jung.*"[18] On the cover below the title stood "collected by Aniela Jaffé," in the same type-size and font as the French translators.

The questionable translation of the title in the English-language editions, meanwhile, created a deliberate impression in order to bolster the autobiography myth. Instead of "*Erinnerungen, Träume, Gedanken von C.G. Jung*" being translated accurately as "Memories, Dreams, Reflections *of* C.G. Jung," the little preposition "of" was replaced with "by" – *Memories, Dreams, Reflections by C.G. Jung.* The sham was consolidated by the cover design: the first three words, "Memories, Dreams, Reflections", were accentuated in large type, with the words "by C.G. Jung" placed underneath in a contrasting color. This title and layout still today gives the impression that Jung is the author of the book. When the Danish version appeared with Biilmann & Eriksen in fall 1965 without Jaffé's name appearing at all on the cover or title pages, Peyer again reacted in representation of the joint legal interests of Aniela Jaffé and the heirs of C.G. Jung. His letter was unequivocal: "I protest against the blatant violation of authors' rights which is deliberately intended to give an entirely false impression of the work."[19] He demanded the immediate correction of the cover and title pages, threatening to claim for damages if they did not comply. On the same date, he also wrote to Pantheon/Random House and criticized their contractual wording: "To my astonishment, Biilmann & Eriksen have used the same dirty trick of *Weltwoche* and have completely omitted to mention Mrs. Aniela Jaffé. [...] Reading the text of your agreement with Biilmann I must state that you yourself did not use there the full correct title."[20] Pantheon had also issued incorrect contracts to the Spanish and Norwegian publishers: in 1967, these versions too

18 Cf. C.G. Jung, *Ma vie*, Paris, 1966, "*Avant-propos de Roland Cahen*" p. 7; the "*souvenirs, rêves et pensées*" are described as "*recueillis par Aniela Jaffé.*" The Swedish translation had already been published two years previously with the main title "C.G. Jung / *Mitt liv*", Natur och Kultur, Stockholm, 1964.

19 Bernhard Peyer to Biilmann & Eriksen, 11.10.1965, AAJD.

20 Bernhard Peyer to Pantheon, 11.10.1965, AAJD (original in English). Even though C.G. Jung had deliberately insisted that he was not to be named as co-author in the original contract with Pantheon, in Pantheon's contract of 11.8.1965 with the Danish publishers Biilmann & Eriksen, Jung and Jaffé were both listed as authors. AAJD. In the first edition published by Biilmann and Eriksen, the book was split into two parts: the first volume which appeared in 1965 contained the four chapters on childhood, school years, student years and psychiatric activities under the authorship of C.G.

appeared without Jaffé's name on the cover, giving the impression that the book was an autobiography by Jung.

Jaffé's attitude toward these infringements, which disregarded both her role and the explicit position of Jung, was nuanced but clear. On the one hand, she was pleased that her text gave readers a feeling of direct connection with the thoughts and words of C.G. Jung – their reactions showed that she had indeed managed to closely reproduce his voice. On the other, she was strongly critical of the disrespect for her work and rights on the part of the publishing houses. In bibliographies in her later writings, she did not list the book under her own publications as editor, but usually directly after Jung's works with no author name, however always indicating her editorial and recording role. Occasionally she listed it in bibliographies as having joint authorship.[21]

The unexpected success and positive reception of the book outweighed to a large extent Jaffé's disappointment at the violations of her rights. In correspondence with Kurt Wolff several years earlier, she had once called the book a "*Schmerzenskind*" (a child born after much pain), because of the many difficulties during its long inception. In the same sentence, however, she added how well known it was that such children were closest to one's heart.[22] That this creation now generated a more profound interest in Jung and his work on an international scale was for Jaffé the highest reward.

Jung only, the second volume which appeared in 1966 contained the remaining chapters under the authorship of Aniela Jaffé and C.G. Jung.

21 Cf. *Schweizerische Zeitschrift für Psychologie und ihre Anwendungen*, no. 24, 1965, where the listing in the bibliography is given with the double name "Jung-Jaffé."

22 In a letter to Laurens van der Post, who had written to her about Franz Jung's criticisms of a film project of his, she replied that in her experience, work about or even with Jung was strangely always accompanied by pain and suffering. The memoir project had brought an avalanche of difficulties in its wake, and the publication of Jung's letters had caused its fair share of problems; the founding of the Jung Institute had also been a stormy affair – as if the unknown gods required a sacrifice, like in the construction of new buildings in ancient times. Aniela Jaffé to Laurens van der Post, 8.12.1971, AAJD

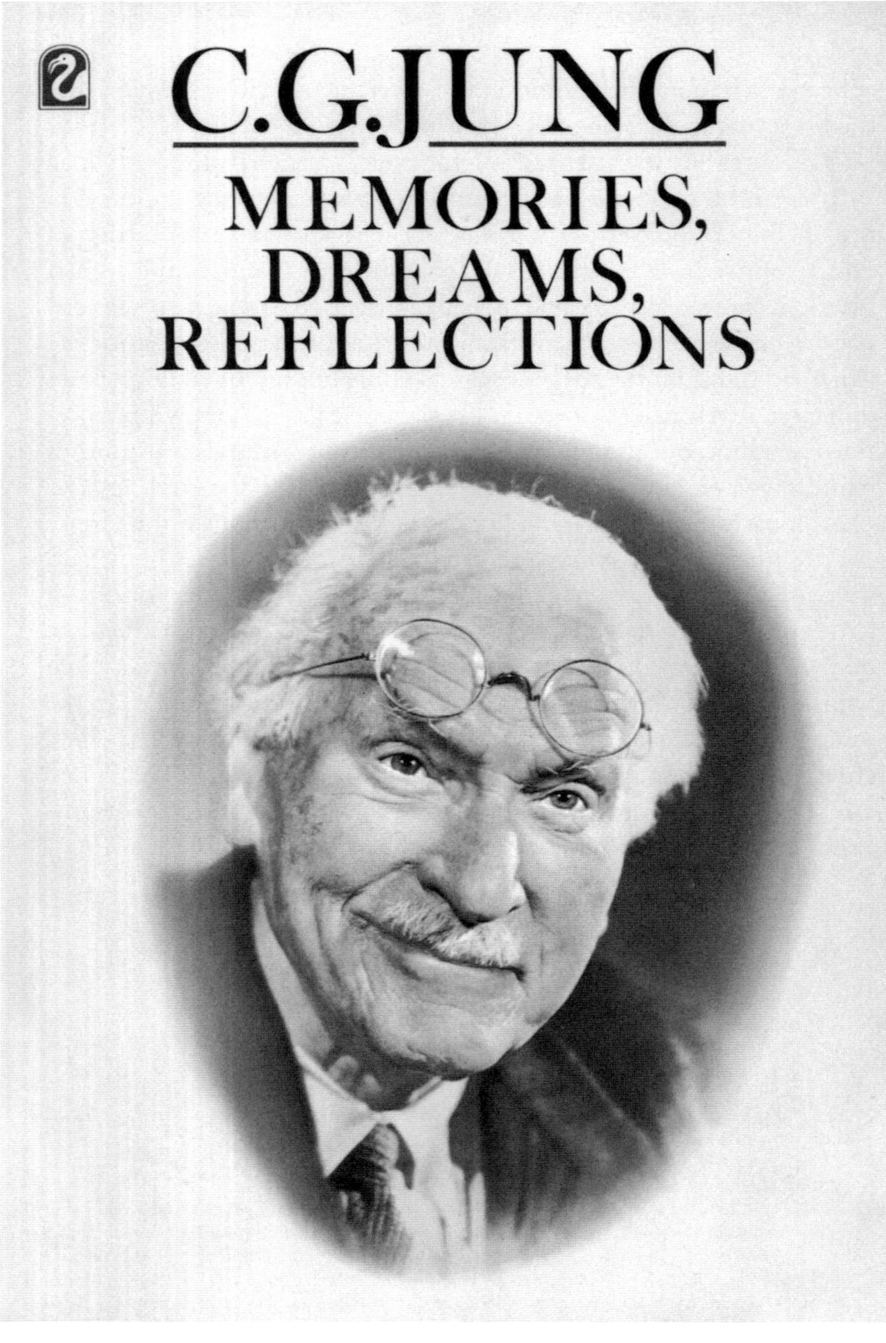

Cover of the 1983 English edition, Flamingo/Fontana Paperbacks

Cover of the 1966 French edition, Editions Gallimard

A far-reaching promise

Since January 1962, Jaffé had been occupied with the preparation of C.G. Jung's letters for publication,[23] in addition to her activities as an author, lecturer and analyst. The English edition of *Geistererscheinungen und Vorzeichen,* published in 1963 entitled *Apparitions and Precognition*, was so successful that a second edition came out only a year later.[24] In 1964, her essay "Symbolism in the Visual Arts" in *Man and his Symbols* met with acclaim.[25] This book, which included C.G. Jung's last piece of writing, became another of the main introductions to Jungian psychology for a wide readership over many years.

It came as no surprise to her that following the publication of *Memories, Dreams, Reflections by C.G. Jung*, she was repeatedly asked to complement Jung's revealings of his "inner personality," which he had called "number two," with depictions of his outer personality, the socially connected "number one." She met this wish by writing a piece called "From Jung's Last Years," drawing upon her personal memories of Jung, mainly from their years of almost daily contact, but emphasized that these were merely sidelights and subjective snapshots of individual moments. At the end of this essay, written in 1965/66, Jaffé disclosed a moving request by Jung and a momentous promise on her part: "One autumn morning in Bollingen, after intense work, Jung asked me to give my word to speak and answer in his stead questions about his life and work when he would no longer be there. The

23 Aniela Jaffé to her friend Karl Schmid, letter of 11.11.1962: "At the moment I am working on ordering Jung's letters and, together with Jung's daughter Mrs. Marianne Niehus and Dr. G. Adler of London, preparing them for publication in two volumes. Thus I am still working in the same old rooms and with the same material as before." ETH.

24 New York, University Books, 1963, second edition 1964. Today in its fifth English edition, revised by the author, under the amended title *An Archetypal Approach to Death Dreams and Ghosts*, Daimon, Einsiedeln, 1999. Translations into numerous languages followed.

25 1964, London. In writing the essay, Jaffé had had access to the comprehensive inventory of the *Bibliothèque nationale de France* which was partially housed in the Château de Beaumesnil, home of her uncle Hans Fürstenberg. Fürstenberg published several books on art history and philosophy such as *Einführung in die Ästhetik. Betrachtungen über die Malkunst,* 1978 and *Dialektik des XXI. Jahrhunderts. Der neue Weg des Denkens von der Atomphysik bis zu den Wissenschaften vom Menschen*, 1972. His home in Normandy was a place of retreat for Jaffé in the post-war years, and she often went there to write.

brief conversation was sober, almost casual; Jung was no friend of big words."[26]

A brief look at Jaffé's editorial and writing endeavors between 1963 and 1978 will show how seriously she took her promise. It became the primary task of the latter part of her life, leading to her finally, in her last years, dedicating herself to the yet unpublished records of her biographical conversations with Jung.

But first, the publication of the selected letters of C.G. Jung entailed more than ten years of work. With the death of Marianne Niehus-Jung, Jaffé and Gerhard Adler lost a valued co-worker on the challenging project. Alongside the editorial work, Jaffé was responsible for translating into German the numerous letters that were in English or French. Her aim in selecting the letters was to shed light on Jung's thought processes during the writing of his individual works or after their publication, as well as to show his capacity for relatedness and connection with people. *MDR* had revealed much about his inner nature. In the letters, however, Jaffé also saw his human warmth and his "jocularity, his extraordinarily charming, almost extroverted side" coming to the fore.[27] The volumes were positively received, not only with regard to the compilation and selection of correspondence from the long time span of 1906 to 1961, but also for the comprehensive, careful and helpful editorial notes. Thanks to the latter, providing a "significant orientation aid," the collection of letters would henceforth be widely perceived as a valuable complement and accompaniment to Jung's academic works.[28] Several reviewers regretted that Jaffé's small selection of affectionate and often humorous letters to his mother, his wife and his children had been excluded from publication by his heirs. Jaffé was particularly praised in reviews for not having tried to white-wash C.G. Jung's image by leaving out certain letters which contained

26 Jaffé, A., 1989, *Aus C.G. Jungs letzten Jahren,* Daimon, Einsiedeln, 1987, p. 159; English edition: *From the Life and Work of C.G. Jung*, Daimon, Einsiedeln, 1989, p. 153. Newly translated here from the German.

27 Aniela Jaffé to Bruno Klopfer, 31.12.1963, ETH.

28 Cf. Jürg Fierz in *Tages-Anzeiger der Stadt Zürich*, 15.11.1972, Alfred Ribi in *Zürichsee-Zeitung*, no. 263, 10.11.1972. C.A. Meier to Aniela Jaffé, 26.3.1973: "Your work is an immense, immensely thorough, sound, careful, reliable, dedicated, valuable achievement. The impression is stupendous." AAJD.

contradictory or controversial remarks,[29] thus allowing both his light and shadow sides to appear.

One such shadow aspect became the subject of a further essay by Jaffé: an extensive scholarly investigation into "C.G. Jung and National Socialism." In it, she researched Jung's own publications and public statements on this topic, as well as letters from 1933 to 1946. Her deep gratitude for the support Jung had shown her notwithstanding, Jaffé's thorough research led her to conclude that he had in fact gone somewhat astray in judgment. That in 1933 – at a time when "being a Jew was enough to put one in danger of one's life" – Jung chose to discuss supposed Jewish "differentnesses" and placed the topic of racial psychology on the scientific agenda was seen by her as "a grave human error."[30] Although the worst consequences of anti-Semitism became public knowledge only later, wrote Jaffé, the slightest hint of Jewish "differentness" served at that time as fuel for further fanaticism. "In this respect (...) silence [in German: *Schweigen*] would have been the order of the day."[31] She also concluded that Jung, in some of his writings of that period, expressed views on the Jewish character and Judaism which, although widespread at the time, were false and based on ignorance of the Jewish culture. She detected a manifestation of the shadow which... "clings to every person and is often all the darker the brighter the light [the] personality sheds."[32] In Jaffé's assessment, criticism of Jung's attitude, particularly during 1933 and 1934, was justified in light of certain facts, but she also recognized that Jung had been neither a National Socialist nor anti-Semitic. This, she felt, was confirmed not only by his commitment as a physician and human to helping Jews and non-Jews alike, but also by many of his writings. Only after completion of her essay did she admit to her friend Laurens van der Post how long she had struggled with immersing herself into this complex topic. Jaffé's awareness and appreciation of her own Jewish heritage had increased through her contact with Gershom Scholem

29 "When Gerhard Adler and I selected C.G. Jung's letters for publication, we were certain that we did not want to fall into the common trap of attempting to eliminate errors and lapses. We wanted the letters to paint a picture of the whole person." Jaffé A. in *Süddeutsche Zeitung*, no. 269, 18.11.1972.

30 Jaffé, A., 1989, p. 86.

31 Ibid., p. 87, translation modified.

32 Ibid., p. 98.

and his writings about the Kabbalah. An extended trip to Israel to visit surviving relatives and friends had also left a deep impression on her.[33]

Despite her personal conviction that Jung was no anti-Semite, she found certain statements of his made in the thirties "inexcusable."[34] However, she never accepted sweeping judgments leveled against Jung and, until her life's end, tirelessly rejected one-sided criticisms of him in this regard and argued for a balanced evaluation with neither polemics nor idealization.[35] Just a year before her death – by then nearly blind – Jaffé penned her final words on the subject. In order to gain a complete picture of Jung's attitude to Judaism, she found it necessary to understand the deep impression which the ambivalence of the Jewish God-image had made on the mature Jung. By virtue of its antinomy, he saw this image as superior to the Christian image of a loving God. The Jewish understanding of the inherent contradictory nature of God was seen as leading to a transformation and new significance of human responsibility. Jung found this expressed above all in the writings of the Kabbalist Isaac Luria: "The Jew has the advantage of having long since anticipated the development of consciousness in his own spiritual history."[36]

---

33 Cf. Scholem, Gershom, *Major Trends in Jewish Mysticism*, 1941. Aniela Jaffé had become acquainted with Gershom Scholem and the physicist and science historian Shmuel Sambursky through the Eranos conferences. She and Sambursky had a close friendship lasting until his death. See also Aniela Jaffé to Ingaret Giffard, 6.11.1968: "I felt completely transformed in my Jewishness after my stay in Israel, which is archaic, antique and modern at the same time." AAJD (original in English).

34 In a letter to Laurens van der Post of 26.5.1976, Jaffé wrote that she found some of Jung's formulations deeply depressing, especially his adoption in the thirties of the typical Nazi terminology about the "corrosive character of the specific Jewish viewpoints of Freud and Adler" from which he had never self-critically distanced himself later: "What I really criticize is the fact that in his book *'Aufsätze zur Zeitgeschichte'* (1946) Jung excluded the article containing the (few) sentences always quoted against him. If he would have published it and added – in a sort of epilogue – some explanations about his standpoint at that time and why he changed his opinion, he would have made things clearer and easier for all of us. I can find no excuses for the formulations in question, but one should not ignore the totality of the personality. One should not judge a man and his work from his errors alone (...) Once Jung told me: 'Die wahre Beziehung zwischen zwei Menschen beruht nie auf ihrer Stärke, sondern geht über ihre Schwäche'." ["The true relationship between two people is never based on their strengths, but on their weaknesses."] AAJD (original letter mostly in English).

35 The following question nevertheless remained unresolved for Jaffé: would it not have been more important to clearly separate from the *"Allgemeine ärztliche Gesellschaft für Psychotherapie"* in the years 1933 to 1939, than to continue working with the society, hoping to control the damage? Cf. Jaffé, A., 1989, p. 82.

36 Cf. Jaffé, A., 1989, p. 100ff., C.G. Jung to James Kirsch, 16.2.1954, *Letters II*, p. 154f., Scholem Gershom, 1941, *Major Trends in Jewish Mysticism*, chapter 7, "Isaac Luria and his School."

In addition to various essays on other subjects, including the phenomenon of synchronicity or the significance of alchemy in Jung's psychology,[37] Jaffé also wrote a new book, *The Myth of Meaning in the Work of C.G. Jung*, published in German with Rascher in 1967 and a few years later in English, translated by R.F.C. Hull.[38] Here she presented several essential aspects of Jung's search for insight and illustrated what had emerged for him from the interaction of consciousness and the unconscious as the purpose of human existence – in short, what he proposed as the possible meaning to counter the "meaningless of life." Toward the end of her life, she referred to this book as her most important work. In 1968, Rascher published a collection of several of her essays under the title *Aus Leben und Werkstatt C.G. Jungs*. An English version – again translated by R.F.C. Hull – was published a short time later in the US and the UK.[39] The German editions of Jung's letters were published in 1972 and 1973 in three volumes.[40]

In the seventies, Aniela Jaffé gave several lectures at the Eranos conferences on various aspects of the work and *vita* of C.G. Jung. Her first talk was on "The Creative Phases in Jung's Life," in which she presented his writings and researches as stations in his individuation process.[41] That same summer she was interviewed for a film made by Jonathan Stedall and Laurens van der Post, *The Story of Carl Gustav Jung*.[42] In 1973, she opened the Eranos conference on "Synchronizität

37 Jaffé, A., "Parapsychology: Experience and Theory" in From the Life and Work of C.G. Jung, Daimon, Einsiedeln, 1989; first published in Smythies, J.R. (Ed.), *Science and ESP*, Routledge & Kegan Paul, London, 1967. Jaffé, A., "Alchemy" in *From the Life and Work of C.G. Jung,* Daimon, Einsiedeln, 1987; first published as "The Influence of Alchemy on the Work of C.G. Jung," foreword to *The Mellon Collection of Alchemy and the Occult,* 1966 (Yale University Press); cf. also *Spring,* 1967, p. 7–25.

38 Jaffé, A. *Der Mythus vom Sinn im Werk von C.G. Jung*, Daimon, Einsiedeln, 5. ed., 2018. *The Myth of Meaning in the Work of C.G. Jung*, Hodder & Stoughton, London, 1970/ G.P. Putnam Son's, New York, 1971.

39 *From the Life and Work of C.G. Jung*, Harper & Row, New York, 1971/Hodder & Stoughton, London, 1971, subsequent expanded edition, Daimon, Einsiedeln, 1989.

40 *C.G. Jung, Briefe*, vol. I, II, III, ed. Aniela Jaffé in collaboration with Gerhard Adler, Walter, Olten, 1972, 1973. Jaffé received no royalties for her editorial work on the letters and after an initial fee worked unpaid on the collection for many years. After the volumes were published, as an "expression of the very best thanks" for the "great work" that Jaffé had done with "such care and self-sacrifice," the community of heirs of C.G. Jung presented her with three leather-bound copies and gave her "a gift of Fr. 5,000"; Franz Jung to Aniela Jaffé, 31.8.1973, AAJD.

41 Jaffé, A., 1989, p. 154–188; first published in *Eranos Jahrbuch 1971*, vol. 40.

42 The documentary was filmed in summer 1971 and broadcast by the BBC in three parts in 1972. Alongside Jaffé, C.A. Meier and C.G. Jung's grandson Dieter Baumann were also interviewed.

After her stay in Israel, Aniela Jaffé, who was cosmopolitan throughout her life, continued her journey by cargo ship – and camel – along the North African coast.

und Kausalität in der Parapsychologie" [Synchronicity and Causality in Parapsychology].[43] Her lecture gave an overview of the most recent research into parapsychology and its connection with Freud's and Jung's theories, as well as venturing more deeply into Jung's ideas about synchronicity. This topic had also often been the subject of discussion in her conversations with Wolfgang Pauli.

The year 1973 marked a significant personal milestone for Jaffé. For the first time in more than thirty years, she again set foot on German soil, traveling to Berlin via Freiburg. In a contribution for a *Festschrift* for Professor Hans Bender, director of the Institute for Frontier Areas of Psychology and Mental Health in Freiburg, written at a later date, Jaffé recalled her strong emotions upon crossing the border once again at Basel. Her nervousness and tension were able to fade thanks to the very warm welcome she received at the institute in Freiburg, making her onward journey to Berlin easier. In Berlin, she gave a lecture on Jung's ideas about death as part of a conference organized by Wilhelm Bitter and the *Internationale Gemeinschaft Arzt und Seelsorger.*[44]

Her initial feelings on rediscovering the once-familiar city of her childhood and youth were very painful, but she soon began to feel at home again in her old milieu. One year later, in 1974, she returned to Berlin to speak at a conference of the *Internationale Gesellschaft für Tiefenpsychologie*. On the two occasions Jaffé visited Berlin in the seventies, the city was still divided. In her old age, she was greatly moved to witness from afar the fall of the Berlin Wall in 1989.

For her lecture at the Eranos conference of 1974, Jaffé chose to address the collective process of humanity becoming conscious in the course of history, comparing the path of individual self-actualization with a collective individuation process.[45] The inspiration for the subject had come from the laudation for Jung's honorary doctorate awarded by the ETH Zürich in 1955, in which he was seen as "the interpreter

43 Jaffé, A., 1985, p. 47–87; First published in *Eranos Jahrbuch 1973*, vol. 42.

44 Jaffé, A.,"Der Tod in der Sicht von C.G. Jung" in *Im Umkreis des Todes*, Daimon, Einsiedeln, 2013. First published in Bitter, Wilhelm (ed.), *Alter und Tod – verdrängen oder bewältigen*, Stuttgart, Klett, 1974.

45 Jaffé, A., "Individuation der Menschheit," in *Parapsychologie, Individuation, Nationalsozialismus – Themen bei C.G. Jung*, Daimon, Einsiedeln, 1985. First published in *Eranos Jahrbuch 1974*, vol. 43. English version: "The Individuation of Mankind" in: Jaffé, A., *Was C.G. Jung a Mystic?*, Daimon, Einsiedeln, 1983, pp. 57ff.

of the individuation process of humankind." Central to Jaffé's thesis was the transformation of both the God-image and the human image in the Judaeo-Christian context. For Jaffé, following the thought of Jung, a religious and psychological examination of and confrontation with the dual aspect of a God-image containing both good and evil could lead to an altered understanding of the role of humankind: it became both our privilege and duty to, as far as possible, consciously recognize and integrate the opposing forces. In the latter part of her manuscript for the first half of the present book, Jaffé returned to Jung's reflections on this subject.[46] The following year, Jaffé gave her last Eranos lecture on Jung's contributions to the annual gathering at Lake Maggiore.[47] She described how the founder of the conferences, Olga Fröbe-Kapteyn, had initially intended to create a meeting place for representatives of Eastern and Western philosophy and spirituality. With Jung's active participation, however, Eranos had evolved into a place of interdisciplinary and interfaith exchange combining the natural sciences and humanities.

Also in 1975, on the occasion of the 100th anniversary of C.G. Jung's birth, a major exhibition was staged at the *Helmhaus* in Zürich, organized by the City of Zürich in cooperation with the C.G. Jung Institute and the Psychology Club. The publisher Walter Verlag asked Aniela Jaffé to compile a selection of one hundred of C.G. Jung's letters for an accompanying publication.[48] This she did on a voluntary basis, with no royalties. Jaffé worked in a small team together with Cornelia Brunner, Liliane Frey-Rohn and Magda Pestalozzi to help prepare the exhibition, which took place from March 14 to April 13, 1975, and attracted so many visitors that it was subsequently also shown in Basel and Bern.[49] With the support of the Swiss arts council Pro Helvetia, international exhibitions followed in more than forty cities around the world, leading to another large editorial project for Jaffé.

46 See in particular p. 183ff.

47 Jaffé, A., "C.G. Jung und die Eranos-Tagungen," in *Aus C.G. Jungs letzten Jahren*, Daimon, Einsiedeln, 1987; first published in *Eranos Jahrbuch 1975*, vol. 44. English translation in *Spring*, 1977, pp. 201ff.

48 Jaffé, A., Ed., *C.G. Jung – 100 Briefe. Eine Auswahl.* Olten, Walter-Verlag, 1975. From a conversation with Robert Hinshaw, audio file, AAJD.

49 Cornelia Brunner, Annual Report 1975, Psychology Club Zürich.

At the request of Walter Verlag, which had taken over the program of Jungian publications from Rascher in 1971, she put together a large hardbound volume of text and images entitled *C.G. Jung – Bild und Wort.*[50] The publisher linked the book with the exhibition: "Visitors to the exhibition were asking for a book that would give a generally comprehensible and illustrated overview of the research, experiences and findings of the great psychiatrist. Now this unique illustrated volume is available." As Jung's colleague of many years, Jaffé was seen as presenting a view of the researcher "from her direct knowledge of his intellectual world, his life and his plans."[51]

The work was very well received by readers and the press.[52] Jaffé was particularly pleased that Jung's daughters personally congratulated her on the publication. Readers appreciated the book for the many references to the Collected Works and the inclusion of some hitherto unpublished letters, diary entries and paintings from *The Red Book*, which was inaccessible at that time. A few lone voices, however, felt the book was not critical enough of Jung, decrying "it has once again been left to his opponents to deal with his shortcomings," opponents who had accused him of having "fascist (Bloch), psychotic (Stern) or downright unscientific (Balmer) traits."[53] One year after the initial publication, a second edition of *C.G. Jung – Bild und Wort* was released. Princeton University Press, which since 1969 had taken over responsibility for the *Collected Works* and the Bollingen Series, commissioned Krishna Winston, daughter of Clara and Richard Winston, to translate the text into English. The English edition, *C.G. Jung – Word and Image*, was then published in the winter of 1979.[54] Only in the second Ger-

50 Jaffé, A., Ed., *C.G. Jung: Bild und Wort*, Walter-Verlag, Olten, 1977; Jaffé, A., Ed., *C.G. Jung: Word and Image*, Princeton, 1979.

51 Editor Joseph Rast in the book description, ibid.

52 The book gave "an admirable insight into Jung's outer and inner development" and was "among the best works available about Jung," Neue Zürcher Zeitung, 13.12.1977; it was "a successful introduction and an easy first step into the complicated cosmos of the most important Swiss psychologist," Weltwoche, 3.8.1977, ETH.

53 Mehren, Günther in Stuttgarter Zeitung, 4.1.1978, AAJD. The review refers to claims made by Ernst Bloch in „Imago als Schein aus der Tiefe" in Erbschaft dieser Zeit, Gesammelte Werkausgabe Bd. 4, 1977, by Paul Stern in *C.G. Jung – Prophet des Unbewussten*, 1977, English edition: Stern, P., *The Haunted Prophet,* George Braziller, New York, 1976, and by Heinrich Balmer in *Die Archetypentheorie von C.G. Jung. Eine Kritik*, 1972.

54 C.G. Jung: Word and Image, ed. and prologue by Aniela Jaffé, Bollingen Series XCVII:2, Princeton University Press, 1979.

man edition of 1985 is Aniela Jaffé named as the author and the book described as "a biography".

Next, Jaffé wrote a contribution for a journal dedicated to her prematurely deceased friend of many years, Erich Neumann – like Jaffé, a Jew born in Berlin shortly after the turn of the century and a close colleague of C.G. Jung over many decades.[55] After the completion of this essay, she devoted her attention to what would be her final work.

55 "Die Einheitswirklichkeit und das Schöpferische" [the unitary reality and creativity] in Dieckmann, H. et al., (ed.), *Kreativität des Unbewussten: zum 75. Geburtstag von Erich Neumann*, Zeitschrift für Analytische Psychologie, vol. 11, Basel, Karger, 1980.

"A manuscript came to be, small in size but great in impact"

In the fifteen years since the publication of *Memories, Dreams, Reflections by C.G. Jung*, the now seventy-five-year-old Aniela Jaffé had gained international renown as an author and continued her work as a lecturer and training analyst. In her twilight years, she set herself the task of sorting through the many papers in her hands and tying up loose ends on pending projects. One impetus for doing so was the planned archiving of valuable Jung-related documents, either at the Jung Institute or in the long-discussed C.G. Jung archive at the ETH Zürich. In the course of this evaluation and sorting, she looked more closely at some folders containing records from her biographical conversations with Jung. The thematically ordered folders contained texts from her base material that had not been published – unused "remnants" as she called them in a letter to Guido Elber of Walter Verlag.[1] She had earlier referred to the fragments as "pieces of a mosaic" for creating a more all-encompassing picture. She now decided to edit a few of these unused notes, varying in length and significance but providing additional glimpses into Jung's life and ideas, and to combine them into a manuscript as a sort of "addendum to the *Memories*."[2] No longer bound by a publisher's requirement for a coherent chronological order, she chose to arrange the "mosaic pieces" in a loose structure. The selected notes were placed in four thematic sections, with chapters of varying length. By indicating the date of each chapter, she endeavored

1 Aniela Jaffé to Guido Elber, 9.8.1978: "I recently came across remaining protocols of my conversations with Jung for the Memories book and found a great deal of material that was not included in the book. I have put together some of these 'remnants' and a manuscript came to be, small in size but great in impact." AAJD

2 Ibid.

to highlight the spontaneous nature of the remarks. Where possible, the situational context was explained with short introductory comments.[3] By August 1978, an initial draft of the new manuscript was ready, though Jaffé would edit it several more times.

Jaffé's motivation for embarking on this new project was in large part a feeling of responsibility to C.G. Jung and the growing new generation of readers interested in his psychology and life story. However, the long legal complications that had beset the creation of *Memories*, the interference of others in her work, and the subsequent disregard for her authorial rights by some publishers remained fresh in her memory. She therefore decided to clarify her rights in advance with a neutral party. She contacted Mathis Baechi, the lawyer responsible for a series of publications from the Jung Institute, to obtain "an outsider's opinion from a legal specialist in publishing matters."[4] He came to the conclusion that she was clearly within her rights to publish the manuscript, basing his assessment on the document of October 21, 1957 in which C.G. Jung had explicitly transferred the rights for the conversation records to Aniela Jaffé. In this document, Jung had not only transferred the copyright to the recorded notes, but had also authorized Jaffé to use her "records of conversations with me at your discretion," i.e., the extent and manner in which she used the records was left to her own judgment and consideration.[5]

Jung had also extended this transfer of rights to Jaffé to include autobiographical texts which he did not count as part of his scientific work, granting her permission to publish them as complements and additions to the conversation records as she saw fit.[6] Regarding the content of the new manuscript, Baechi saw nothing that could be considered defamatory and believed authorization from the heirs was not required.[7] In fact, Jaffé had made very little use of the authorization granted by Jung to use extracts from his autobiographical writings, either in this volume or in earlier writings, and the new manuscript

3 See also Jaffé's introduction to the present volume, p. 6ff.
4 Aniela Jaffé to Gerda Niedieck, copy to Mathis Baechi, 9.11.1980, AAJD.
5 C.G. Jung to Aniela Jaffé, 21.10.1957, AAJD, YBL.
6 Ibid. "...I permit you to complement and add to these records with extracts and selections from autobiographical papers of my own."
7 Cf. Mathis Baechi to Berthold Gaupp, copy to Aniela Jaffé, 24.4.1980, AAJD.

was based almost exclusively on her own notes (much more so than the earlier *Memories, Dreams, Reflections by C.G. Jung*). Nevertheless, it was her wish to grant the heirs of C.G. Jung fifty percent of the royalties for this book too, as had been the case for *Memories.*[8] Despite Baechi's assurances, Jaffé was worried that Jung's family might object to some contents – the attempts to veto certain passages in the previous book were still very present in her mind. Her presentiment would soon be confirmed.

When she initially informed Guido Elber of Walter Verlag about the project, she added: "In order to avoid any complications regarding permissions, I would like to suggest that this slim volume not be published until *x* years after my death – if at all – although of course I do not know whether Walter Verlag would be willing to undertake this."[9] This proviso notwithstanding, she made it clear that she felt a responsibility to make the material available to readers interested in Jung. Elber's curiosity was piqued and he promised to read the manuscript immediately. At the beginning of November 1978, they met to discuss it. He was keen to release the book already as part of the spring 1979 program, which Jaffé felt was precipitous. As a next step, she wanted to inform the Jung heirs about the planned publication and the proposed fifty percent royalties, and was not confident that this would go smoothly. She granted Walter Verlag a rights option until December 31, 1979. Elber suggested that Jaffé write a supplementary directive to her will regulating what was to happen with the manuscript after her death: the directive should nominate Walter Verlag as the owner of the manuscript with a stipulation that the publisher would undertake to publish it within a "specified time." Jaffé accordingly drew up a document and sent it to the publishing house and to the executor of her will, writing "property of Walter Verlag" on the manuscript.[10]

After a year went by with no news from Elber about the project, Jaffé discovered in conversation with him that no decision about pub-

8 Aniela Jaffé to Guido Elber, 15.11.1978; Aniela Jaffé to Helmut Hungerbühler, 26.11.1978; Mathis Baechi to Berthold Gaupp, 24.4.1980, AAJD.

9 Aniela Jaffé to Guido Elber, 9.8.1978, AAJD.

10 At the end she added that this manuscript, which at that point had the working title "C.G. Jung erzählt" ("C.G. Jung narrates"), was among the most valuable material that remained of her records of Jung. Aniela Jaffé to Guido Elber, Walter Verlag, 15.11.1978, AAJD.

lication had yet been made, due to the publishers' reluctance to get on the wrong side of the Jung heirs; Walter Verlag now felt they could not risk losing the heirs' goodwill over a manuscript which Jaffé might not be entitled to use without their approval. She confirmed to Elber once more that she was "free to publish the manuscript," as it was based only on her own notes, but now asked him to destroy his copy of the testamentary directive or to mark it as "invalid." "It causes me great pain that our agreement about a manuscript so important to me has been forgotten, and that I have been waiting in vain for a decision since the summer of last year," she wrote to Elber.[11] Jaffé had been in negotiations for some time with German publishing house Bonz Verlag regarding another book,[12] and Bonz now showed great interest in taking over the new manuscript should Walter decide not to publish it. Jaffé agreed with Bonz Verlag that once a contract was signed, a copy would be sent to the Jung heirs to inform them.[13]

"As she is the author, in effect, her attitude is central"[14]

Unbeknownst to Jaffé, while sorting through her papers and preparing the new manuscript, on the other side of the Atlantic some copies of her notes and other documents passed on by her had unexpectedly come to light and were the subject of intensive discussions: copies of Jaffé's records of conversations from September 21, 1956 to September 19, 1958 and other material given by her to Kurt Wolff in the late fifties. As will become clear from the following, William McGuire

11 Aniela Jaffé to Guido Elber, Walter Verlag, 22.11.1979, AAJD.

12 Jaffé, Aniela *Religiöser Wahn und schwarze Magie. Das tragische Leben der Anna Kingsford*, first published by Bonz, Fellbach, 1980. "Jung first gave me her biography to edit, around a thousand pages written by her friend [Edward Maitland] whose light vision Jung had reproduced in 'The Secret of the Golden Flower.' Anna Kingsford (1848–1888) was a medical doctor, mystic, theosophist, visionary – and murderer. The indescribably dark, somewhat grotesque or even sick life story would be a psychological thriller at best, were it not for the wealth of dreams, visions and active imaginations contained in Maitland's biography." Aniela Jaffé to Ines Buhofer and Guido Elber, 4.3.1979, AAJD. The editor Ines Buhofer at Walter Verlag found the story too "unnerving" and thought it would barely be profitable, whereupon Bonz Verlag took on the project. 2nd edition, Daimon, Einsiedeln, 1986.

13 Correspondence on behalf of Aniela Jaffé to Bonz Verlag, 24.4.1980, AAJD.

14 William McGuire to Herbert Bailey, Princeton University Press, 29.6.1977, LoC, Manuscript Division (original in English).

played a key role in the affair. McGuire was the only employee of the Bollingen Series who had been retained after the transfer of the series to Princeton University Press. His many years of work on the *Collected Works of C.G. Jung* were coming to an end with the publication of volume 18 in 1976. The series' long-time financial backer Paul Mellon had decided at the end of 1963 that, while he would still finance the already-planned volumes, he would withdraw his support once they were published. His foundation had invested several million dollars for the *Collected Works* by that point, and Mellon now felt he had done enough. John Barrett, director of the Bollingen Series for many years, had retired in July 1969 when the series officially became part of Princeton University Press.

In the late seventies, John Barrett was paid a visit by Kurt Wolff's widow Helene. She pressed a heavy package into his hands and begged him to protect her from any possible subsequent legal difficulties.[15] The package, she claimed, contained valuable unpublished autobiographical material – original texts by C.G. Jung. Barrett therefore decided to pass it on to Paul Mellon and Mellon's lawyer, Donald Osborn. From there, the material found its way to the director of Princeton University Press, Herbert Bailey, who asked William McGuire to assess its content. The central question was whether there really were unpublished texts written by C.G. Jung here.[16] The most significant contents in the package were the copies of Aniela Jaffé's records of conversations with C.G. Jung from September 21, 1956 to September 19, 1958 (the last one incorrectly dated by Jaffé as October 19). Further documents included an edited version of the first three chapters of *Memories, Dreams, Reflections by C.G. Jung* based on Jung's text "From the Earliest Experiences of My Life" and several other draft chapters. The collection documents the extent to which Kurt Wolff, supported by Wolfgang Sauerländer, had tried to interfere in the book's creation process. After their arrival in New York, Jaffé's notes were not only annotated with comments and deletions, but often cut up and com-

15 Cf. William McGuire to Paul Mellon, 4.4.1979, Library of Congress, Manuscript Division (LoC/MD).

16 Cf. William McGuire to Herbert Bailey, 29.6.1977, Donald Osborn to Herbert Bailey, 13.7.1977, both LoC/MD.

bined with extracts from earlier or later conversation notes. Among the papers were also many different drafts of chapters – not only those composed by Jaffé, but also several put together by Kurt Wolff with the assistance of Sauerländer.

Why were these documents only now given to Barrett by Helene Wolff? And why to him and not to Jaffé or to Jung's family? Why did Barrett emphasize the moral obligation to protect the donor of the papers during her lifetime?[17] Helene Wolff was most likely aware, through her husband and others at Pantheon, that Jaffé's lawyer Peyer had requested the return of the protocols and other related texts. One reason for Kurt Wolff's failure to accommodate this demand might have been because of his long surreptitious editorial attempts, but it could also have been due to lingering resentment against Jaffé and Jung or against Pantheon Books. As a publisher, Wolff clearly knew that Pantheon's contract with Jaffé only gave the publishing house legal right to the finished work agreed upon with her, not to her base material and working notes – a fact which even she had explicitly stated.[18] She had given Wolff the conversation records and further documents at his insistence and as a gesture of goodwill, for information purposes only, as pointed out earlier, but had never granted him any rights to them.

After examining the material and discussing it with Barrett, McGuire informed his boss Bailey at the end of June 1977 about the contents: the package contained seven folders with notes, drafts and research documents relating to the book *Memories, Dreams, Reflections by C.G. Jung*, primarily in German. As well as looking through the material, McGuire labeled the folders with the letters A to G and inserted page numbers. Folder A, he claimed, had the most important contents: the "so-called protocols" with "Mrs. Jaffé's transcripts of her (shorthand?) notes of her conversations with Jung, each dated, from 21 Sept. 1956 to 23 May 1958."[19] The text in folder C, said McGuire, was

17 William McGuire to Paul Mellon, 4.4.1979, LoC.

18 See p. 262. Aniela Jaffé to Kurt Wolff, 2.11.1957, YBL; this restriction was also expressly made by Jung. The advance payments that Kurt Wolff had sent to Aniela Jaffé from November 1957, and that she had later stopped, were advances on her author's royalties and in no way payments for these documents.

19 W. McGuire to Herbert Bailey, 29.6.1977, LoC (original in English). Page numbers typed on

based on the essay written by Jung about his early years, but had been edited and expanded in such a way that one could not assume it was an original text by Jung; the folder also contained extracts from Jaffé's protocols about this stage of Jung's life. McGuire here for the first time labeled the protocols a "dictated version."[20] The other folders contained compositions of chapters that had been edited or put together in Zürich and New York, along with documents about C.G. Jung. "In other words, I believe there is no typescript here which can be considered pure Jung," concluded McGuire.[21] He found no excluded chapters, but only certain passages that had been left out for editorial reasons or due to family objections. McGuire claimed there were only one or two pages relating to Toni Wolff and a short section with Jung's reflections on his deceased wife Emma.

In McGuire's opinion, there were actually only two people capable of structuring and evaluating this precious biographical material today: Aniela Jaffé and Wolfgang Sauerländer. But of the two, McGuire thought it would be best to approach only Sauerländer, and to ask him to also translate the unpublished passages. Mellon and Barrett were interested in an English translation, McGuire told Bailey. McGuire's further explanations hint indirectly at possible motives for his nominating Sauerländer ahead of Jaffé for the task. Jaffé's attitude toward the papers was unpredictable, he thought. She could have "silently [...] kept a copy of them also" as the documents in the package were mostly "carbon copies." McGuire felt certain Jaffé would be in favor of preserving the papers, but believed she would probably be opposed to publishing them at present: "As she is the author, in effect, her attitude is central."[22]

What McGuire now held back from Bailey was significant: he had already contacted Sauerländer, who had agreed to look through the material and translate selected parts.[23] The two men had worked to-

top right of each page. McGuire's assessment was evidently not very thorough, perhaps due to his limited grasp of German: the pagination does not follow an exact chronological order, and in Kurt Wolff's documents there were copies of conversations between Jaffé and Jung up to 19.9.1958.

20 Ibid.

21 Ibid.

22 Ibid.

23 Cf. William McGuire to Herbert Bailey, 21.4.1980, LoC.

gether on the 1974 publication of the correspondence between Freud and Jung. It is possible that McGuire saw the potential for another prestigious project in the newly discovered material, which he might realize with Sauerländer's help.[24] His reservations about informing and involving Jaffé, the author of the protocols, may have been connected with as yet undisclosed plans which he did not want to see blocked by a veto on her part or on the part of the Jung heirs, whom she might inform: plans to use the new biographical information to write his own biography of Jung in the future, or possibly even to publish the complete protocols.[25]

McGuire's report to Bailey concluded that, because Kurt Wolff had played an active role as editor of *Memories, Dreams, Reflections by C.G. Jung*, the documents should be considered the property of Pantheon. As far as McGuire was aware, Wolff had left Pantheon after the final version of the book had been approved. Both were, in fact, incorrect assumptions.[26] Wolff had probably silently kept the files with him in Switzerland, not wishing to return them to Jaffé or to Jung's heirs, according to McGuire. Whether right or wrong, he said, Wolff's holding them back had saved the papers. McGuire neglected to mention the demand by the Swiss lawyer Peyer in the early sixties for the return of the documents. However, he probably was aware of the request, since his second wife Paula van Doren had worked at Pantheon in a managerial role during the period in question and it is highly unlikely that she would not have known about this explicit demand.[27] The question now was what to do with the material. McGuire suggested provisionally storing it with the Bollingen files at Princeton University Press where he worked. Later, he ventured, they could consider creating a special archive for it: rather than the Library of Congress, as proposed by Mellon and Osborn, where many documents from the Bollingen

24 Sauerländer, however, died unexpectedly in the fall of 1977. After Sauerländer's death, McGuire approached Richard Winston, who said he would be willing to take on the project after completing his biography of Thomas Mann, but Winston then became ill and died on December 22, 1979. Cf. William McGuire to Herbert Bailey, 21.4.1980, LoC. The Freud/Jung letters were published in English by Princeton University Press and in German by S. Fischer Verlag in 1974.

25 The plan to publish the material becomes even clearer from subsequent correspondence in the US.

26 Kurt Wolff was the publisher, the editor/author was Aniela Jaffé; Wolff left Pantheon on October 1, 1960, before the final version was finished.

27 See p. 324.

Foundation were already stored,[28] McGuire felt it would more suitably belong in the planned C.G. Jung archive at the ETH in Zürich. However, he felt it would be prudent to wait until the Jung archive was no longer in the hands or under the control of the Jung family, who might choose to dispose of the material. While it would be necessary to consult with Aniela Jaffé and the erstwhile program director of Pantheon André Schiffrin regarding the transfer of the documents, McGuire nevertheless advised against surrendering the material to either of them, regardless of their possible claims to it. If Pantheon and Jaffé should decide to publish the hitherto undisclosed material, that decision could probably not be legally challenged by the Jung family, according to McGuire.[29] Both Herbert Bailey and the lawyer Donald Osborn now were of the opinion that neither the Bollingen Foundation nor Princeton University Press had literary rights to the material. Bailey was willing to inform André Schiffrin of Pantheon and to turn the documents over to him on the condition that a copy be placed in the Jung archive in Zürich. But in order not to upset the Jung family, Bailey also thought it advisable to hold off on publication, even though the material didn't appear to contain anything "very explosive." In his reply, Osborn, who believed the provisional custody of the materials at Princeton University Press was legally defensible, proposed a meeting between himself, Bailey, Paul Mellon and John Barrett, but did not consider the matter urgent.[30] Further discussion about it was kept on hold until spring 1979. McGuire had his hands full with a number of concomitant projects: the English edition of Aniela Jaffé's *C.G. Jung: Word and Image*, his anthology, *C.G. Jung Speaking*, an article entitled "Jung in America 1924/25" for *Spring 1978*, the preparation of a collection of Jung's seminars, and research for his book on the history of the Bollingen Foundation.[31] He dedicated the anthology *C.G. Jung Speaking* to Aniela Jaffé, and in the foreword gave her particular

28 Paul Mellon to William McGuire, 26.3.1979, LoC.
29 William McGuire to Herbert Bailey, 29.6.1977, LoC.
30 Herbert Bailey to Donald Osborn, 7.7.1977; Donald Osborn to Herbert Bailey, 13.7.1977, both letters LoC.
31 Jaffé, A., Ed., *C.G. Jung: Word and Image*, 1979, McGuire, W., Ed., *C.G. Jung Speaking*, 1977, McGuire, W., Ed., *Dream Analysis. Notes of the Seminar given in 1928-1930*, 1984, McGuire, W., *Bollingen. An Adventure in Collecting the Past*, 1982.

Aniela Jaffé in 1978.
Photo © Frank Herrmann.

DAS GROSSE
GERALD B.
WIESINGER OKKULTE PHÄNOMENE

thanks for her advice and help. The dedication also served as thanks for her tireless support with editorial questions concerning the *Collected Works,* now nearing completion. Despite his frequent correspondence with Aniela Jaffé during this time, McGuire never mentioned her material in Helene Wolff's package of documents.

Jaffé, believing they had a friendly and trusting relationship, informed McGuire in a letter in July 1978 that she had finally found time to sort through her "Jungiana" and had found some interesting things.[32] At the beginning of 1979, James Hillman, with whom Aniela Jaffé had had a warm friendship since the early fifties, brought out a new edition of her book *Apparitions and Precognition,* at Spring Publications. The English edition of *C.G. Jung: Word and Image* was published at the same time, receiving very positive reviews.[33]

Paul Mellon, after seeing a copy of *Word and Image,* wrote to McGuire congratulating him on the publication, but expressed hesitation about McGuire's plans to publish C.G. Jung's seminars. He was also not pleased with McGuire's intention to give the recently-surfaced documents in connection with *Memories, Dreams, Reflections by C.G. Jung* to the Jung archive at the ETH Zürich.[34] Mellon still thought the Library of Congress would be the better option, in view of the material already archived there. This would also circumvent any confrontation with the Jung family, whom Mellon believed doubtless exerted a degree of control over the Jung archive, even though it was ostensibly under Swiss government auspices.[35] Although McGuire had initially regarded the ETH archive as a suitable option because the material was primarily in German, in his present reply to Mellon he now expressed his fear that the papers could be "buried there in more than one sense." He disclosed that he was searching for an expert to analyze and translate these documents, which he deemed important for the study of Jung's life, theoretical development and working methods. They would also reveal how *Memories, Dreams, Reflections by C.G.*

32 Aniela Jaffé to William McGuire, 17.7.1978, AAJD.

33 Aniela Jaffé to William McGuire, 10.3.1979: "I got some excellent book-reviews about it." AAJD. Harry Wilmer called it "A sophisticated, unsurpassed introduction," *American Journal of Psychiatry,* no. 137, 1.1.1980, ETH. (Original quotes in English).

34 Cf. William McGuire to Paul Mellon, 21.3.1979, LoC.

35 Paul Mellon to William McGuire, 26.3.1979, LoC.

Jung was not only the creation of Jung and Jaffé, but had also been shaped by Kurt Wolff, wrote McGuire. He believed Pantheon Books to be the legal proprietor, although Aniela Jaffé and the Jung heirs might have proprietary rights to certain parts.[36] A short time later, McGuire informed Jaffé that he had inquired of Franz Jung "whether the Freud Archive [sic] had now been established at the ETH."[37] In the same letter, he also asked Jaffé in passing whether the Jung family were in possession of the "*Vita protocols*" and whether they were planning to place them in the ETH archive.

As he could no longer ask Sauerländer or Winston to help, McGuire sent selected protocol extracts to Cary Baynes' daughter Ximena de Angulo in Switzerland, asking her to translate them. He instructed her to keep the matter completely confidential. The selection he sent suggests that he was particularly curious about Jung's unpublished comments regarding his personal life: they were passages about Toni Wolff, Emma Jung, Sigmund Freud and C.G. Jung's family of origin. At the beginning of October 1959, Ximena de Angulo reported enthusiastically on the records, saying they approximated C.G. Jung's style of speaking very closely. She felt it was like hearing him speak with his typical cadence; Aniela Jaffé's notes seemed to reproduce Jung's speech very accurately. However, she would need more time for the translation, as she wanted to reproduce all the nuances as precisely as possible.[38] In early March 1980, she returned the translated passages to McGuire.

Meanwhile, Jaffé had published three of her Eranos lectures in the volume *Aus C.G. Jungs Welt. Gedanken und Politik* with Berlin-based Claassen Verlag, and brought out an extended version of her article on the subject of "C.G. Jung and National Socialism." She had also been working on her book *Anna Kingsford – Religiöser Wahn und Magie*. Still completely oblivious to the recent discovery of her protocols in the United States, she informed McGuire in spring 1980 that the C.G. Jung archive at the ETH in Zürich had now been established under

36 William McGuire to Paul Mellon, 4.4.1979, LoC.
37 William McGuire to Aniela Jaffé, 25.4.1979, AAJD.
38 Ximena de Angulo to William McGuire, 1.10.1979, LoC.

the management of Dr. Beat Glaus. McGuire had no scruples about enlisting Jaffé's further help for his projects. He asked her to transcribe a diary and some handwritten letters written by Sigmund Freud to his family during his American journey in the fall of 1909, and in addition to let him know what information they contained about Jung.[39] Ever helpful, she undertook the task for no payment other than four complimentary copies of her own book *C.G. Jung: Word and Image*. After a second inquiry from McGuire asking whether a copy of the "Vita protocols" existed and if so, whether it would be archived at ETH, she replied that there were no longer any copies.[40]

Dictation by Jung to secretary Jaffé? Pure Jung?

After receiving de Angulo's translations of the protocol extracts, McGuire sent them on to Paul Mellon and John Barrett. As in his initial assessment, he again referred to Jaffé's notes as "dictation": "Jung's dictation taken down in shorthand and transcribed by Aniela Jaffé."[41] McGuire now described this material – unlike the heavily edited *Memories, Dreams, Reflections by C.G. Jung* or the seminars – as "pure Jung."[42] The remaining, untranslated material was, he said, of little personal interest – for example Jung's descriptions of travels or meeting people – but he hoped the complete protocols could be published within a few years. He would now commence the process of archiving them in the Library of Congress, and planned to personally deposit the material there in April 1980.[43] Paul Mellon responded immediately. The extracts were fascinating, he said, one could hear Jung's spontaneous, direct, enthusiastic style of speaking. Nevertheless, he ventured, might it not be advisable to place the material in the

39 William McGuire to Aniela Jaffé, 29.2.1980, AAJD.
40 Cf. message from William McGuire to Herbert Bailey, 21.4.1980, LoC.
41 William McGuire to Paul Mellon and Jack (John) Barrett, with copy to Herbert Bailey, 10.3.1980, LoC, (original in English).
42 Ibid
43 Ibid.

Library of Congress under seal for around twenty-five years, to avoid unnecessarily upsetting the Jung family?[44]

McGuire was not only opposed to this long sealing, but now also had scruples about giving the documents to the Library of Congress without first informing Pantheon Books. His wife Paula, who had been responsible for *Memories, Dreams, Reflections by C.G. Jung* at Pantheon until 1972, still worked for the publishing house in a freelance capacity and had moral misgivings about the matter. McGuire therefore now suggested informing André Schiffrin of Pantheon in person that the documents were in the possession of Princeton University Press, without specifying from where they had come. For McGuire, it was of utmost importance that the material be made available for research or publication in due course. He proposed utilizing the opportunity to try and learn from Schiffrin whether Jaffé or the Jung heirs held rights to the records.[45] For the time being, he suggested, the papers could temporarily be housed either on the premises of Princeton University Press or in the university's Firestone Library. Some of McGuire's views had changed since 1977: he was no longer in favor of giving the material to the Jung archive in Zürich. Even less did he favor informing Jaffé and sending her a copy.[46]

McGuire's actions here are worthy of brief examination in the context of his professional and personal circumstances. His employment as Editor of the *Collected Works* had largely been financed by the Bollingen Foundation. With the publication of the last volume and Paul Mellon's funding set to stop, McGuire's financial prospects therefore looked less than secure. Although close to retirement age, he was interested in taking on further assignments and projects. One of his projects, for example, involved editing historical material with regard to Freud and Jung. He also pushed for publication of the majority of C.G. Jung's seminars and previously unpublished lectures.[47] For

44 Paul Mellon to William McGuire, 17.3.1980, LoC.
45 William McGuire to Herbert Bailey, 21.4.1980, LoC.
46 Ibid.
47 Carotenuto, A., *A Secret Symmetry. Sabina Spielrein between Jung and Freud*, 1982. Burnham, J., McGuire, W. (ed.), *Jelliffe: American Psychoanalyst and Physician and His Correspondence with Sigmund Freud and C.G. Jung*, 1983. McGuire, W. (ed.), *C.G. Jung: The Zofingia Lectures*, 1983. McGuire, W. (ed.), *Analytical Psychology. Notes of the Seminar Given in 1925 by C.G. Jung*, 1989.

McGuire, especially after receiving Ximena de Angulo's enthusiastic response and her translations of the protocol extracts, the idea of publishing the protocols – or at least using them for a biographical work of his own – may have been an increasingly enticing prospect. This would explain his reluctance to accept Mellon's suggestion of placing the documents under seal, as well as his resistance to informing Jaffé – he needed to keep access to the files and exclude the possibility of opposition or competition from Jaffé regarding the use of the materials.

Herbert Bailey, doubtful about Pantheon possibly having a valid legal claim, turned to Mellon's legal counsel Donald Osborn for advice: would the *literary rights* not belong to the Jung heirs, or possibly to Aniela Jaffé, and might the *physical property* possibly also belong to both or either party? As he was generally against the publication of private documents that could cause hurt to living people, wrote Bailey to Osborn, he was rather opposed to publishing the material, irrespective of the legal situation. Furthermore: should he inform the Jung heirs about the documents in his possession so that they could decide what should be done with them? As the words came from Jung and were taken down by his secretary, the literary rights most likely belonged to his heirs, thought Bailey. In his view, any rule regarding their sealing should be limited to fifteen years maximum. Bailey moreover assumed that, because Jaffé had apparently been paid by Pantheon to take down Jung's words, i.e., presumably was employed by Pantheon, she was unlikely to have any literary rights to the protocols.[48] This assumption was based on McGuire's incorrect assertion that Jaffé had worked "for hire" and then later received royalties. In fact, no employment relationship ever existed between Jaffé and Pantheon.[49] McGuire, for his part, was against informing the Jung heirs and declared that anything discussed with the heirs would also have to be agreed with Jaffé. He now conceded, however, that because she

48 Herbert Bailey to Donald Osborn, 28.4.1980, LoC.

49 In addition, the majority of the conversation notes contained in the package were written before the author contract had been drawn up. Once the contract was signed, Jaffé had turned down advance payment of royalties – money, she thought, was not compatible with creative work. When Kurt Wolff, against her wishes, transferred an initial installment in November 1957, she opened a *Sperrkonto* (blocked account) which was not to be touched until the book had been published.

knew the material best, she should be given the opportunity to write an accompanying commentary in case of publication. Unlike Bailey, McGuire considered the contents to be not particularly intimate, and certainly suitable for publication.[50]

Osborn replied to three principal questions: Who owned the *physical property* rights? Who owned the *literary property* rights? What *obligations* did Princeton University Press and the Bollingen Foundation have with regard to the documents? In the absence of sufficient factual information, he was unable to answer the important question of *physical property*. According to Osborn, it was not known whether Kurt Wolff or his wife Helene had been correctly in possession of the documents. If Kurt Wolff held them only in his capacity as an employee of Pantheon, the publishing house could have a justified claim. Osborn neglected to even consider the possibility that certain documents might be the physical property of Aniela Jaffé. As possible owners of the *literary property rights*, he named "the Jung Estate, Pantheon and Mrs. Jaffé." According to Osborn, it was "most doubtful" that Jung had a contract with Jaffé with respect to the literary property rights for the transcribed interviews. She would seem to have no claim to the literary rights, although that was also in doubt. On balance, he concluded that the Jung heirs probably had the primary claim. Osborn saw no obligation on the part of Princeton University Press or the Bollingen Foundation to do anything with the documents at that time. Should, however, the material be donated to the Library of Congress, they would be obliged to advise both the Jung heirs and Pantheon Books and to request their consent. He therefore concurred with Bailey's proposal to simply hold the documents for the time being and wait until such time as "passions are less likely to be inflamed."[51] Bailey then informed McGuire via internal memo that after thorough consultation it had been decided to do "absolutely nothing" about the protocols, and to inform neither the Jung heirs nor Pantheon, nor "anyone else." He asked McGuire merely to ensure safe storage of the documents.[52] One look at the contract between Pantheon and Aniela

50 William McGuire to Herbert Bailey, 29.4.1980, LoC.
51 Donald Osborn to Paul Mellon, with copy to Herbert Bailey, 22.5.1980, LoC.
52 Herbert Bailey to William McGuire, 9.6.1980, LoC.

Jaffé, including the assignment of rights by C.G. Jung, would have been sufficient to clarify the questions of literary property and rights to use the material. Had anyone informed Jaffé and asked her about the origin of the documents in Helene Wolff's package, or had Pantheon been able to give information about the legal arrangements, many of Osborn's conjectures would have fallen by the wayside. Astonishingly for a lawyer, Osborn seems to have given no consideration to the fact that preparatory notes and drafts of a book project are generally protected by copyright law and are the property of their creator/author.

A few months later, McGuire again attempted to indirectly elicit from Jaffé whether there were still any copies of her biographical notes in Switzerland, calling them "the Protocols that he [Jung] dictated to you."[53] She responded with a clear and succinct "Jung never 'dictated me protocols'," adding how much easier her work would have been if he had.[54] She would have to emphatically refute the "dictation myth" several times more during her final years of life.

Jung exposed?

In the meantime back in Zürich, several members of the Jung family had been able to read Aniela Jaffé's new manuscript. Although some were in favor of the publication and found nothing objectionable in the contents, the prevailing sentiment was one of opposition. Two topics in particular were deemed problematic. The first stumbling block was the passages about Toni Wolff and Emma Jung. It was felt that these contributed nothing to an understanding of C.G. Jung's work and were indiscreet. Wasn't Jaffé here making public confidential remarks

53 William McGuire to Aniela Jaffé, 9.12.1980, AAJD (original in English).

54 Aniela Jaffé to William McGuire, 24.12.1980, AAJD (original in English). To a later question from McGuire about whether she still had a copy of the protocols, she replied that she did not and specified: "I never protocolled everything Jung told me. Impossible if someone speaks as in everyday-life. It was not dictated as one pretends now so often. Completely ridiculous! He spoke and followed a sort of Freudian line of associations." Following the conversations she had copied the notes and filled them out with "what was still in my ears." Jung had never spoken in a ready-to-print way, she said – "printing and speaking are different." Aniela Jaffé to William McGuire, 26.11.1981, AAJD (original in English). A copy of the letter was later given by McGuire to the Library of Congress.

without authorization, disregarding the requirement for discretion and exposing Jung? Jaffé was unfortunately seen to be confirming inaccurate, clichéd preconceptions.[55] A second area of contention was the final chapters of the manuscript concerning Jung's thoughts about life after death and the God image.[56] It was feared that these ideas would damage Jung's reputation as a scientist. A further obstacle was the legal situation, as the heirs questioned Jaffé's legal right to publish the manuscript, which now had the new working title "*Erlebtes und Gedachtes bei C.G. Jung*" ("Experiences and Thoughts of C.G. Jung").

The accusation of indiscretion and of a clichéd portrayal of Emma Jung affected Jaffé deeply. In her response, she first expressed understanding for the family's feelings, acknowledging the difficulty of being the son or daughter of a man whose influence "extends far beyond the personal and family sphere."[57] But she went on to refute any breaching of loyalty or discretion. "There is nothing in the manuscript that was told to me in confidence," she wrote, and explained that she and Jung had had a "silent agreement" about what could or could not be said in public.[58] From the start, Jung had left it up to her to decide what to record, write and publish. She saw the collection of these fragments as an attempt to convey "something of Jung's whole human personality." Jaffé purposely included some of the particularly moving things Jung had said about his wife's "superior human character and strong intellect" precisely in order to break down the cliché of Emma Jung as housewife and homemaker.[59] Regarding the sections about Toni Wolff, Jaffé was willing to consider a compromise: she thought it might be possible to leave out Jung's thoughts and the few dreams about Toni Wolff and instead indicate in her commentary how Jung had struggled with the decision to enter into and live out the relationship. But because so much had already been published and speculated on the matter – including false and defamatory information – she believed people ought perhaps to know what Jung himself had said about it. After all, wrote Jaffé, nothing attracted "projections and mythologizing"

55 Messages from the heirs of C.G. Jung to Aniela Jaffé, 2.2.1981, 9.7.1981, AAJD.
56 Cf. p. 147ff.
57 Aniela Jaffé to a representative of the family, 16.2.1981, AAJD.
58 Ibid.
59 Ibid.

more than the "half-known" or "concealed."[60] Jaffé had anticipated that the family might have some objections or doubts, and therefore had vacillated about whether to show the family the manuscript before it went to print. But these reactions left her now disheartened. Having already drawn up a testamentary directive granting permission for the manuscript to be published after her death, she was inclined not to press the matter any further. She wrote to her friend Laurens van der Post that she did not know whether she had the strength to resist the objections of the family – "I am too old." But she held out some hope nonetheless: "The right moment to publish the manuscript will come, I hope, sooner or later. (...) A book is a slow growth and doesn't suffer hurry."[61] Her lawyer saw no reason to give up yet. He believed C.G. Jung's letter of October 21, 1957 provided a solid legal base for the publication rights: Jung had assigned sole copyright for the conversation records to Jaffé and given her permission to publish from them at her own discretion. The only restriction in the authorization and assignment of rights was that autobiographical writings by C.G. Jung were not to be included in his Collected Works.[62] Jaffé was therefore entitled to publish the manuscript at hand.

"The attempt to eliminate me is being repeated"

The Jung heirs' literary agent and their legal representative now also adopted the view that Jaffé's records were "only a dictation of autobiographical material" by Jung. Moreover, they claimed that the material Jaffé now wished to use had not been previously published at

60 Ibid. In fact, a comparison of the carefully edited text of *Memories, Dreams, Reflections by C.G. Jung* and of the current book with the base material, the so-called protocols, reveals how circumspect and tactful Jaffé had been in her editing of the material. After accusations in the 1980s that she wanted to expose Jung, two or three decades later she would be accused of the opposite in works of popular science and medical history claiming that she had not sufficiently revealed the "real, direct" Jung. It is clear from her published writings that even when taking a critical, analytical look at certain aspects of Jung, she did so always with a nuanced and respectful attitude.

61 Aniela Jaffé to Laurens van der Post, 15.2.1981; in a further letter to the latter on 8.3.1981 she wrote: "My lawyer is glad that I did not withdraw my plans to publish. He is quite optimistic. I hesitated because I do not wish to offend the family and, coward that I am, fear their animosity. It is about the question of the copyright of my notes." Both letters AAJD (originals in English).

62 Cf. C.G. Jung to Aniela Jaffé, 21.10.1957, AAJD, YBL, ETH.

"the express wish of C.G. Jung."[63] The fragments had been rightly excluded from the published manuscript because they would damage the personality rights of the heirs. They saw Jaffé as a mere stenographer of Jung's speech, and believed therefore that Jung could possibly even be regarded as "the sole creator of the planned book."[64]

Jaffé again reiterated how, during their biography sessions, Jung had "never, as has sometimes been falsely assumed, 'dictated' to me," but had spoken freely on a variety of topics in everyday language in more or less depth. It had been completely up to her to make notes as she wished. "It has also often been falsely assumed that Jung followed a systematic train of thought and systematically dealt with one topic after another. Jung's thought processes during our conversations were quite associative." Every conversation "played out differently, so that it is hardly possible to say that Jung had one single speaking style."[65] Already the act of writing up the conversation protocols from her cursory notes had involved her transferring them into a first readable and coherent form. The material that had led to the chapters in *Memories* and to the current publication/manuscript *Reflections* had been through a further editing process by Jaffé. "The notes in the new manuscript are not identical with the protocols, even though I did attempt to maintain Jung's idiomatic style to a large extent."[66] Jung had trusted her and granted her free rein in the selection and final form of the manuscript.[67] It was distressing to her that her editorial role and authorship were now again being denied, and a painful reminder of how she had earlier been misjudged and disregarded: "By claiming that the manuscript is not my work but C.G. Jung's, the attempt to eliminate me, which I already experienced with Memories, is being repeated."[68]

Lost in the conflict was the point that for her there was no question regarding Jung's collaborative creative role on the biographical work. What she however found difficult to swallow was the fact that Jung's

63 Gerda Niedieck to Mathis Baechi, 2.3.1981, AAJD.
64 Martin Lutz to Mathis Baechi, 23.4.1981, AAJD.
65 Aniela Jaffé to Mathis Baechi, 7.3.1981; Aniela Jaffé to Mathis Baechi, copy to Martin Lutz, 7.4.1981, AAJD.
66 Aniela Jaffé to Mathis Baechi, 26.4.1981, AAJD.
67 Aniela Jaffé to Mathis Baechi, 7.3.1981, AAJD.
68 Aniela Jaffé to Mathis Baechi, May 1981, AAJD.

explicit assignment of the copyright to her conversation notes, and her co-author and editor role, was being invalidated and ignored. In vain she reiterated that the manuscript was based on these very records: not Jung's notes, but her own, rendered and edited from statements and remarks made by Jung.[69] In order to avoid delaying the book going to press with Bonz Verlag, Jaffé's lawyer suggested a compromise agreement: half of any profits from the book would go to Jung's heirs, an arrangement Jaffé had specified all along. Baechi emphasized that this agreement would have no bearing on the question of copyright, which should be evaluated and resolved by a neutral third-party authority.[70]

The attempt to reach an agreement was in vain. When the compromise offer was rejected, Jaffé finally withdrew the planned publication.[71] It saddened her deeply that assumptions had been presented as facts despite her untiring attempts to ensure transparency and clarity, that such important documents as Jung's authorization and assignment of rights had been overridden, and that her role and work had yet again been questioned. She had experienced similar opposition with the publication of *Memories*, but "at that time Jung stood up for me and had the power to ensure the truth was upheld."[72]

A good year later, when the Jung family's literary agent again questioned Jaffé's work and rights with regard to *Memories, Dreams, Reflections by C.G. Jung* and cast doubt upon Jung's demarcation of Jaffé's responsibility, Jaffé took up her pen in self-defense once again. She felt an "obligation to correct the facts," she wrote to the family representatives, lest silence itself becomes wrongdoing. If the book had often been incorrectly read as Jung's work, it was in some ways "the best compliment for the success of my task, namely to shape the book in the form of an autobiography." But in terms of the legal situation of her rights and her authorship, the "actual facts" were what mattered. The book's form had been created at the express wish of the publisher Kurt Wolff. She reiterated that she had never comprehensively retained Jung's speech word-for-word.[73]

69 Aniela Jaffé to Lorenz Jung, 3.9.1985, AAJD.
70 Cf. Mathis Baechi to Gerda Niedieck, copy to Franz Jung and Aniela Jaffé, 9.3.1981, AAJD.
71 Meeting notes, 19.6.1981, AAJD. Cf. Also Aniela Jaffé to William McGuire, 24.6.1981, AAJD.
72 Aniela Jaffé to Mathis Baechi, May 1981, AAJD.
73 Aniela Jaffé to N. Baumann, 6.10.1982, 7.11.1982, AAJD.

While not concealing her disappointment at the outcome, Jaffé told others that she felt an inner readiness to let go of the matter – letting go, she said, was after all one of the tasks of old age. But it was far from easy. She had done everything in her power to make important contents from the conversations with Jung available to readers. More than that she could not do. Jung had once said to her that what counted was the effort, not the result – this had been one of the most important things he understood during his near-fatal illness in 1944.[74] She had not yet resigned altogether, however. In the summer of 1981, she gave the manuscript draft and some other documents to the Jung Institute along with a deed of donation for the copy of *The Red Book* in her possession. In the hope that it might be possible to deal with the matter more openly a few decades into the future, she continued to work on the manuscript, but also devoted time to a new essay with thoughts on transcendence.[75] In the meantime, the team at Princeton University Press had heard about the conflict in Zürich from the Jungs' literary agent. The director Herbert Bailey now informed William McGuire that Princeton University Press was "not interested in publishing the Protocols." They wanted to keep out of the matter and avoid any legal controversy. Regarding Jung's unpublished seminars, on the other hand, they intended to vigorously defend their right to publish the material, according to Bailey.[76] Over the course of the next year, however, Bailey's interest in the seminars waned, and after the publication of the 1928–30 seminars, he decided not to publish any additional unpublished works of C.G. Jung – also due to the fact that the *Collected Works* were not selling well. To promote the *Collected Works*, McGuire prepared two paperbacks containing extracts from various volumes: *Aspects of the Feminine* and *Aspects of the Masculine*. He wrote to Jaffé that while he did not find Jung's comments on the subject particularly

74 Aniela Jaffé to Mathis Baechi, 21.6.1981, Aniela Jaffé to William McGuire, 24.6.1981, both letters AAJD.

75 Aniela Jaffé, "Transzendenz", in Jaffé, A., 1985, *Themen bei C.G. Jung*, p. 91-102; English version in Jaffé, A., '*Was C.G. Jung a Mystic?' and other essays*, trans. Diana Dachler and Fiona Cairns, p. 103, Daimon Verlag, 1989.

76 "We ought to stay out of the controversy over the Protocols. The rights situation is unclear. As for the Seminars, the reverse is true, and we ought to protect that copyright vigorously." Memorandum from Herbert Bailey to William McGuire, 11.2.1981, LoC (original in English).

impressive, there was a market for such books.[77] After Jaffé had sent him positive and detailed feedback on his book about the Bollingen Foundation, she received a letter from him in November 1982 with surprising news: he was retiring from Princeton University Press at the end of the year. He wrote that it had been a happy turn of fate to get to know her and work with her, and he thanked her for her many years of competent support: "No one is closer to the Jung corpus than you."[78]

At this news, Jaffé wrote to McGuire advocating one last time for publication of the *complete* works of Jung. At least the "Zarathustra" seminar ought to be published as an appendix to the Collected Works, as should *Wandlungen und Symbole der Libido* from 1912.[79] McGuire replied, expressing his frustration: despite means still being available in the Bollingen Fund, Bailey had arbitrarily decided, without consulting him, to cancel the publication of further volumes.[80] In their exchange of letters, McGuire still made no mention whatsoever to Jaffé of the copies of the protocols and the associated documents, even as he was compiling a dossier for their archiving in the Library of Congress. He and Bailey had now decided to place them under restriction for ten years. The correspondence between Princeton University Press, Paul Mellon and Mellon's lawyer Donald Osborn, which gave insight into the "history of the Jung 'protocols'," was filed alongside the material and also sealed for ten years. The only people permitted to access the files during those ten years were McGuire and Bailey. As donor of the material, Bailey had stipulated that he would have the right to decide whether to release the material earlier.[81]

Finally, at the urging of Violet S. de Laszlo (an analyst friend of Aniela Jaffé's who had lived in New York for many years and was now returning to Zürich), in the fall of 1983 McGuire informed Jaffé about the package handed over by Helene Wolff six years previously. The notes and documents relating to *Memories, Dreams, Reflections by*

77 W. McGuire to Aniela Jaffé, 27.4.1982, AAJD (original in English). *Aspects of the Masculine* was published in 1989 under the editorship of John Beebe.

78 See W. McGuire to Aniela Jaffé, 10.12.1982, 18.2.1983, both letters AAJD (originals in English).

79 William McGuire to Aniela Jaffé, 18.2.1983. Aniela Jaffé to William McGuire, 29.12.1982, AAJD. (Originals in English)

80 Initially Bailey had also wanted to cancel McGuire's project for the publication of C.G. Jung's "Zofingia" lectures, a decision which was then reversed.

81 Handwritten note by W. McGuire, 7.3.1983, LoC.

C.G. Jung had now been deposited under seal in the Library of Congress, he wrote, asking her to sign a confidentiality agreement: she was to say nothing about the documents.[82] This news – "that the protocols of my conversations with Jung have been declared to be his 'dictation', that it was forbidden to inform me that they had been deposited in the Library of Congress, and that the access is restricted" – cut Jaffé to the core. She was deeply shocked that McGuire, whom she had supported and assisted over decades, could have acted in such a manner behind her back. Only at the dogged insistence of a third party had he been persuaded to "inform me secretly that I have been betrayed. And to go so far as to make me sign a document promising not to talk about it to anyone." Her personal diary entries from October 1983 are a moving testimony of how she tried to come to terms with what had been done. "During the day I find myself gradually thinking about it less, but it still comes up in my dreams. A sign of how deeply hurt I am? I ask myself: why can I not accept it? Why is the truth so important to me? Since the protocols are now *under restriction* for ten years, meaning they are inaccessible, they won't be my concern anyway – I'll be dead before I have a chance to see them. Why all the secrecy? Why yet again these attempts to eliminate me?"

After a few weeks, even confessing to feeling slightly ashamed that she lacked the wisdom of age which ought to allow her to rise above matters, the "miracle of time" began to work: "The affair is receding into the mist, or I am moving further away from it. Is that the benevolent gift of old age? Perhaps. After all it's not the first time in my life that I've been betrayed. Today I can think of it but it no longer hurts. Or no longer hurts so much. It's strange: physical pain, even severe, excruciating pain, I have forgotten. With the soul's emotional pain, it is different. Such pain digs itself in deep. But the further it fades into the past, the more calmly I can think of it, *deo gratia*."[83]

Jaffé nevertheless refused to acquiesce to McGuire's demand for silence, and at the end of October 1983 sent a declaration to the Library of Congress, requesting that it be filed with the protocol copies.

82 Aniela Jaffé, personal diary entry, 23.10.1983, AAJD.
83 Aniela Jaffé, personal diary entries, October 1983, AAJD.

In the statement she underscored that the protocols were based on her notes of interviews with C.G. Jung and specified: "The protocols do not correspond *verbatim* to what Jung told me during the interviews in a free talk. In working out my notes I did an immediate editing, in order to formulate a readable and coherent text." The declaration was written not only for the purpose of transparency about her role in the editing process, but also to correct the assumption that these were original texts of C.G. Jung. Her questions and comments had not been included in the notes, she explained, because the publisher Kurt Wolff had from the outset wished for a book that would be as close as possible to an autobiography. "The Protocols were the beginning of the co-authorship between C.G. Jung and myself, which Jung stipulated for the whole book."[84]

Despite McGuire promising to send Jaffé the explanatory text he had written to accompany the material, he never did so. The Jung heirs had agreed with Bailey that the Library of Congress would provide the Jung archive at the ETH Zürich with a microfilm of the protocol copies. Jaffé informed Bailey that her co-authorship with Jung also applied to the protocol contents and again pointed out that C.G. Jung had explicitly transferred his copyright for them to her, meaning she had the right to publish extracts from them. After she heard from others that Bailey and McGuire had granted themselves exclusive access to the documents, and that Bailey held the right to lift the access restriction early if he wished, she wrote to Bailey: "C.G. Jung and myself being the authors of the 'Protocols', his heirs and myself (or my heirs) alone have the responsibility and the right to make the material available to the public or not."[85]

In the preceding years, Princeton University Press had done good business with titles edited by Aniela Jaffé. In spring 1983, a paperback edition of her book *C.G. Jung: Word and Image* was published and the first print-run sold out within a month; a second paperback edition followed in the fall. An English-language anthology of hundreds of

84 Aniela Jaffé to the Library of Congress, "Concerning the Protocols for *Memories, Dreams, Reflections by C.G. Jung* recorded and edited by Aniela Jaffé," October 1983, LoC, AAJD (original in English).

85 Aniela Jaffé to Herbert Bailey, 3.1.1985, AAJD (original in English).

C.G. Jung's letters, similar to the German one also compiled by Jaffé and based on the letter volumes edited by Jaffé and Gerhard Adler, was published in the fall of 1984 with the title *Selected Letters of C.G. Jung 1909–1961.*

Jaffé, in the interest of transparency and following her own conscience, now also contacted Pantheon Books about the matter. She informed the publishing house that protocols and further documents which had been incorrectly kept by Helene and Kurt Wolff had found their way into the hands of representatives of the Bollingen Foundation and Princeton University Press and were now deposited in the Library of Congress.[86] A copy of the above-mentioned declaration was enclosed with the letter.

"This work has filled my final years with meaning"

Jaffé meanwhile quietly continued to work on the withdrawn manuscript. She drew strength from the encouragement of friends who read her additional text and found it to be of great value. She was also motivated by what she perceived as the unjust confidentiality requirement and the underhanded way her primary material for *Memories* had been dealt with in the USA. Last but not least, her friendly relationship with Lorenz Jung, a son of Franz Jung, who represented the Jung heirs and was contact person for the Jung archive at the ETH, provided a good feeling. She was now eighty-two years old and still working as an analyst. As she became more occupied with thoughts of her own approaching death, she wrote an essay about C.G. Jung's epistemological standpoint regarding popular ideas of a transcendental reality, in particular fantasies about a post-mortal existence.[87] The essay included extracts from the last two sections of *Reflections*. She felt that at least in this way she had managed to publish a small portion of the remaining material from her conversations with Jung. At the same time, this increased her awareness of the value of Jung's more

86 Aniela Jaffé to the director of Random House, Division Pantheon Books, 21.3.1984, AAJD (original in English).
87 "Transcendence" in Jaffé, A., 1989, p. 103ff.

(Previous page) Aniela Jaffé in September, 1988. Photo © Robert Hinshaw.
(Top left:) Aniela Jaffé, 1989, almost blind, but still actively deciphering with her magnifying glass fondly named "Türmchen" (little tower).
(Below left:) Aniela Jaffé, 1990, still lively in old age, and interested in her conversation partners; photos © by Robert Hinshaw.

comprehensive remarks from the unpublished manuscript – she continued to be convinced of the importance of their being made available as completely as possible to interested readers.

As her correspondence and writing attest, Jaffé's intellectual faculties remained sharp in the final phase of her life, but her physical health steadily declined. Her deteriorating eyesight caused her the most difficulty. Yet, even when almost blind, she continued to type her own letters, apologizing for the numerous typos. At the end of 1986, she drew up a handwritten document transferring her author's rights relating to the protocol records to Robert Hinshaw of Daimon Verlag, and added the following provision to C.G. Jung's authorization of October 21, 1957: "I hereby transfer the copyright to the records made by me as mentioned in the above letter, under the conditions specified by C.G. Jung, to Dr. Robert Hinshaw."[88] The current volume, with its deliberately fragmentary character, differs significantly in style from *Memories, Dreams, Reflections by C.G. Jung,* which, in the words of Lorenz Jung, had become a valuable standard work.[89] For Jaffé, these fragments of further memories, dreams and reflections of C.G. Jung had varying degrees of significance, however all parts were too valuable to be tossed aside. Jaffé's short introductory comments, many of which she added in response to questions from the Daimon Verlag editors, provide useful additional information and reveal some of the context in which certain statements were made. No longer bound by Kurt Wolff's demands that her role as conversation partner, author and editor remain as invisible as possible, Jaffé also added editorial notes referring to Jung's *Collected Works* and other sources – it was important to her that future readers understand the connections to Jung's body of work. Some of the chapters contain extracts from records made from late 1958 up to May 1961. As mentioned previously, Jaffé ceased sending protocol copies to Kurt Wolff after October 1958, due to his interference and intrusive treatment of the material. Following Jaffé's death, no copies of the later conversation records could

88 Aniela Jaffé to Robert Hinshaw, 18.12.1986, transfer of copyright to the records of her conversations with C.G. Jung. AAJD.

89 Lorenz Jung to Aniela Jaffé, 20.2.1987, AAJD. In the same letter he wrote that Jaffé had "performed an extraordinary service in bringing to fruition this appealing title."

be found. She had stated on multiple occasions in the eighties that she had not retained any complete protocol copies, but merely "remnants" ordered thematically in folders. No protocols or fragments of protocols were found in her papers after her death.

Asked by Robert Hinshaw what she felt had been her most important contribution for C.G. Jung's legacy, she responded: "The memory book, the published correspondence and these additional *Streiflichter*."[90] As her own most significant work, she cited her book *The Myth of Meaning in the Work of C.G. Jung*. In a conversation a few months before her death when asked what in retrospect held the most important place in her life, she notably did not answer "my contact with C.G. Jung," but said: "Everything was important at the time. First my work with children. My time as a student. My work with disabled children. The relationship with my husband was precious and saved my life, my experience of marriage was very important. One thing led to another. My work for Jung and his *oeuvre* strongly shaped many years..." The personal relationship between them was the most cherished part, but she "paid dearly for the richness experienced with Jung." At this late stage in her life, her dreams were described as clear, simple and beautiful and she felt secure: "I knew the path I wanted to take and I took it, without shying from conflict."[91]

In this state of calm, Aniela Jaffé passed away in October, 1991, confident that her unpublished manuscript would eventually see the light of day.

Elena Fischli
April 22, 2021

90 Trans. note: "*Streiflichter*" is a word Aniela Jaffé used to describe her manuscript, and it became the title of this book in German. It translates roughly as "snapshots", "sidelights", or "rapidly moving beams of light."
91 Aniela Jaffé in conversation with Robert Hinshaw, 12.4.1991, 17.6.1991, AAJD.

List of Illustrations

Acknowledgments

We are very grateful to the following persons for their invaluable participation on this project: Heidy Fässler, Sandro Fischli, Thomas Föhl, Torsten Haeffner, Frank und Patricia Herrmann, Luke und Georgina Herrmann, Nicole Hofmann-Kotsonis, Robert Imhoff, Ann Lammers, Karl Saurer, Caitlin Stephens, Laurens van der Post and Peter Volkart. Each of them has contributed with expertise, knowledge and other forms of support to the success of this project: thank you!

Bibliography

Aalders, Gerard, 2004, *Nazi Looting. The Plunder of Dutch Jewry During the Second World War*. Trans. Pomerans, Arnold/Pomerans, Erica. Berg Publishers, Oxford.

Adler, Gerhard/Jaffé, Aniela (ed.), 1973, *Letters of C.G. Jung: Volume I, 1906-1950*. Trans. Hull, Richard F.C. Princeton University Press, New Jersey / Routledge & Kegan Paul, London.

Adler, Gerhard/Jaffé, Aniela (ed.), 1975, *Letters of C.G. Jung: Volume II, 1951-1961*. Trans. Hull, Richard F.C. Princeton University Press, New Jersey / Routledge & Kegan Paul, London.

Adler, Gerhard/Jaffé, Aniela (ed.), 1984, *Selected Letters of C.G. Jung 1909-1961*. Trans. Hull, Richard F.C. Princeton University Press, New Jersey.

Anders-Stern, Günther, 1952, Introduction to unrevised 7th edition of: Stern, William, 1914, *Psychologie der frühen Kindheit bis zum sechsten Lebensjahr*.

Bachofen, Johann Jakob, 1967, *Myth, Religion and Mother Right, Selected Writings*. Introduction by J. Campbell. Routledge & Kegan Paul, London.

Bair, Deirdre, 2003, *Jung – A Biography*. Little/Brown, New York.

Balmer, Heinrich, 1972, *Die Archetypentheorie von C.G. Jung. Eine Kritik*. Springer, Berlin.

BBC Broadcast, *Carl Gustav Jung: 1875–1961*. Edited by Ean Begg. Recording 14 July 1975.

Beebe, John (ed.), 1989, *Aspects of the Masculine*. Princeton University Press, New Jersey.

Bennet, Edward A., 1961, *C.G. Jung*. Barrie and Rockliff, London.

Beriger, Kurt, 1927, *Der Meskalinrausch. Seine Geschichte und Erscheinungsweise*. Springer, Berlin.

Berthelot, Marcellin, 1877/88, *Collection des anciens alchimistes grecs*. Paris.

– 1893, *La Chimie au moyen âge*. Paris.

– 1885, *Les Origines de l'alchimie*. Paris.

Bilsky, Emily D., 2000, *Berlin Metropolis: Jews and the New Culture 1890–1918*. University of California Press, Oakland.

Bitter, Wilhelm (ed.), 1974, *Alter und Tod – Verdrängen oder Bewältigen*. With a contribution by Jaffé, Aniela: Der Tod in der Sicht von C.G. Jung. Klett, Stuttgart.

Bloch, Ernst, 1977, *Erbschaft dieser Zeit*, Gesammelte Werke Bd. 4. Suhrkamp, Frankfurt.

Bolliger, Silvia, 2019, *Im Zeichen der Nationalisierung. Die Haltung der Universität Zürich gegenüber ausländischen Studierenden in der Zwischenkriegszeit*. Zürcher Beiträge zur Geschichtswissenschaft, Bd. 11. Böhlau, Vienna/Cologne.

Burnham, John/McGuire, William (ed.), 1983, *Jelliffe: American Psychoanalyst and Physician and His Correspondence with Sigmund Freud and C.G. Jung*. University of Chicago Press, Chicago.

C.G Jung Institute (ed.), 1955, *Studien zur analytischen Psychologie C.G. Jungs*. Festschrift for the eightieth birthday of C.G. Jung, Zürich.

Campbell, Joseph/Heyer-Grote, Lucy (ed.), 1973, *Heinrich Zimmer. Philosophie und Religion Indiens*. Suhrkamp, Frankfurt.

Carlyle, Thomas, 1894, *Past and Present*. Chapman and Hall, London.

– 1896, *Sartor Resartus*. Ginn & Company, Massachusetts.

Carotenuto, Aldo, 1982, *A Secret Symmetry. Sabina Spielrein between Jung and Freud*. Foreword by William McGuire. Trans. Pomerans, Arno/Shepley, John/Winston, Krishna. Pantheon, New York.

Cassirer, Ernst, 1923-1929, *The Philosophy of Symbolic Forms*. 3 Volumes. Trans. Manheim, Ralph. Yale University Press, New Haven and London.

Cassirer, Toni, 2003, *Mein Leben mit Ernst Cassirer*. Meiner, Hamburg. New edition of 1948 typoscript.

Castell, Rolf et al., 2003, *Geschichte der Kinder- und Jugendpsychiatrie in Deutschland in den Jahren 1937 bis 1961*. Vandenhoeck & Ruprecht, Göttingen.

Claudel, Paul/Amrouche, Jean, 1954, *Mémoires Improvisées*. Gallimard, Paris.

Cole, Stewart (ed.), 1956, *This is my Faith. The Convictions of Representative Americans today*. Harper, New York.

Deutsch, Werner (ed.), 1991, *Über die verborgene Aktualität von William Stern*. Peter Lang, Frankfurt.

Dieckmann, Hans et al. (ed.), 1980, *Kreativität des Unbewussten: Zum 75. Geburtstag von Erich Neumann*. With a contribution by Jaffé, Aniela: Die Einheitswirklichkeit und das Schöpferische (Erich Neumann und C.G. Jung). S. Karger, Basel.

Diels, Hermann, 1903, *Die Fragmente der Vorsokratiker*. Weidmann, Berlin.

Dru, Alexander (ed.), 1955, *The Letters of Jacob Burckhardt*. Routledge & Kegan Paul, London.

Eckermann, Johann P., 1852, *Conversations with Goethe in the Last Years of His Life*. Trans. Fuller, S.M. James Munroe and Company, Boston and Cambridge.

Einstein Albert/Freud Sigmund, 1972, *Warum Krieg? – Ein Briefwechsel.* 1933, Internationales Institut für geistige Zusammenarbeit, Paris. Diogenes, Zürich.

Einstein, Albert, 1988, *Einstein on Peace.* Ed. Nathan, Otto/Norden, Heinz. Random House, New York.

Fierz-David, Linda, 1957, Typoskript: *Psychologische Betrachtungen zu der Freskenfolge der Villa dei Misteri in Pompeji. Ein Versuch.*

– 1988, *Women's Dionysian Initiation: the Villa of Mysteries in Pompei.* Trans. Phelan, Gladys. Spring Publications, Dallas.

Fleig, Horst (ed.), 1993, *J.W. Goethe, Sämtliche Werke.* Deutscher Klassiker Verlag, Frankfurt.

Foundation of the Works of C.G. Jung (ed. Hoerni, Ulrich; Fischer, Thomas; Kaufmann, Bettina), 2019, *The Art of C.G. Jung.* W.W. Norton, New York/London.

Freud, Sigmund/Jung, C.G., 1974, *The Freud-Jung Letters. The Correspondence between Sigmund Freud and C.G. Jung.* Ed. McGuire, William/Sauerländer, Wolfgang. Trans. Manheim, Ralph/Hull, Richard F.C. Princeton University Press, New Jersey.

Freud, Sigmund, 2000, Psychoanalytische Bemerkungen über einen autobiographisch beschriebenen Fall von Paranoia (Dementia paranoides*)*. In: *Studienausgabe, vol. 8: Zwang, Paranoia und Perversion.* Fischer, Frankfurt. See: Schreber, 1903, *Memoirs of My Nervous Illness.*

Friedländer, Saul, 2010, *Das Dritte Reich und die Juden.* Beck, Munich.

Fröbe-Kapteyn, Olga (ed.), 1952, *Mensch und Zeit. Eranos-Jahrbuch 1951,* vol. 20. Rhein-Verlag, Zürich.

Fürstenberg, Hans, 1928, *Erinnerungen an Walther Rathenau. Ein Kommentar.* In: Kessler, *Walther Rathenau, sein Leben und sein Werk.*

– 1931, *Carl Fürstenberg. Die Lebensgeschichte eines deutschen Bankiers 1870-1914.* Ullstein, Berlin.

– 1978, *Einführung in die Ästhetik. Betrachtungen über die Malkunst.* Econ, Vienna.

– 1972, *Dialektik des 21. Jahrhunderts. Der neue Weg des Denkens von der Atomphysik bis zu den Wissenschaften vom Menschen.* Econ, Vienna.

Goethe, Johann W., 1898, *Faust, Part 1.* Trans. Swanwick, Anna. D. McKay, Philadelphia.

Goethe, Johann W., 1989, *Wilhelm Meister's Journeyman Years, or the Renunciants.* Trans. Winston, Krishna. Suhrkamp, New York.

Graf-Nold, Angela, 1991, Stern versus Freud. Die Kontroverse um die Kinder–Psychoanalyse. In Deutsch, *Über die verborgene Aktualität von William Stern.*

Gsell, Yael Naomi Berit, 2019, *Lucy Heyer-Grote Biographie. Eine emanzipierte Frau im Wandel der Zeit.* Master's Thesis, University of Basel.

Hannah, Barbara, 1976, *Jung, his Life and Work.* Putnam, New York. Neuauflage 1997. Chiron, Wilmette.

Häsler, Alfred A., 2008, *Das Boot ist voll. Die Schweiz und die Flüchtlinge 1933-1945*. Diogenes, Zürich.

Heinemann, Rebecca, 2016, *Das Kind als Person. William Stern als Wegbereiter der Kinder- und Jugendforschung 1900 – 1933*. Klinkhardt, Bad Heilbronn.

Herrmann, Frank, 2002, *Low Profile. A Life in the World of Books*. Plough Press, Nottingham.

Heyer, Gustav R., 1935, *Eine Einführung in die Psychotherapie für Ärzte und Studierende*. J.F. Lehmanns, München.

Heyer, Gustav R./Seifert, Friedrich (ed.), 1937, *Reich der Seele*. J.F. Lehmanns, München.

Heyer-Grote, Lucy, 1970, *Atemschulung als Element der Psychotherapie*. Wissenschaftliche Buchgemeinschaft, Darmstadt.

Hillman, James, 1983, *Healing Fiction. On Freud, Jung, Adler*. Station Hill Press, Barrytown, N.Y.

– 1978, *Suicide and the Soul*. Spring Publications, Dallas.

Hinshaw, Robert (ed.), 1989, *The Rock Rabbit and the Rainbow. Laurens van der Post among Friends*. Daimon, Einsiedeln.

Hinshaw, Robert/Hinshaw-Fischli, Elena (ed.), 1986, *C.G. Jung im Gespräch*. Daimon, Einsiedeln.

Hinshaw, Robert/Hinshaw-Fischli, Elena (ed.), 2013, *Im Umkreis des Todes*. With a contribution by Jaffé, Aniela. Daimon, Einsiedeln. New edition of: Von Franz et al., 1980.

Hoffmann, William S., 1974, *Paul Mellon: Portrait of an Oil Baron*. Follett, Chicago.

Hölderlin, Friedrich, 1803, *Patmos*. In: 1998, *Selected Poems and Fragments*. Trans. Hamburger, Michael. Penguin Books, London.

Holenstein, André/Kury, Patrick/Schulz, Kristina (ed.), 2018, *Schweizer Migrationsgeschichte*. Hier und Jetzt, Baden.

Independent Commission of Experts Switzerland – Second World War, 2001, *Die Schweiz und die Flüchtlinge zur Zeit des Nationalsozialismus*. Chronos, Zürich.

Jacobi, Jolande (ed.), 1945, *Psychologische Betrachtungen. Eine Auswahl aus den Schriften von C.G. Jung*. Rascher, Zürich.

– 1951, *Paracelsus: Selected Writings*. Trans. Guterman, Norbert. Bollingen Series, Princeton University Press, New Jersey.

– 1952, *C.G. Jung. Symbole der Wandlung. Analyse des Vorspiels zu einer Schizophrenie*. Rascher, Zürich. 4th revised edition of: Jung, 1911-1912, *Wandlungen und Symbole der Libido. Beitrag zur Entwicklungsgeschichte des Denkens*.

Jacobi, Jolande, 1942, *The Psychology of C.G. Jung*. Trans. Bash, K.W. Routledge & Kegan Paul, London.

–1969, *Vom Bilderreich der Seele*. Walter, Olten.

Jaffé, Aniela, 1950, *Bilder und Symbole aus E.T.A. Hoffmanns Märchen „Der goldne Topf"*. In: Jung, 1950, *Gestaltungen des Unbewussten. Psychologische Abhandlungen*, vol. VII. And as single publication in: Jaffé, 1978, *Bilder und Symbole aus E.T.A. Hoffmanns Märchen „Der goldne Topf"*.

Jaffé, Aniela/Vettiger, Gretel/Vogt, Alban, 1951, *Alte Menschen im Altersheim*. Benno Schwabe, Basel.

Jaffé, Aniela/Zacharias, Gerhard P. (ed.), 1954, *Welt der Psyche. Eine Auswahl zur Einführung*. Rascher, Zürich.

– 1965, *Geist und Psyche*. New edition of "Welt der Psyche" with amended title. Kindler, München.

Jaffé, Aniela, 1955, Carl Gustav Jung. In: DU. Schweizerische Monatsschrift, vol. 15/no. 4. Conzett & Huber, Zürich.

– 1955, Hermann Brochs ‚Der Tod des Vergil' – Ein Beitrag zum Problem der Individuation. In: Jung-Institut (ed.), 1955. *Studien zur Analytischen Psychologie C.G. Jungs. Band II*. And in: Jaffé, 1988, *Mystik und Grenzen der Erkenntnis*.

Jaffé, Aniela (ed.), 1957, C.G. Jung. *Bewusstes und Unbewusstes. Beiträge zur Psychologie*. Postscript by Aniela Jaffé. Fischer, Frankfurt.

Jaffé, Aniela, 1957, Zur Psychologie des alten Menschen. In: *Zeitschrift für Präventivmedizin*, January 1957, no. 2. Birkhäuser, Basel.

– 1958, *Geistererscheinungen und Vorzeichen. Eine psychologische Deutung*. Rascher, Zürich.

Jaffé, Aniela (ed.), 1962, *Erinnerungen, Träume, Gedanken von C.G. Jung*. Rascher, Zürich.

– 1962, *Memories, Dreams, Reflections by C.G. Jung*. Trans. Winston, Richard/ Winston, Clara. Pantheon, New York.

Jaffé, Aniela, 1963, *Apparitions and Precognition. A Study from the Point of View of C.G. Jungs Analytical Psychology*. University Books, New York.

– 1964, Symbolism in the Visual Arts. In: Jung et al., 1964, *Man and his Symbols*.

Jaffé, Aniela (ed.), 1966, *C.G. Jung, Ma Vie. Souvenirs, Rêves et Pensées*. Trans. Le Lay, Yves/Cahen, Roland. Gallimard, Paris.

Jaffé, Aniela, 1966, *The Influence of Alchemy in the Work of C.G. Jung*. In: MacPhail (ed.), 1968, *Alchemy and the Occult. A Catalogue of Books and Manuscripts from the Collection of Paul and Mary Mellon given to Yale University Library*. And in: Jaffé, 1988. *Mystik und Grenzen der Erkenntnis*.

– 1967, *Der Mythus vom Sinn*. Rascher, Zürich.

– 1968, *Aus Leben und Werkstatt von C.G. Jung*. Rascher, Zürich. With the essay "C.G. Jung und der Nationalsozialismus".

– 1968, Bildende Kunst als Symbol. In: Jung et al., 1968, *Der Mensch und seine Symbole*.

– 1970, *The Myth of Meaning in the Work of C.G. Jung*. Trans. Hull, Richard F.C. Hodder & Stoughton, London / Putnam's Sons, 1971, New York.

– 1971, *From the Life and Work of C.G. Jung.* Trans. Hull, Richard F.C. Hodder & Stoughton, London / Harper & Row, New York.

Jaffé, Aniela/Adler, Gerhard (ed.), 1972, *C.G. Jung: Briefe, Bd. 1, 1906-1945.*

– 1972, *C.G. Jung: Briefe, Bd. 2, 1946-1955.*

– 1973, *C.G. Jung: Briefe,* Bd. 3, *1956-1961.* All volumes Walter, Olten/Freiburg i. Br.

Jaffé, Aniela/Adler, Gerhard (ed.), 1973, *Letters of C.G. Jung Vol. I, 1906-1950.* Trans. Hull, Richard F.C. Princeton University Press, New Jersey / Routledge & Kegan Paul, London.

– 1975, *Letters of C.G. Jung Vol. II, 1951-1961.* Trans. Hull, Richard F.C. Princeton University Press, New Jersey / Routledge & Kegan Paul, London.

Jaffé, Aniela, 1973, *Schöpferische Phasen im Leben von C.G. Jung.* In: Portmann/ Ritsema (ed.), *Das Lebensalter im schöpferischen Prozess.* Eranos Jahrbuch 1971, vol. 40.

– 1974, *Der Tod aus der Sicht C.G. Jungs.* In: Bitter, 1974, *Alter und Tod – Annehmen oder Verdrängen.* And in: von Franz et al., 1980, *Im Umkreis des Todes.*

– 1975, *Synchronizität und Kausalität in der Parapsychologie.* In: Portmann/Ritsema (ed.), *Die Welt der Entsprechungen.* Eranos Jahrbuch 1973, vol. 42. And in: Jaffé, 1985, *Parapsychologie, Individuation, Nationalsozialismus. Themen bei C.G. Jung.*

Jaffé, Aniela (ed.), 1975, C.G. Jung – 100 Briefe. Eine Auswahl. Walter, Olten.

– 1977, *C.G. Jung. Bild und Wort.* Walter, Olten/Freiburg i. Br.

Jaffé, Aniela, 1977, *C.G. Jungs Auffassung einer Individuation der Menschheit.* In: Portmann/Ritsema (ed.), *Normen im Wandel der Zeit.* Eranos Jahrbuch 1974, vol. 43: And in: Jaffé, 1985, *Parapsychologie, Individuation, Nationalsozialismus. Themen bei C.G. Jung.*

– 1977, *C.G. Jung und die Eranos-Tagungen.* In: Portmann/Ritsema (ed.), *Die Vielheit der Welten.* Eranos Jahrbuch 1975, vol. 44: And in: Jaffé, 1977, "C.G. Jung and the Eranos Conferences" in *Spring, An Annual of Archetypal Psychology and Jungian Thought,* Zürich.

– 1978, *Apparitions. An Archetypal Approach to Death Dreams and Ghosts.* Spring Publications, Dallas.

– 1978, *Bilder und Symbole aus E.T.A. Hoffmanns Märchen „Der goldne Topf".* Gerstenberg, Hildesheim.

– 1979, *Aus C.G. Jungs Welt. Gedanken und Politik.* Werner Claassen, Zürich.

– 1979, *C.G: Jung: Word and Image.* Bollingen Series XCVII Vol. 2. Princeton University Press, New Jersey.

– 1980, *Anna Kingsford – Religiöser Wahn und Magie.* Bonz, Stuttgart.

– 1980, *Die Einheitswirklichkeit und das Schöpferische (Erich Neumann und C.G. Jung).* In: Dieckmann, 1980, *Kreativität des Unbewussten. Zum 75. Geburtstag von Erich Neumann.* And in: Jaffé, 1987, *Aus C.G. Jungs letzten Jahren und andere Aufsätze.*

– 1982, *Aufsätze zur Psychologie C.G. Jungs.* Daimon, Zürich.
– 1984, Details about C.G. Jung's Family. Trans. Weber, R.G.S. In: *Spring 1984, An Annual of Archetypal Psychology and Jungian Thought.* Spring Publications, Dallas.
– 1985, *Parapsychologie, Individuation, Nationalsozialismus. Themen bei C.G. Jung.* Daimon, Einsiedeln.
– 1986, *Religiöser Wahn und schwarze Magie – das tragische Leben der Anna Kingsford.* 2nd edition with amended title. Daimon, Einsiedeln.
– 1986, *The Myth of Meaning in the Life of C.G. Jung.* Trans. Hull, Richard F.C. Daimon, Einsiedeln.
– 1987, *Aus C.G. Jungs letzten Jahren und andere Aufsätze.* Daimon, Einsiedeln.
– 1988, *Mystik und Grenzen der Erkenntnis.* Daimon, Einsiedeln.
– 1989, C.G. Jung and National Socialism. In: Jaffé, 1989, *From the Life and Work of C.G. Jung.*
– 1989, *From the Life and Work of C.G. Jung.* Expanded edition trans. Hull, Richard F.C/Stein, Murray. Daimon, Einsiedeln.
– 1989, A Last Look at a First Encounter. In: *The Rock Rabbit and the Rainbow. Laurens van der Post among Friends.* Ed. Hinshaw, Robert.
– 1989, *Was C.G. Jung a Mystic? and Other Essays.* Trans. Dachler, Diana Dachler/ Cairns, Fiona. Daimon, Einsiedeln.
– 1999, *An Archetypal Approach to Death Dreams and Ghosts.* Daimon, Einsiedeln. Revised new edition by Jaffé, 1963, *Apparitions and Precognition.*
Jarret, James L. (ed.), 1989, C.G. Jung. The Seminars. Vol. 2, Part I, Part II. *Nietzsche's Zarathustra. Notes of the Seminar Given in 1934-1939.* Routledge, London.
Jones, Ernest, 1953, *The Life and Work of Sigmund Freud. 1856–1900: The Formative Years and the Great Discoveries.* Vol. 1.
– 1955, *The Life and Work of Sigmund Freud. Years of Maturity 1901-1919.* Vol. 2.
– 1957, *The Life and Work of Sigmund Freud. The Last Phase 1919-1939.* Vol. 3. All volumes Basic Books, New York.
Jung, C.G., 1911/1912, *Wandlungen und Symbole der Libido. Beiträge zur Entwicklungsgeschichte des Denkens.* Deuticke, Leipzig und Wien. Revised 4th edition by Jacobi (ed.), 1952, *C.G. Jung. Symbole der Wandlung. Analyse des Vorspiels zu einer Schizophrenie.*
– 1929, Ein europäischer Kommentar. In: Wilhelm, 1929, *Das Geheimnis der Goldenen Blüte.*
– 1939, Foreword to: Suzuki, *Die große Befreiung. Einführung in den Zen-Buddhismus.*
– 1940, *Psychologie und Religion. Die Terry Lectures 1937 gehalten an der Yale University.* Rascher, Zürich.
– 1948, *Symbolik des Geistes.* Psychologische Abhandlungen Bd. VI. With a contribution by Rivkah Schärf. Rascher, Zürich.

– 1950, Foreword to: Wilhelm, Richard/Baynes, Cary F., *The I Ching, or Book of Change. The Richard Wilhelm Translation, rendered into English by Cary F. Baynes.*

– 1950, *Gestaltungen des Unbewussten.* Psychologische Abhandlungen Bd. VII. With a contribution by Aniela Jaffé. Rascher, Zürich.

– 1951, *Aion. Untersuchungen zur Symbolgeschichte.* Psychologische Abhandlungen Band VIII. Rascher, Zürich. And in: Jung, 1976, Gesammelte Werke, Band 9/II.

– 1952, *Symbole der Wandlung. Analyse des Vorspiels zu einer Schizophrenie.* Rascher, Zürich. Ed. Jacobi, Jolande.

– 1952, *Antwort auf Hiob.* Rascher, Zürich. And in: Jung, 1963, Gesammelte Werke, Band 11: *Zur Psychologie westlicher und östlicher Religion.*

– 1952, Über Synchronizität. In: Fröbe-Kapteyn, Olga (ed.), *Mensch und Zeit.* Eranos Jahrbuch 1951, Bd. 20. Rhein-Verlag, Zürich. And in: Jung, 1976, Gesammelte Werke Band 8: *Dynamik des Unbewussten.*

– 1954, *Welt der Psyche. Eine Auswahl zur Einführung.* Rascher, Zürich. Ed. Jaffé, Aniela/Zacharias, Gerhard P.

Jung, C.G. / Pauli, Wolfgang, 1955, *The Interpretation of Nature and the Psyche.* Trans. Hull, Richard F.C. Bollingen Foundation/Pantheon Books, New York. And in: Jung, 1976, Collected Works Volume 8: *The Structure and Dynamics of the Psyche.*

Jung, C.G., 1955, Mandalas. Mit Kommentar zur Abbildung „Systema mundi totius", 1916. In: DU, Monatszeitschrift. Issue 15/no. 4. Conzett & Huber, Zürich.

– 1957, *Bewusstes und Unbewusstes. Beiträge zur Psychologie.* Fischer, Frankfurt. Ed. Jaffé, Aniela.

– 1957, *Gegenwart und Zukunft.* Rascher, Zürich. And in: Jung, 1974, Gesammelte Werke, Band 10: *Zivilisation im Übergang.*

– 1958, *Ein moderner Mythus. Von Dingen, die am Himmel gesehen werden.* Rascher, Zürich. And in: Jung, 1974, Gesammelte Werke, Band 10: *Zivilisation im Übergang.*

Jung, C.G. et al., 1964, *Man and his Symbols.* Aldus, London.

Jung, C.G., 1964, Approaching the Unconscious. In: Jung et al., 1964, *Man and his Symbols.*

– 1965, *Geist und Psyche.* New edition of "Welt der Psyche" with amended title. Kindler, München. Ed. Jaffé, Aniela/Zacharias, Gerhard P.

Jung, C.G. et al., 1968, *Der Mensch und seine Symbole.* Walter, Olten.

Jung, C.G., 1968, Zugang zum Unbewussten. In: Jung et al., 1968, *Der Mensch und seine Symbole.*

– 1972, *Briefe. Band 1, 1906-1945.*

– 1972, *Briefe. Band 2, 1946-1955.*

– 1973, *Briefe. Band 3, 1956-1961.* All volumes Walter, Olten/Freiburg i. Br. Ed. Jaffé, Aniela/Adler Gerhard P.

– 1973, *Letters of C.G. Jung Vol. I, 1906-1950.* Trans. Hull, Richard F.C. Princeton University Press, New Jersey/Routledge & Kegan Paul, London. Ed. Adler, Gerhard/Jaffé, Aniela.

– 1974, *The Freud-Jung-Letters. The correspondence between Sigmund Freud and C.G. Jung.* Trans. Manheim, Ralph Manheim/Hull, Richard F.C. Princeton University Press, New Jersey. Ed. McGuire, William/Sauerländer, Wolfgang.

– 1974, *Sigmund Freud – C.G. Jung. Briefwechsel.* Fischer, Frankfurt. Ed. McGuire, William/ Sauerländer, Wolfgang.

– 1975, *Letters of C.G. Jung Vol. II, 1951-1961.* Trans. Hull, Richard F.C. Princeton University Press, New Jersey/Routledge & Kegan Paul, London. Ed. Adler, Gerhard/Jaffé, Aniela.

– 1975, *C.G. Jung – 100 Briefe. Eine Auswahl.* Walter, Olten. Ed. Jaffé, Aniela.

– 1977, *C.G. Jung. Bild und Wort.* Walter Olten/Freiburg i. Br. Ed. Jaffé, Aniela.

– 1977, *C.G. Jung Speaking.* Princeton University Press, New Jersey. Ed. McGuire, William.

– 1983, *The Zofingia Lectures. Collected Works of C.G. Jung, Supplementary Volume A.* Princeton University Press, New Jersey/Routledge, London. Ed. McGuire, William.

– 1983, *Aspects of the Feminine.* Princeton University Press, New Jersey.

– 1984, *Selected Letters of C.G. Jung 1909-1961.* Trans. Hull, Richard F.C. Princeton University Press, New Jersey. Ed. Adler, Gerhard/Jaffé Aniela.

– 1984, *Dream Analysis. Notes of the Seminars given in 1928-30 by C.G. Jung.* The Seminars Vol. 1. Princeton University Press, New Jersey. Ed. McGuire, William.

– 1986, *C.G. Jung im Gespräch.* Daimon, Einsiedeln. Ed. Hinshaw, Robert/Hinshaw-Fischli, Elena.

– 1989, *Nietzsche's Zarathustra. Notes of the Seminar given in 1934-1939.* The Seminars. Vol. 2, Part I/Part II. Routledge, London. Ed. Jarrett, James L.

– 1989, *Analytical Psychology. Notes of the Seminar given in 1925.* The Seminars, Vol. 3. Princeton University Press, New Jersey/Routledge, London. Ed. McGuire, William.

– 1989, *Aspects of the Masculine.* Princeton University Press, New Jersey. Ed. Beebe John.

– 1991, *Traumanalyse.* Nach Aufzeichnungen des Seminars 1928-1930. Walter, Olten. Ed. McGuire, William.

– 1995, *Analytische Psychologie. Nach Aufzeichnungen des Seminars 1925.* Walter, Solothurn/Düsseldorf. Ed. McGuire, William.

– 1997, *Die Zofingia-Vorträge.* Patmos, Ostfilden.

– 2009, *C.G. Jung. Das Rote Buch. Liber Novus.* Patmos, Düsseldorf. Ed. Shamdasani, Sonu.

– 2009, *C.G. Jung. The Red Book. Liber Novus.* Trans. Kyburz, Mark/Peck, John/Shamdasani, Sonu. W. W. Norton, New York/London. Ed. Shamdasani, Sonu.

– 2010, *Children's Dreams: Notes from the Seminar Given in 1936-1940.* Trans. Falzeder Ernst/Woolfson, Tony. Princeton University Press, New Jersey. Ed. Jung, Lorenz/Meyer-Grass, Maria.

– 2012, *Introduction to Jungian Psychology. Notes of the Seminar given in 1925 by C.G. Jung.* Princeton University Press, New Jersey. Ed. Shamdasani, Sonu.

– 2020, *C.G. Jung. The Black Books 1913-1932: Notebooks of Transformation.* Trans. Liebscher, Martin/Peck, John/Shamdasani, Sonu. W.W. Norton, New York/London. Ed. Shamdasani, Sonu.

Jung, C.G., *The Collected Works of C.G. Jung* (CW). Trans. Hull, Richard F.C. except CW 2, parts of CW 18 and writings originally published English. Princeton University Press, New Jersey/Routledge & Kegan Paul, London. Ed. Read, Herbert et al.

– CW 1. *Psychiatric Studies.* 1970.

– CW 2. *Experimental Researches.* Trans. Stein, Leopold/Riviere Diana. 1973.

– CW 3. *The Psychogenesis of Mental Disease.* 1972.

– CW 4. *Freud and Psychoanalysis.* 1970.

– CW 5. *Symbols of Transformation.* 1967.

– CW 6. *Psychological Types.* 1971.

– CW 7. *Two Essays on Analytical Psychology.* 1966.

– CW 8. *The Structure and Dynamics of the Psyche.* 1972.

– CW 9/I. *The Archetypes of the Collective Unconscious.* 1968.

– CW 9/II. *Aion: Researches into the Phenomenology of the Self.* 1968.

– CW 10. *Civilization in Transition.* 1970.

– CW 11. *Psychology and Religion: West and East.* 1969.

– CW 12. *Psychology and Alchemy.* 1968.

– CW 13. *Alchemical Studies.* 1967.

– CW 14. *Mysterium Coniunctionis.* 1970.

– CW 15. *The Spirit in Man, Art and Literature.* 1966.

– CW 16. *The Practice of Psychotherapy.* 1966.

– CW 17. *The Development of Personality.* 1970.

– CW 18. *The Symbolic Life.* 1976.

Jung, Emma/von Franz, Marie-Louise, 1970, *The Grail Legend.* Trans. Dykes, Andrea. C.G. Jung Foundation for Analytical Psychology, Inc., New York.

Jungk, Robert, 1958, *Brighter than a Thousand Suns.* Trans. Cleugh, James. Harcourt, New York.

Kessler, Harry Graf, 1928, *Walther Rathenau. Sein Leben und sein Werk.* Hermann Klemm, Berlin.

Keyserling, Count Hermann, 1925, *Travel Diary of a Philosopher.* Trans. Reece, J. Holroyd. Harcourt, New York.

Klibansky, Raymond/Panowsky, Erwin/Saxl, Fritz, 1990, *Saturn und Melancholie: Studien zur Geschichte der Naturphilosophie und Medizin, der Religion und der Kunst.* New edition of 1964, Suhrkamp, Frankfurt a.M.

Lammers, Ann, 2004, Correctio Fatuorum, Re. the Jung-White-Letters. In: *Journal of Analytical Psychology,* no. 49. Society of Analytical Psychology, London.

Lejeune, Robert (ed.), 1964, *William Wolfensberger – Ausgewählte Werke.* Huber, Frauenfeld.

Liebscher, M. (ed.), 2015, *Analytical Psychology in Exile, The Correspondence of Jung, C.G. and Erich Neumann.* Trans. McCartney, Heather. Princeton University Press, New Jersey.

Linsmayer, Charles, Probst, Rudolf (ed.), 2007, *Eingeklemmt zwischen Unmöglichkeit und Sehnsucht. Ein Lesebuch.* Huber, Frauenfeld.

Löhr, Hanns C., 2005, *Das Braune Haus der Kunst. Hitler und der "Sonderauftrag Linz".* Akademie- Verlag, Berlin.

Ludwig, Carl, 1966, *Die Flüchtlingspolitik der Schweiz seit 1933 bis zur Gegenwart.* Peter Lang, Bern.

Maidenbaum, Aryeh/Martin, Stephen A. (ed.), 1991, *Lingering Shadows – Jungians, Freudians and Antisemitism.* Shambala, Boston and London.

Maidenbaum, Aryeh (ed.), 2002, *Jung and the Shadow of Antisemitism.* Nicolas-Hays, Berwick.

Mattioli, Aram, 1998, *Antisemitismus in der Schweiz 1848 – 1960.* Orell Füssli, Zürich.

McGuire, William/Sauerländer, Wolfgang (ed.), 1974, *The Freud-Jung Letters. The Correspondence between Sigmund Freud and C.G. Jung.* Trans. Manheim, Ralph/Hull, Richard F.C. Princeton University Press, New Jersey.

– 1974, *Sigmund Freud – C.G. Jung. Briefwechsel.* Fischer, Frankfurt.

McGuire, William (ed.), 1977, *C.G. Jung Speaking.* Princeton University Press, New Jersey.

McGuire, William, 1978, Jung in America 1924/25. In: *Spring 1978, An Annual of Archetypal Psychology and Jungian Thought.* Spring Publications, Irving.

McGuire, William, 1982, *Bollingen. An Adventure in Collecting the Past.* Princeton University Press, New Jersey.

McGuire, William (ed.), 1983, *The Zofingia Lectures.* Collected Works of C.G. Jung, Supplementary Volume A. Princeton University Press, New Jersey/Routledge, London.

– 1984, *Dream Analysis. Notes of the Seminars given in 1928-30 by C.G. Jung.* The Seminars, Vol. 1. Princeton University Press, New Jersey.

– 1989, *Analytical Psychology. Notes of the Seminar given in 1925. C.G. Jung.* The Seminars, Vol. 3. Princeton University Press, New Jersey.

– 1995, *Analytische Psychologie. Nach Aufzeichnungen des Seminars 1925.* Walter, Solothurn/Düsseldorf.

Meier, Carl A. (ed.), 2001, *Atom and Archetype: The Pauli/Jung Letters, 1932–1958.* Trans. Roscoe, David. Princeton University Press, New Jersey.

Mellon, Paul/Baskett, John, 1992, *Reflections in a Silver Spoon – A Memoir.* Morrow/Harper/Collins, New York.

Mörike, Eduard, 2005, *The Book of Lieder.* Trans. Stokes, Richard. Faber, London.

Moser, Fanny, 1950, *Spuk, Irrglaube oder Wahrglaube?* Gyr, Baden/Zürich.

Muramoto, Shoji, 1987, Completing the Memoirs: The Passages Omitted or Transposed in the English or Japanese Versions of Jung's Autobiography. In: *Spring 1987, An Annual of Archetypal Psychology and Jungian Thought.* Spring Publications, Dallas.

Museum Rietberg (ed.), 2010, *C.G. Jung – Das Rote Buch.* Exhibition Guide, Zürich.

Neumann, Erich, 1956, *Amor and Psyche: The Psychic Development of the Feminine.* Trans. Manheim, Ralph. Princeton University Press, New Jersey/Routledge & Kegan Paul, London.

Neumann, Karl Eugen, 1962, *Also sprach der Erhabene. Eine Auswahl aus den Reden Gotamo Buddhos.* New edition of 1916, Artemis, Zürich/Zsolnay, Vienna.

Nietzsche, Friedrich, 1954, *Thus Spoke Zarathustra. A Book for All and None.* Translated by Walter Kaufmann. Viking Penguin, New York.

Philp, Howard L., 1958, *Jung and the Problem of Evil.* Rockliff, London.

Portmann, Adolf, 1956, *Biologie und Geist.* Rhein-Verlag, Zürich.

Portmann, Adolf/Ritsema, Rudolf (ed.), 1973, *Das Lebensalter im schöpferischen Prozess.* Eranos Jahrbuch 1971, Bd. 40.

– 1975, *Die Welt der Entsprechungen.* Eranos Jahrbuch 1973, vol. 42.

– 1977, *Normen im Wandel der Zeit.* Eranos Jahrbuch 1974, vol. 43.

– 1977, *Die Vielheit der Welten.* Eranos Jahrbuch 1975, vol. 44. All volumes E. J. Brill, Leiden.

Psychologische Gesellschaft Basel (ed.), 1976, *C.G. Jung heute.* Bonz, Stuttgart.

Rathenau, Walther, 1918, Staat und Judentum. Eine Polemik. In *Zur Kritik der Zeit. Mahnung und Warnung.* Fischer, Berlin.

Rössler, Wulf/Danuser, Hans (ed.), 2013, *Das Burghölzli. Von der Irrenanstalt zur Psychiatrischen Universitätsklinik Zürich. Entwicklungen, Innen- und Aussensichten.* NZZ-Verlag, Zürich.

Rousseau, Jean-Jaques, 1762, *Émile ou De l'éducation.*

Schär, Hans, 1952, *C.G. Jung und die Deutung der Geschichte.* Schweizerische Theologische Umschau VIII, Bern.

Schärf, Rivkah, 1948, Die Gestalt des Satans im Alten Testament. In: Jung, 1948, *Symbolik des Geistes.* Psychologische Abhandlungen Band VI.

Schiller, Friedrich, 1991, *Wallenstein*. Trans. Willson, Jeanne. In: *Wallenstein and Mary Stuart*. Ed. Walter Hinderer. The Continuum Publishing Company, New York.

Schoenl, William, 1998, *C.G. Jung: His Friendship with Mary Mellon and J.B. Priestley*. Chiron, North Carolina.

Scholem, Gershom, 1941, *Major Trends in Jewish Mysticism*. Schocken, Jerusalem.

Schopenhauer, Arthur, 1960, *Essay on the Freedom of the Will*. Trans. Kolenda, Konstantin. Bobbs-Merrill Company, Indianapolis.

Schreber, Daniel Paul, 1955. *Memoirs of My Nervous Illness*. Trans. Macalpine, Ida/ Hunter, Richard A. Harvard College, Massachusetts.

Seelig, Carl, 1956, *Albert Einstein. A Documentary Biography*. Staples Press, London.

– 1956, *Helle Zeit – Dunkle Zeit. In memoriam Albert Einstein*. Europa Verlag, Zürich.

Sengupta, Sulagna, 2013, *Jung in India*. Spring Journal Books, New Orleans.

Shamdasani, Sonu, 1995, Memories, Dreams, Omissions. In: *Spring 58. Disillusionment. A Journal of Archetype and Culture*. Spring Publications, Woodstock.

– 2005, *Jung stripped Bare by his Biographers, Even*. Karnac Books, London.

– 2012, *C.G. Jung, A Biography in Books*. W. W. Norton, New York/London.

Shamdasani, Sonu (ed.), 2009, C.G. Jung. *The Red Book. Liber Novus*. Trans. Kyburz, Mark/Peck, John/Shamdasani, Sonu. W. W. Norton, New York/London.

– 2012, *Introduction to Jungian Psychology. Notes of the Seminar given in 1925 by C.G. Jung*. Princeton University Press, New Jersey.

– 2020, *C.G. Jung. The Black Books 1913-1932: Notebooks of Transformation*. Trans. Liebscher, Martin/Peck, John/Shamdasani, Sonu. W. W. Norton, New York/ London.

Sherry, Jay, 2010, *Carl Gustav Jung – Avant Garde Conservative*. Palgrave Macmillan, New York.

Sibold, Noemi, 2010, *Bewegte Zeiten. Zur Geschichte der Juden in Basel 1930–1950*. Chronos, Zürich.

Silesius, Angelus, 1905 (1675), *Cherubinischer Wandersmann*. Diederichs, Jena.

Smythies, John R., 1967, *Science and ESP*. Routledge & Kegan Paul, London.

Spielrein, Sabina, 1986, Diary and Letters. In: Carotenuto (ed.), 1982, *A Secret Symmetry. Sabina Spielrein between Jung and Freud*.

Stedall, Jonathan/Van der Post, Laurens, 1971, *The Story of Carl Gustav Jung*. Film, 1972 broadcast by the BBC in three parts.

Stern, Paul, 1977, *C.G. Jung – Prophet des Unbewussten*. Piper, Munich.

Stern, William, 1900, *Über Psychologie der individuellen Differenzen: Ideen zu einer differentiellen Psychologie*. Barth Verlag, Leipzig.

– 1906, Person und Sache – System der philosophischen Weltanschauung. 1. Band. *Ableitung und Grundlehre*. Barth, Leipzig.

– 1911, *Die differentielle Psychologie in ihren methodischen Grundlagen*. Barth, Leipzig.

– 1914, *Psychologie der frühen Kindheit bis zum sechsten Lebensjahr. Mit Benutzung ungedruckter Tagebücher von Clara Stern*. Quelle & Meyer, Leipzig.

– 1918, Person und Sache – System der philosophischen Weltanschauung. 2. Band. *Die menschliche Persönlichkeit*. Barth, Leipzig.

– 1924, Person und Sache – System des kritischen Personalismus. 3. Band. *Wertphilosophie*. Barth, Leipzig.

– 1924, *Psychology of Early Childhood*. Trans. Barwell, Anna. London: George Allen & Unwin Ltd.

– 1987, Das Kind und die Welt. Lecture 12.2.1932. In: *Geschichte der Psychologie*. Nachrichtenblatt deutschsprachiger Psychologen, issue 4, Springer, Wiesbaden.

Stiftung C.G. Jung Küsnacht (ed.), 2009, *The House of C.G. Jung. The History and Restoration of the Residence of Emma and Carl Gustav Jung-Rauschenbach*. Fo-Print+Media, Zürich/Egg.

Suzuki, Daisetz T., 1939, *Die große Befreiung. Einführung in den Zen-Buddhismus*. With a foreword by C.G. Jung. Weller, Leipzig.

– 1991, *An Introduction to Zen Buddhism*. Grove Press, New York.

Van der Post, Laurens, 1976, *Jung and the Story of our Time*. Hogarth Press, London.

Von Franz, Marie-Louise, 1980, *Die Erlösung des Weiblichen im Manne. Der goldene Esel von* Apuleius *aus tiefenpsychologischer Sicht*. Insel, Frankfurt.

Von Franz, Marie-Louise/Frey-Rohn, Liliane/Jaffé, Aniela, 1980, *Im Umkreis des Todes*. Daimon. Zürich.

Walk, Joseph, 1981, *Das Sonderrecht für die Juden im NS-Staat: Eine Sammlung der gesetzlichen Massnahmen und Richtlinien, Inhalt und Bedeutung*. C.F. Müller, Heidelberg.

Wilhelm, Richard, 1924, *I Ging. Das Buch der Wandlungen*. Eugen Diederichs, Jena.

– 1929, *Das Geheimnis der Goldenen Blüte*. Mit einem europäischen Kommentar von C.G. Jung. Dorn, Munich.

Wilhelm, Richard/Baynes, Cary, 1950, *The I Ching, or Book of Changes. The Richard Wilhelm Translation rendered into English by Cary F. Baynes*. Foreword by C.G. Jung. Bollingen Series XIX, New York.

Wilhelmy, Petra, 1989, *Der Berliner Salon im 19. Jahrhundert 1780-1914*. Walter de Gruyter, Berlin/New York.

Wolff, Toni, 1959, *Studien zu C.G. Jungs Psychologie*. Rhein-Verlag, Zürich.

– 2003, new edition. Daimon, Einsiedeln.

Wolff-Windegg, P., 1976. C.G. Jung – Bachofen, Burckhardt, and Basel. In *Spring, An Annual of Archetypal Psychology and Jungian Thought*. Spring Publications, Irving.

Zahn-Harnack, Agnes, 1928, *Die Frauenbewegung. Geschichte, Probleme, Ziele.* Deutsche Buchgemeinschaft, Berlin.

Zimmer, Heinrich, 1973, *Philosophie und Religion Indiens.* Suhrkamp, Frankfurt. Ed. Campell, Joseph/Heyer-Grote, Lucy.

Aniela Jaffé

Death Dreams and Ghosts

A collection of death dreams and ghost stories were gathered and presented to C.G. Jung and the author, who approaches this fascinating material from the depths of her analytic experience.
We are left in the overpowering presence of a great mystery.

"... among the Swiss, who are commonly regarded as stolid, unimaginative, rationalistic and materialistic, there are just as many ghost stories and suchlike as, say, in England or Ireland. Indeed, as I know from my own experience ... magic as practiced in the Middle Ages ... has by no means died out, but still flourishes today ...
I can recommend it to all those who know how to value things that break through the monotony of daily life with salutary effects, (sometimes!) shaking our certitudes and lending wings to the imagination."

– from the Foreword by C.G. Jung

200 pages, ISBN 978-3-85630-580-2

E.A. Bennet

Meetings with Jung

In this collection of diary entries made by British psychiatrist E.A. Bennet during his visits with the Swiss analyst C.G. Jung over a 15-year period, Bennet's colorfully spontaneous accounts reveal Jung's down-to-earth personality and his extraordinary mind, at ease in his daily surroundings. Meetings with Jung serves as an ideal introduction to Jungian psychology while providing a rare, intimate perspective into Jung's life and work for those already familiar with the more scholarly literature.

125 pages, ISBN 978-3-85630-501-7

RELATED DAIMON TITLES

Aniela Jaffé

The Myth of Meaning

What gives a life its meaning? In this significant volume, one of C.G. Jung's closest associates explores the world of subjective experience in dreams, fantasies and inner images in an illuminating examination of the phenomenon of meaning.

In so doing, she provides further insights into the significance of Jung's work. Aniela Jaffé maintains that any search for meaning ultimately leads into this inner "mythical" realm and must be understood as a limited subjective attempt to answer the unanswerable. Any answer must be one's own, and its formulation one's own myth.

186 pages, ISBN 978-3-85630-500-0

Aniela Jaffé

From the Life and Work of C.G. Jung

with a new Epilogue by Sir Laurens van der Post

Aniela Jaffé was given permission to quote from Jung's highly personal "Red Book," and she does so in her essay on Jung's creative phases. Shortly before her death, the author also updated and expanded her long-famous article addressing the National Socialism accusations leveled against Jung. Sir Laurens van der Post provides a sharp echo in his Epilogue, written especially for this edition.

Chapters: Parapsychology / C.G. Jung and National Socialism / From Jung's Last Years / The Creative Phases in Jung's Life / Alchemy / Epilogue (L. van der Post).

200 pages, ISBN 978-3-85630-515-4

English Titles from Daimon

Ruth Ammann - *The Enchantment of Gardens*
Susan R. Bach - *Life Paints its Own Span*
Diana Baynes Jansen - *Jung's Apprentice: A Biography of Helton Godwin Baynes*
John Beebe (Ed.) - *Terror, Violence and the Impulse to Destroy*
E.A. Bennet - *Meetings with Jung*
W.H. Bleek / L.C. Lloyd (Ed.) - *Specimens of Bushman Folklore*
Tess Castleman - *Threads, Knots, Tapestries*
- *Sacred Dream Circles*
Renate Daniel - *Taking the Fear out of the Night*
- *The Self: Quest for Meaning in a Changing World*
- *Psyche and Soma*
Eranos Yearbook 69 - *Eranos Reborn*
Eranos Yearbook 70 - *Love on a Fragile Thread*
Eranos Yearbook 71 - *Beyond Masters*
Eranos Yearbook 72 - *Soul between Enchantment and Disenchantment*
Eranos Yearbook 73 - *The World and its Shadow*
Eranos Yearbook 74 - *The Age of Immediacy at the Test of Meaning*
Michael Escamilla - *Bleuler, Jung, and the Schizophrenias*
Heinrich Karl Fierz - *Jungian Psychiatry*
John Fraim - *Battle of Symbols*
Liliane Frey-Rohn - *Friedrich Nietzsche, A Psychological Approach*
Marion Gallbach - *Learning from Dreams*
Ralph Goldstein (Ed.) - *Images, Meanings & Connections: Essays in Memory of Susan Bach*
Yael Haft - *Hands: Archetypal Chirology*
Fred Gustafson - *The Black Madonna of Einsiedeln*
Daniel Hell - *Soul-Hunger: The Feeling Human Being and the Life-Sciences*
Siegmund Hurwitz - *Lilith, the first Eve*
Aniela Jaffé - *The Myth of Meaning*
- *Was C.G. Jung a Mystic?*
- *From the Life and Work of C.G. Jung*
- *Death Dreams and Ghosts*
C.G. Jung - *The Solar Myths and Opicinus de Canistris*
Verena Kast - *A Time to Mourn*
- *Sisyphus*
Hayao Kawai - *Dreams, Myths and Fairy Tales in Japan*
James Kirsch - *The Reluctant Prophet*
Eva Langley-Dános - *Prison on Wheels: Ravensbrück to Burgau*
Rivkah Schärf Kluger - *The Gilgamesh Epic*
Yehezkel Kluger & *Nomi Kluger-Nash* - *RUTH in the Light of Mythology, Legend and Kabbalah*
Paul Kugler (Ed.) - *Jungian Perspectives on Clinical Supervision*
Paul Kugler - *The Alchemy of Discourse*
Rafael López-Pedraza - *Cultural Anxiety*
- *Hermes and his Children*
Alan McGlashan - *The Savage and Beautiful Country*
- *Gravity & Levity*
Gregory McNamee (Ed.) - *The Girl Who Made Stars: Bushman Folklore*
- *The North Wind and the Sun & Other Fables of Aesop*
Gitta Mallasz / Hanna Dallos - *Talking with Angels*
C.A. Meier - *Healing Dream and Ritual*
- *A Testament to the Wilderness*
- *Personality: The Individuation Process*
Haruki Murakami - *Haruki Murakami Goes to Meet Hayao Kawai*
Eva Pattis Zoja (Ed.) - *Sandplay Therapy*
Laurens van der Post - *The Rock Rabbit and the Rainbow*

English Titles from Daimon

Psychology Club Zurich - *Stone by Stone: Reflections on Jung*
- *Wisdom has Built her House*
- *Encounters with C.G. Jung. The Journal of Sabi Tauber*

Jane Reid - *Jung, My Mother and I: The Analytic Diaries of Catharine Rush Cabot*

Ingrid Riedel & Christa Henzler - *Painting Therapy on the Basis of C.G. Jung's Analytical Psychology*

R.M. Rilke - *Duino Elegies*

Miguel Serrano - *C.G. Jung and Hermann Hesse*

Helene Shulman - *Living at the Edge of Chaos*

D. Slattery / G. Slater (Eds.) - *Varieties of Mythic Experience*

David Tacey - *Edge of the Sacred: Jung, Psyche, Earth*

Susan Tiberghien - *Looking for Gold*

Ann Ulanov - *Spiritual Aspects of Clinical Work*
- *The Female Ancestors of Christ*
- *Healing Imagination*
- *Picturing God*
- *Receiving Woman*
- *Spirit in Jung*
- *The Wisdom of the Psyche*
- *The Wizards' Gate, Picturing Consciousness*
- *The Psychoid, Soul and Psyche*
- *Knots and their Untying*
- *Back to Basics*

Ann & Barry Ulanov - *Cinderella and her Sisters*

Eva Wertenschlag-Birkhäuser - *Windows on Eternity: The Paintings of Peter Birkhäuser*

Harry Wilmer - *How Dreams Help*
- *Quest for Silence*

Luigi Zoja - *Drugs, Addiction and Initiation*

Luigi Zoja & Donald Williams - *Jungian Reflections on September 11*

Jungian Congress Papers - *Jerusalem 1983: Symbolic & Clinical Approaches*
- *Berlin 1986: Archetype of Shadow in a Split World*
- *Paris 1989: Dynamics in Relationship*
- *Chicago 1992: The Transcendent Function*
- *Zürich 1995: Open Questions*
- *Florence 1998: Destruction and Creation*
- *Cambridge 2001*
- *Barcelona 2004: Edges of Experience*
- *Cape Town 2007: Journeys, Encounters*
- *Montreal 2010: Facing Multiplicity*
- *Copenhagen 2013: 100 Years on*
- *Kyoto 2016: Anima Mundi in Transition*
- *Vienna 2019: Encountering the Other*

Our books are available from your bookstore or from our distributors:

Baker & Taylor
30 Amberwood Parkway
Ashland OH 44805, USA
Phone: 419-281-5100
Fax: 419-281-0200
www.btpubservices.com

Gazelle Book Services Ltd.
White Cross Mills, High Town
Lancaster LA1 4XS, UK
Tel: +44 1524 528500
Email: sales@gazellebookservices.co.uk
www.gazellebookservices.co.uk

Daimon Verlag - Hauptstrasse 85 - CH-8840 Einsiedeln - Switzerland
Phone: (41)(55) 412 2266 Email: info@daimon.ch
For detailed book descriptions visit our website: **www.daimon.ch**